S0-AAC-797

VOLUME 48

Gosho Aoyama

Case Briefing:

Subject:
Occupation:
Special Skills:
Equipment:

Jimmy Kudo, a.k.a. Conan Edogawa
High School Student/Detective
Analytical thinking and deductive reasoning, Soccer
Bow Tie Voice Transmitter, Super Sneakers,
Homing Glasses, Stretchy Suspenders

The subject is hot on the trail of a pair of suspicious men in black
when he is attacked from behind and administered a strange
substance which physically transforms him into a first grader.
When the subject confides in the eccentric inventor Dr. Agasa,
they decide to keep the subject's true identity a secret for the
safety of everyone around him. Assuming the new identity of
first-grader Conan Edogawa, the subject continues to assist the
police force on their most baffling cases. The only problem is that
most crime-solving professionals won't take a little kid's advice!

Table of Contents

CONFIDEN

CASE CLOSED

Volume 48
Shonen Sunday Edition

Story and Art by GOSHO AOYAMA

MEITANTEI CONAN Vol. 48
by Gosho AOYAMA
© 1994 Gosho AOYAMA
All rights reserved.
Original Japanese edition published by SHOGAKUKAN.
English translation rights in the United States of America, Canada,
the United Kingdom and Ireland arranged with SHOGAKUKAN.

Translation
Tetsuichiro Miyaki

Touch-up & Lettering
Freeman Wong

Cover & Graphic Design
Andrea Rice

Editor
Shaenon K. Garrity

Printed in Canada

Published by VIZ Media, LLC
P.O. Box 77010
San Francisco, CA 94107

10 9 8 7 6 5 4 3 2 1
First printing, October 2013

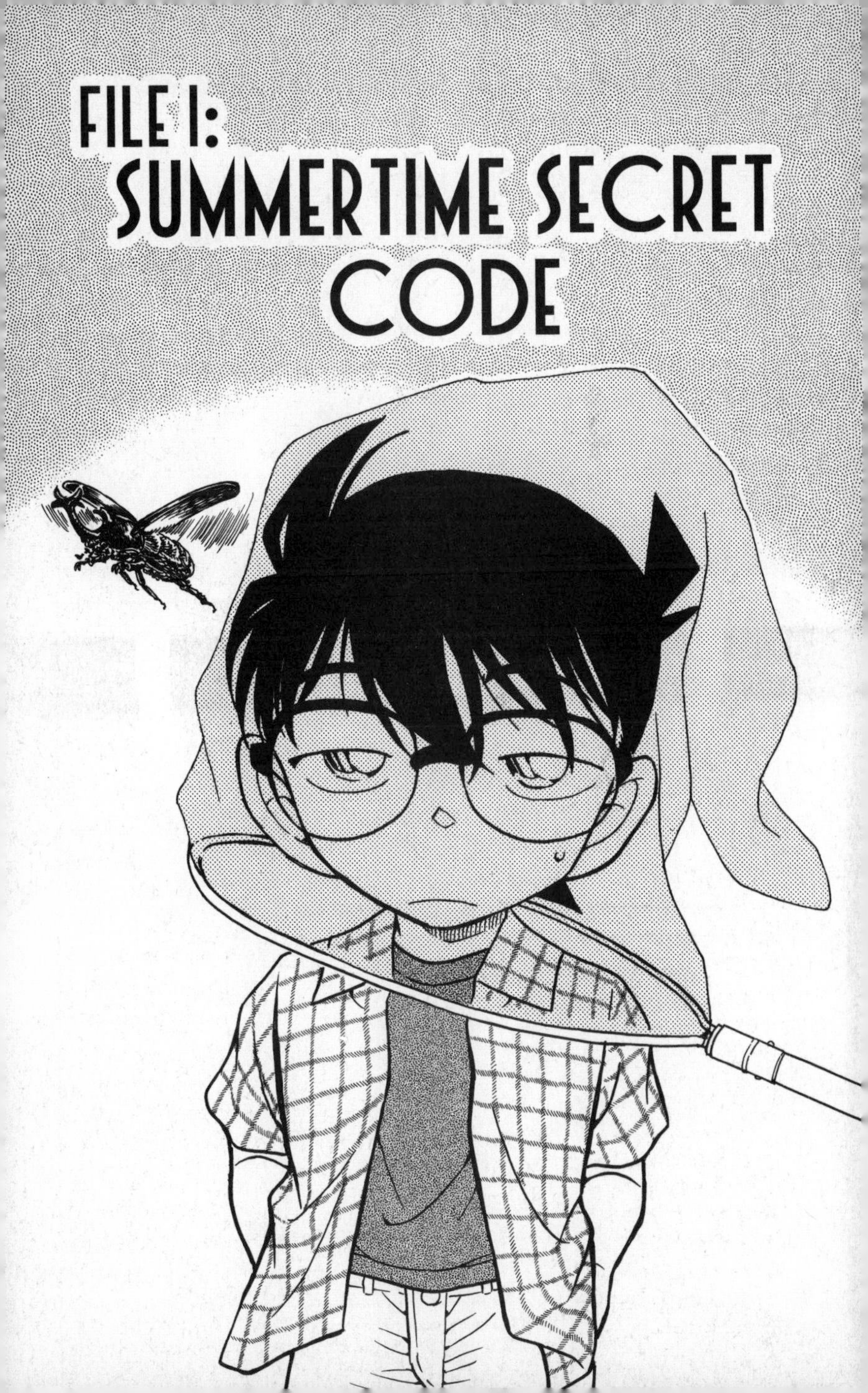
FILE 1:
SUMMERTIME SECRET CODE

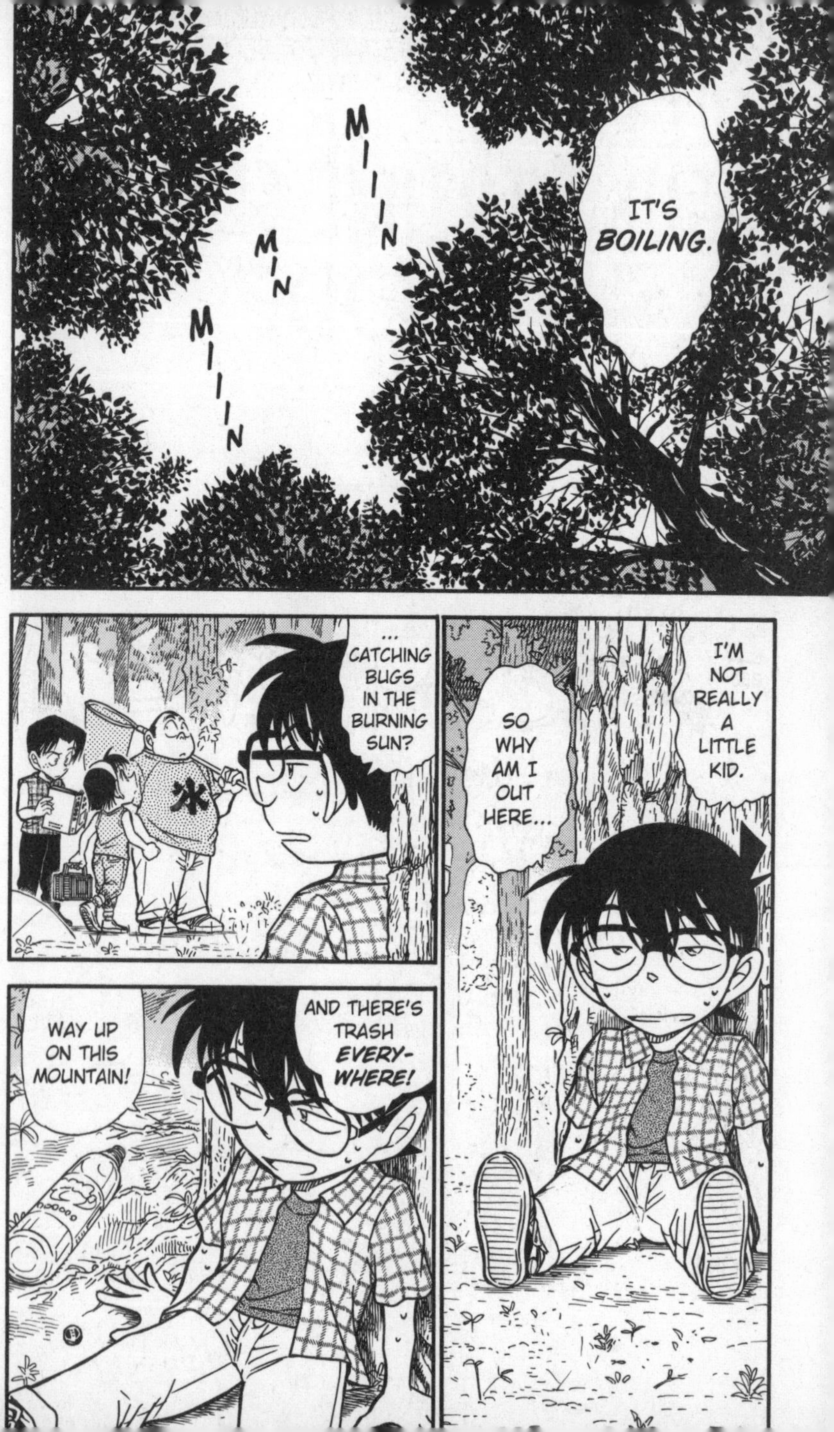
IT'S *BOILING.*
MIIIN
MIN
MIIIN
I'M NOT REALLY A LITTLE KID.
SO WHY AM I OUT HERE...
...CATCHING BUGS IN THE BURNING SUN?
AND THERE'S TRASH *EVERY-WHERE!*
WAY UP ON THIS MOUNTAIN!

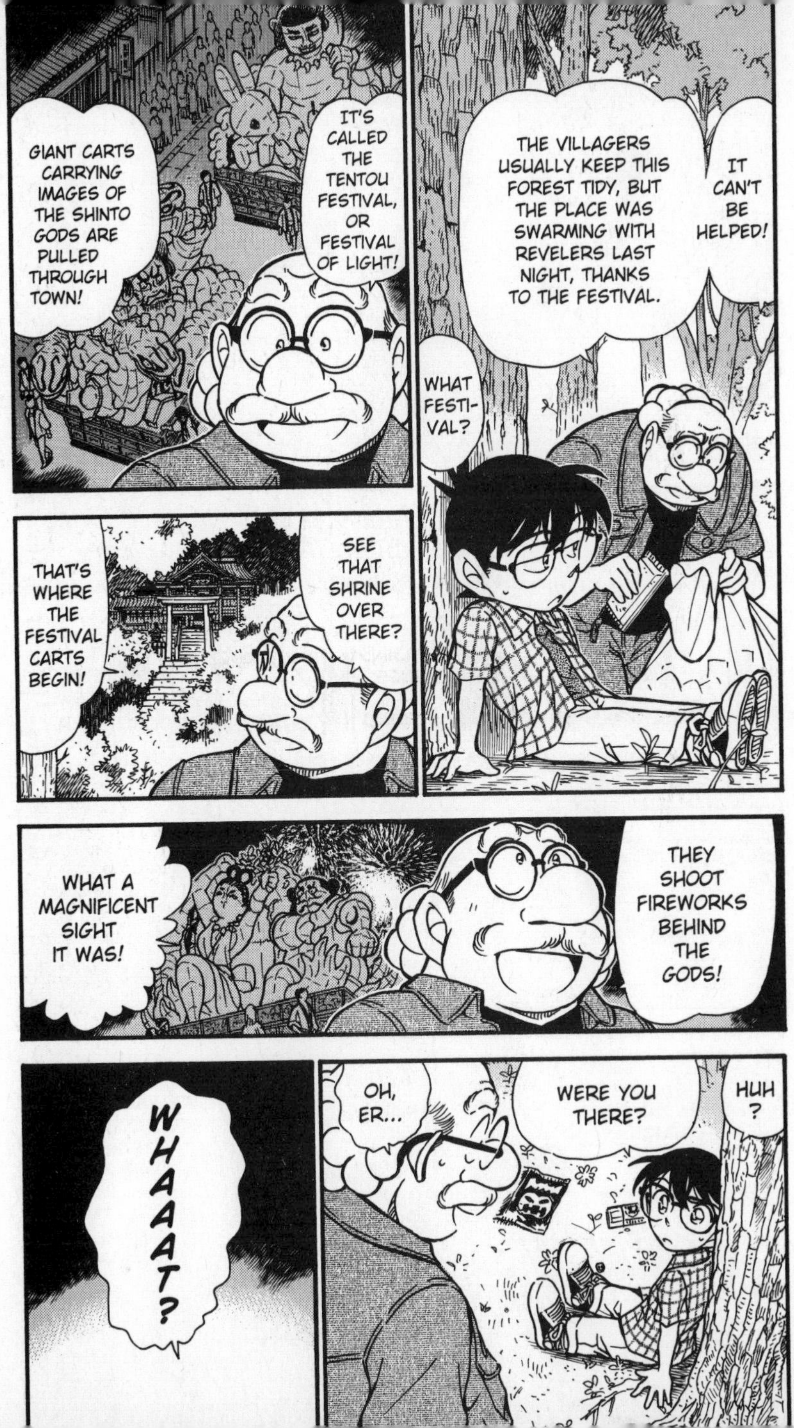
IT CAN'T BE HELPED!
THE VILLAGERS USUALLY KEEP THIS FOREST TIDY, BUT THE PLACE WAS SWARMING WITH REVELERS LAST NIGHT, THANKS TO THE FESTIVAL.
WHAT FESTI-VAL?
IT'S CALLED THE TENTOU FESTIVAL, OR FESTIVAL OF LIGHT!
GIANT CARTS CARRYING IMAGES OF THE SHINTO GODS ARE PULLED THROUGH TOWN!
SEE THAT SHRINE OVER THERE?
THAT'S WHERE THE FESTIVAL CARTS BEGIN!
THEY SHOOT FIREWORKS BEHIND THE GODS!
WHAT A MAGNIFICENT SIGHT IT WAS!
HUH?
WERE YOU THERE?
OH, ER...
WHAAAAT?

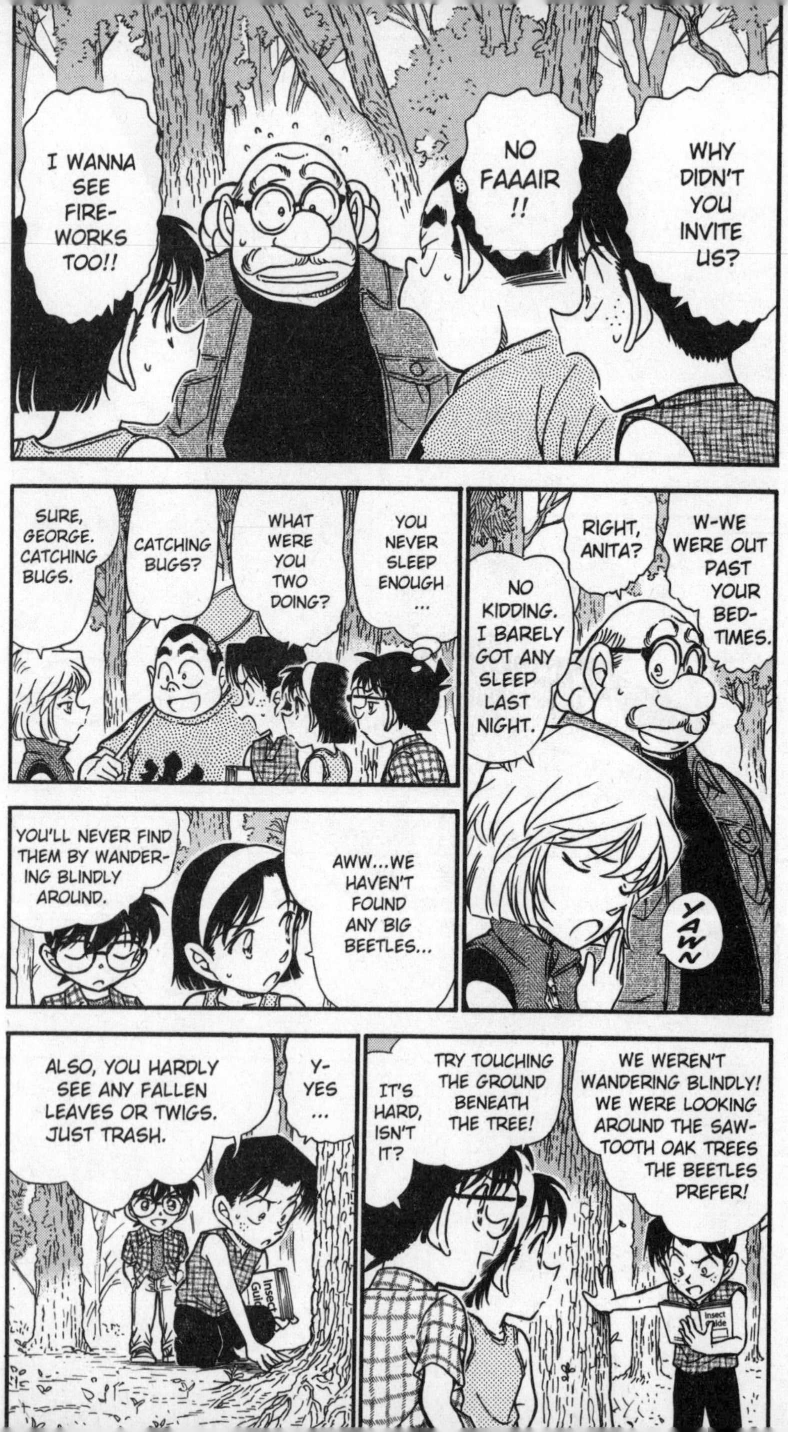
WHY DIDN'T YOU INVITE US?
NO FAAAIR!!
I WANNA SEE FIRE-WORKS TOO!!
W-WE WERE OUT PAST YOUR BED-TIMES.
RIGHT, ANITA?
NO KIDDING. I BARELY GOT ANY SLEEP LAST NIGHT.
YAWN
YOU NEVER SLEEP ENOUGH...
WHAT WERE YOU TWO DOING?
CATCHING BUGS?
SURE, GEORGE. CATCHING BUGS.
AWW...WE HAVEN'T FOUND ANY BIG BEETLES...
YOU'LL NEVER FIND THEM BY WANDER-ING BLINDLY AROUND.
WE WEREN'T WANDERING BLINDLY! WE WERE LOOKING AROUND THE SAW-TOOTH OAK TREES THE BEETLES PREFER!
TRY TOUCHING THE GROUND BENEATH THE TREE!
IT'S HARD, ISN'T IT?
Y-YES...
ALSO, YOU HARDLY SEE ANY FALLEN LEAVES OR TWIGS. JUST TRASH.
Insect Guide

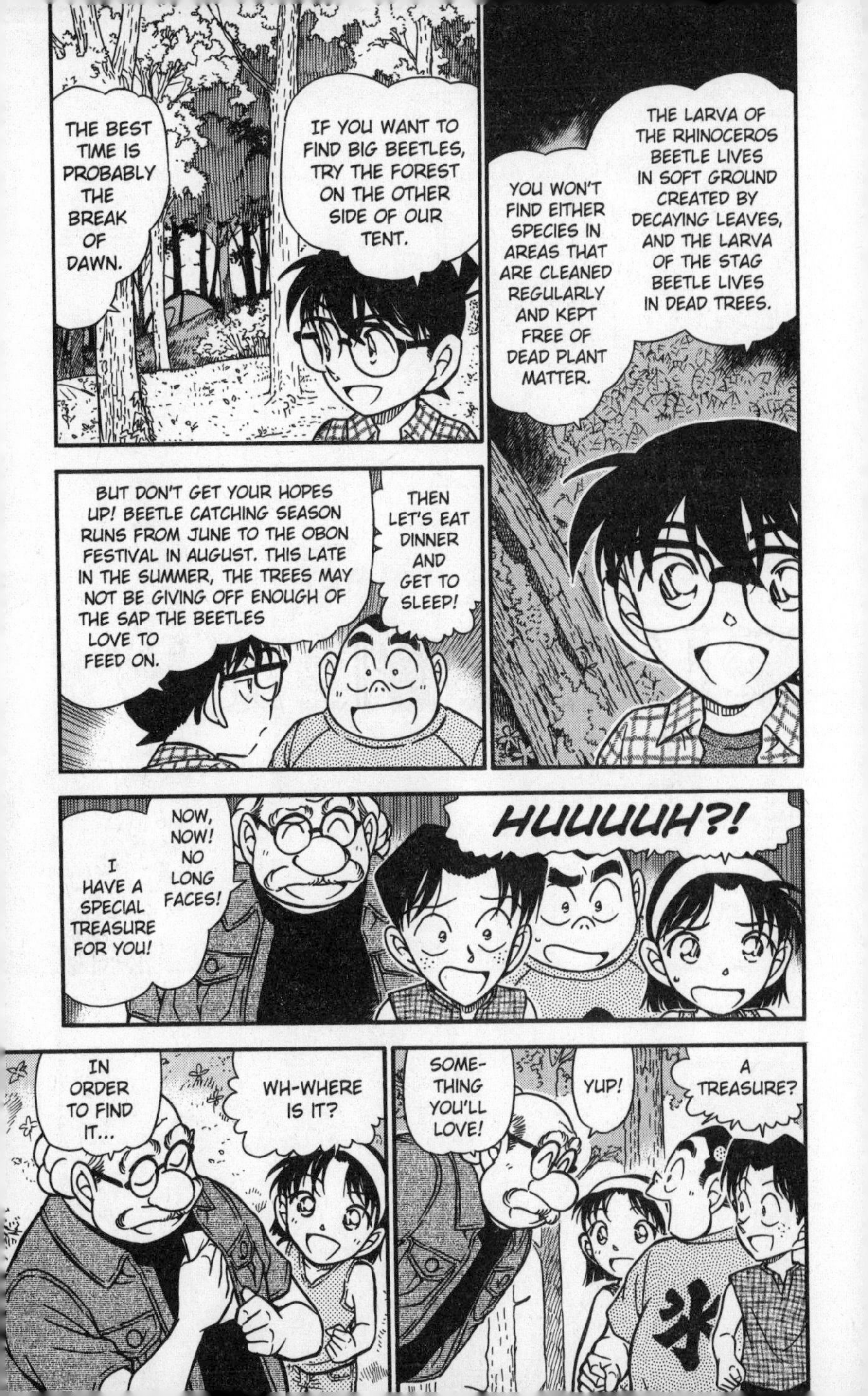
THE LARVA OF THE RHINOCEROS BEETLE LIVES IN SOFT GROUND CREATED BY DECAYING LEAVES, AND THE LARVA OF THE STAG BEETLE LIVES IN DEAD TREES.
YOU WON'T FIND EITHER SPECIES IN AREAS THAT ARE CLEANED REGULARLY AND KEPT FREE OF DEAD PLANT MATTER.
IF YOU WANT TO FIND BIG BEETLES, TRY THE FOREST ON THE OTHER SIDE OF OUR TENT.
THE BEST TIME IS PROBABLY THE BREAK OF DAWN.
THEN LET'S EAT DINNER AND GET TO SLEEP!
BUT DON'T GET YOUR HOPES UP! BEETLE CATCHING SEASON RUNS FROM JUNE TO THE OBON FESTIVAL IN AUGUST. THIS LATE IN THE SUMMER, THE TREES MAY NOT BE GIVING OFF ENOUGH OF THE SAP THE BEETLES LOVE TO FEED ON.
HUUUUUH?!
NOW, NOW! NO LONG FACES!
I HAVE A SPECIAL TREASURE FOR YOU!
A TREASURE?
YUP!
SOME-THING YOU'LL LOVE!
WH-WHERE IS IT?
IN ORDER TO FIND IT...

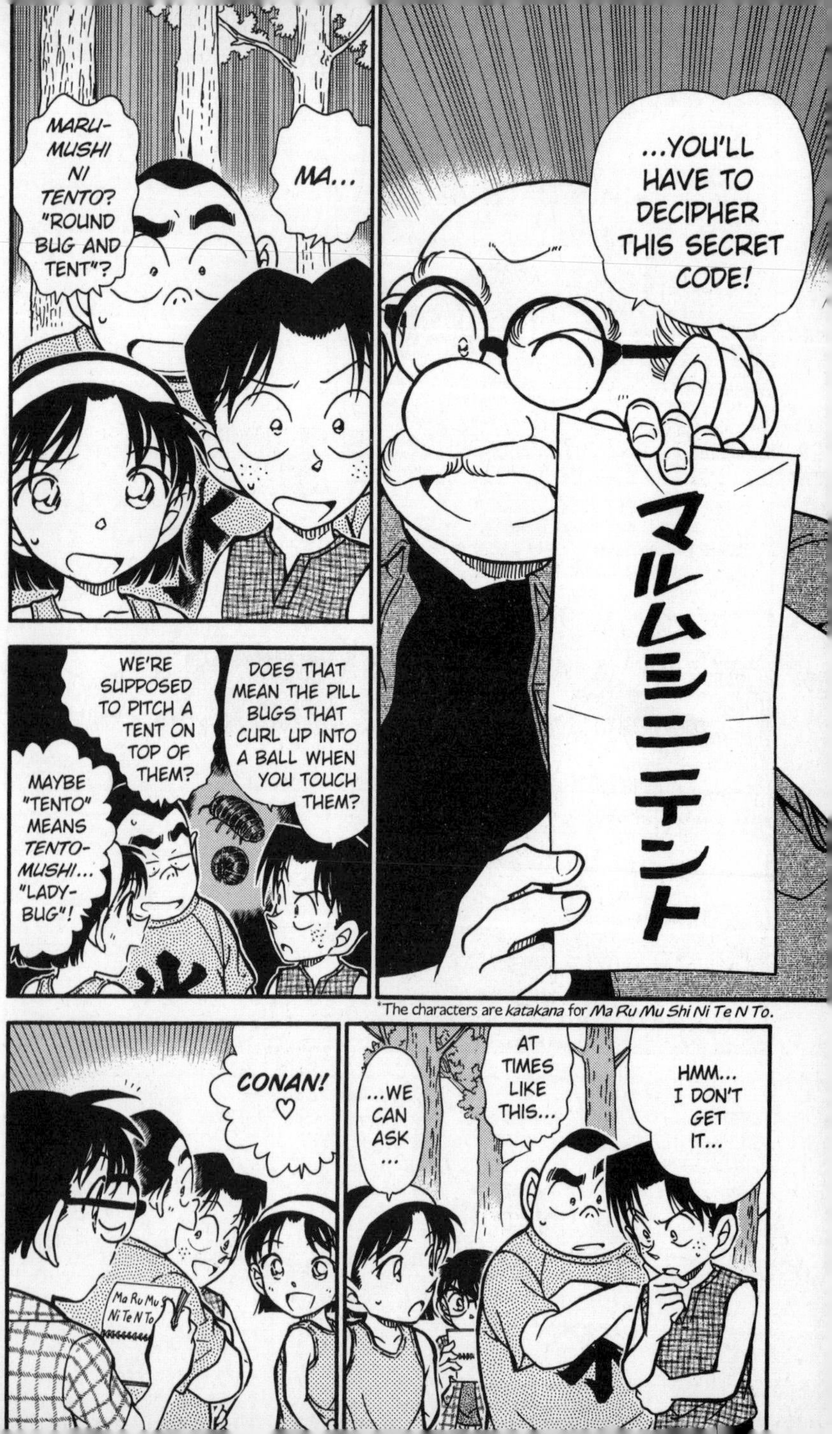
...YOU'LL HAVE TO DECIPHER THIS SECRET CODE!
マルムシニテント
MA...
MARU-MUSHI NI TENTO? "ROUND BUG AND TENT"?
DOES THAT MEAN THE PILL BUGS THAT CURL UP INTO A BALL WHEN YOU TOUCH THEM?
WE'RE SUPPOSED TO PITCH A TENT ON TOP OF THEM?
MAYBE "TENTO" MEANS TENTO-MUSHI... "LADY-BUG"!
*The characters are katakana for Ma Ru Mu Shi Ni Te N To.
HMM... I DON'T GET IT...
AT TIMES LIKE THIS...
...WE CAN ASK ...
CONAN! ♡
Ma Ru Mu Ni Te N To

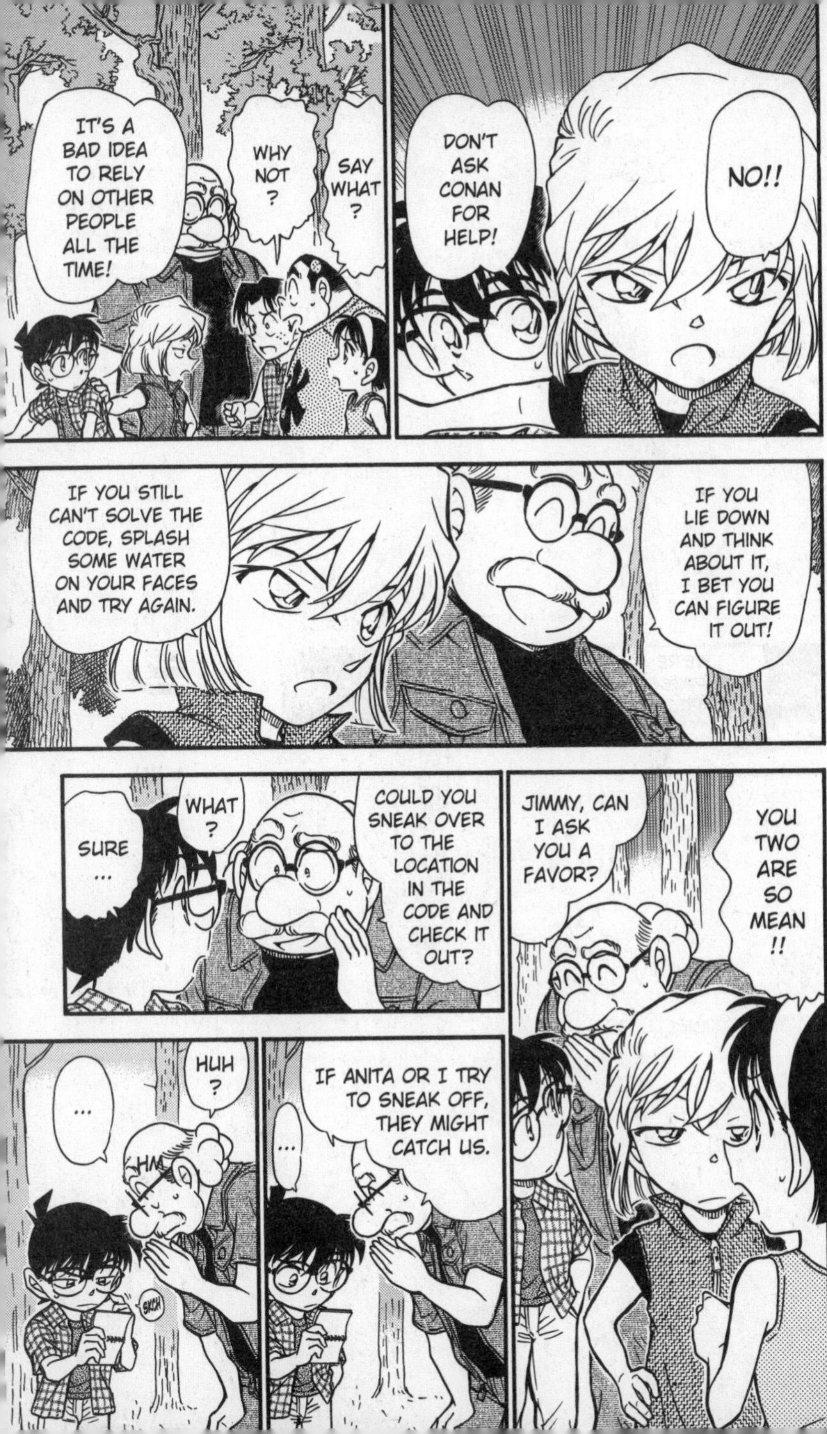
NO!!
DON'T ASK CONAN FOR HELP!
SAY WHAT?
WHY NOT?
IT'S A BAD IDEA TO RELY ON OTHER PEOPLE ALL THE TIME!
IF YOU LIE DOWN AND THINK ABOUT IT, I BET YOU CAN FIGURE IT OUT!
IF YOU STILL CAN'T SOLVE THE CODE, SPLASH SOME WATER ON YOUR FACES AND TRY AGAIN.
YOU TWO ARE SO MEAN!!
JIMMY, CAN I ASK YOU A FAVOR?
COULD YOU SNEAK OVER TO THE LOCATION IN THE CODE AND CHECK IT OUT?
WHAT?
SURE ...
IF ANITA OR I TRY TO SNEAK OFF, THEY MIGHT CATCH US.
...
HUH?
HM
...
SKCH

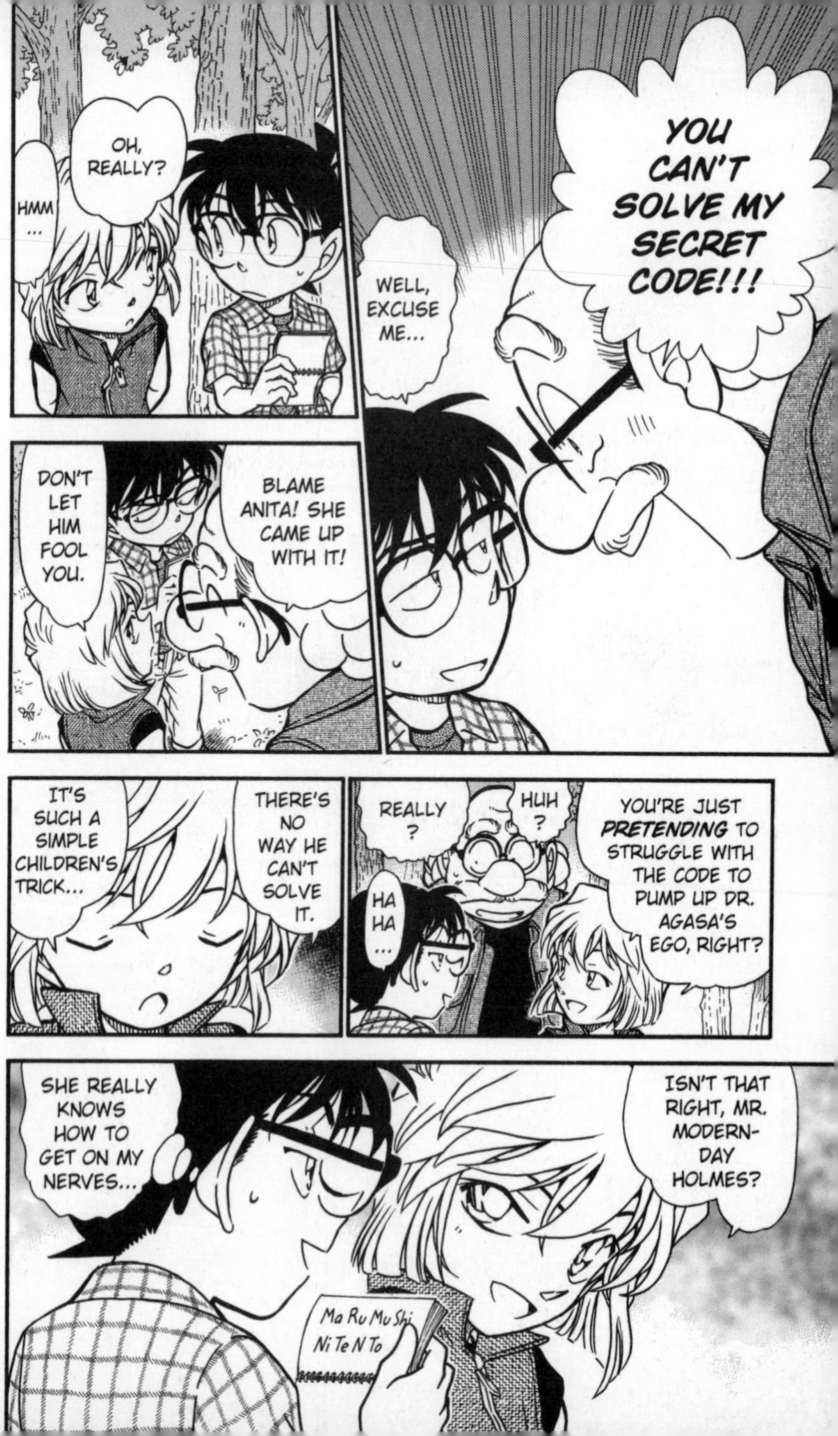
YOU CAN'T SOLVE MY SECRET CODE!!!
WELL, EXCUSE ME...
OH, REALLY?
HMM ...
BLAME ANITA! SHE CAME UP WITH IT!
DON'T LET HIM FOOL YOU.
YOU'RE JUST PRETENDING TO STRUGGLE WITH THE CODE TO PUMP UP DR. AGASA'S EGO, RIGHT?
HUH ?
REALLY ?
HA HA ...
THERE'S NO WAY HE CAN'T SOLVE IT.
IT'S SUCH A SIMPLE CHILDREN'S TRICK...
ISN'T THAT RIGHT, MR. MODERN-DAY HOLMES?
SHE REALLY KNOWS HOW TO GET ON MY NERVES...
Ma Ru Mu Shi
Ni Te N To

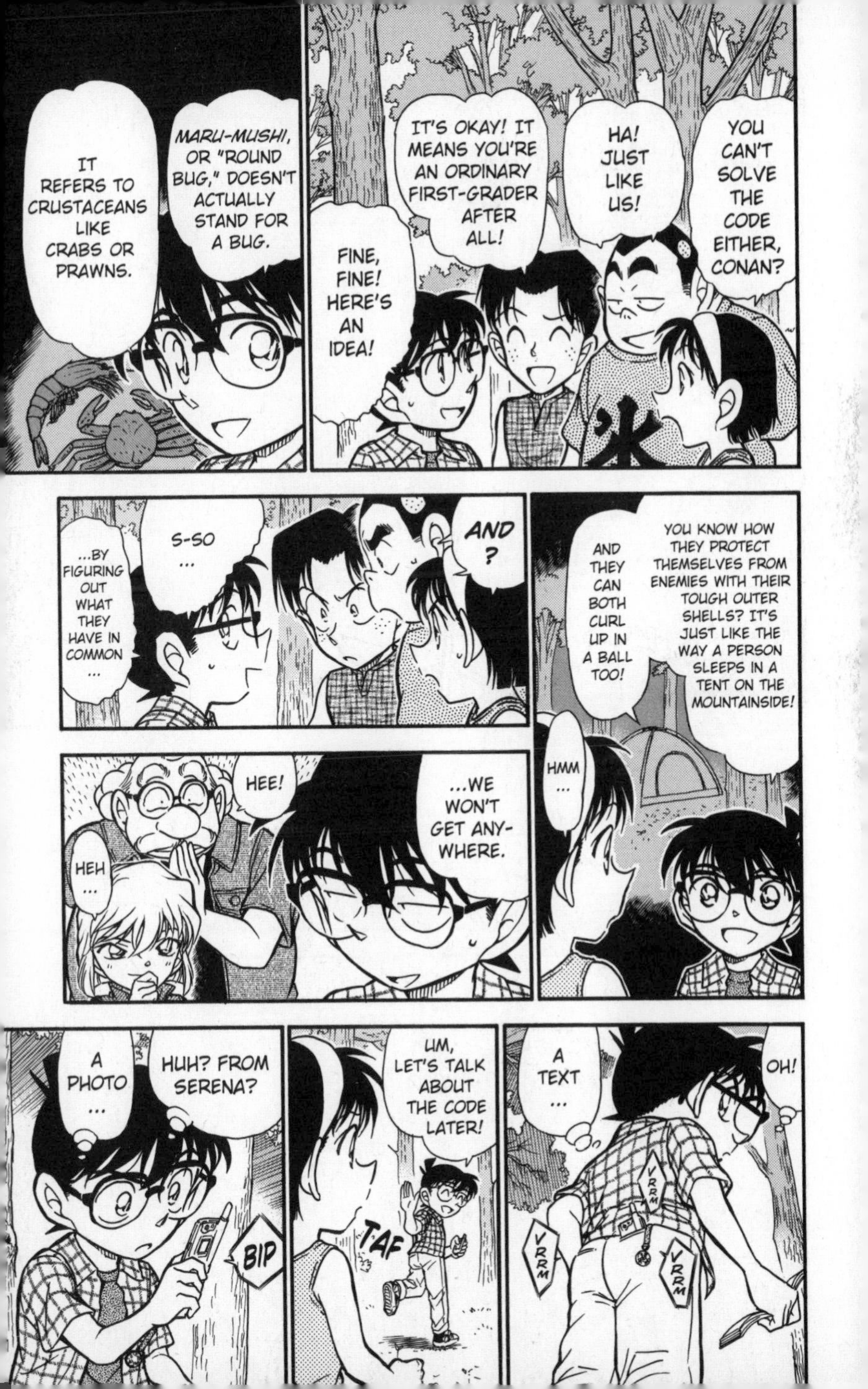
YOU CAN'T SOLVE THE CODE EITHER, CONAN?
HA! JUST LIKE US!
IT'S OKAY! IT MEANS YOU'RE AN ORDINARY FIRST-GRADER AFTER ALL!
FINE, FINE! HERE'S AN IDEA!
MARU-MUSHI, OR "ROUND BUG," DOESN'T ACTUALLY STAND FOR A BUG.
IT REFERS TO CRUSTACEANS LIKE CRABS OR PRAWNS.
YOU KNOW HOW THEY PROTECT THEMSELVES FROM ENEMIES WITH THEIR TOUGH OUTER SHELLS? IT'S JUST LIKE THE WAY A PERSON SLEEPS IN A TENT ON THE MOUNTAINSIDE!
AND THEY CAN BOTH CURL UP IN A BALL TOO!
HMM...
AND?
S-SO...
...BY FIGURING OUT WHAT THEY HAVE IN COMMON...
...WE WON'T GET ANYWHERE.
HEE!
HEH...
OH!
A TEXT...
VRRM
VRRM
VRRM
UM, LET'S TALK ABOUT THE CODE LATER!
TAF
HUH? FROM SERENA?
A PHOTO...
BIP

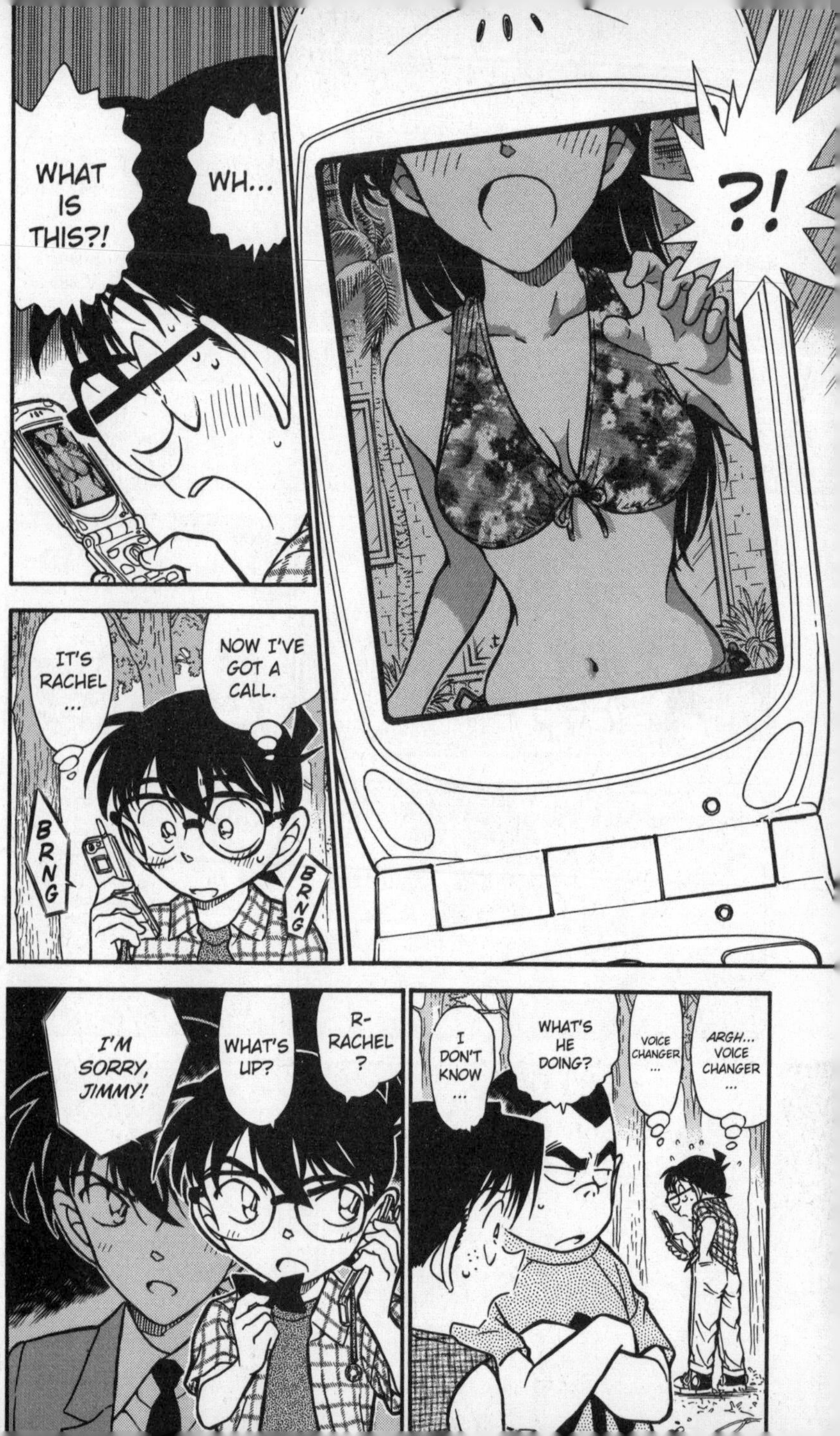
?!
WH...
WHAT IS THIS?!
NOW I'VE GOT A CALL.
IT'S RACHEL ...
BRNG
BRNG
ARGH... VOICE CHANGER ...
VOICE CHANGER ...
WHAT'S HE DOING?
I DON'T KNOW ...
R-RACHEL?
WHAT'S UP?
I'M SORRY, JIMMY!

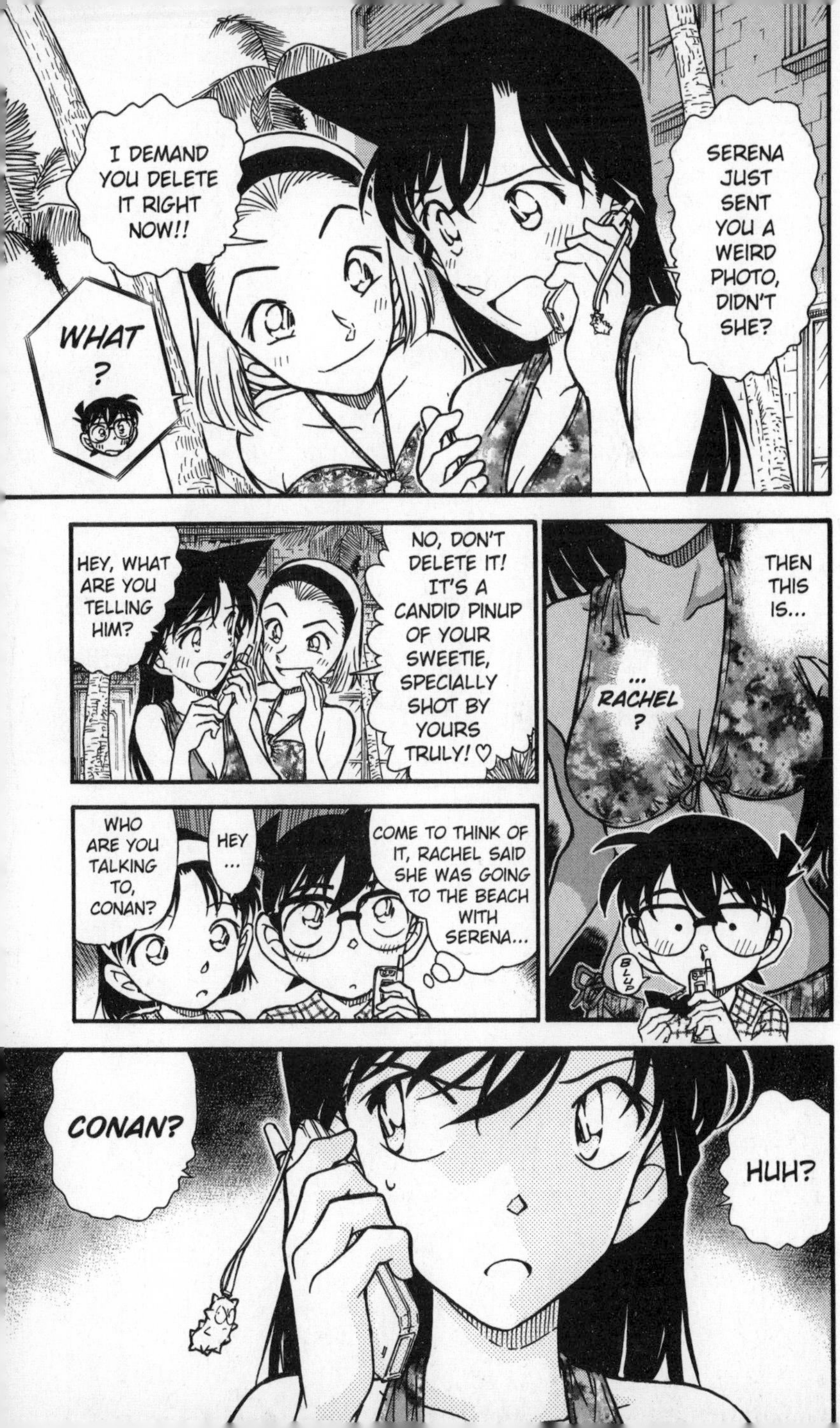
SERENA JUST SENT YOU A WEIRD PHOTO, DIDN'T SHE?
I DEMAND YOU DELETE IT RIGHT NOW!!
WHAT ?
THEN THIS IS...
... RACHEL ?
BLUP
NO, DON'T DELETE IT! IT'S A CANDID PINUP OF YOUR SWEETIE, SPECIALLY SHOT BY YOURS TRULY! ♡
HEY, WHAT ARE YOU TELLING HIM?
COME TO THINK OF IT, RACHEL SAID SHE WAS GOING TO THE BEACH WITH SERENA...
HEY ...
WHO ARE YOU TALKING TO, CONAN?
HUH?
CONAN?

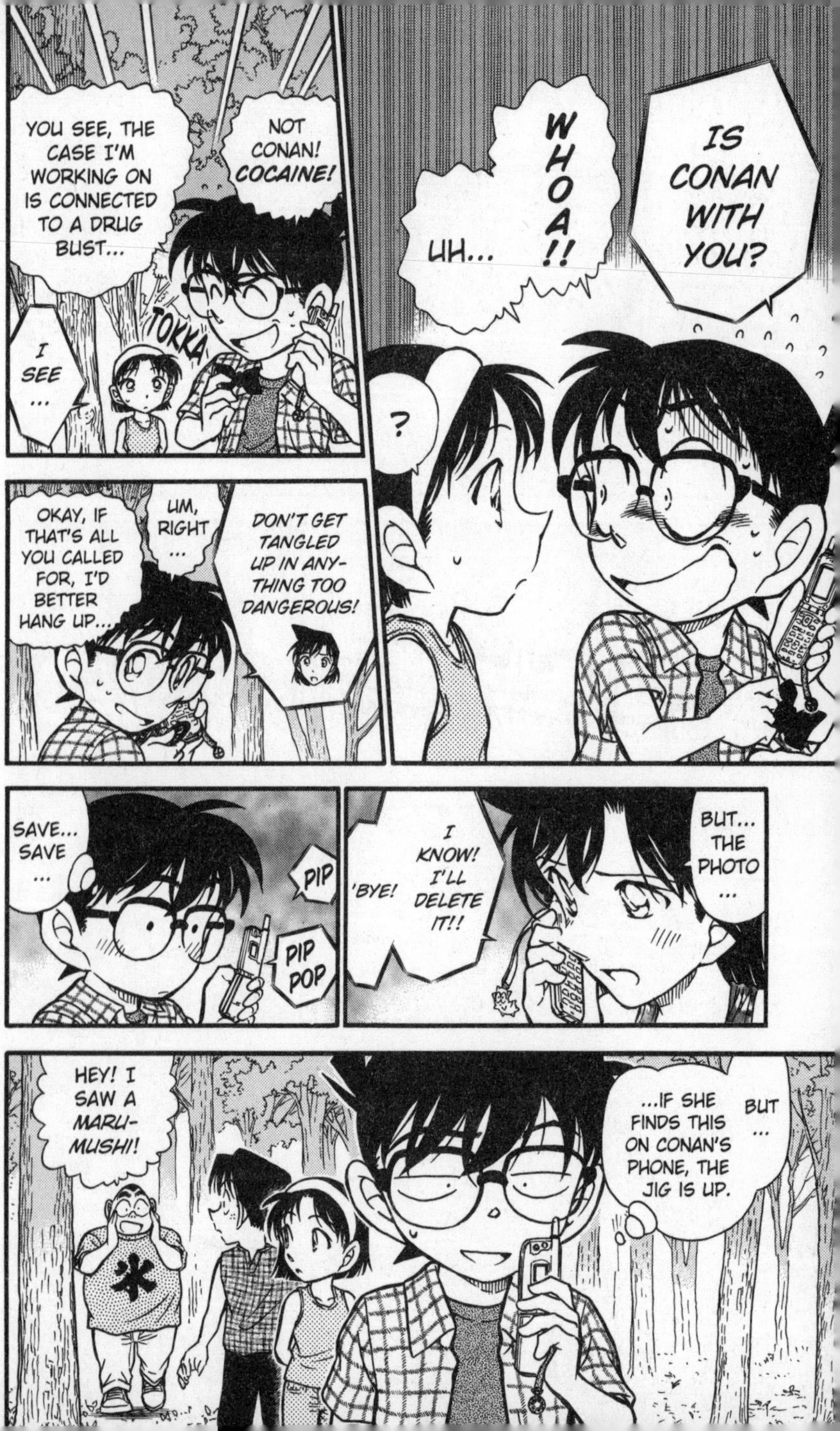
IS CONAN WITH YOU?
UH... WHOA!!
?
NOT CONAN! COCAINE!
YOU SEE, THE CASE I'M WORKING ON IS CONNECTED TO A DRUG BUST...
TOKKA
I SEE ...
DON'T GET TANGLED UP IN ANYTHING TOO DANGEROUS!
UM, RIGHT ...
OKAY, IF THAT'S ALL YOU CALLED FOR, I'D BETTER HANG UP...
BUT... THE PHOTO ...
I KNOW! I'LL DELETE IT!!
'BYE!
SAVE... SAVE ...
PIP
PIP POP
BUT ...
...IF SHE FINDS THIS ON CONAN'S PHONE, THE JIG IS UP.
HEY! I SAW A MARU-MUSHI!

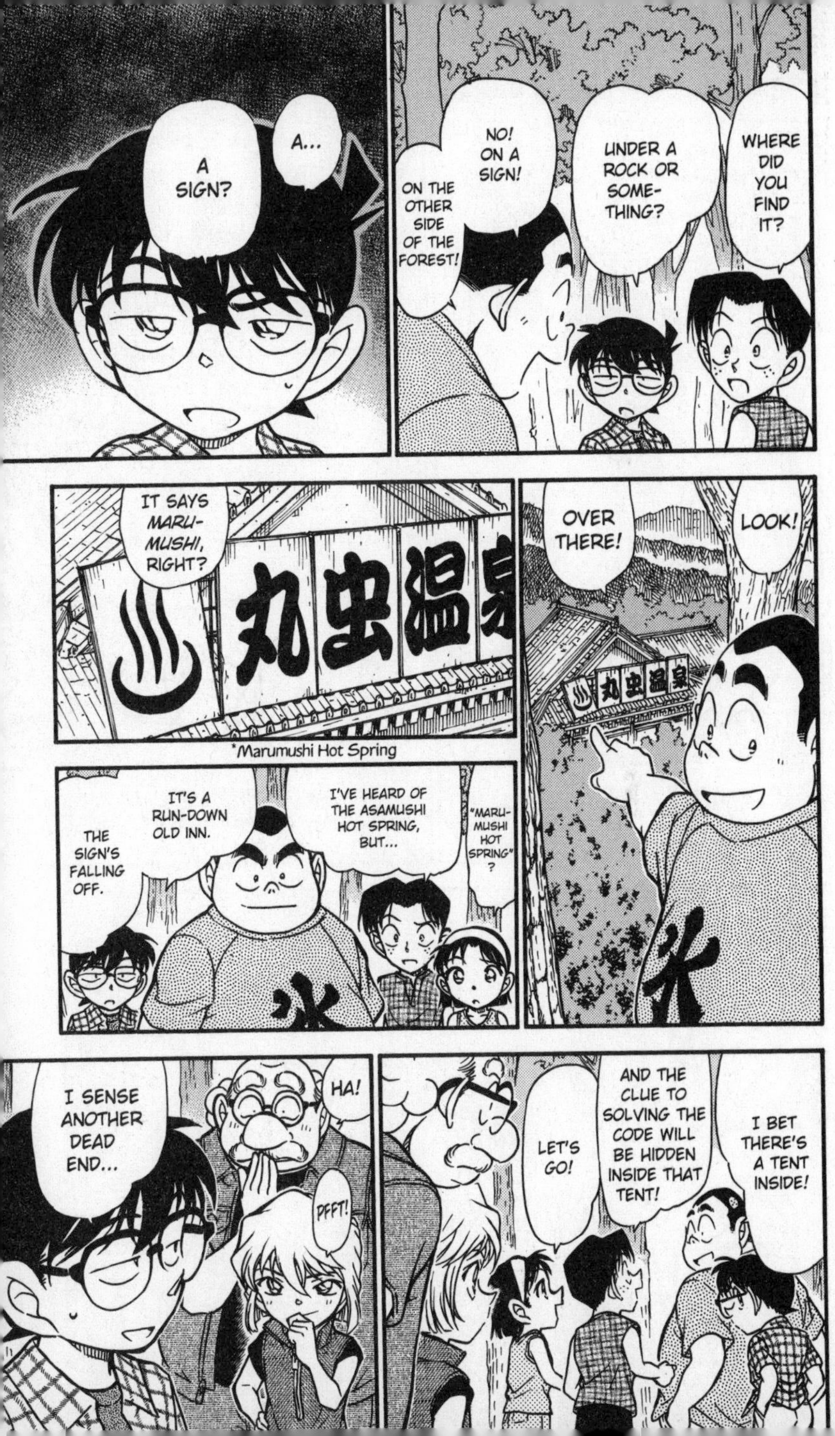
WHERE DID YOU FIND IT?
UNDER A ROCK OR SOMETHING?
NO! ON A SIGN!
ON THE OTHER SIDE OF THE FOREST!
A...
A SIGN?
LOOK!
OVER THERE!
丸虫温泉
IT SAYS MARUMUSHI, RIGHT?
丸虫温泉
*Marumushi Hot Spring
"MARUMUSHI HOT SPRING"?
I'VE HEARD OF THE ASAMUSHI HOT SPRING, BUT...
IT'S A RUN-DOWN OLD INN.
THE SIGN'S FALLING OFF.
I BET THERE'S A TENT INSIDE!
AND THE CLUE TO SOLVING THE CODE WILL BE HIDDEN INSIDE THAT TENT!
LET'S GO!
HA!
I SENSE ANOTHER DEAD END...
PFFT!

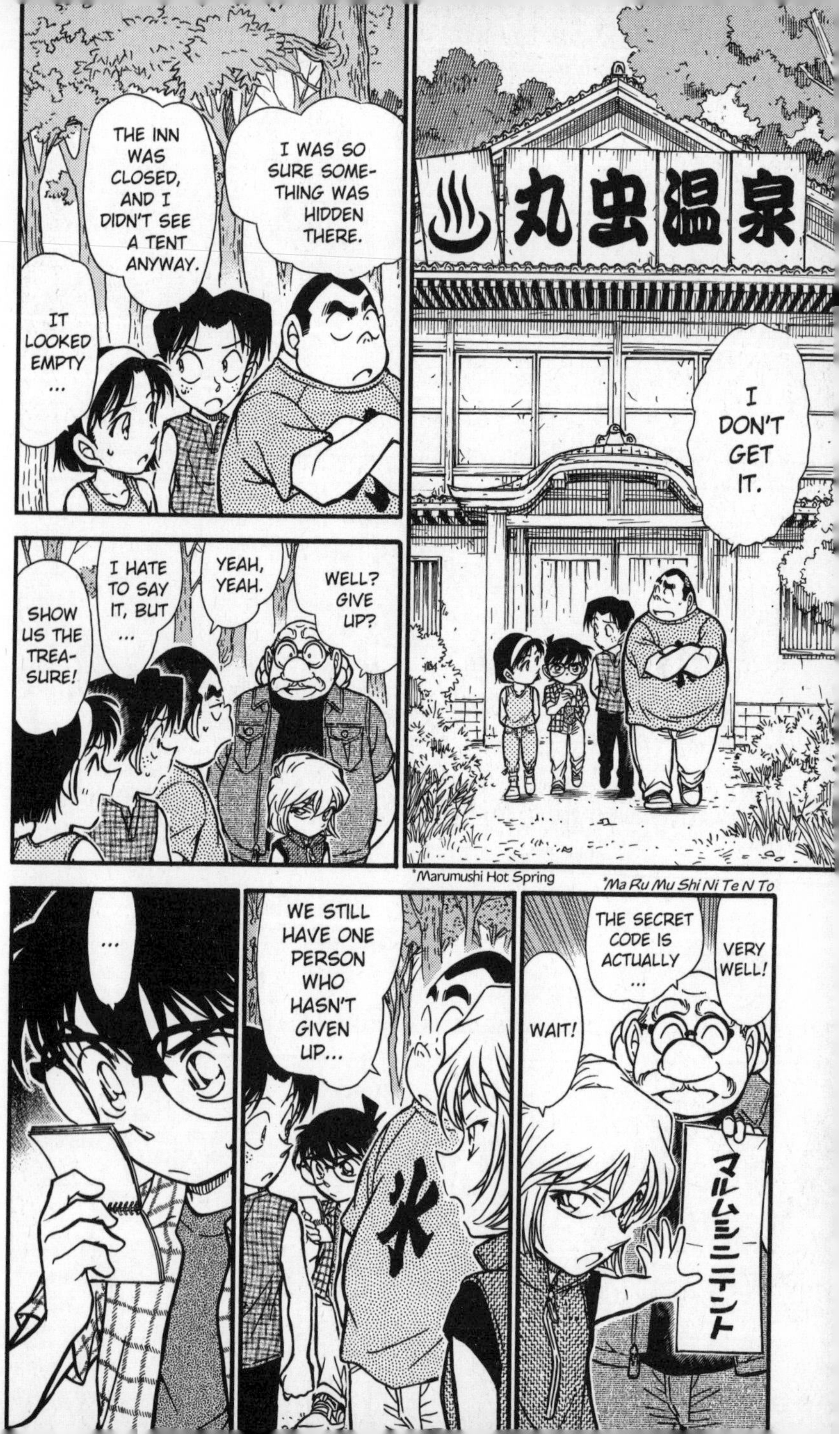
丸虫温泉
I DON'T GET IT.
I WAS SO SURE SOME-THING WAS HIDDEN THERE.
THE INN WAS CLOSED, AND I DIDN'T SEE A TENT ANYWAY.
IT LOOKED EMPTY ...
WELL? GIVE UP?
YEAH, YEAH.
I HATE TO SAY IT, BUT ...
SHOW US THE TREA-SURE!
VERY WELL!
THE SECRET CODE IS ACTUALLY ...
WAIT!
マルムシニテント
WE STILL HAVE ONE PERSON WHO HASN'T GIVEN UP...
...
*Marumushi Hot Spring
*Ma Ru Mu Shi Ni Te N To

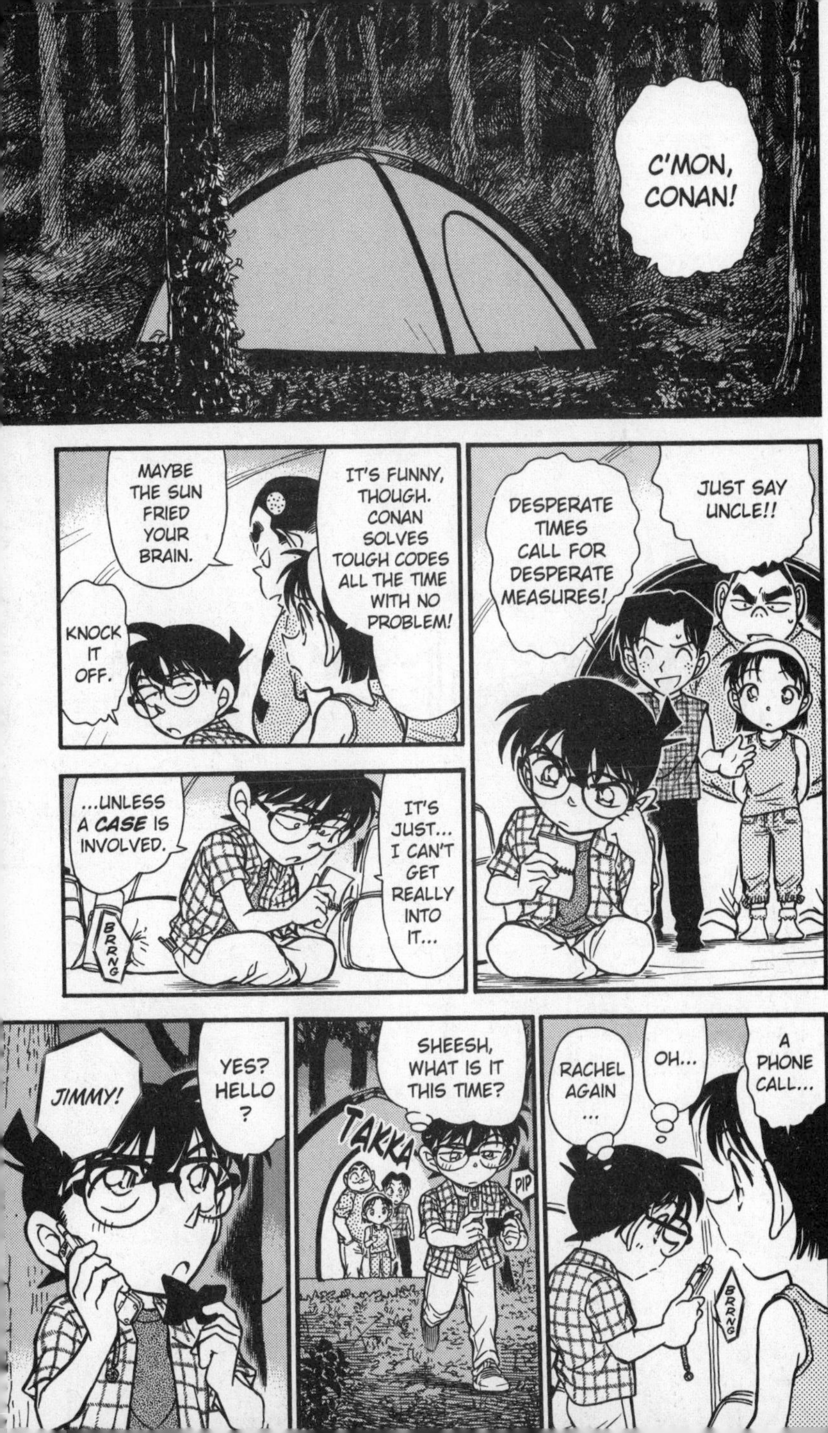
C'MON, CONAN!
JUST SAY UNCLE!!
DESPERATE TIMES CALL FOR DESPERATE MEASURES!
IT'S FUNNY, THOUGH. CONAN SOLVES TOUGH CODES ALL THE TIME WITH NO PROBLEM!
MAYBE THE SUN FRIED YOUR BRAIN.
KNOCK IT OFF.
IT'S JUST... I CAN'T GET REALLY INTO IT...
...UNLESS A CASE IS INVOLVED.
BRRNG
A PHONE CALL...
OH...
RACHEL AGAIN ...
BRRNG
SHEESH, WHAT IS IT THIS TIME?
TAKKA
PIP
YES? HELLO ?
JIMMY!

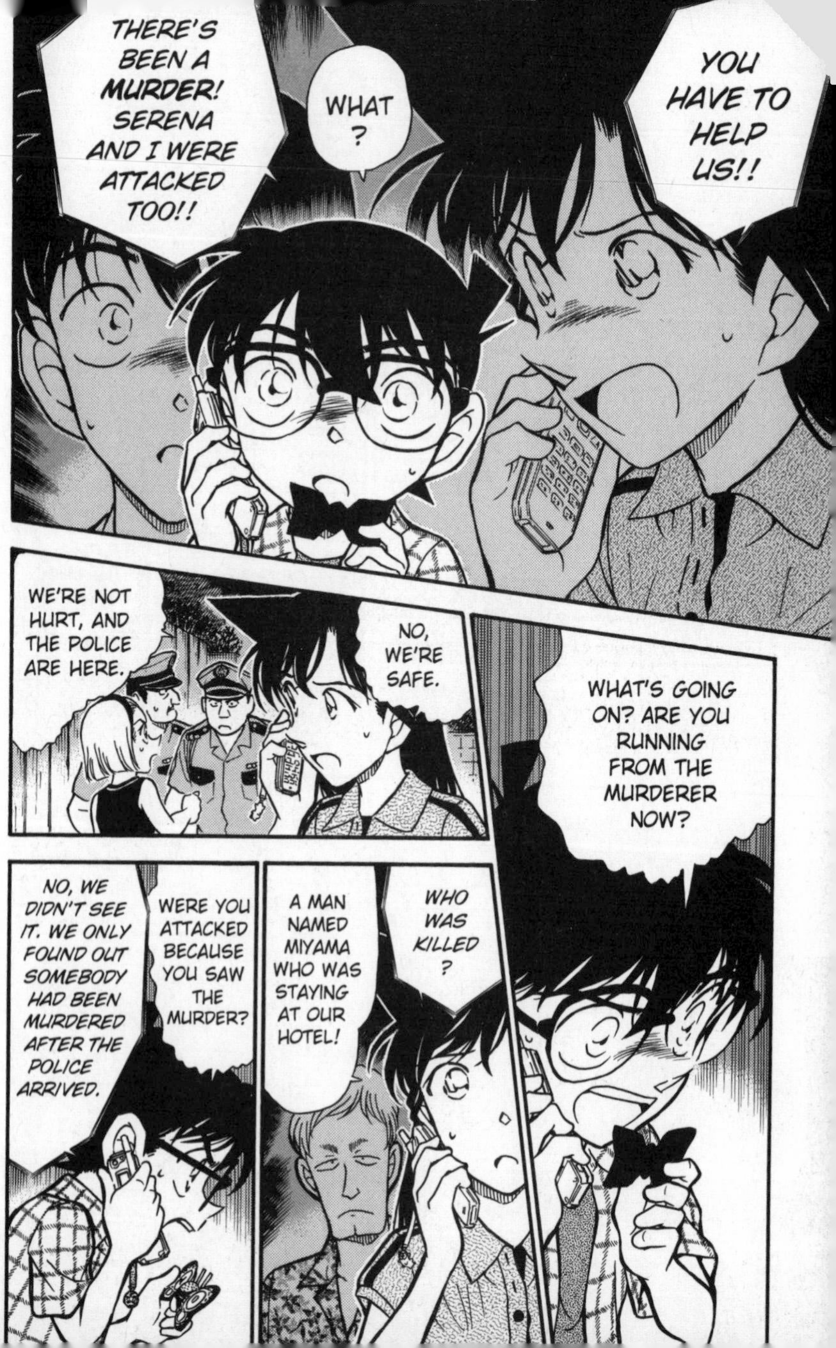
YOU HAVE TO HELP US!!
WHAT?
THERE'S BEEN A MURDER! SERENA AND I WERE ATTACKED TOO!!
WHAT'S GOING ON? ARE YOU RUNNING FROM THE MURDERER NOW?
NO, WE'RE SAFE.
WE'RE NOT HURT, AND THE POLICE ARE HERE.
WHO WAS KILLED?
A MAN NAMED MIYAMA WHO WAS STAYING AT OUR HOTEL!
WERE YOU ATTACKED BECAUSE YOU SAW THE MURDER?
NO, WE DIDN'T SEE IT. WE ONLY FOUND OUT SOMEBODY HAD BEEN MURDERED AFTER THE POLICE ARRIVED.

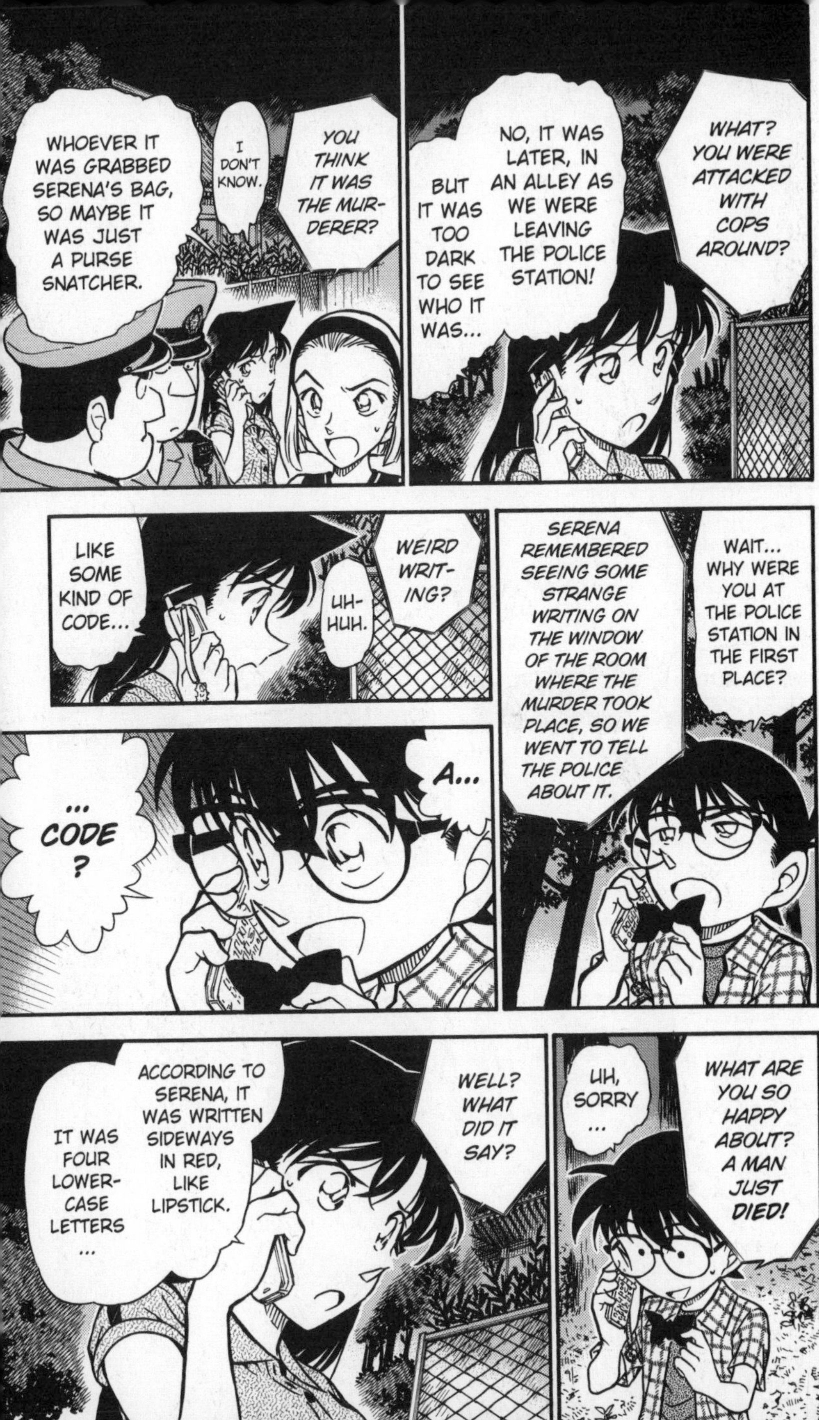
WHAT? YOU WERE ATTACKED WITH COPS AROUND?
NO, IT WAS LATER, IN AN ALLEY AS WE WERE LEAVING THE POLICE STATION!
BUT IT WAS TOO DARK TO SEE WHO IT WAS...
YOU THINK IT WAS THE MURDERER?
I DON'T KNOW.
WHOEVER IT WAS GRABBED SERENA'S BAG, SO MAYBE IT WAS JUST A PURSE SNATCHER.
WAIT... WHY WERE YOU AT THE POLICE STATION IN THE FIRST PLACE?
SERENA REMEMBERED SEEING SOME STRANGE WRITING ON THE WINDOW OF THE ROOM WHERE THE MURDER TOOK PLACE, SO WE WENT TO TELL THE POLICE ABOUT IT.
WEIRD WRITING?
UH-HUH.
LIKE SOME KIND OF CODE...
A...
...CODE?
WHAT ARE YOU SO HAPPY ABOUT? A MAN JUST DIED!
UH, SORRY...
WELL? WHAT DID IT SAY?
ACCORDING TO SERENA, IT WAS WRITTEN SIDEWAYS IN RED, LIKE LIPSTICK.
IT WAS FOUR LOWER-CASE LETTERS...

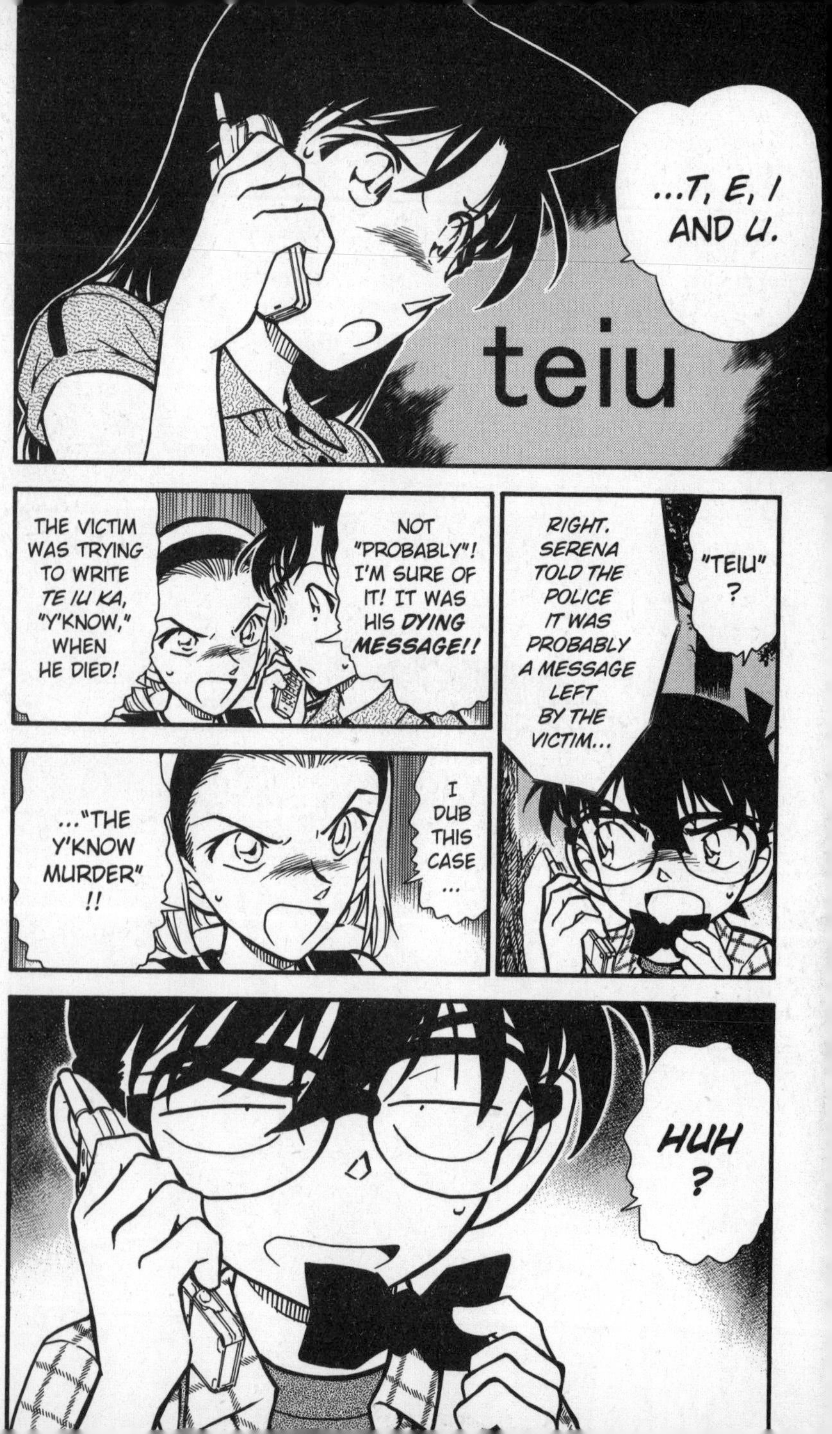
...T, E, I AND U.
teiu
"TEIU"?
RIGHT. SERENA TOLD THE POLICE IT WAS PROBABLY A MESSAGE LEFT BY THE VICTIM...
NOT "PROBABLY"! I'M SURE OF IT! IT WAS HIS DYING MESSAGE!!
THE VICTIM WAS TRYING TO WRITE TE IU KA, "Y'KNOW," WHEN HE DIED!
I DUB THIS CASE...
..."THE Y'KNOW MURDER"!!
HUH?

FILE 2: IT'S A WASH

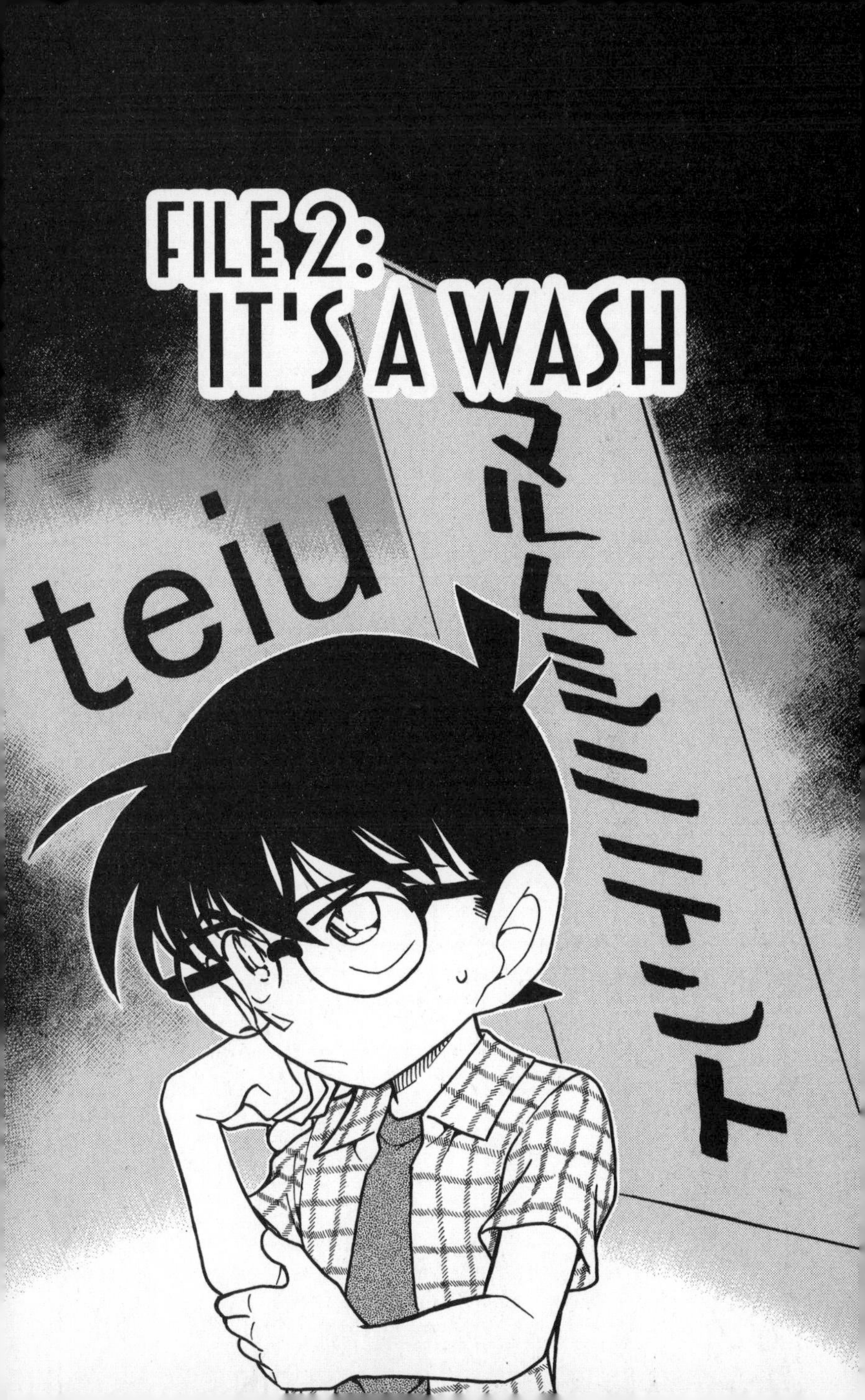

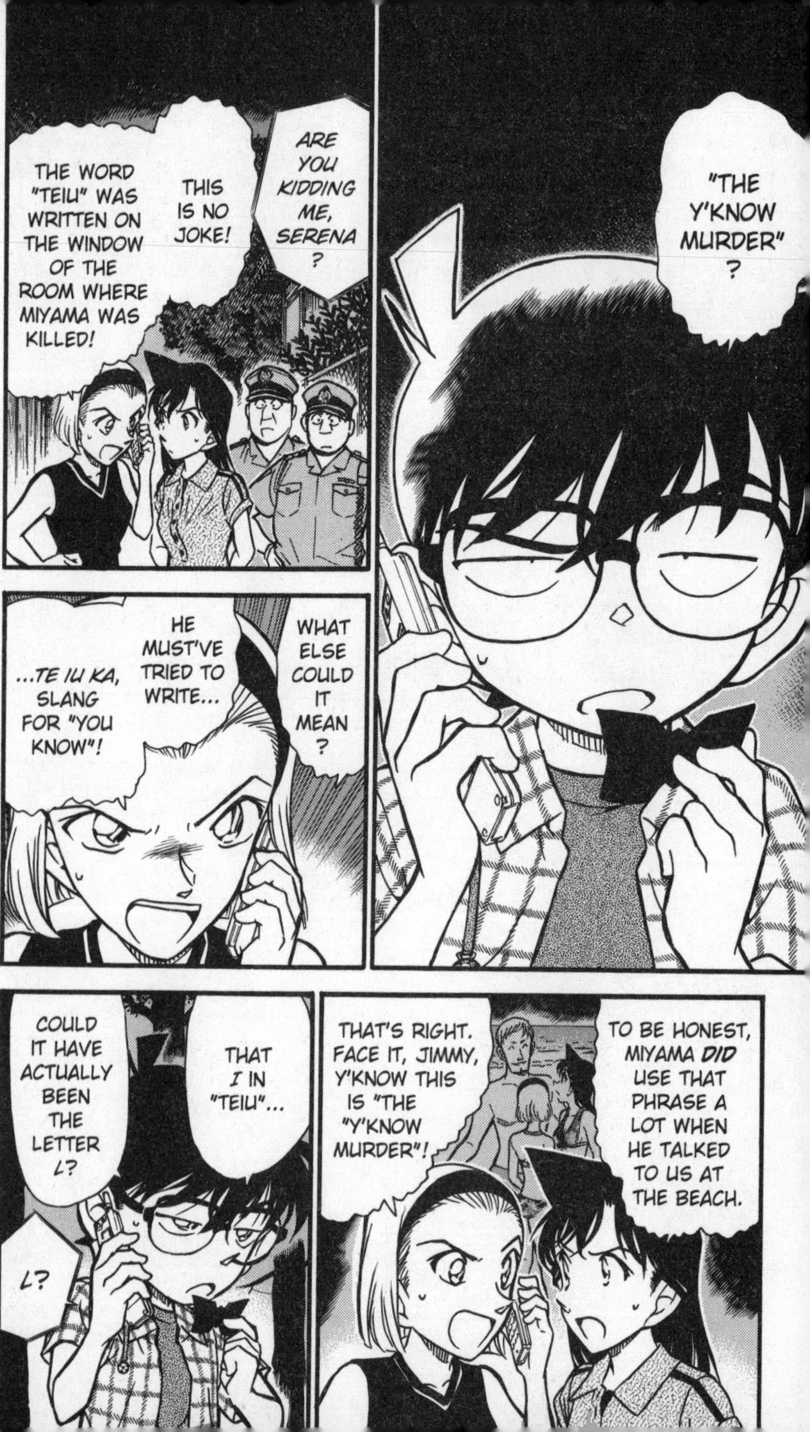
"THE Y'KNOW MURDER"?
ARE YOU KIDDING ME, SERENA?
THIS IS NO JOKE!
THE WORD "TEIU" WAS WRITTEN ON THE WINDOW OF THE ROOM WHERE MIYAMA WAS KILLED!
WHAT ELSE COULD IT MEAN?
HE MUST'VE TRIED TO WRITE...
...*TE IU KA*, SLANG FOR "YOU KNOW"!
TO BE HONEST, MIYAMA *DID* USE THAT PHRASE A LOT WHEN HE TALKED TO US AT THE BEACH.
THAT'S RIGHT. FACE IT, JIMMY, Y'KNOW THIS IS "THE "Y'KNOW MURDER"!
THAT *I* IN "TEIU"...
COULD IT HAVE ACTUALLY BEEN THE LETTER *L*?
L?

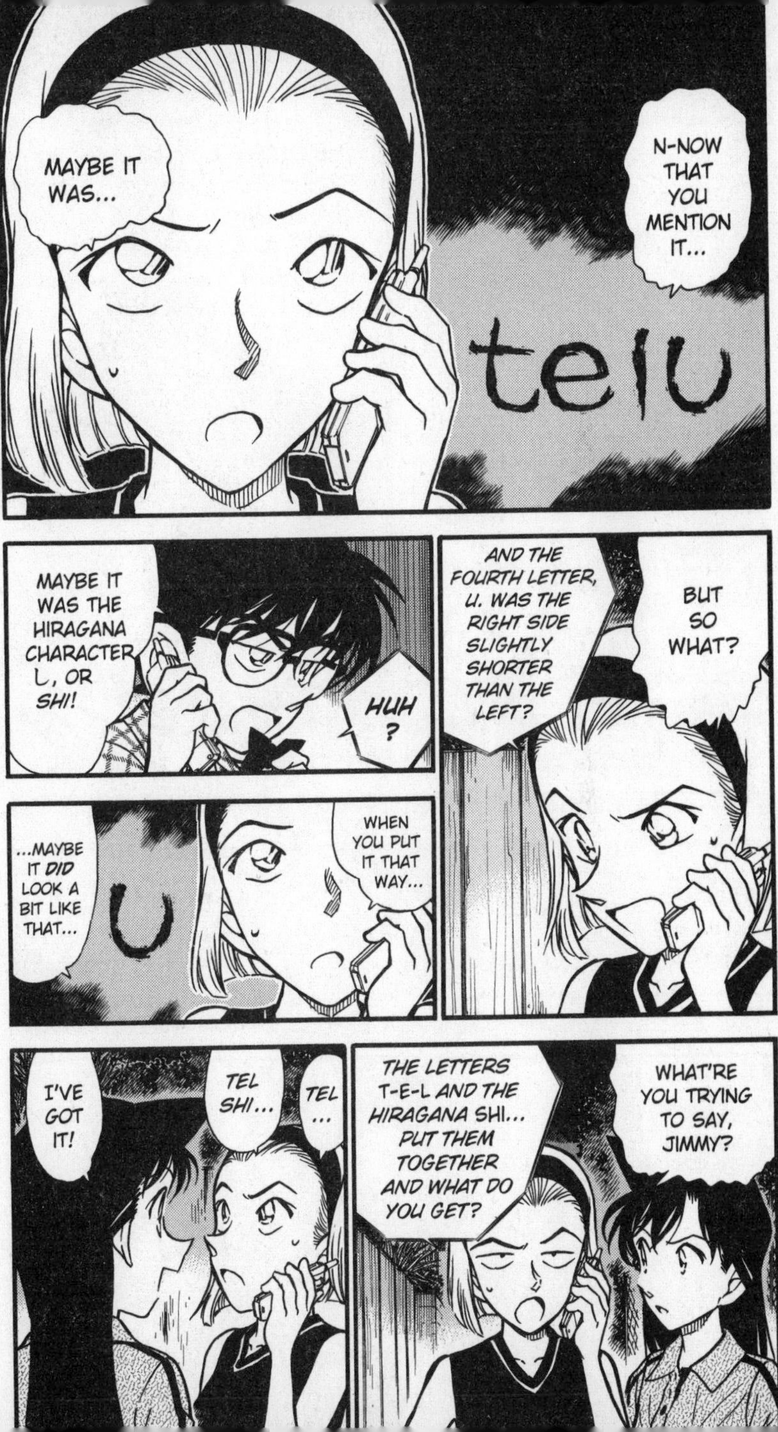
N-NOW THAT YOU MENTION IT...
MAYBE IT WAS...
teIU
AND THE FOURTH LETTER, U. WAS THE RIGHT SIDE SLIGHTLY SHORTER THAN THE LEFT?
BUT SO WHAT?
MAYBE IT WAS THE HIRAGANA CHARACTER し, OR SHI!
HUH?
WHEN YOU PUT IT THAT WAY...
...MAYBE IT DID LOOK A BIT LIKE THAT...
WHAT'RE YOU TRYING TO SAY, JIMMY?
THE LETTERS T-E-L AND THE HIRAGANA SHI... PUT THEM TOGETHER AND WHAT DO YOU GET?
TEL...
TEL SHI...
I'VE GOT IT!

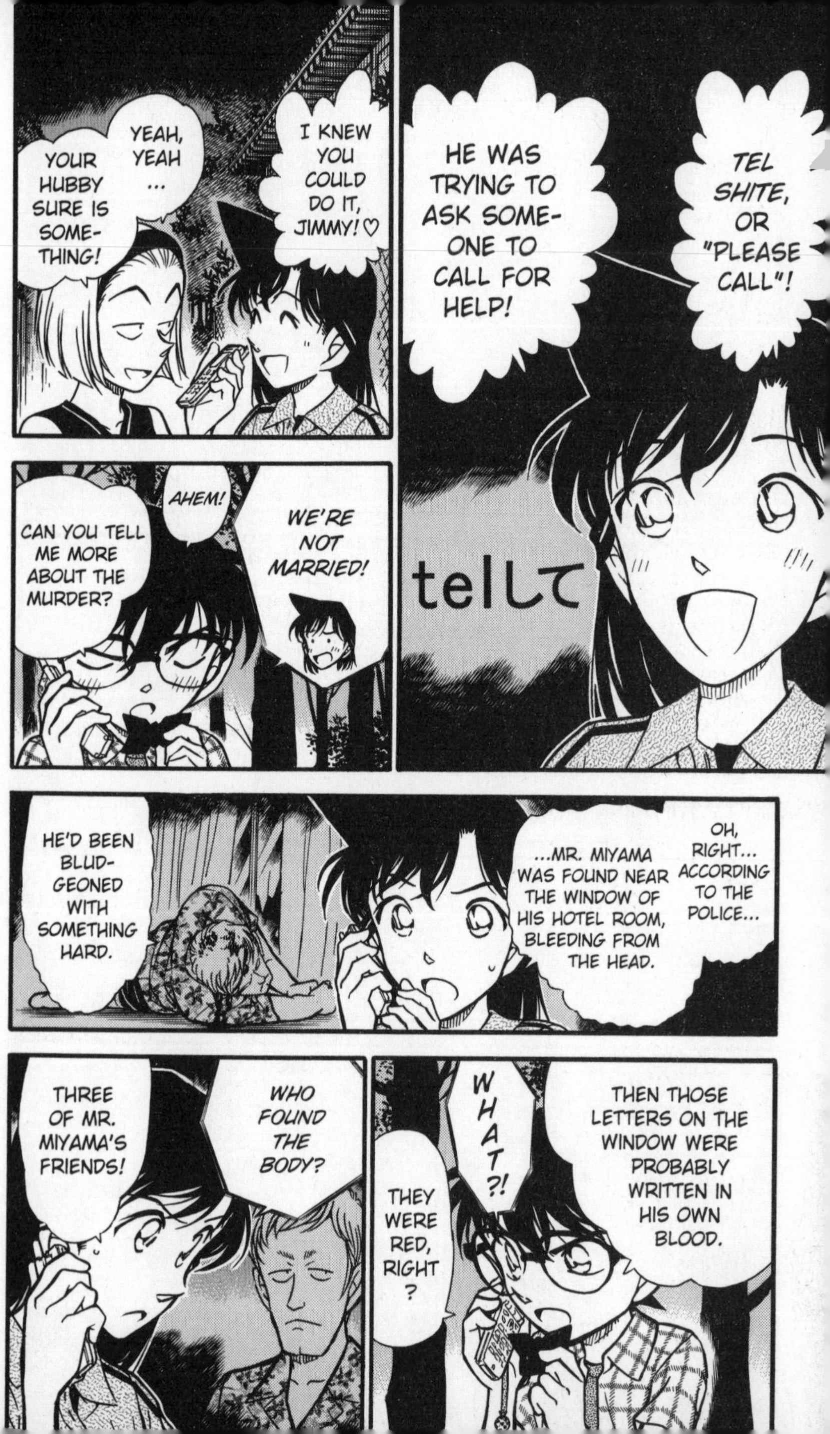
TEL SHITE, OR "PLEASE CALL"!
HE WAS TRYING TO ASK SOMEONE TO CALL FOR HELP!
tellして
I KNEW YOU COULD DO IT, JIMMY!♡
YEAH, YEAH ...
YOUR HUBBY SURE IS SOMETHING!
WE'RE NOT MARRIED!
AHEM!
CAN YOU TELL ME MORE ABOUT THE MURDER?
OH, RIGHT... ACCORDING TO THE POLICE...
...MR. MIYAMA WAS FOUND NEAR THE WINDOW OF HIS HOTEL ROOM, BLEEDING FROM THE HEAD.
HE'D BEEN BLUDGEONED WITH SOMETHING HARD.
THEN THOSE LETTERS ON THE WINDOW WERE PROBABLY WRITTEN IN HIS OWN BLOOD.
WHAT?!
THEY WERE RED, RIGHT?
WHO FOUND THE BODY?
THREE OF MR. MIYAMA'S FRIENDS!

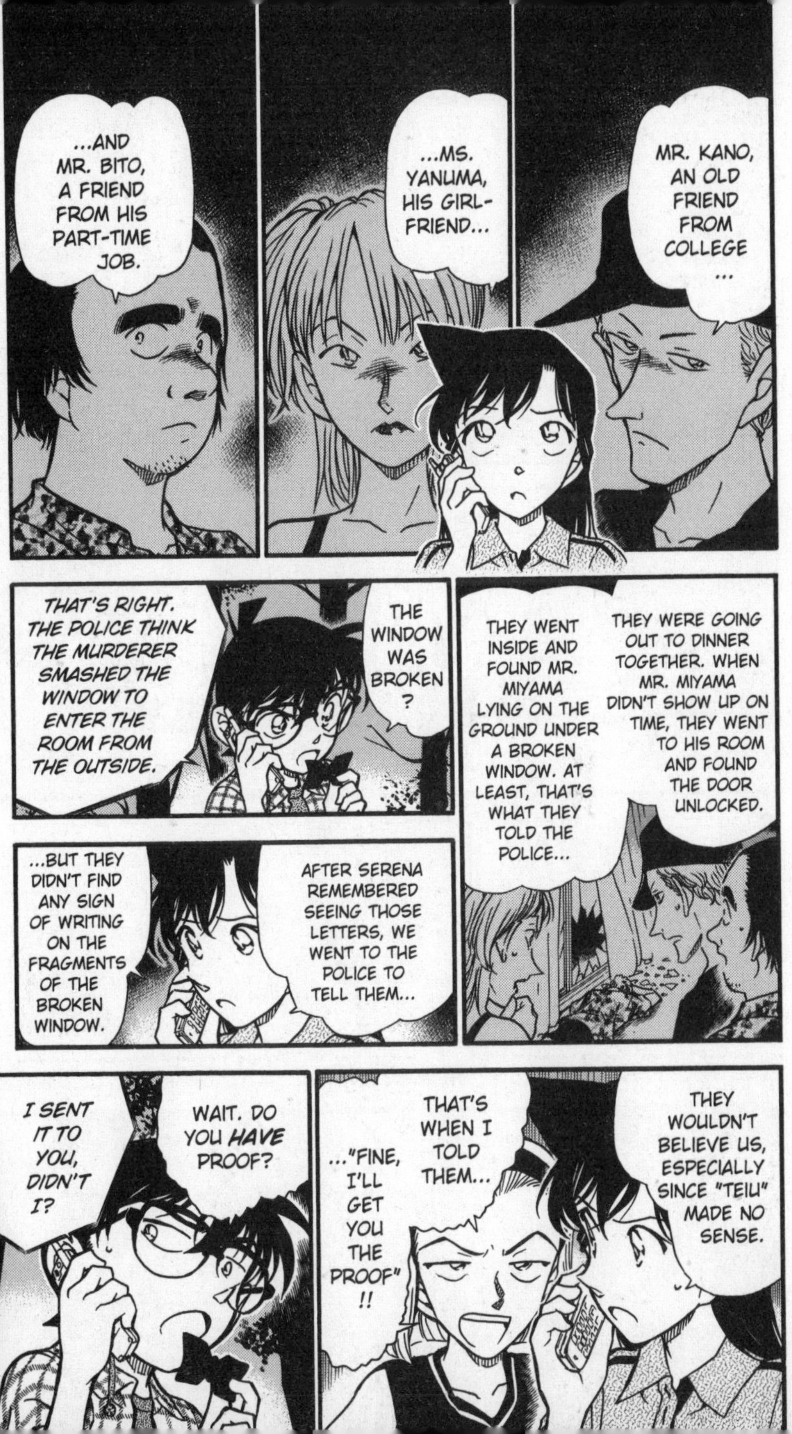
MR. KANO, AN OLD FRIEND FROM COLLEGE ...
...MS. YANUMA, HIS GIRL-FRIEND...
...AND MR. BITO, A FRIEND FROM HIS PART-TIME JOB.
THEY WERE GOING OUT TO DINNER TOGETHER. WHEN MR. MIYAMA DIDN'T SHOW UP ON TIME, THEY WENT TO HIS ROOM AND FOUND THE DOOR UNLOCKED.
THEY WENT INSIDE AND FOUND MR. MIYAMA LYING ON THE GROUND UNDER A BROKEN WINDOW. AT LEAST, THAT'S WHAT THEY TOLD THE POLICE...
THE WINDOW WAS BROKEN?
THAT'S RIGHT. THE POLICE THINK THE MURDERER SMASHED THE WINDOW TO ENTER THE ROOM FROM THE OUTSIDE.
AFTER SERENA REMEMBERED SEEING THOSE LETTERS, WE WENT TO THE POLICE TO TELL THEM...
...BUT THEY DIDN'T FIND ANY SIGN OF WRITING ON THE FRAGMENTS OF THE BROKEN WINDOW.
THEY WOULDN'T BELIEVE US, ESPECIALLY SINCE "TEIU" MADE NO SENSE.
THAT'S WHEN I TOLD THEM...
..."FINE, I'LL GET YOU THE PROOF" !!
WAIT. DO YOU *HAVE* PROOF?
I SENT IT TO YOU, DIDN'T I?

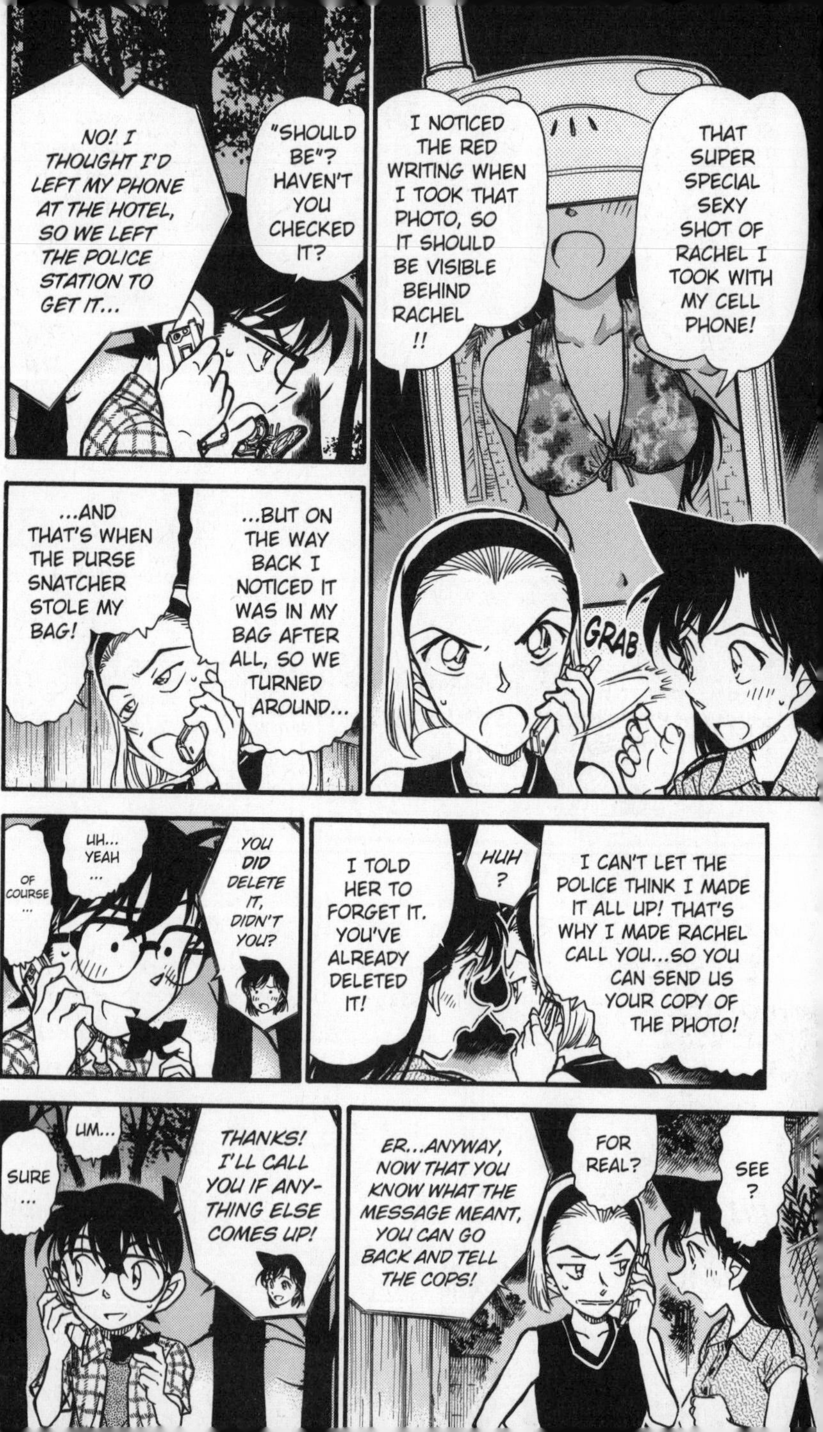
THAT SUPER SPECIAL SEXY SHOT OF RACHEL I TOOK WITH MY CELL PHONE!
I NOTICED THE RED WRITING WHEN I TOOK THAT PHOTO, SO IT SHOULD BE VISIBLE BEHIND RACHEL !!
GRAB
"SHOULD BE"? HAVEN'T YOU CHECKED IT?
NO! I THOUGHT I'D LEFT MY PHONE AT THE HOTEL, SO WE LEFT THE POLICE STATION TO GET IT...
...BUT ON THE WAY BACK I NOTICED IT WAS IN MY BAG AFTER ALL, SO WE TURNED AROUND...
...AND THAT'S WHEN THE PURSE SNATCHER STOLE MY BAG!
I CAN'T LET THE POLICE THINK I MADE IT ALL UP! THAT'S WHY I MADE RACHEL CALL YOU...SO YOU CAN SEND US YOUR COPY OF THE PHOTO!
HUH ?
I TOLD HER TO FORGET IT. YOU'VE ALREADY DELETED IT!
YOU DID DELETE IT, DIDN'T YOU?
UH... YEAH ...
OF COURSE ...
SEE ?
FOR REAL?
ER...ANYWAY, NOW THAT YOU KNOW WHAT THE MESSAGE MEANT, YOU CAN GO BACK AND TELL THE COPS!
THANKS! I'LL CALL YOU IF ANYTHING ELSE COMES UP!
UM...
SURE ...

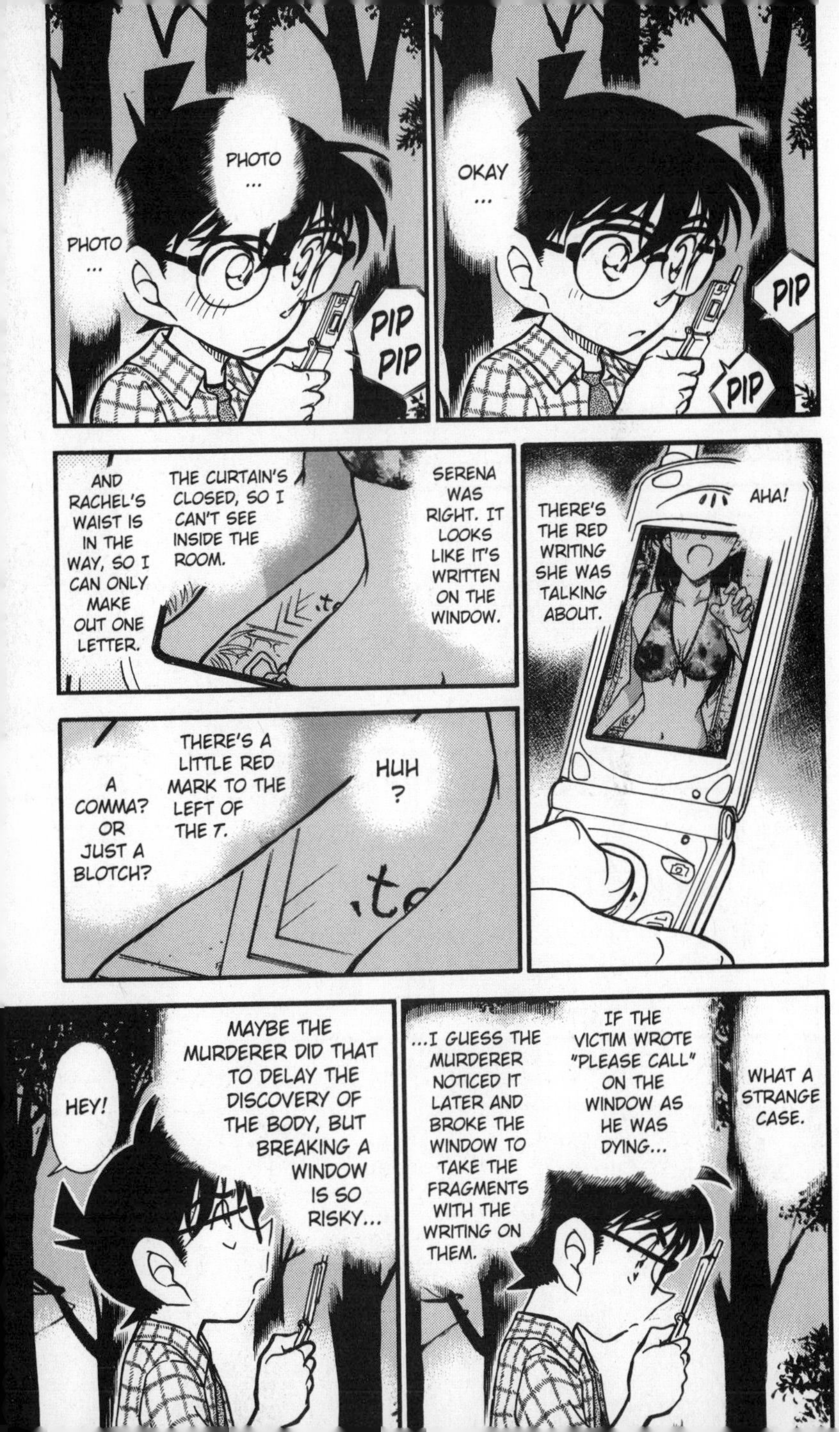
OKAY ...
PIP
PIP
PHOTO ...
PHOTO ...
PIP PIP
AHA!
THERE'S THE RED WRITING SHE WAS TALKING ABOUT.
SERENA WAS RIGHT. IT LOOKS LIKE IT'S WRITTEN ON THE WINDOW.
THE CURTAIN'S CLOSED, SO I CAN'T SEE INSIDE THE ROOM.
AND RACHEL'S WAIST IS IN THE WAY, SO I CAN ONLY MAKE OUT ONE LETTER.
HUH ?
THERE'S A LITTLE RED MARK TO THE LEFT OF THE *T*.
A COMMA? OR JUST A BLOTCH?
WHAT A STRANGE CASE.
IF THE VICTIM WROTE "PLEASE CALL" ON THE WINDOW AS HE WAS DYING...
...I GUESS THE MURDERER NOTICED IT LATER AND BROKE THE WINDOW TO TAKE THE FRAGMENTS WITH THE WRITING ON THEM.
MAYBE THE MURDERER DID THAT TO DELAY THE DISCOVERY OF THE BODY, BUT BREAKING A WINDOW IS SO RISKY...
HEY!

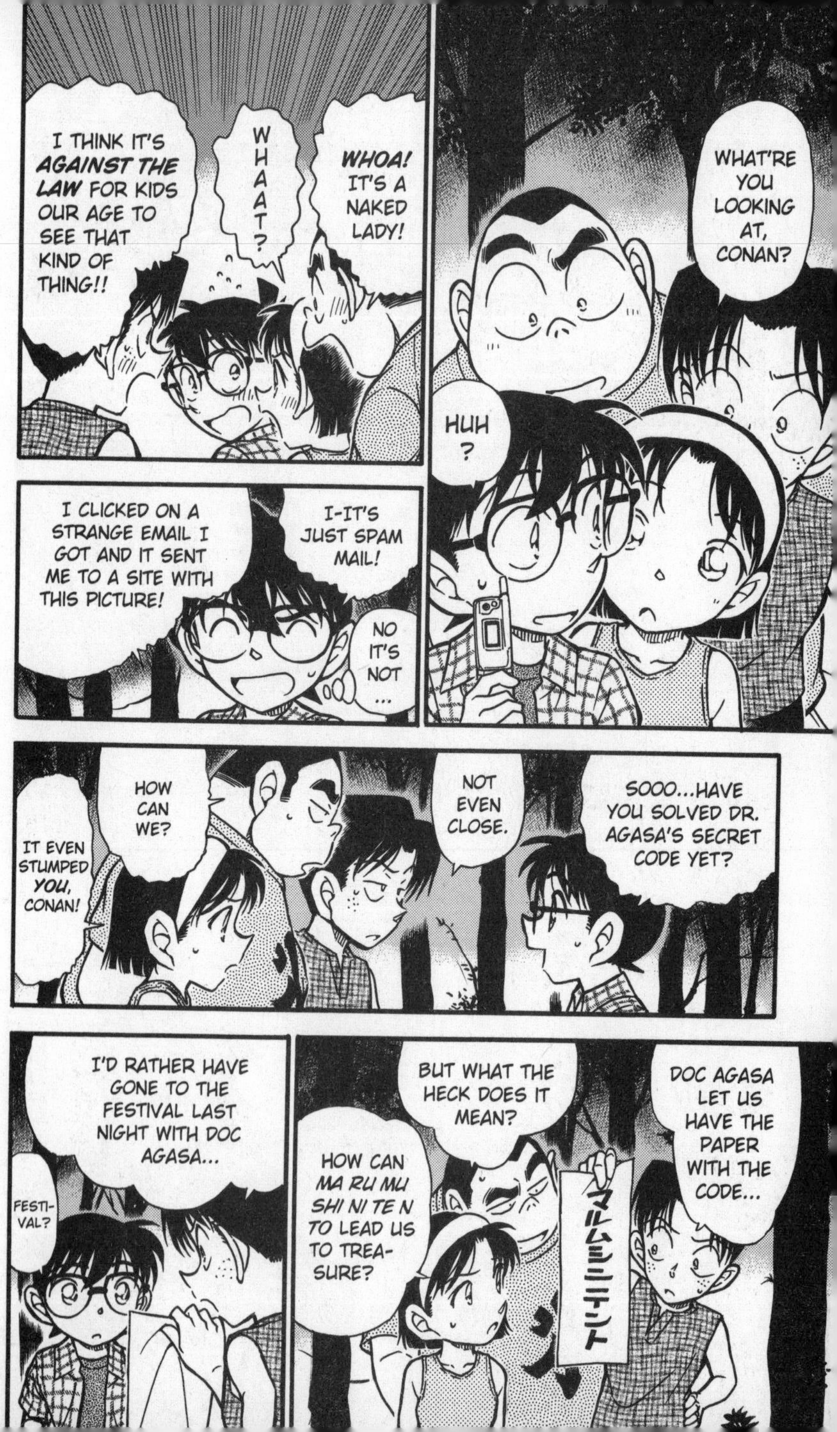
WHAT'RE YOU LOOKING AT, CONAN?
HUH?
WHOA! IT'S A NAKED LADY!
WHAAAT?
I THINK IT'S ***AGAINST THE LAW*** FOR KIDS OUR AGE TO SEE THAT KIND OF THING!!
I-IT'S JUST SPAM MAIL!
I CLICKED ON A STRANGE EMAIL I GOT AND IT SENT ME TO A SITE WITH THIS PICTURE!
NO IT'S NOT...
SOOO...HAVE YOU SOLVED DR. AGASA'S SECRET CODE YET?
NOT EVEN CLOSE.
HOW CAN WE?
IT EVEN STUMPED *YOU*, CONAN!
DOC AGASA LET US HAVE THE PAPER WITH THE CODE...
BUT WHAT THE HECK DOES IT MEAN?
HOW CAN *MA RU MU SHI NI TE N* TO LEAD US TO TREASURE?
マルムシニテント
I'D RATHER HAVE GONE TO THE FESTIVAL LAST NIGHT WITH DOC AGASA...
FESTIVAL?

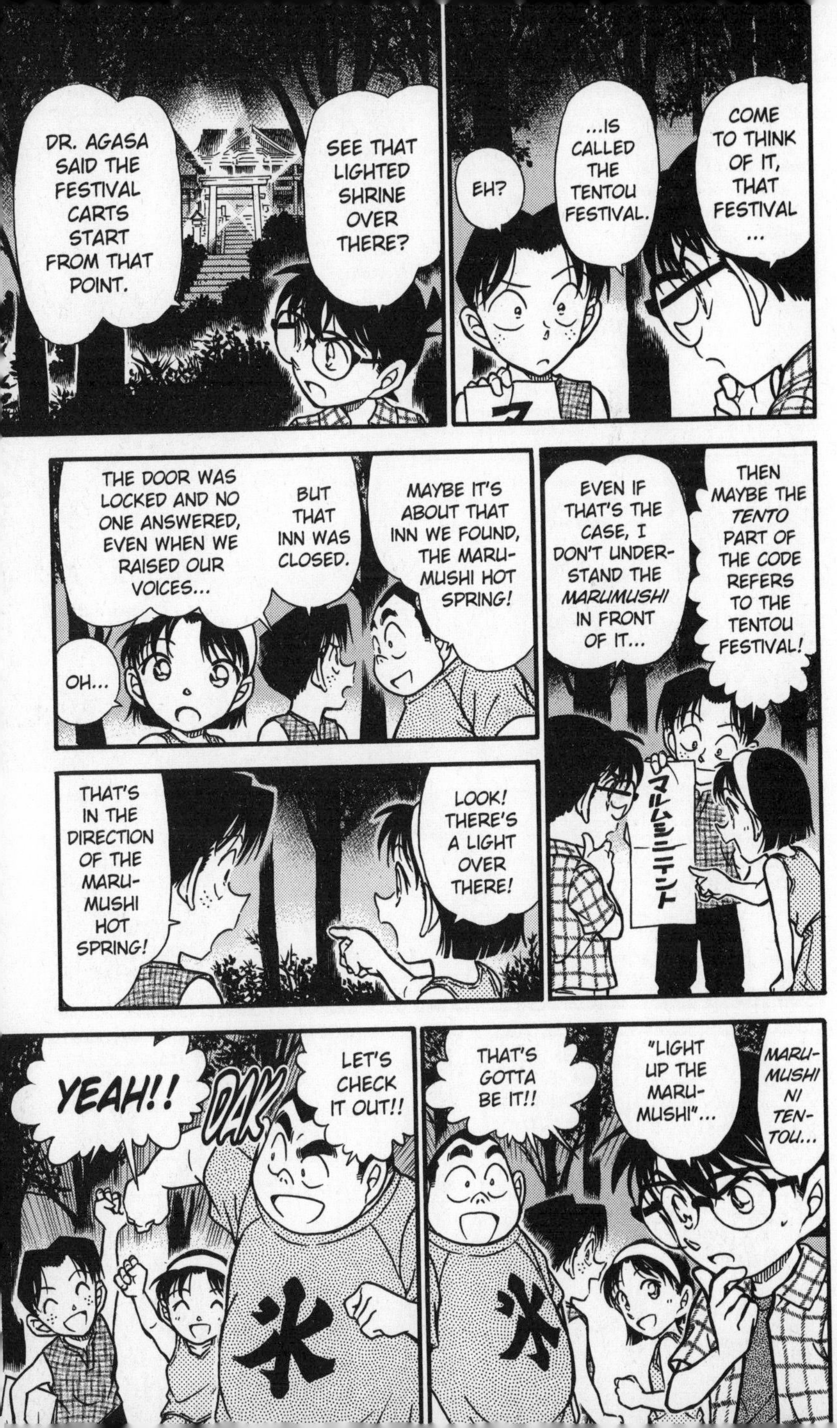
COME TO THINK OF IT, THAT FESTIVAL...
...IS CALLED THE TENTOU FESTIVAL.
EH?
SEE THAT LIGHTED SHRINE OVER THERE?
DR. AGASA SAID THE FESTIVAL CARTS START FROM THAT POINT.
THEN MAYBE THE *TENTO* PART OF THE CODE REFERS TO THE TENTOU FESTIVAL!
EVEN IF THAT'S THE CASE, I DON'T UNDERSTAND THE *MARUMUSHI* IN FRONT OF IT...
マルムシニテント
MAYBE IT'S ABOUT THAT INN WE FOUND, THE MARUMUSHI HOT SPRING!
BUT THAT INN WAS CLOSED.
THE DOOR WAS LOCKED AND NO ONE ANSWERED, EVEN WHEN WE RAISED OUR VOICES...
OH...
LOOK! THERE'S A LIGHT OVER THERE!
THAT'S IN THE DIRECTION OF THE MARUMUSHI HOT SPRING!
MARUMUSHI NI TENTOU...
"LIGHT UP THE MARUMUSHI"...
THAT'S GOTTA BE IT!!
LET'S CHECK IT OUT!!
DAK
YEAH!!

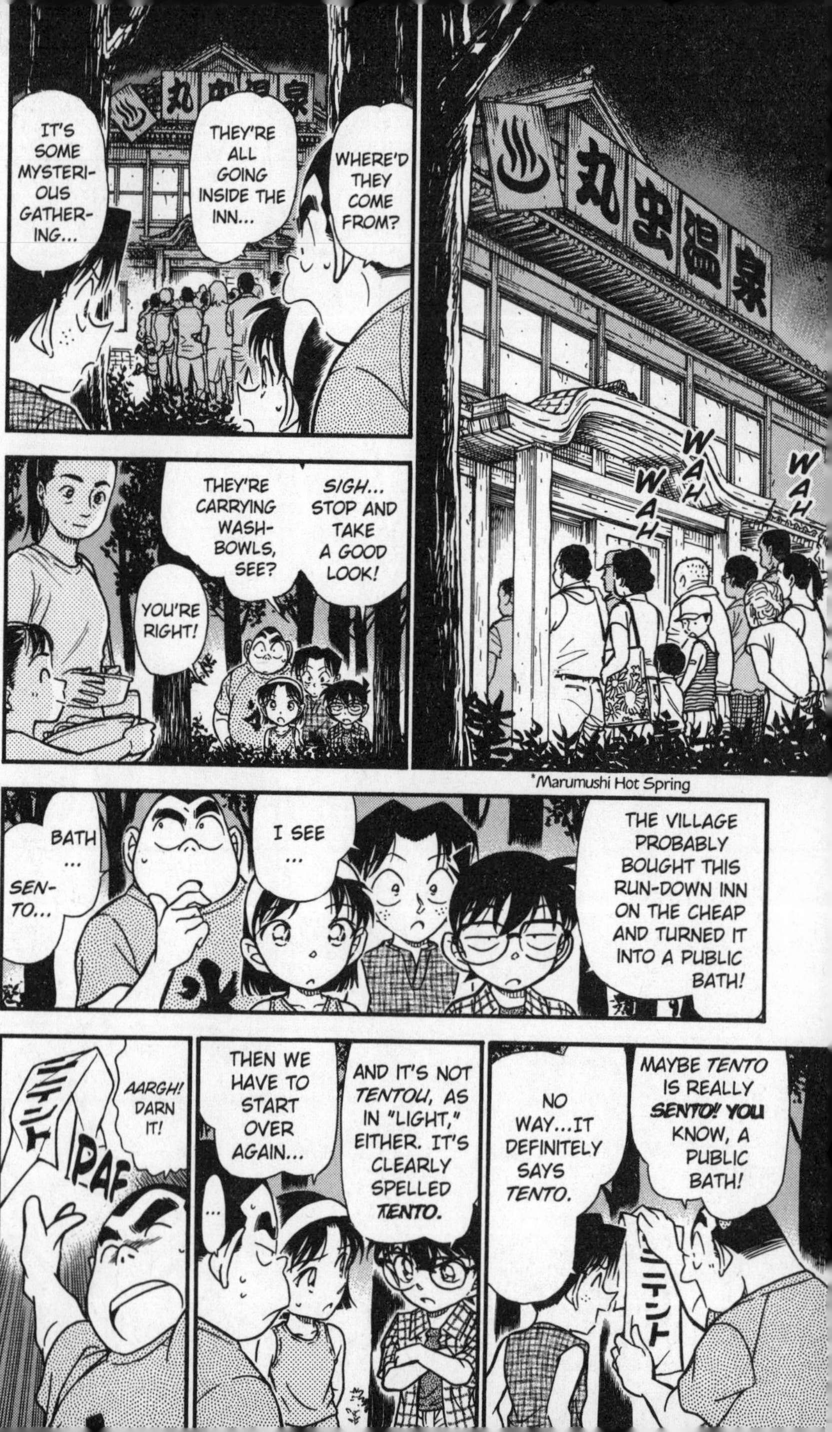
丸虫温泉
WAH WAH
WAH
*Marumushi Hot Spring
WHERE'D THEY COME FROM?
THEY'RE ALL GOING INSIDE THE INN...
IT'S SOME MYSTERIOUS GATHERING...
SIGH... STOP AND TAKE A GOOD LOOK!
THEY'RE CARRYING WASH-BOWLS, SEE?
YOU'RE RIGHT!
THE VILLAGE PROBABLY BOUGHT THIS RUN-DOWN INN ON THE CHEAP AND TURNED IT INTO A PUBLIC BATH!
I SEE...
BATH... SEN-TO...
MAYBE *TENTO* IS REALLY ***SENTO!* YOU** KNOW, A PUBLIC BATH!
NO WAY...IT DEFINITELY SAYS *TENTO*.
テント
AND IT'S NOT *TENTOU*, AS IN "LIGHT," EITHER. IT'S CLEARLY SPELLED ***TENTO***.
THEN WE HAVE TO START OVER AGAIN...
...
AARGH! DARN IT!
PAF
テント

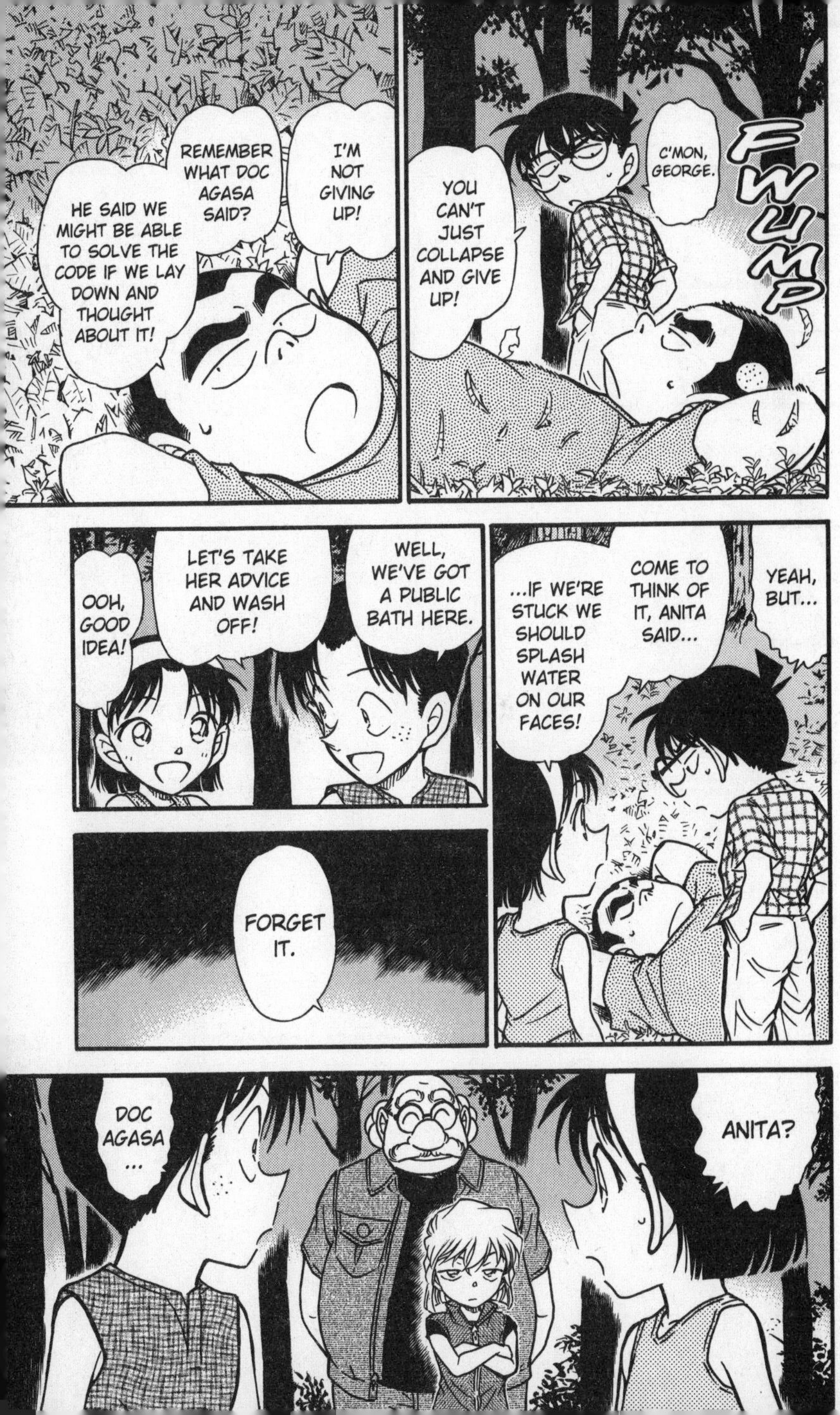
C'MON, GEORGE.
FWUMP
YOU CAN'T JUST COLLAPSE AND GIVE UP!
I'M NOT GIVING UP!
REMEMBER WHAT DOC AGASA SAID?
HE SAID WE MIGHT BE ABLE TO SOLVE THE CODE IF WE LAY DOWN AND THOUGHT ABOUT IT!
YEAH, BUT...
COME TO THINK OF IT, ANITA SAID...
...IF WE'RE STUCK WE SHOULD SPLASH WATER ON OUR FACES!
WELL, WE'VE GOT A PUBLIC BATH HERE.
LET'S TAKE HER ADVICE AND WASH OFF!
OOH, GOOD IDEA!
FORGET IT.
ANITA?
DOC AGASA ...

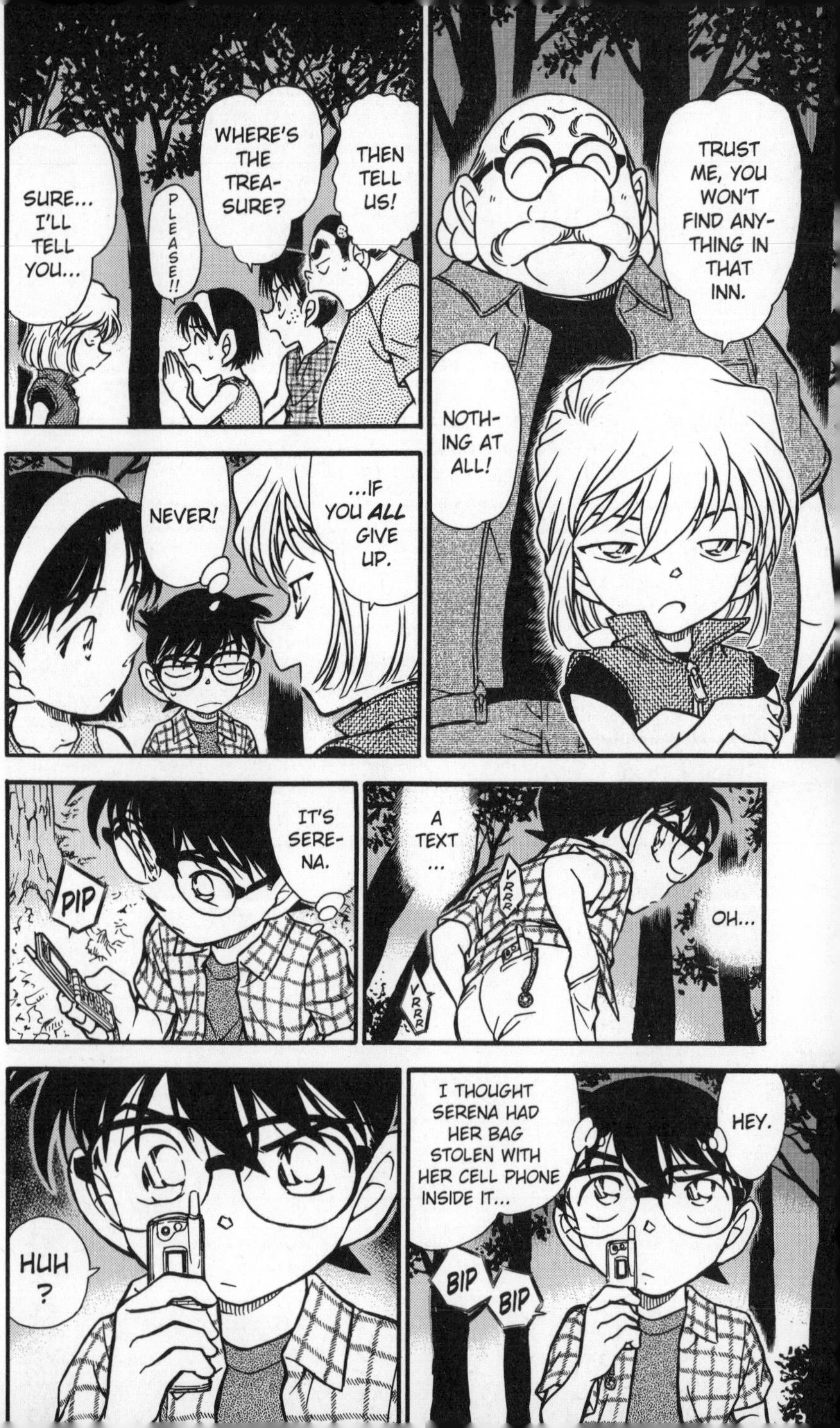
TRUST ME, YOU WON'T FIND ANYTHING IN THAT INN.
NOTHING AT ALL!
THEN TELL US!
WHERE'S THE TREASURE?
PLEASE!!
SURE... I'LL TELL YOU...
...IF YOU **ALL** GIVE UP.
NEVER!
A TEXT ...
VRRR
OH...
VRRR
IT'S SERENA.
PIP
HEY.
I THOUGHT SERENA HAD HER BAG STOLEN WITH HER CELL PHONE INSIDE IT...
BIP
BIP
HUH?

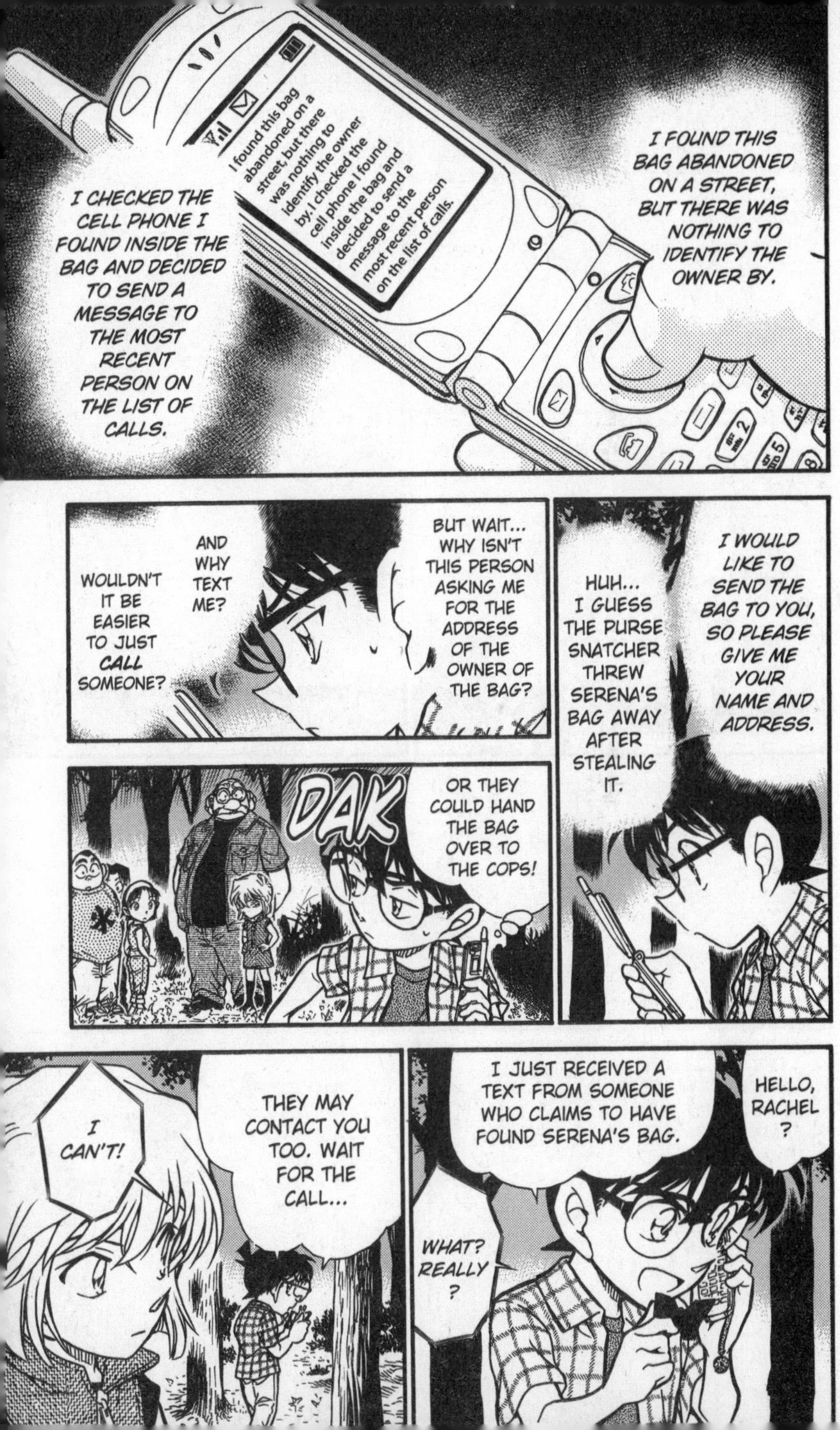
I found this bag abandoned on a street, but there was nothing to identify the owner by. I checked the cell phone I found inside the bag and decided to send a message to the most recent person on the list of calls.
I FOUND THIS BAG ABANDONED ON A STREET, BUT THERE WAS NOTHING TO IDENTIFY THE OWNER BY.
I CHECKED THE CELL PHONE I FOUND INSIDE THE BAG AND DECIDED TO SEND A MESSAGE TO THE MOST RECENT PERSON ON THE LIST OF CALLS.
I WOULD LIKE TO SEND THE BAG TO YOU, SO PLEASE GIVE ME YOUR NAME AND ADDRESS.
HUH... I GUESS THE PURSE SNATCHER THREW SERENA'S BAG AWAY AFTER STEALING IT.
BUT WAIT... WHY ISN'T THIS PERSON ASKING ME FOR THE ADDRESS OF THE OWNER OF THE BAG?
AND WHY TEXT ME?
WOULDN'T IT BE EASIER TO JUST CALL SOMEONE?
OR THEY COULD HAND THE BAG OVER TO THE COPS!
DAK
HELLO, RACHEL?
I JUST RECEIVED A TEXT FROM SOMEONE WHO CLAIMS TO HAVE FOUND SERENA'S BAG.
WHAT? REALLY?
THEY MAY CONTACT YOU TOO. WAIT FOR THE CALL...
I CAN'T!

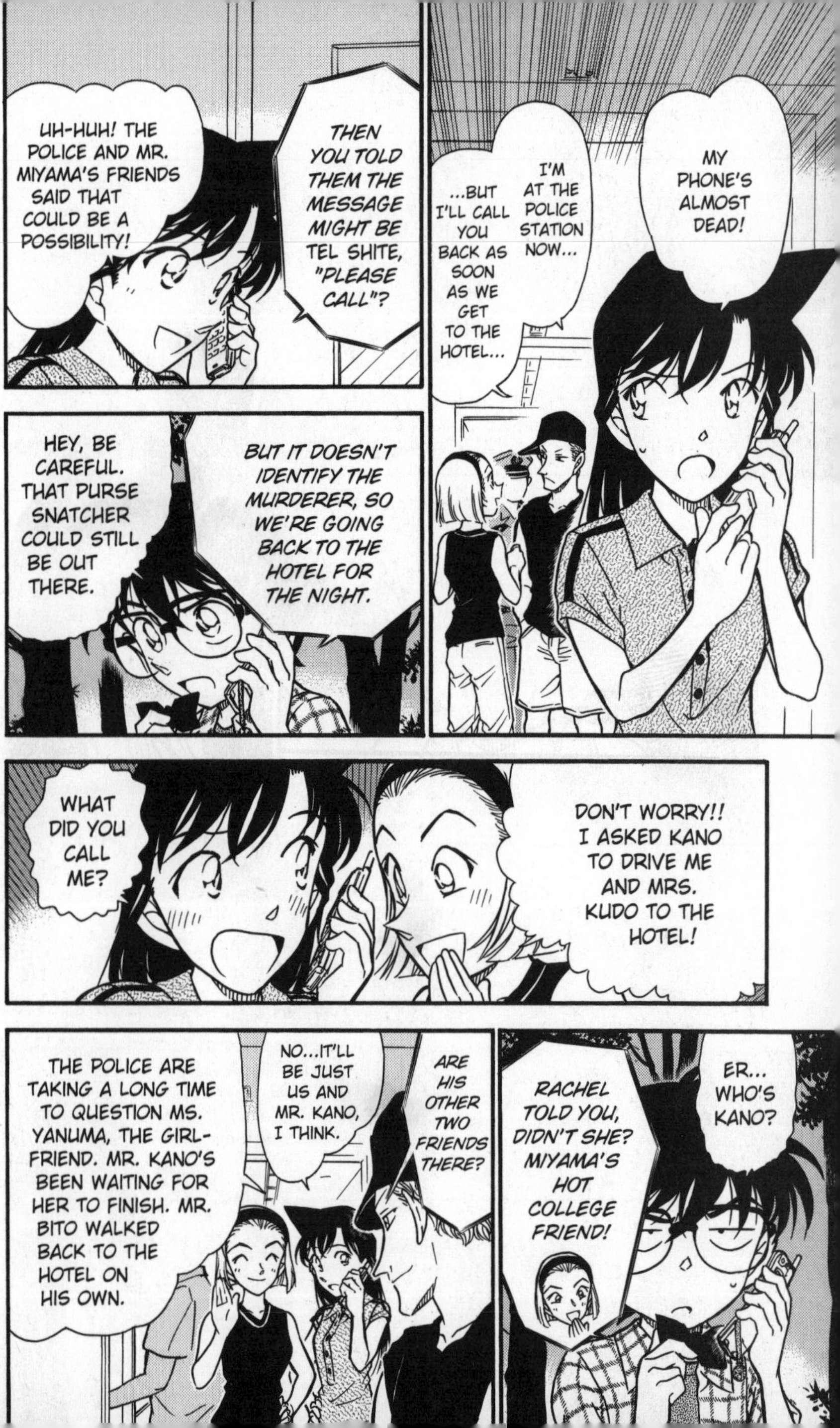
MY PHONE'S ALMOST DEAD!
I'M AT THE POLICE STATION NOW...
...BUT I'LL CALL YOU BACK AS SOON AS WE GET TO THE HOTEL...
THEN YOU TOLD THEM THE MESSAGE MIGHT BE TEL SHITE, "PLEASE CALL"?
UH-HUH! THE POLICE AND MR. MIYAMA'S FRIENDS SAID THAT COULD BE A POSSIBILITY!
BUT IT DOESN'T IDENTIFY THE MURDERER, SO WE'RE GOING BACK TO THE HOTEL FOR THE NIGHT.
HEY, BE CAREFUL. THAT PURSE SNATCHER COULD STILL BE OUT THERE.
DON'T WORRY!! I ASKED KANO TO DRIVE ME AND MRS. KUDO TO THE HOTEL!
WHAT DID YOU CALL ME?
ER... WHO'S KANO?
RACHEL TOLD YOU, DIDN'T SHE? MIYAMA'S HOT COLLEGE FRIEND!
ARE HIS OTHER TWO FRIENDS THERE?
NO...IT'LL BE JUST US AND MR. KANO, I THINK.
THE POLICE ARE TAKING A LONG TIME TO QUESTION MS. YANUMA, THE GIRL-FRIEND. MR. KANO'S BEEN WAITING FOR HER TO FINISH. MR. BITO WALKED BACK TO THE HOTEL ON HIS OWN.

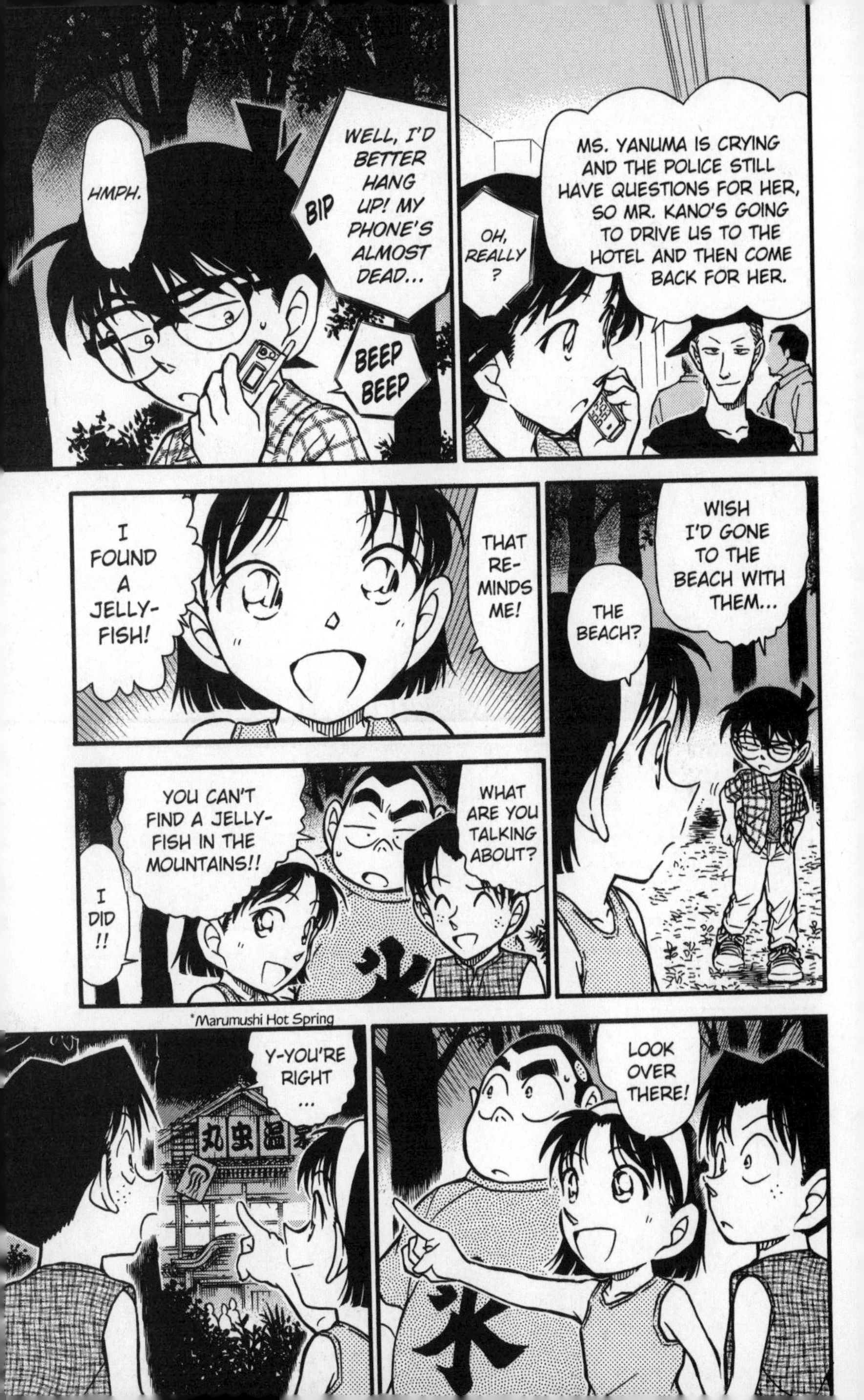
MS. YANUMA IS CRYING AND THE POLICE STILL HAVE QUESTIONS FOR HER, SO MR. KANO'S GOING TO DRIVE US TO THE HOTEL AND THEN COME BACK FOR HER.
OH, REALLY?
WELL, I'D BETTER HANG UP! MY PHONE'S ALMOST DEAD...
BIP
BEEP BEEP
HMPH.
WISH I'D GONE TO THE BEACH WITH THEM...
THE BEACH?
THAT RE- MINDS ME!
I FOUND A JELLY- FISH!
WHAT ARE YOU TALKING ABOUT?
YOU CAN'T FIND A JELLY- FISH IN THE MOUNTAINS!!
I DID!!
LOOK OVER THERE!
Y-YOU'RE RIGHT ...
丸虫温泉
*Marumushi Hot Spring

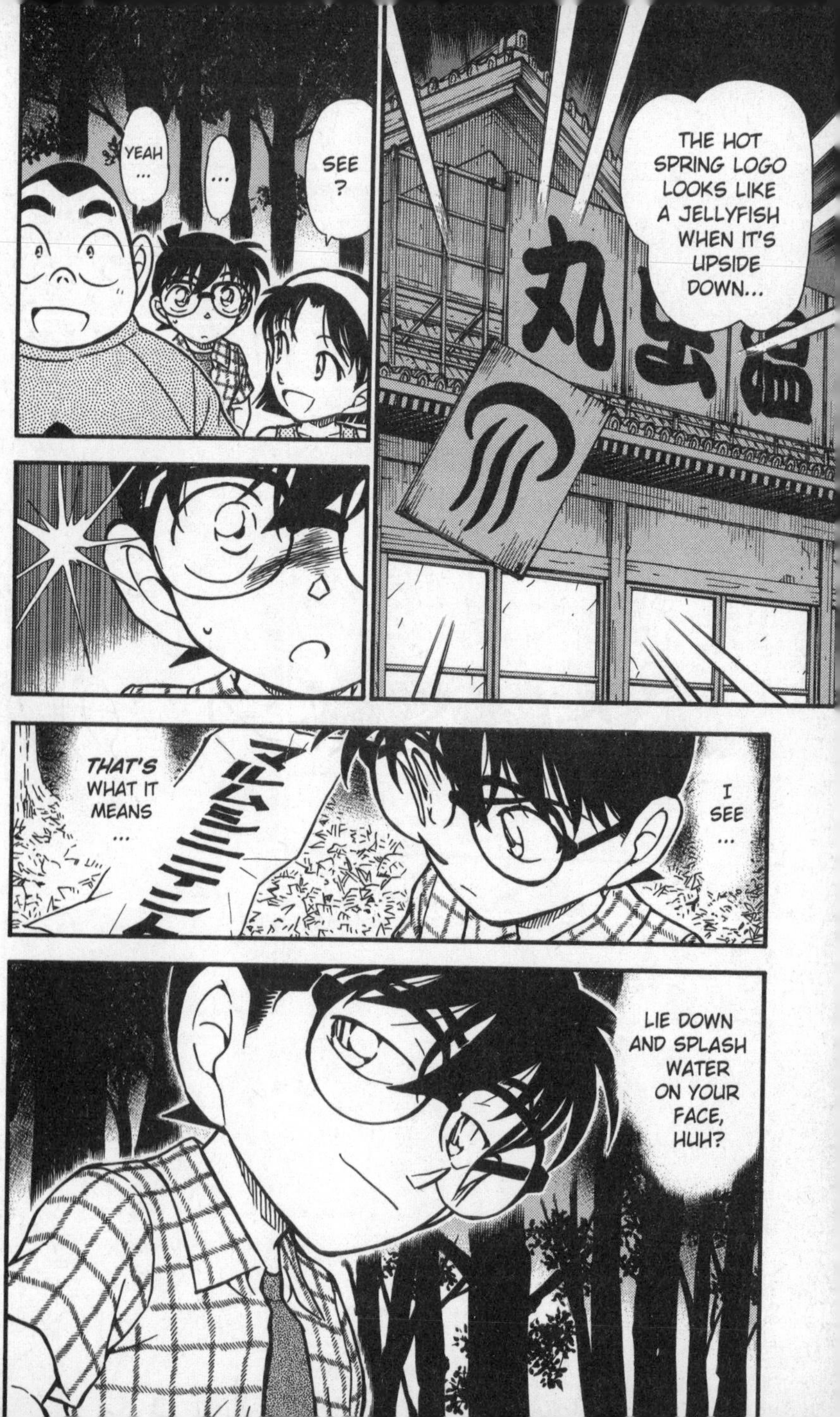
THE HOT SPRING LOGO LOOKS LIKE A JELLYFISH WHEN IT'S UPSIDE DOWN...
SEE?
...
YEAH ...
I SEE ...
THAT'S WHAT IT MEANS ...
LIE DOWN AND SPLASH WATER ON YOUR FACE, HUH?

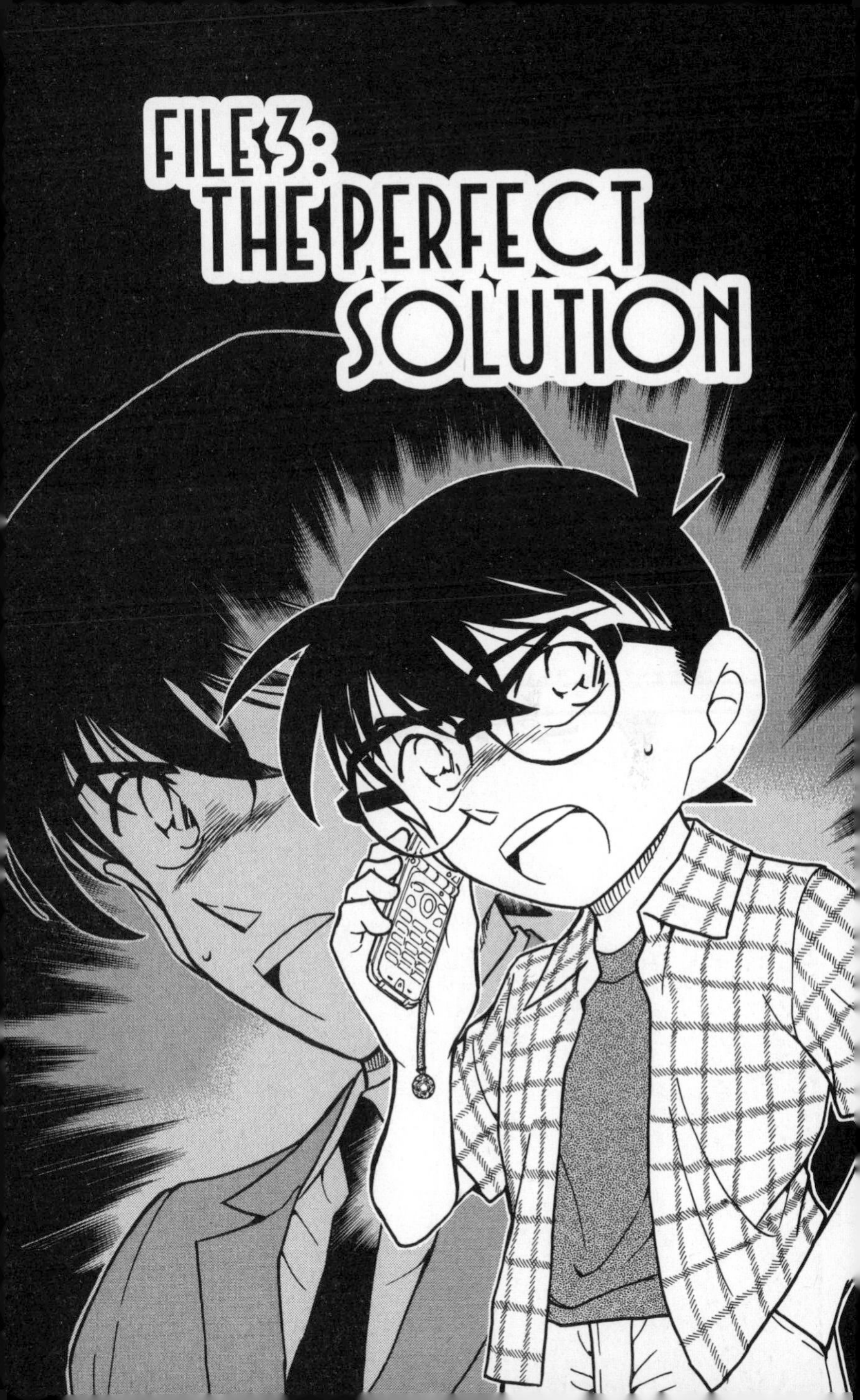
FILE 3:
THE PERFECT SOLUTION

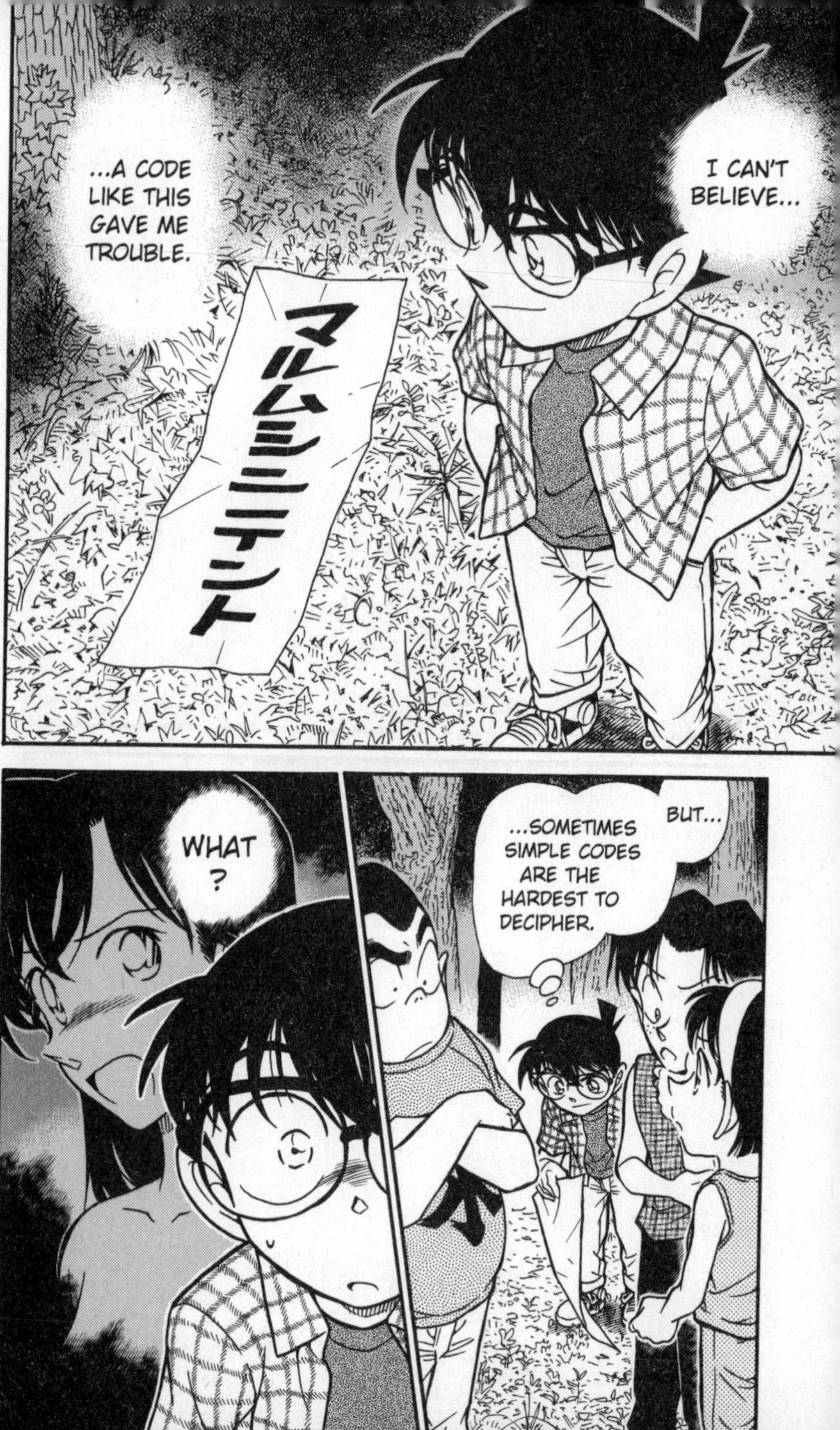
I CAN'T BELIEVE...
...A CODE LIKE THIS GAVE ME TROUBLE.
マルムミニテント
BUT...
...SOMETIMES SIMPLE CODES ARE THE HARDEST TO DECIPHER.
WHAT?

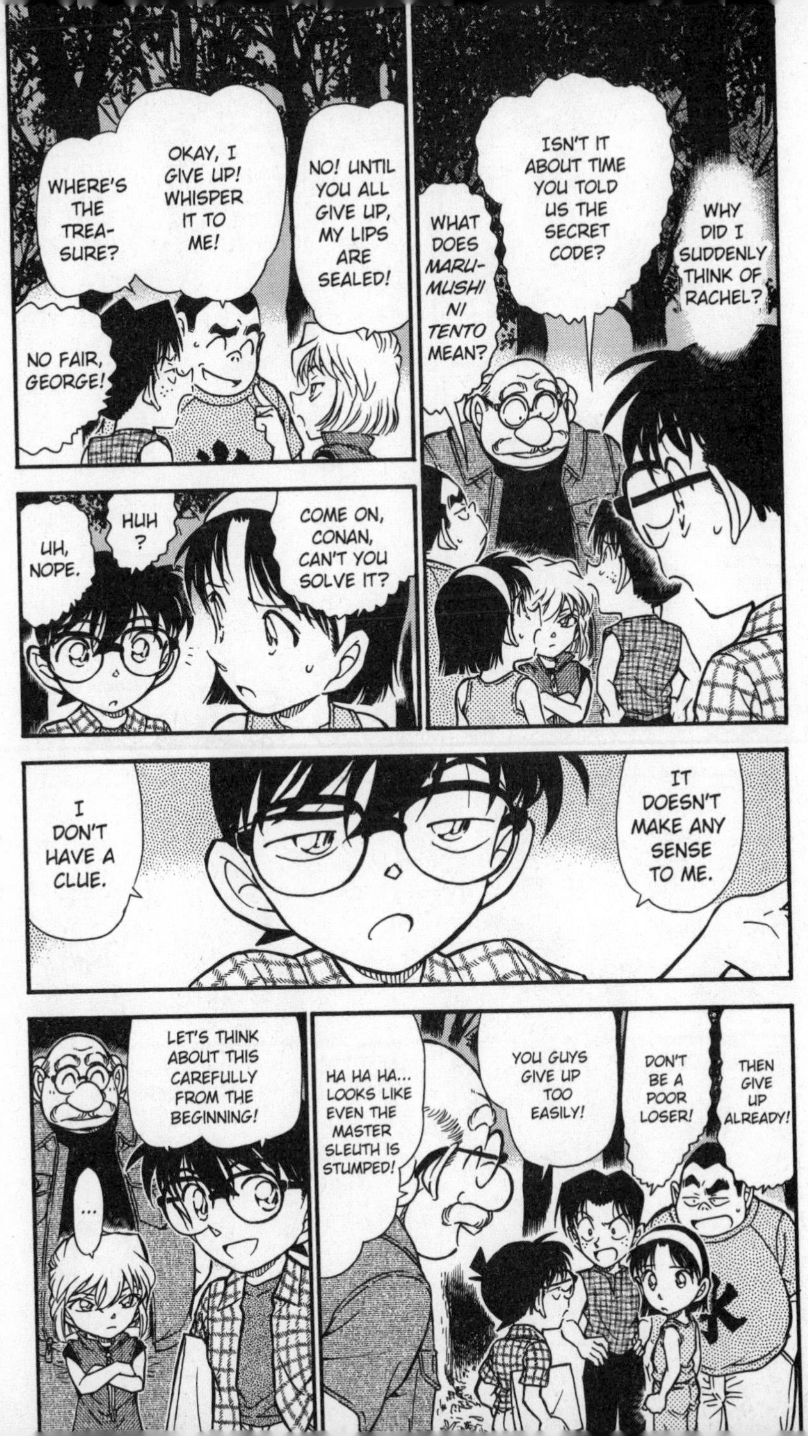
WHY DID I SUDDENLY THINK OF RACHEL?
ISN'T IT ABOUT TIME YOU TOLD US THE SECRET CODE?
WHAT DOES *MARU-MUSHI NI TENTO* MEAN?
NO! UNTIL YOU ALL GIVE UP, MY LIPS ARE SEALED!
OKAY, I GIVE UP! WHISPER IT TO ME!
WHERE'S THE TREA-SURE?
NO FAIR, GEORGE!
COME ON, CONAN, CAN'T YOU SOLVE IT?
HUH?
UH, NOPE.
IT DOESN'T MAKE ANY SENSE TO ME.
I DON'T HAVE A CLUE.
THEN GIVE UP ALREADY!
DON'T BE A POOR LOSER!
YOU GUYS GIVE UP TOO EASILY!
HA HA HA... LOOKS LIKE EVEN THE MASTER SLEUTH IS STUMPED!
LET'S THINK ABOUT THIS CAREFULLY FROM THE BEGINNING!
...

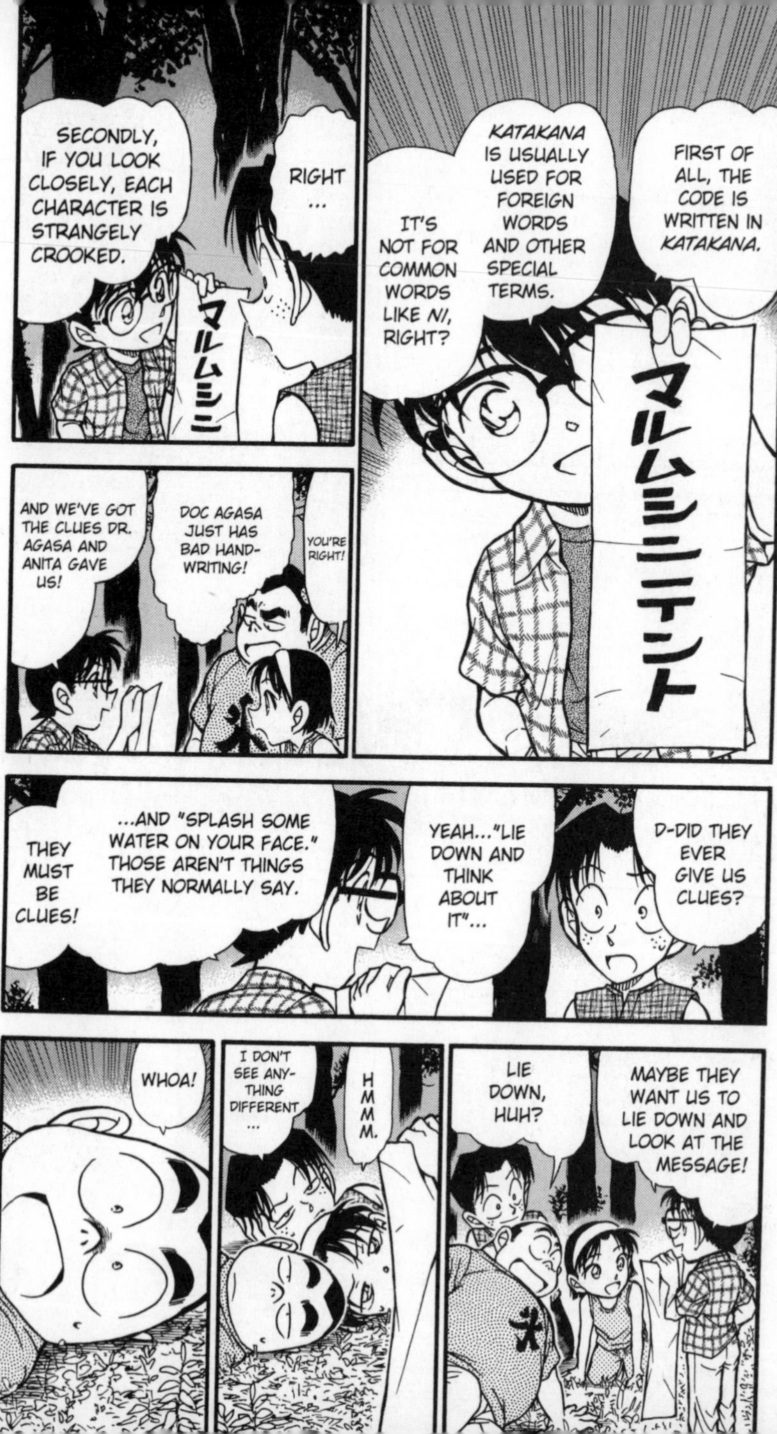
FIRST OF ALL, THE CODE IS WRITTEN IN *KATAKANA*.
KATAKANA IS USUALLY USED FOR FOREIGN WORDS AND OTHER SPECIAL TERMS.
IT'S NOT FOR COMMON WORDS LIKE *NI*, RIGHT?
マルムシニテント
RIGHT ...
SECONDLY, IF YOU LOOK CLOSELY, EACH CHARACTER IS STRANGELY CROOKED.
マルムシニ
YOU'RE RIGHT!
DOC AGASA JUST HAS BAD HAND-WRITING!
AND WE'VE GOT THE CLUES DR. AGASA AND ANITA GAVE US!
D-DID THEY EVER GIVE US CLUES?
YEAH..."LIE DOWN AND THINK ABOUT IT"...
...AND "SPLASH SOME WATER ON YOUR FACE." THOSE AREN'T THINGS THEY NORMALLY SAY.
THEY MUST BE CLUES!
MAYBE THEY WANT US TO LIE DOWN AND LOOK AT THE MESSAGE!
LIE DOWN, HUH?
HMMM.
I DON'T SEE ANY-THING DIFFERENT ...
WHOA!

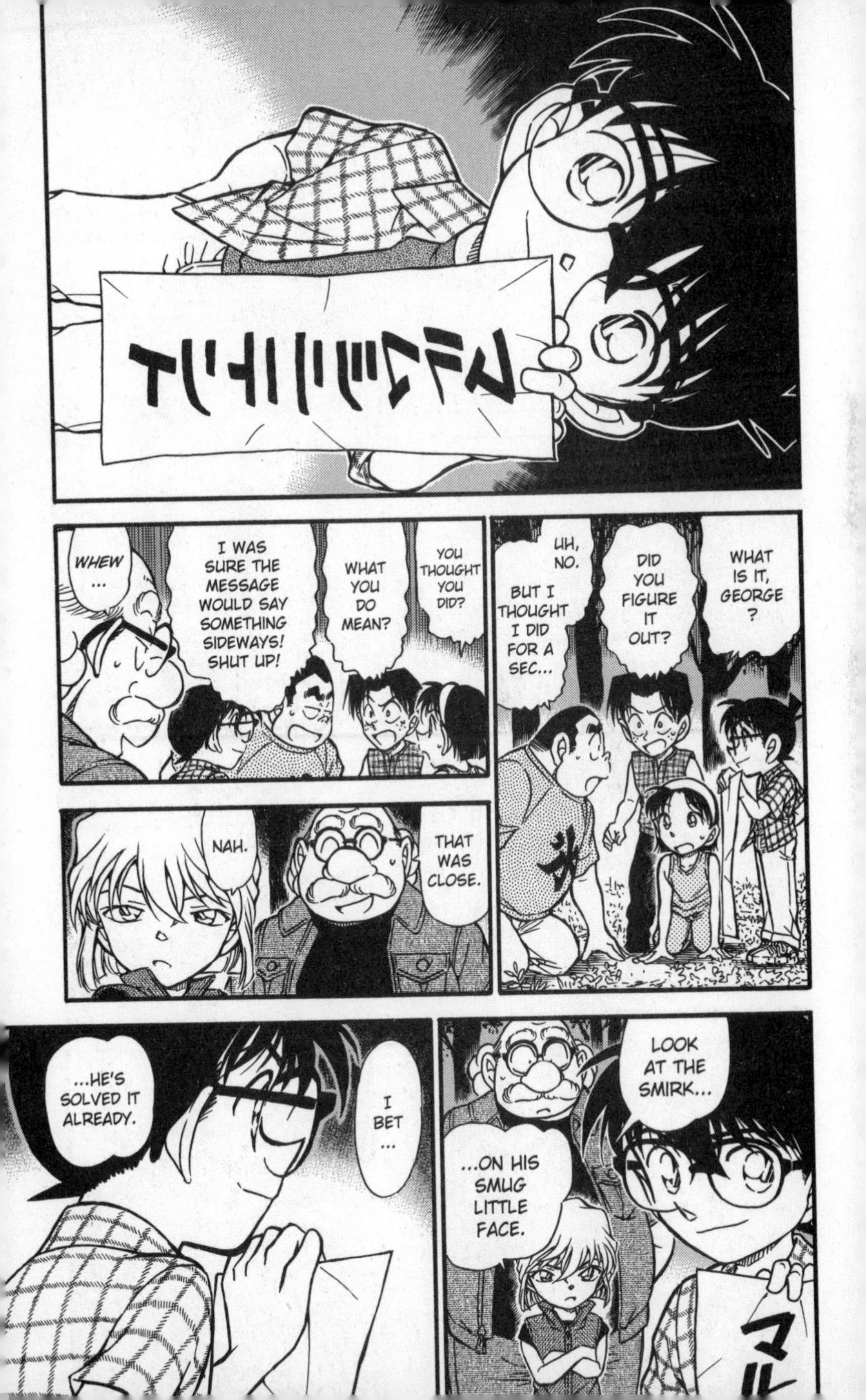
WHAT IS IT, GEORGE?
DID YOU FIGURE IT OUT?
UH, NO.
BUT I THOUGHT I DID FOR A SEC...
YOU THOUGHT YOU DID?
WHAT YOU DO MEAN?
I WAS SURE THE MESSAGE WOULD SAY SOMETHING SIDEWAYS! SHUT UP!
WHEW...
THAT WAS CLOSE.
NAH.
LOOK AT THE SMIRK...
...ON HIS SMUG LITTLE FACE.
マル
I BET...
...HE'S SOLVED IT ALREADY.

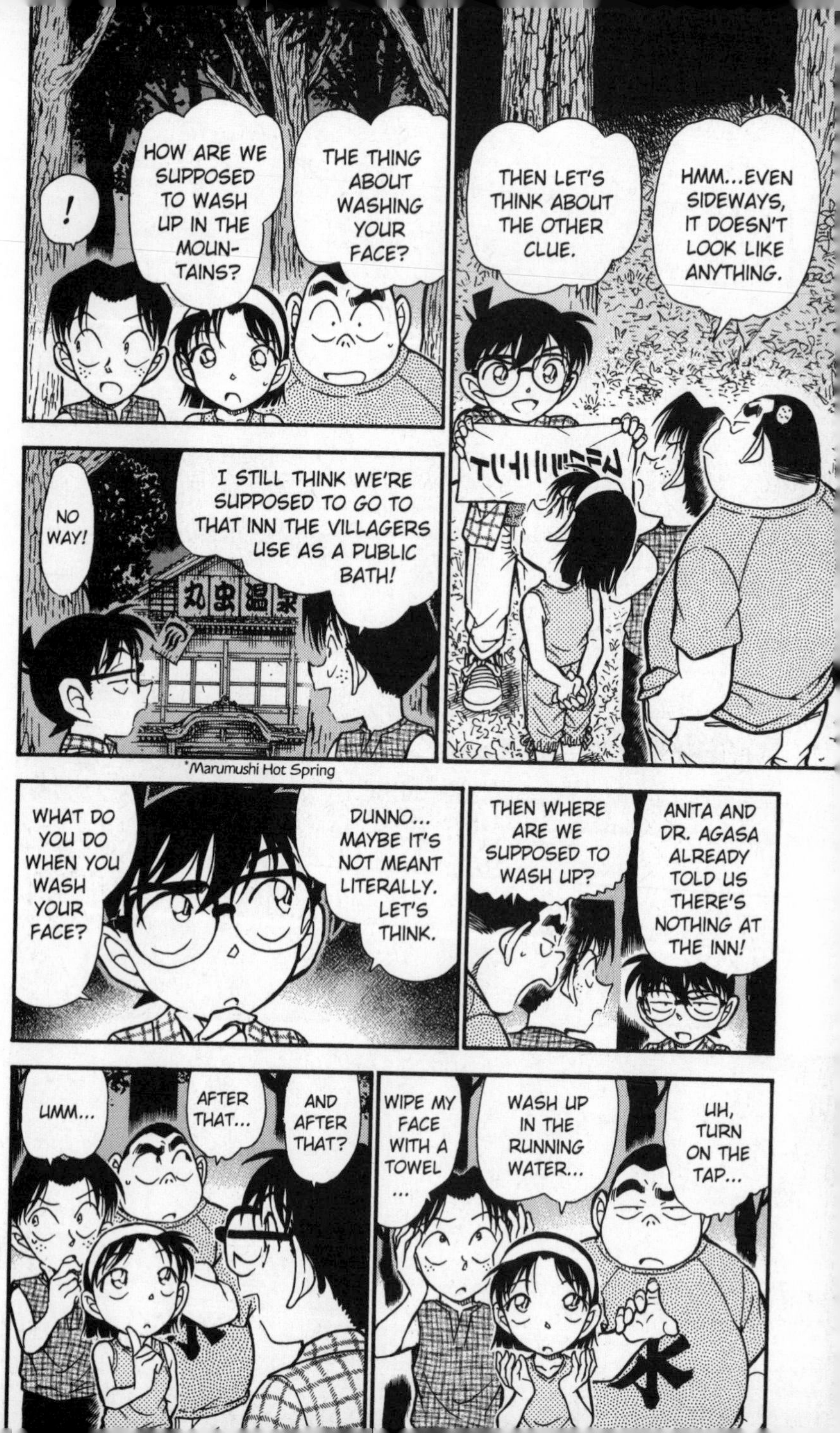
HMM...EVEN SIDEWAYS, IT DOESN'T LOOK LIKE ANYTHING.
THEN LET'S THINK ABOUT THE OTHER CLUE.
THE THING ABOUT WASHING YOUR FACE?
HOW ARE WE SUPPOSED TO WASH UP IN THE MOUNTAINS?
!
I STILL THINK WE'RE SUPPOSED TO GO TO THAT INN THE VILLAGERS USE AS A PUBLIC BATH!
NO WAY!
丸虫温泉
*Marumushi Hot Spring
ANITA AND DR. AGASA ALREADY TOLD US THERE'S NOTHING AT THE INN!
THEN WHERE ARE WE SUPPOSED TO WASH UP?
DUNNO... MAYBE IT'S NOT MEANT LITERALLY. LET'S THINK.
WHAT DO YOU DO WHEN YOU WASH YOUR FACE?
UH, TURN ON THE TAP...
WASH UP IN THE RUNNING WATER...
WIPE MY FACE WITH A TOWEL ...
AND AFTER THAT?
AFTER THAT...
UMM...

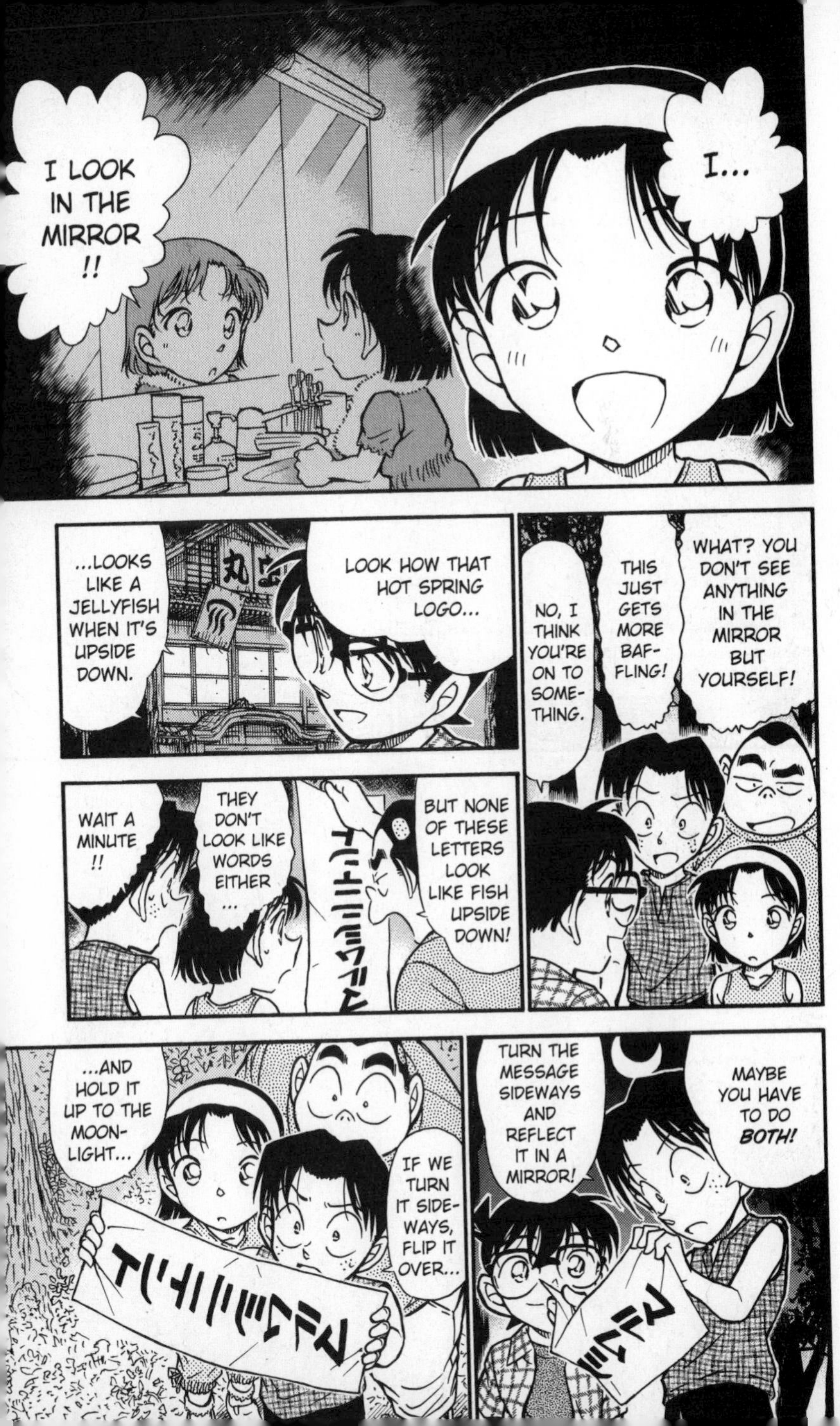
I...
I LOOK IN THE MIRROR !!
WHAT? YOU DON'T SEE ANYTHING IN THE MIRROR BUT YOURSELF!
THIS JUST GETS MORE BAF-FLING!
NO, I THINK YOU'RE ON TO SOME-THING.
LOOK HOW THAT HOT SPRING LOGO...
...LOOKS LIKE A JELLYFISH WHEN IT'S UPSIDE DOWN.
BUT NONE OF THESE LETTERS LOOK LIKE FISH UPSIDE DOWN!
THEY DON'T LOOK LIKE WORDS EITHER...
WAIT A MINUTE !!
MAYBE YOU HAVE TO DO *BOTH!*
TURN THE MESSAGE SIDEWAYS AND REFLECT IT IN A MIRROR!
IF WE TURN IT SIDE-WAYS, FLIP IT OVER...
...AND HOLD IT UP TO THE MOON-LIGHT...

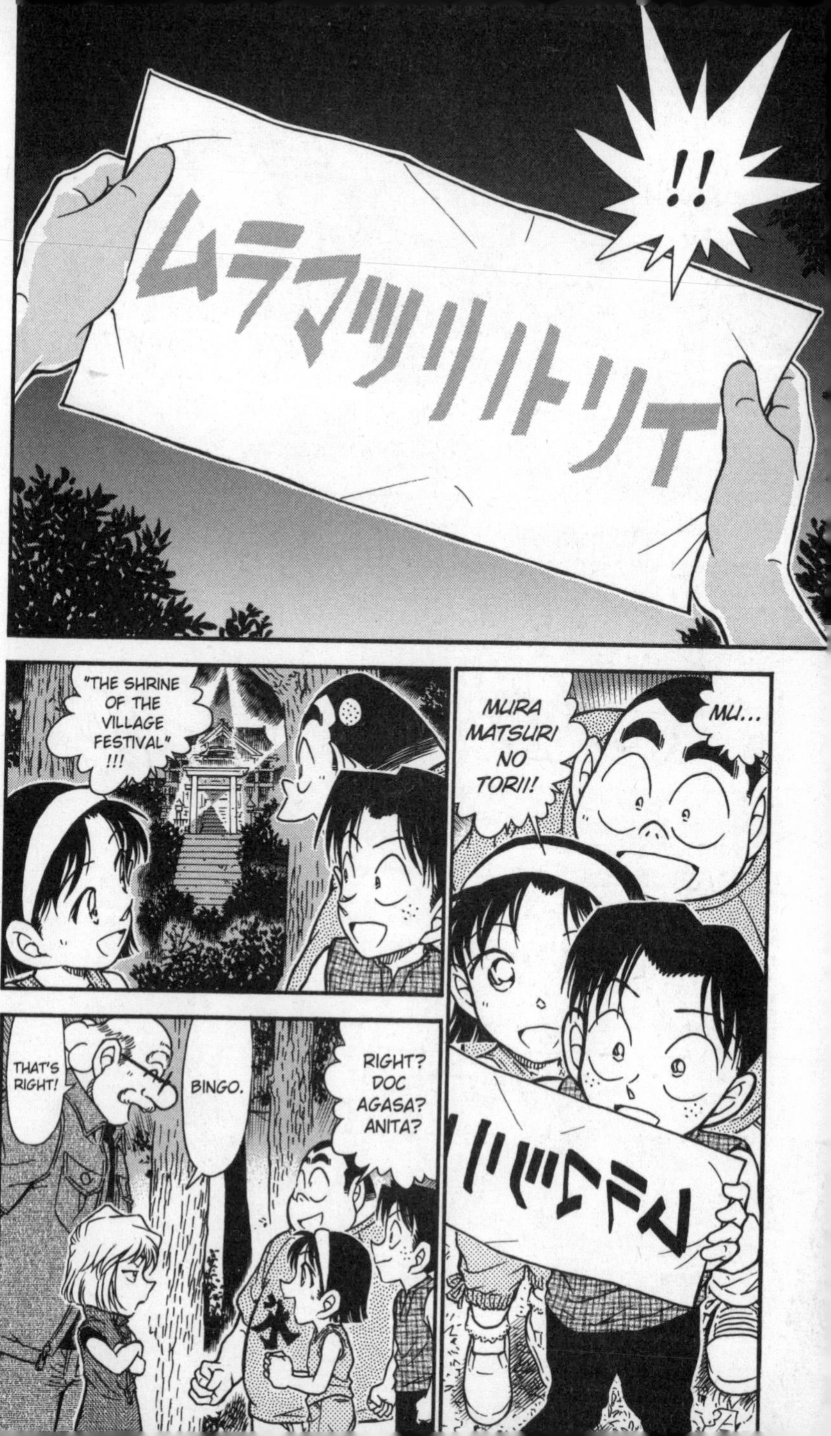
!!
ムラマツリトリイ
MU...
MURA MATSURI NO TORII!
"THE SHRINE OF THE VILLAGE FESTIVAL" !!!
RIGHT? DOC AGASA? ANITA?
BINGO.
THAT'S RIGHT!

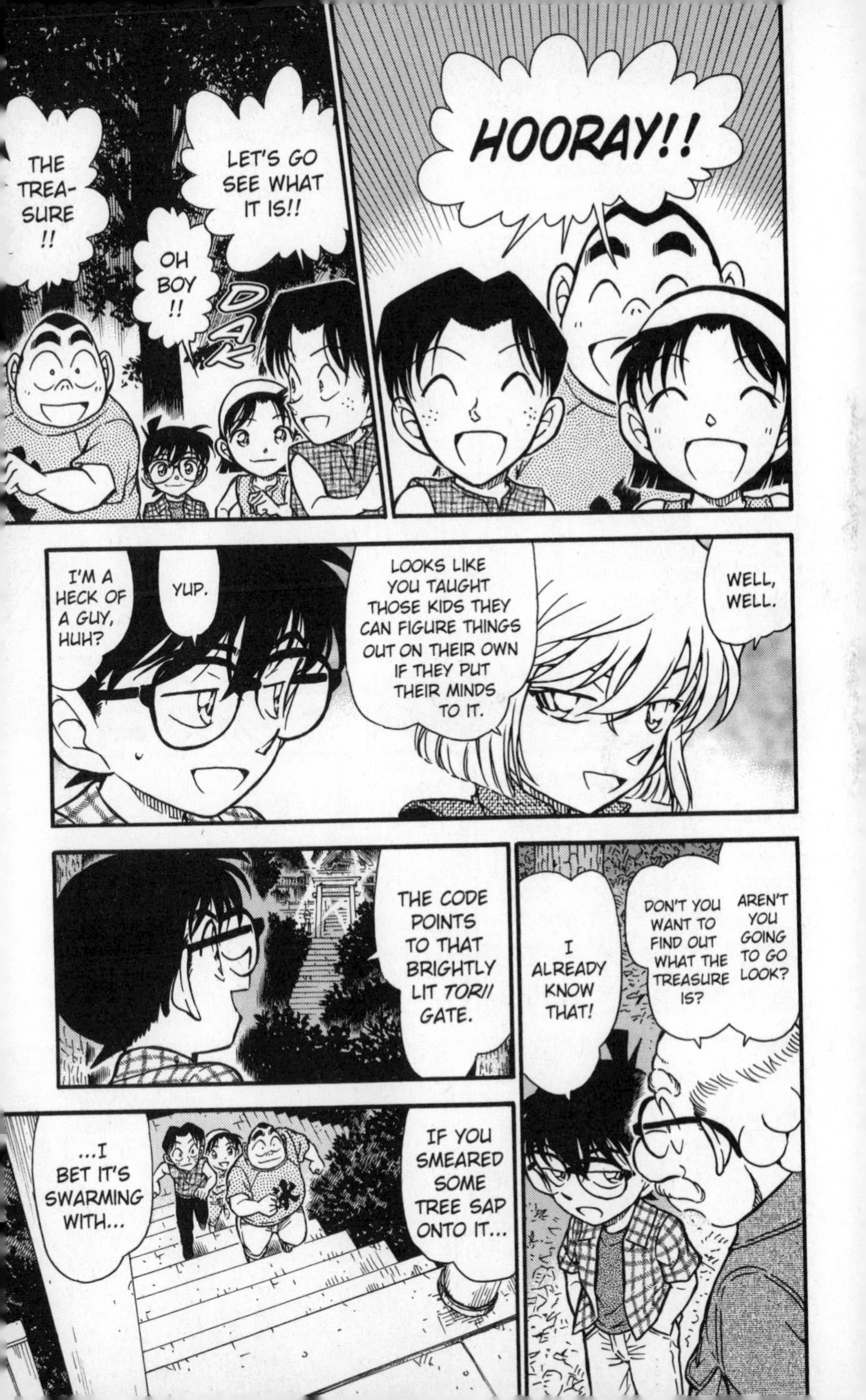
HOORAY!!
LET'S GO SEE WHAT IT IS!!
THE TREASURE!!
OH BOY!!
DAK
WELL, WELL.
LOOKS LIKE YOU TAUGHT THOSE KIDS THEY CAN FIGURE THINGS OUT ON THEIR OWN IF THEY PUT THEIR MINDS TO IT.
YUP.
I'M A HECK OF A GUY, HUH?
AREN'T YOU GOING TO GO LOOK?
DON'T YOU WANT TO FIND OUT WHAT THE TREASURE IS?
I ALREADY KNOW THAT!
THE CODE POINTS TO THAT BRIGHTLY LIT *TORII* GATE.
IF YOU SMEARED SOME TREE SAP ONTO IT...
...I BET IT'S SWARMING WITH...

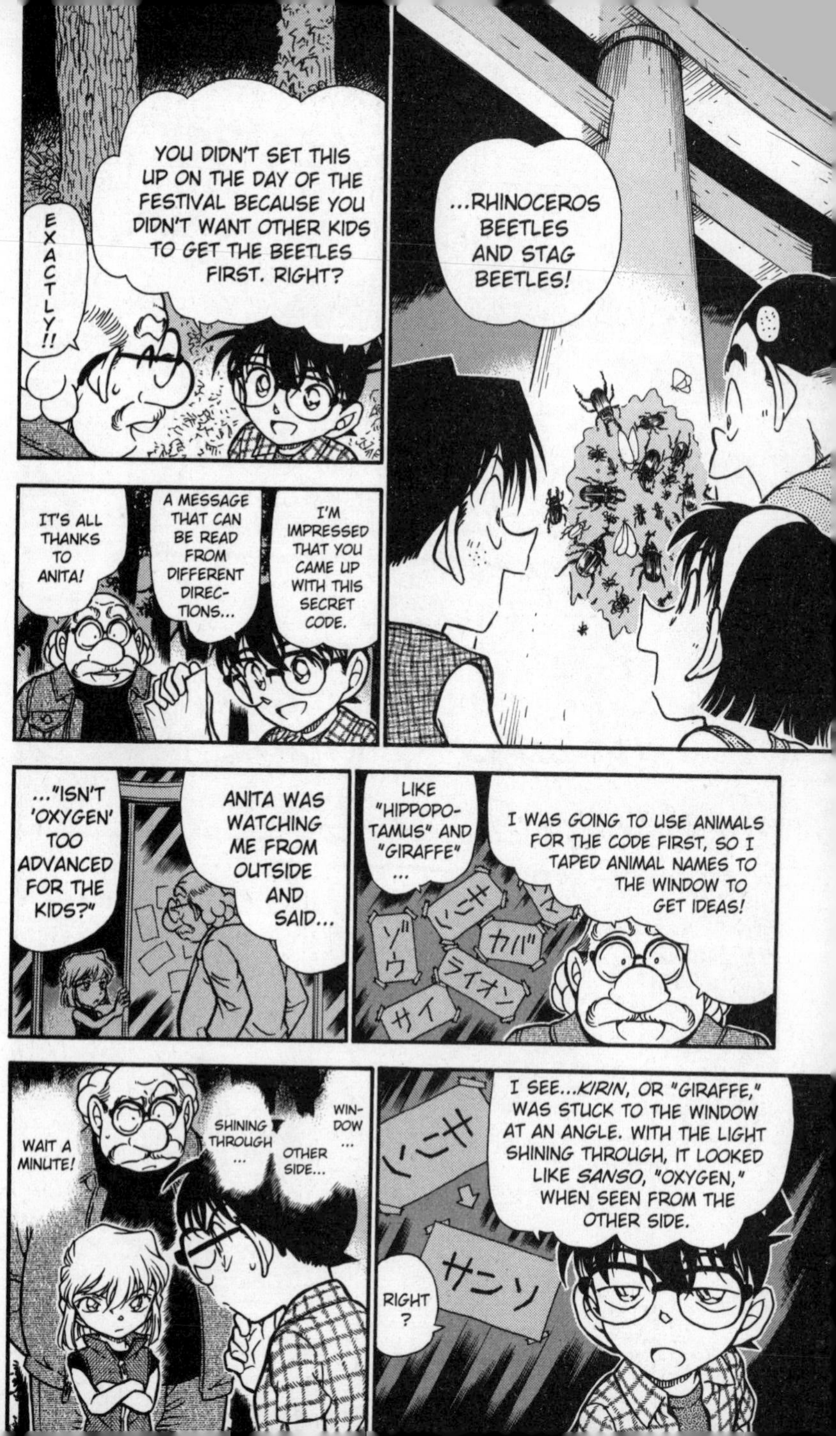
...RHINOCEROS BEETLES AND STAG BEETLES!
YOU DIDN'T SET THIS UP ON THE DAY OF THE FESTIVAL BECAUSE YOU DIDN'T WANT OTHER KIDS TO GET THE BEETLES FIRST. RIGHT?
EXACTLY!!
I'M IMPRESSED THAT YOU CAME UP WITH THIS SECRET CODE.
A MESSAGE THAT CAN BE READ FROM DIFFERENT DIRECTIONS...
IT'S ALL THANKS TO ANITA!
I WAS GOING TO USE ANIMALS FOR THE CODE FIRST, SO I TAPED ANIMAL NAMES TO THE WINDOW TO GET IDEAS!
LIKE "HIPPOPOTAMUS" AND "GIRAFFE"...
カバ
ゾウ
ライオン
サイ
ANITA WAS WATCHING ME FROM OUTSIDE AND SAID...
..."ISN'T 'OXYGEN' TOO ADVANCED FOR THE KIDS?"
I SEE...*KIRIN*, OR "GIRAFFE," WAS STUCK TO THE WINDOW AT AN ANGLE. WITH THE LIGHT SHINING THROUGH, IT LOOKED LIKE *SANSO*, "OXYGEN," WHEN SEEN FROM THE OTHER SIDE.
サンソ
RIGHT?
WINDOW...
OTHER SIDE...
SHINING THROUGH...
WAIT A MINUTE!

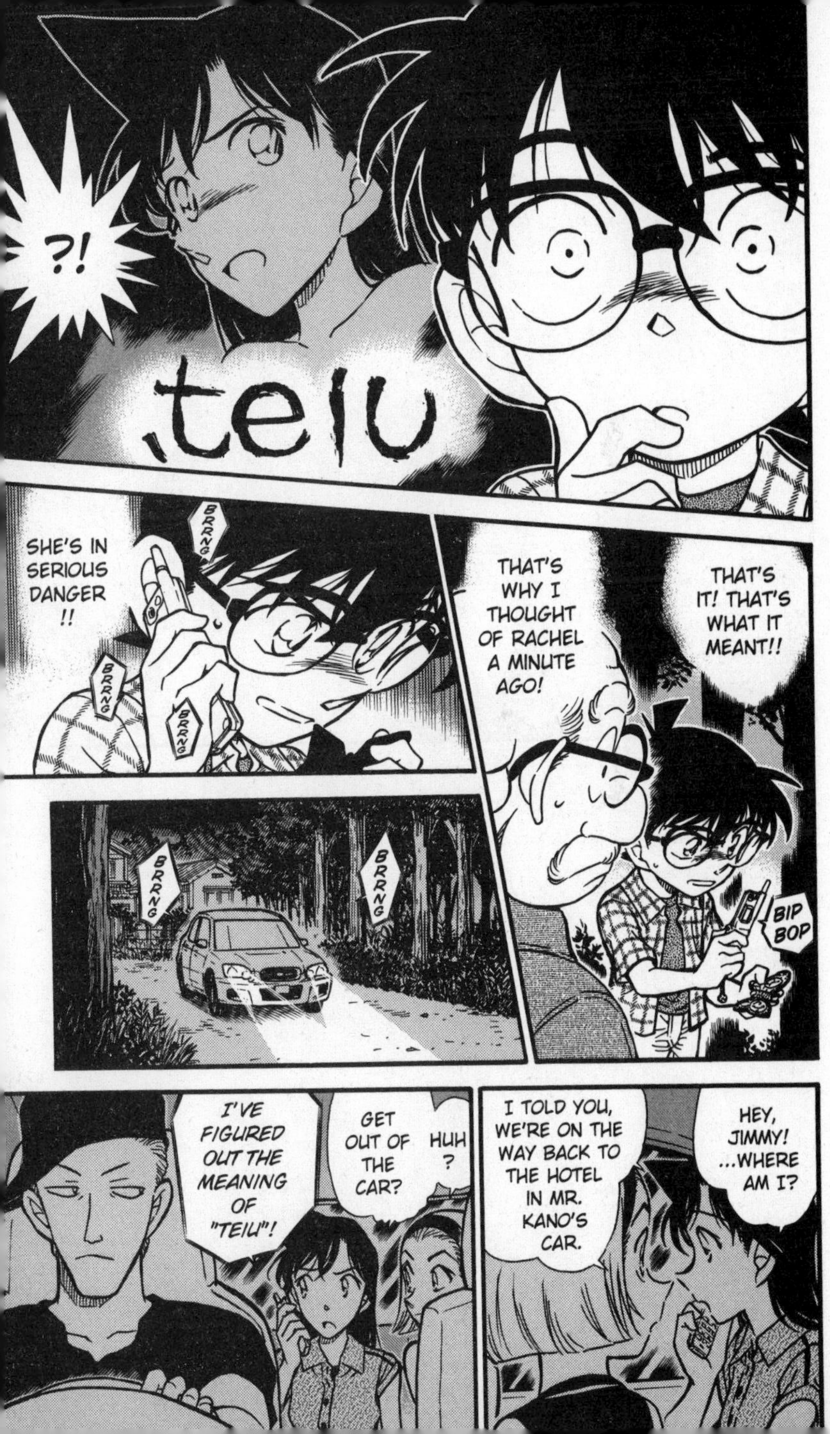
?!
teiu
THAT'S IT! THAT'S WHAT IT MEANT!!
THAT'S WHY I THOUGHT OF RACHEL A MINUTE AGO!
BIP BOP
BRRNG
SHE'S IN SERIOUS DANGER!!
BRRNG
BRRNG
BRRNG
BRRNG
HEY, JIMMY! ...WHERE AM I?
I TOLD YOU, WE'RE ON THE WAY BACK TO THE HOTEL IN MR. KANO'S CAR.
HUH?
GET OUT OF THE CAR?
I'VE FIGURED OUT THE MEANING OF "TEIU"!

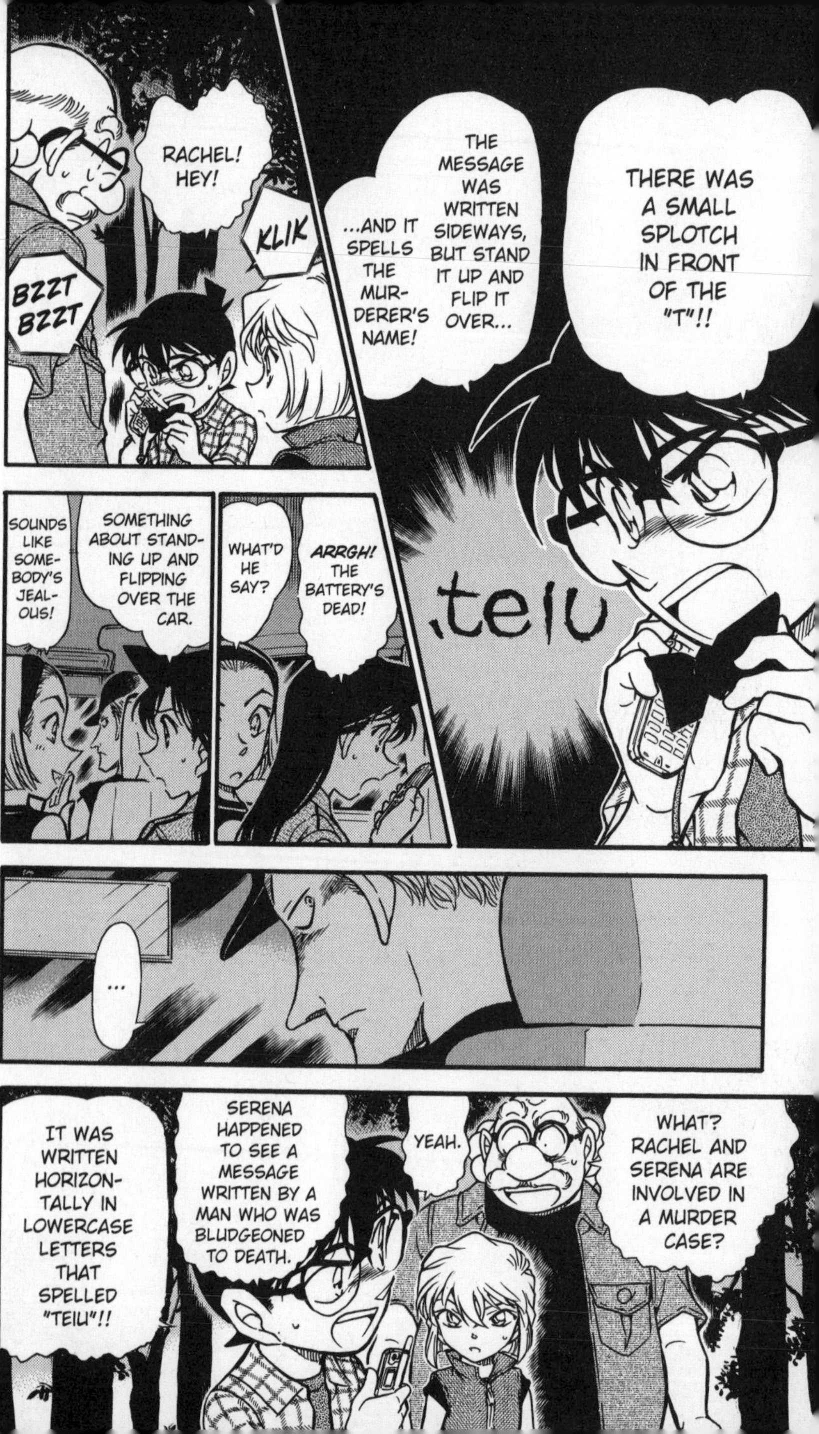
THERE WAS A SMALL SPLOTCH IN FRONT OF THE "T"!!
THE MESSAGE WAS WRITTEN SIDEWAYS, BUT STAND IT UP AND FLIP IT OVER...
...AND IT SPELLS THE MURDERER'S NAME!
.teiu
KLIK
RACHEL! HEY!
BZZT BZZT
ARRGH! THE BATTERY'S DEAD!
WHAT'D HE SAY?
SOMETHING ABOUT STANDING UP AND FLIPPING OVER THE CAR.
SOUNDS LIKE SOMEBODY'S JEALOUS!
...
WHAT? RACHEL AND SERENA ARE INVOLVED IN A MURDER CASE?
YEAH.
SERENA HAPPENED TO SEE A MESSAGE WRITTEN BY A MAN WHO WAS BLUDGEONED TO DEATH.
IT WAS WRITTEN HORIZONTALLY IN LOWERCASE LETTERS THAT SPELLED "TEIU"!!

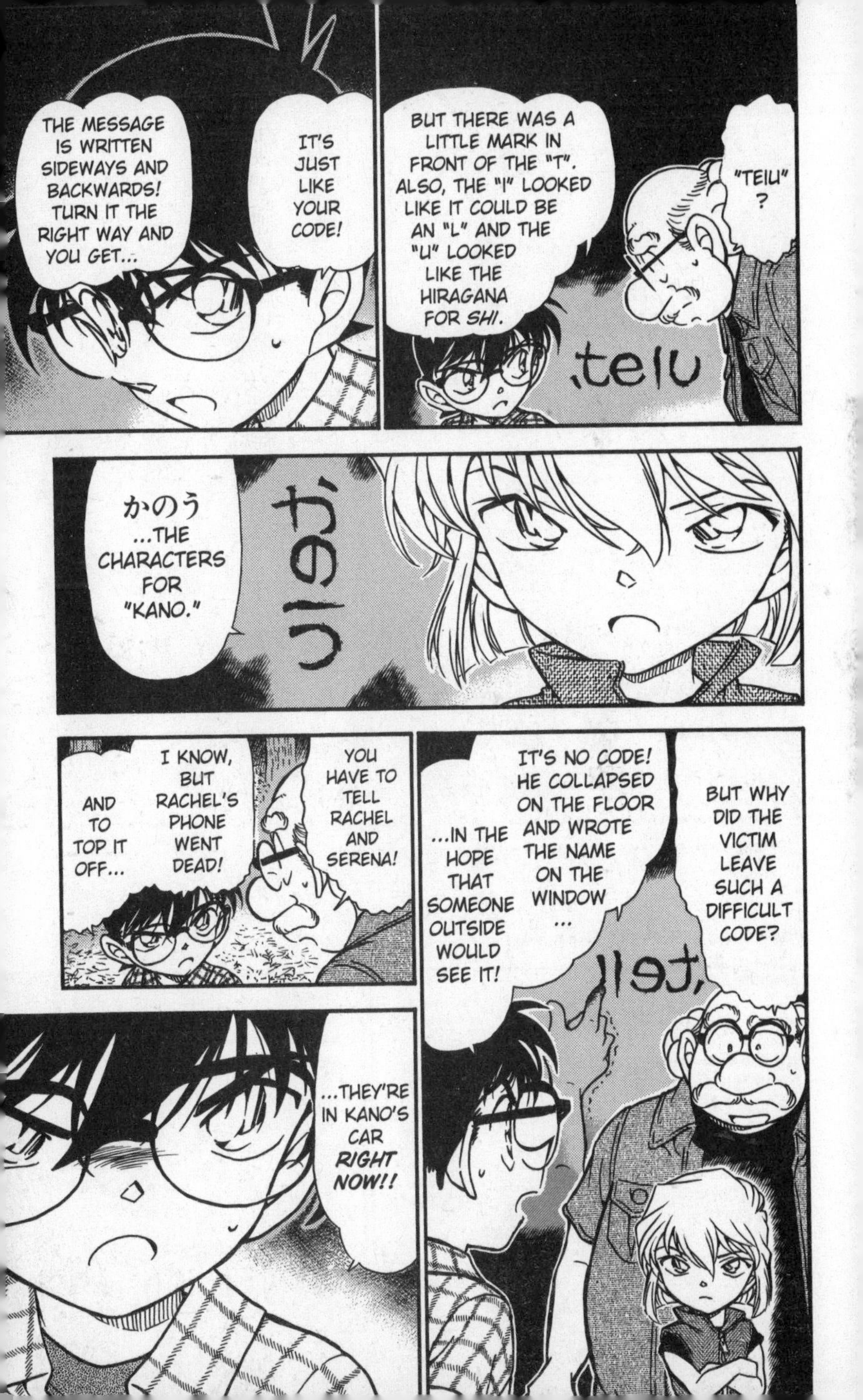
"TEIU" ?
BUT THERE WAS A LITTLE MARK IN FRONT OF THE "T". ALSO, THE "I" LOOKED LIKE IT COULD BE AN "L" AND THE "U" LOOKED LIKE THE HIRAGANA FOR *SHI*.
IT'S JUST LIKE YOUR CODE!
THE MESSAGE IS WRITTEN SIDEWAYS AND BACKWARDS! TURN IT THE RIGHT WAY AND YOU GET...
かのう ...THE CHARACTERS FOR "KANO."
BUT WHY DID THE VICTIM LEAVE SUCH A DIFFICULT CODE?
IT'S NO CODE! HE COLLAPSED ON THE FLOOR AND WROTE THE NAME ON THE WINDOW ...
...IN THE HOPE THAT SOMEONE OUTSIDE WOULD SEE IT!
YOU HAVE TO TELL RACHEL AND SERENA!
I KNOW, BUT RACHEL'S PHONE WENT DEAD!
AND TO TOP IT OFF...
...THEY'RE IN KANO'S CAR ***RIGHT NOW!!***

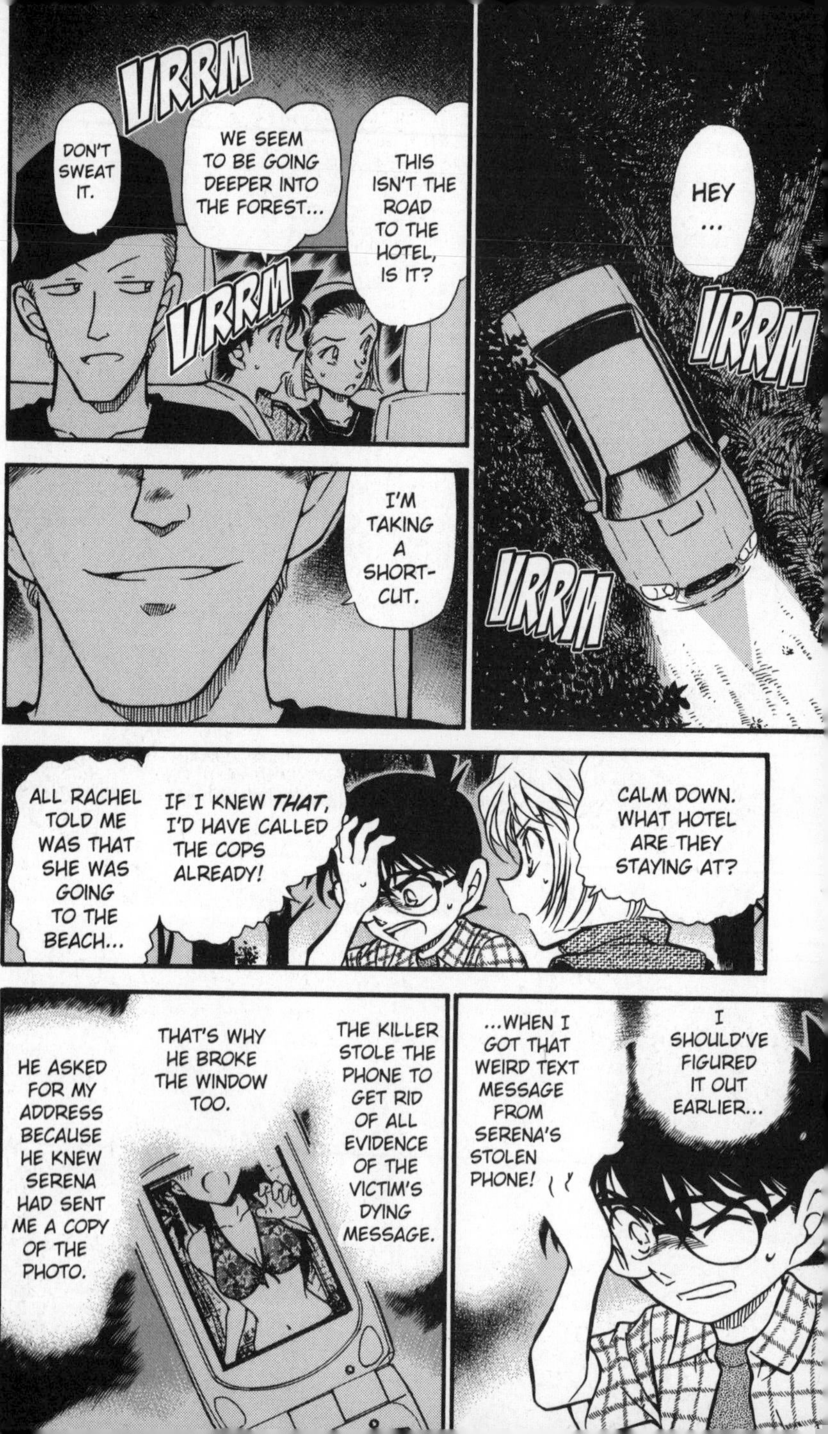
HEY ...
VRRM
VRRM
VRRM
THIS ISN'T THE ROAD TO THE HOTEL, IS IT?
WE SEEM TO BE GOING DEEPER INTO THE FOREST...
VRRM
DON'T SWEAT IT.
I'M TAKING A SHORT-CUT.
CALM DOWN. WHAT HOTEL ARE THEY STAYING AT?
IF I KNEW *THAT*, I'D HAVE CALLED THE COPS ALREADY!
ALL RACHEL TOLD ME WAS THAT SHE WAS GOING TO THE BEACH...
I SHOULD'VE FIGURED IT OUT EARLIER...
...WHEN I GOT THAT WEIRD TEXT MESSAGE FROM SERENA'S STOLEN PHONE!
THE KILLER STOLE THE PHONE TO GET RID OF ALL EVIDENCE OF THE VICTIM'S DYING MESSAGE.
THAT'S WHY HE BROKE THE WINDOW TOO.
HE ASKED FOR MY ADDRESS BECAUSE HE KNEW SERENA HAD SENT ME A COPY OF THE PHOTO.

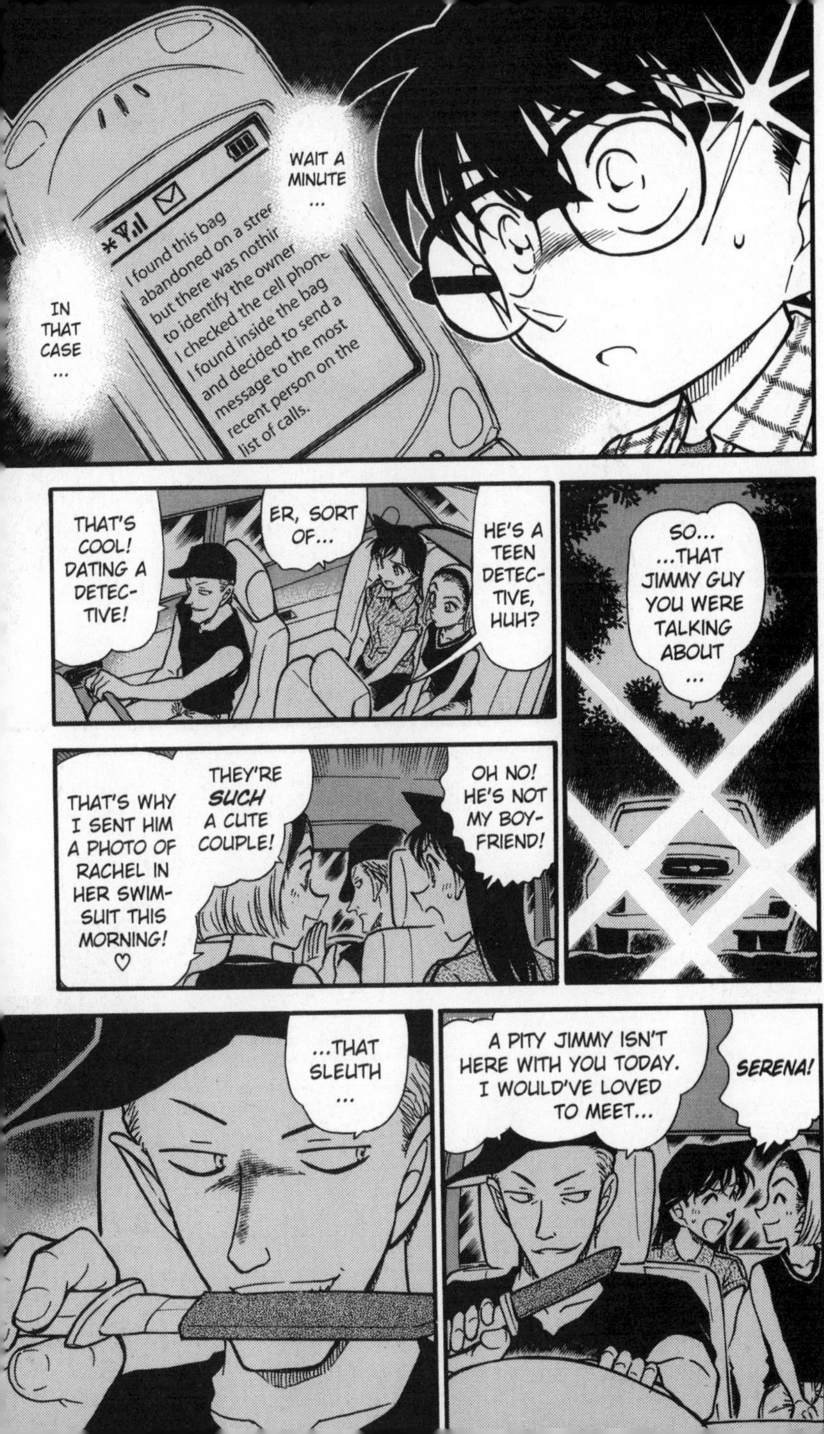
WAIT A MINUTE ...
I found this bag abandoned on a stre but there was nothir to identify the owner I checked the cell phone I found inside the bag and decided to send a message to the most recent person on the list of calls.
IN THAT CASE ...
SO... ...THAT JIMMY GUY YOU WERE TALKING ABOUT ...
HE'S A TEEN DETEC-TIVE, HUH?
ER, SORT OF...
THAT'S COOL! DATING A DETEC-TIVE!
OH NO! HE'S NOT MY BOY-FRIEND!
THEY'RE *SUCH* A CUTE COUPLE!
THAT'S WHY I SENT HIM A PHOTO OF RACHEL IN HER SWIM-SUIT THIS MORNING! ♡
SERENA!
A PITY JIMMY ISN'T HERE WITH YOU TODAY. I WOULD'VE LOVED TO MEET...
...THAT SLEUTH ...

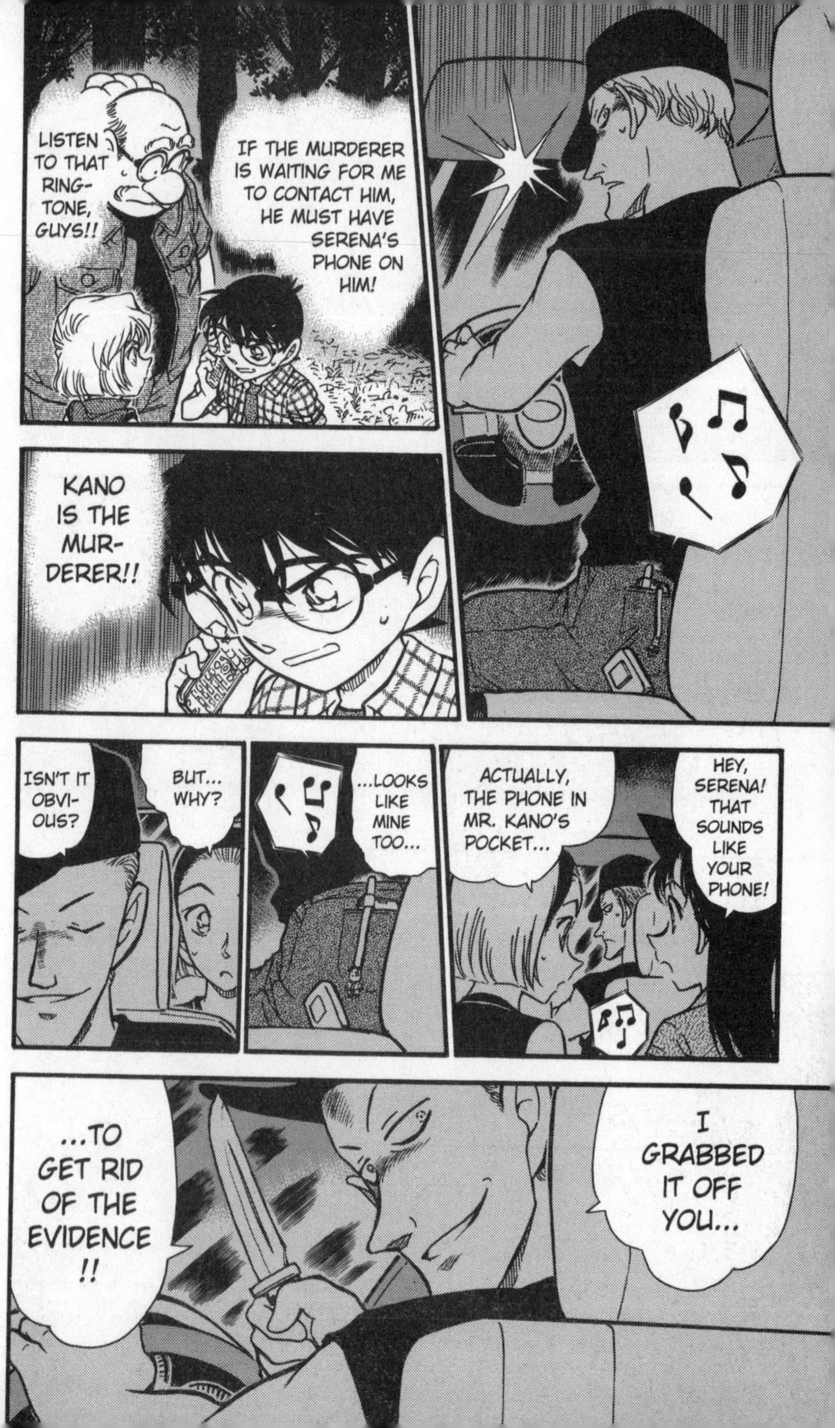
IF THE MURDERER IS WAITING FOR ME TO CONTACT HIM, HE MUST HAVE SERENA'S PHONE ON HIM!
LISTEN TO THAT RING-TONE, GUYS!!
KANO IS THE MUR-DERER!!
HEY, SERENA! THAT SOUNDS LIKE YOUR PHONE!
ACTUALLY, THE PHONE IN MR. KANO'S POCKET...
...LOOKS LIKE MINE TOO...
BUT... WHY?
ISN'T IT OBVI-OUS?
I GRABBED IT OFF YOU...
...TO GET RID OF THE EVIDENCE!!

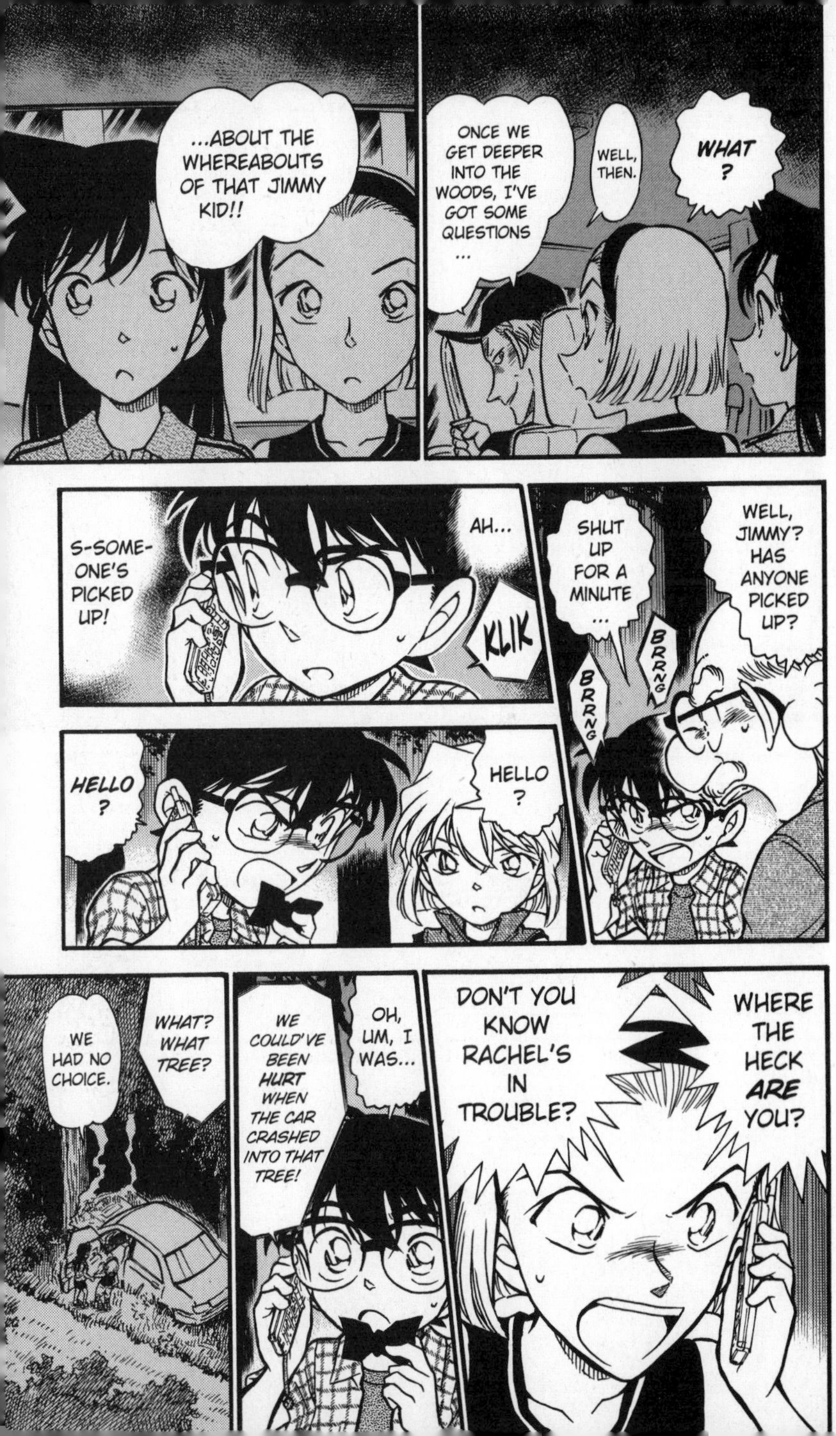
WHAT ?
WELL, THEN.
ONCE WE GET DEEPER INTO THE WOODS, I'VE GOT SOME QUESTIONS ...
...ABOUT THE WHEREABOUTS OF THAT JIMMY KID!!
WELL, JIMMY? HAS ANYONE PICKED UP?
SHUT UP FOR A MINUTE ...
BRRNG
BRRNG
AH...
KLIK
S-SOME-ONE'S PICKED UP!
HELLO ?
HELLO ?
WHERE THE HECK ARE YOU?
DON'T YOU KNOW RACHEL'S IN TROUBLE?
OH, UM, I WAS...
WE COULD'VE BEEN HURT WHEN THE CAR CRASHED INTO THAT TREE!
WHAT? WHAT TREE?
WE HAD NO CHOICE.

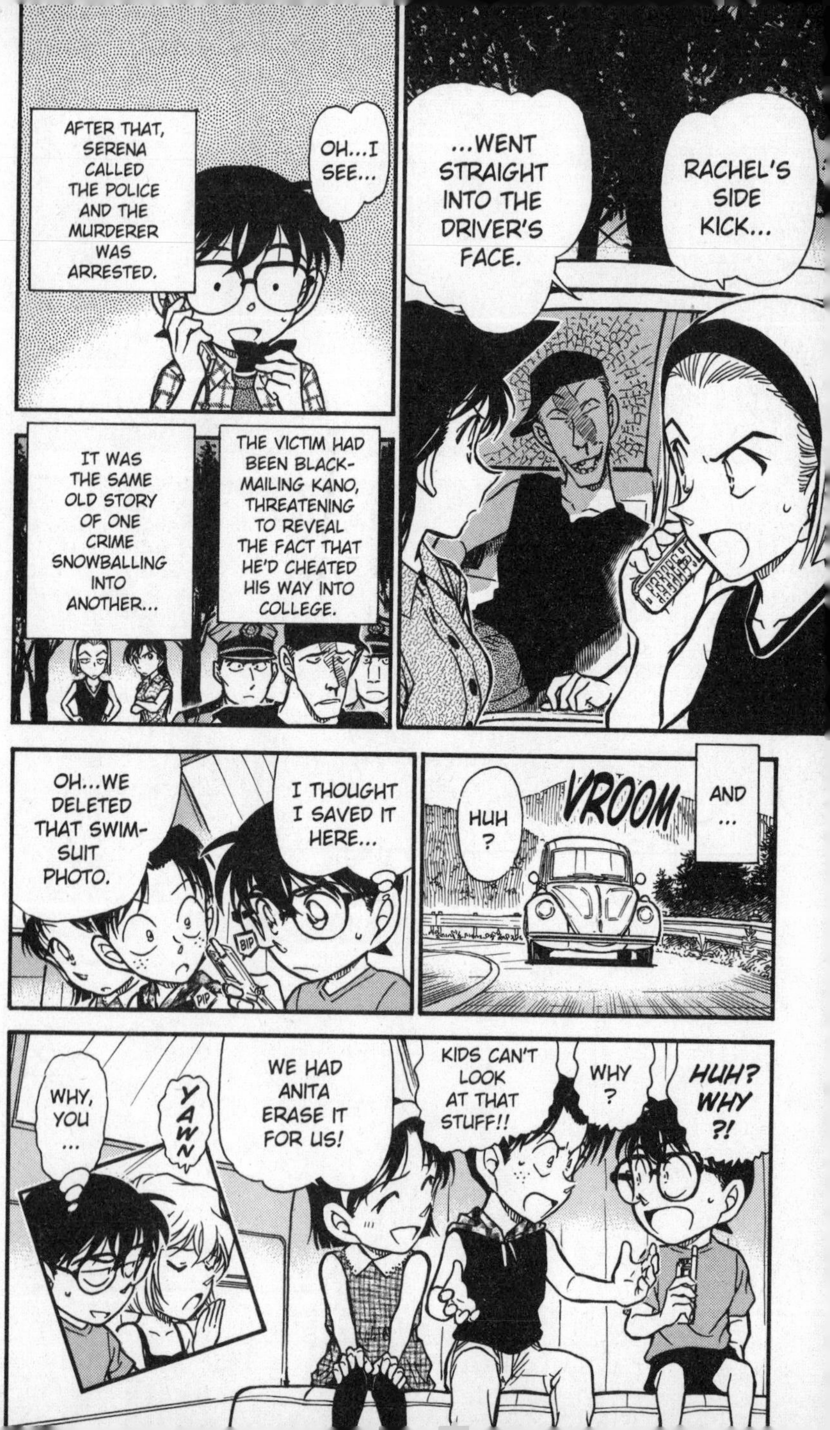
RACHEL'S SIDE KICK...
...WENT STRAIGHT INTO THE DRIVER'S FACE.
OH...I SEE...
AFTER THAT, SERENA CALLED THE POLICE AND THE MURDERER WAS ARRESTED.
THE VICTIM HAD BEEN BLACK-MAILING KANO, THREATENING TO REVEAL THE FACT THAT HE'D CHEATED HIS WAY INTO COLLEGE.
IT WAS THE SAME OLD STORY OF ONE CRIME SNOWBALLING INTO ANOTHER...
AND ...
VROOM
HUH ?
I THOUGHT I SAVED IT HERE...
BIP
OH...WE DELETED THAT SWIM-SUIT PHOTO.
PIP
HUH? WHY ?!
WHY ?
KIDS CAN'T LOOK AT THAT STUFF!!
WE HAD ANITA ERASE IT FOR US!
YAWN
WHY, YOU ...

FILE 4:
THE HOUSE OF THE EVIL SPIRIT

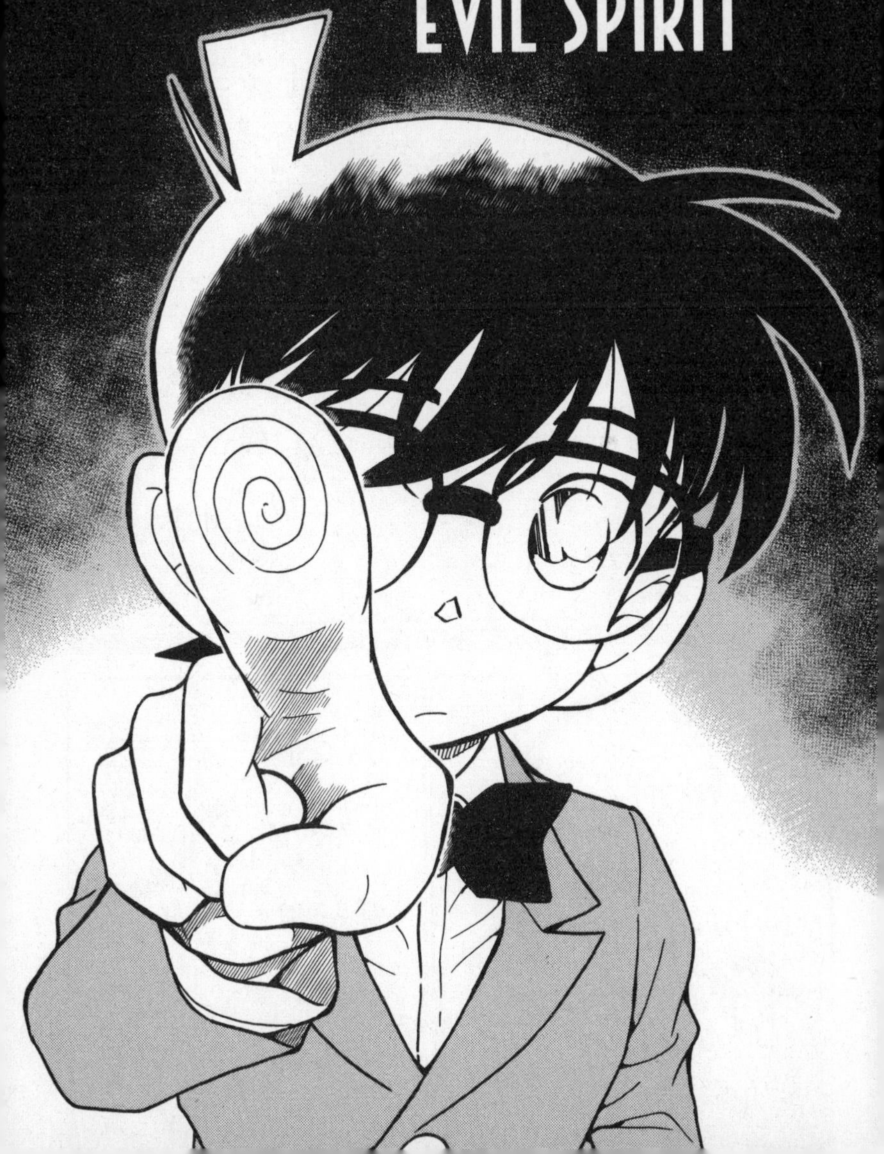

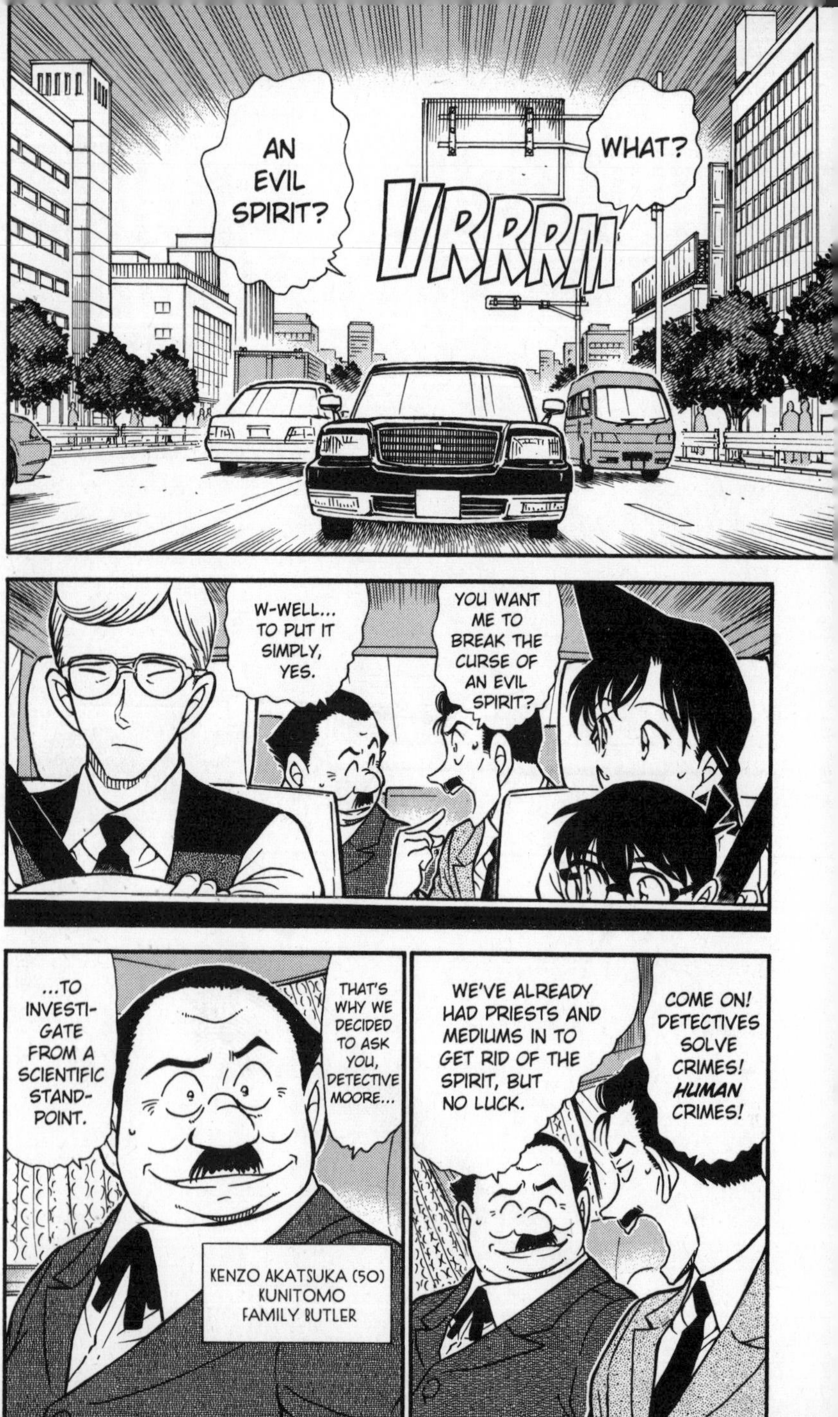
WHAT?
URRRM
AN EVIL SPIRIT?
YOU WANT ME TO BREAK THE CURSE OF AN EVIL SPIRIT?
W-WELL... TO PUT IT SIMPLY, YES.
COME ON! DETECTIVES SOLVE CRIMES! *HUMAN* CRIMES!
WE'VE ALREADY HAD PRIESTS AND MEDIUMS IN TO GET RID OF THE SPIRIT, BUT NO LUCK.
THAT'S WHY WE DECIDED TO ASK YOU, DETECTIVE MOORE...
...TO INVESTIGATE FROM A SCIENTIFIC STANDPOINT.
KENZO AKATSUKA (50) KUNITOMO FAMILY BUTLER

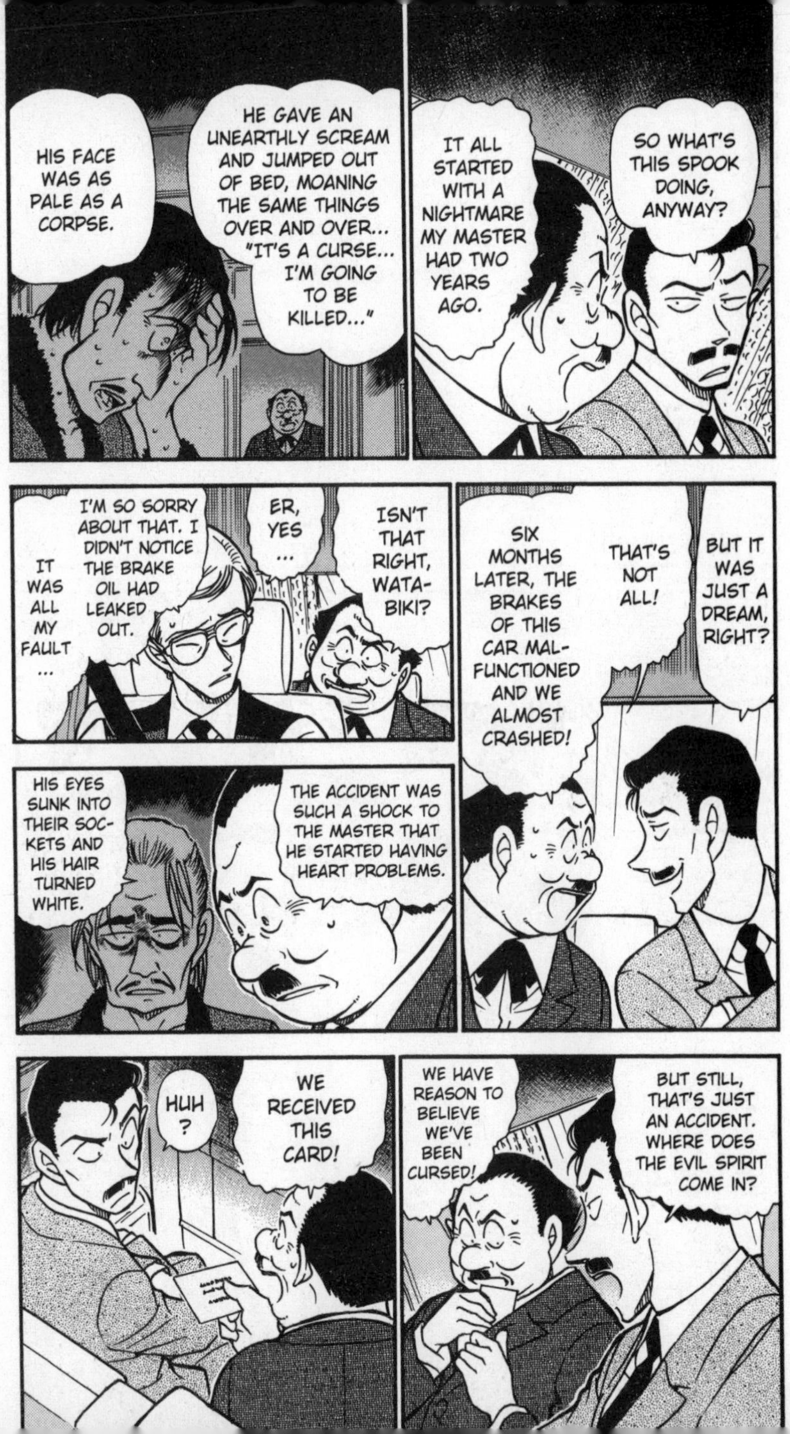
SO WHAT'S THIS SPOOK DOING, ANYWAY?
IT ALL STARTED WITH A NIGHTMARE MY MASTER HAD TWO YEARS AGO.
HE GAVE AN UNEARTHLY SCREAM AND JUMPED OUT OF BED, MOANING THE SAME THINGS OVER AND OVER... "IT'S A CURSE... I'M GOING TO BE KILLED..."
HIS FACE WAS AS PALE AS A CORPSE.
BUT IT WAS JUST A DREAM, RIGHT?
THAT'S NOT ALL!
SIX MONTHS LATER, THE BRAKES OF THIS CAR MAL-FUNCTIONED AND WE ALMOST CRASHED!
ISN'T THAT RIGHT, WATA-BIKI?
ER, YES ...
I'M SO SORRY ABOUT THAT. I DIDN'T NOTICE THE BRAKE OIL HAD LEAKED OUT.
IT WAS ALL MY FAULT ...
THE ACCIDENT WAS SUCH A SHOCK TO THE MASTER THAT HE STARTED HAVING HEART PROBLEMS.
HIS EYES SUNK INTO THEIR SOC-KETS AND HIS HAIR TURNED WHITE.
BUT STILL, THAT'S JUST AN ACCIDENT. WHERE DOES THE EVIL SPIRIT COME IN?
WE HAVE REASON TO BELIEVE WE'VE BEEN CURSED!
WE RECEIVED THIS CARD!
HUH ?

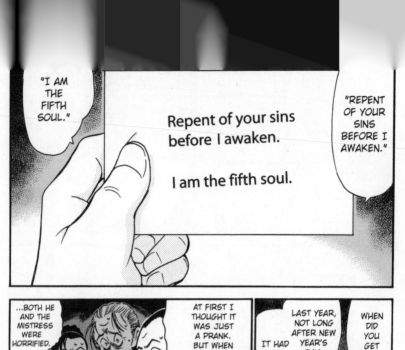

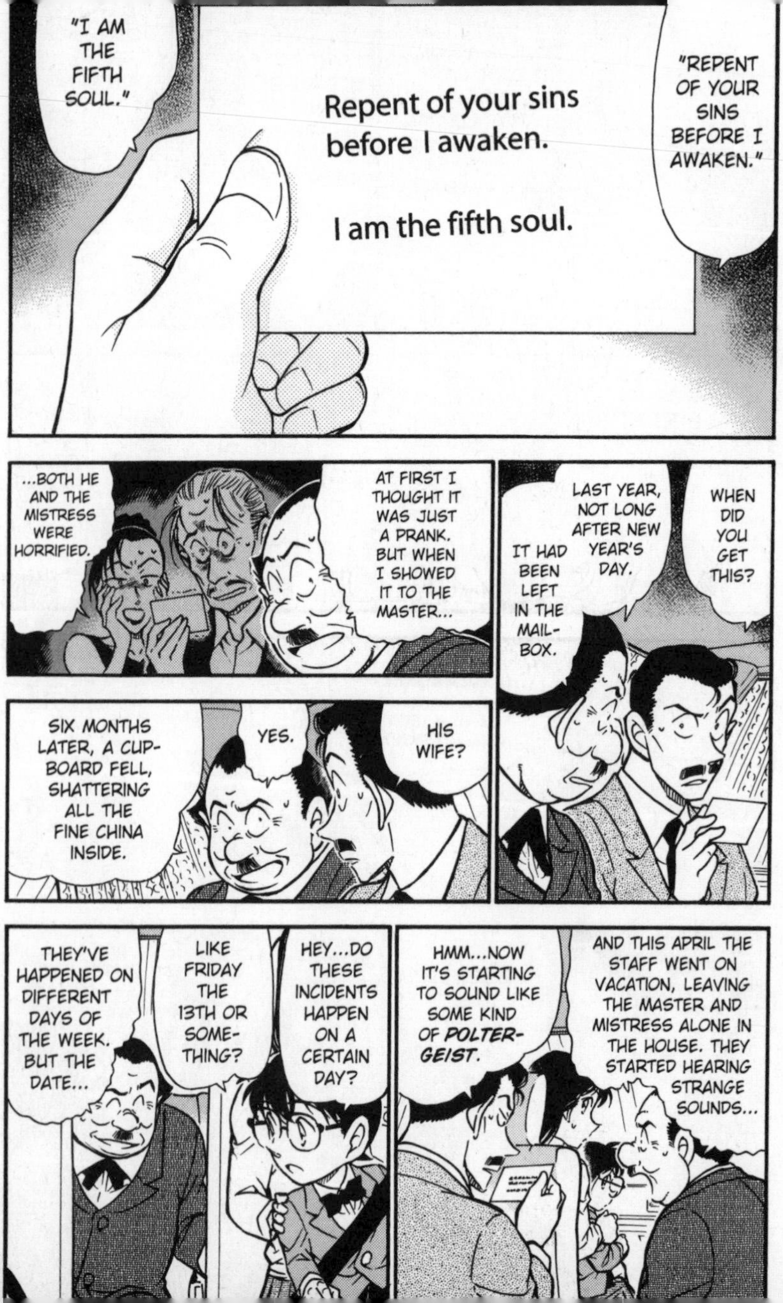
"REPENT OF YOUR SINS BEFORE I AWAKEN."
Repent of your sins before I awaken.
I am the fifth soul.
"I AM THE FIFTH SOUL."
WHEN DID YOU GET THIS?
LAST YEAR, NOT LONG AFTER NEW YEAR'S DAY.
IT HAD BEEN LEFT IN THE MAILBOX.
AT FIRST I THOUGHT IT WAS JUST A PRANK. BUT WHEN I SHOWED IT TO THE MASTER...
...BOTH HE AND THE MISTRESS WERE HORRIFIED.
HIS WIFE?
YES.
SIX MONTHS LATER, A CUPBOARD FELL, SHATTERING ALL THE FINE CHINA INSIDE.
AND THIS APRIL THE STAFF WENT ON VACATION, LEAVING THE MASTER AND MISTRESS ALONE IN THE HOUSE. THEY STARTED HEARING STRANGE SOUNDS...
HMM...NOW IT'S STARTING TO SOUND LIKE SOME KIND OF POLTERGEIST.
HEY...DO THESE INCIDENTS HAPPEN ON A CERTAIN DAY?
LIKE FRIDAY THE 13TH OR SOMETHING?
THEY'VE HAPPENED ON DIFFERENT DAYS OF THE WEEK. BUT THE DATE...

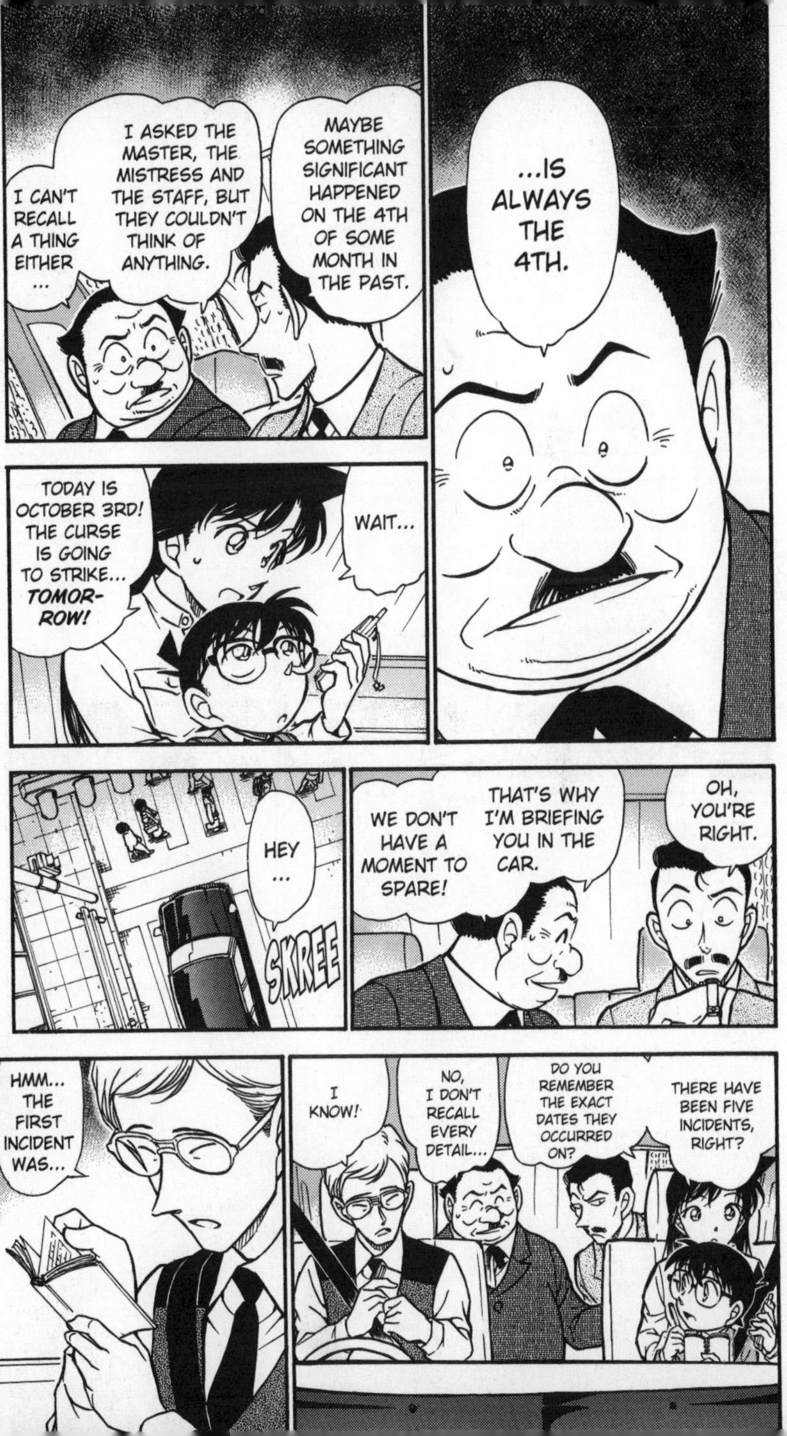
...IS ALWAYS THE 4TH.
MAYBE SOMETHING SIGNIFICANT HAPPENED ON THE 4TH OF SOME MONTH IN THE PAST.
I ASKED THE MASTER, THE MISTRESS AND THE STAFF, BUT THEY COULDN'T THINK OF ANYTHING.
I CAN'T RECALL A THING EITHER ...
WAIT...
TODAY IS OCTOBER 3RD! THE CURSE IS GOING TO STRIKE... *TOMORROW!*
OH, YOU'RE RIGHT.
THAT'S WHY I'M BRIEFING YOU IN THE CAR.
WE DON'T HAVE A MOMENT TO SPARE!
HEY ...
SKREE
THERE HAVE BEEN FIVE INCIDENTS, RIGHT?
DO YOU REMEMBER THE EXACT DATES THEY OCCURRED ON?
NO, I DON'T RECALL EVERY DETAIL...
I KNOW!
HMM... THE FIRST INCIDENT WAS...

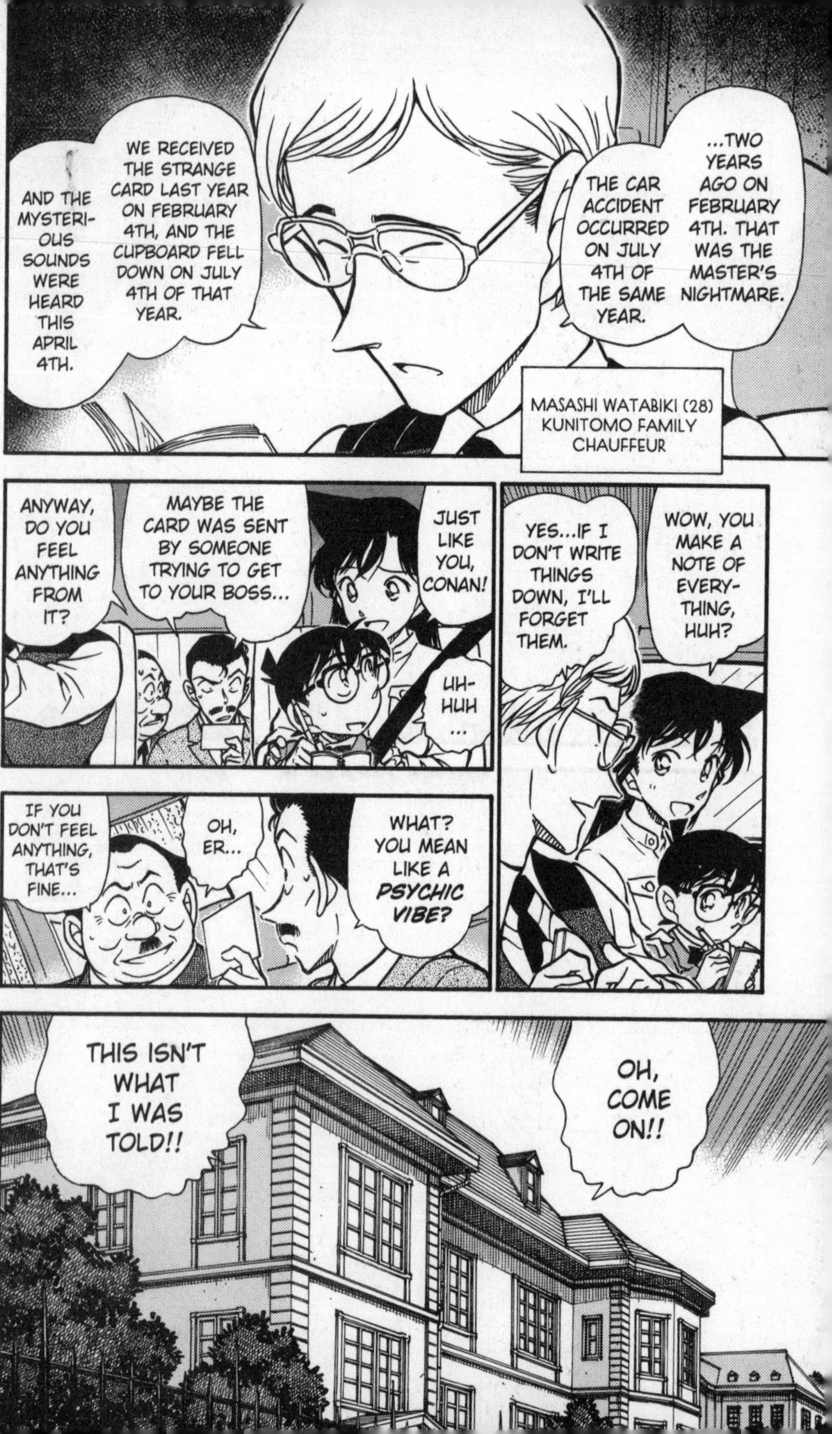
...TWO YEARS AGO ON FEBRUARY 4TH. THAT WAS THE MASTER'S NIGHTMARE.
THE CAR ACCIDENT OCCURRED ON JULY 4TH OF THE SAME YEAR.
MASASHI WATABIKI (28) KUNITOMO FAMILY CHAUFFEUR
WE RECEIVED THE STRANGE CARD LAST YEAR ON FEBRUARY 4TH, AND THE CUPBOARD FELL DOWN ON JULY 4TH OF THAT YEAR.
AND THE MYSTERIOUS SOUNDS WERE HEARD THIS APRIL 4TH.
WOW, YOU MAKE A NOTE OF EVERYTHING, HUH?
YES...IF I DON'T WRITE THINGS DOWN, I'LL FORGET THEM.
JUST LIKE YOU, CONAN!
UH-HUH...
MAYBE THE CARD WAS SENT BY SOMEONE TRYING TO GET TO YOUR BOSS...
ANYWAY, DO YOU FEEL ANYTHING FROM IT?
WHAT? YOU MEAN LIKE A *PSYCHIC VIBE?*
OH, ER...
IF YOU DON'T FEEL ANYTHING, THAT'S FINE...
OH, COME ON!!
THIS ISN'T WHAT I WAS TOLD!!

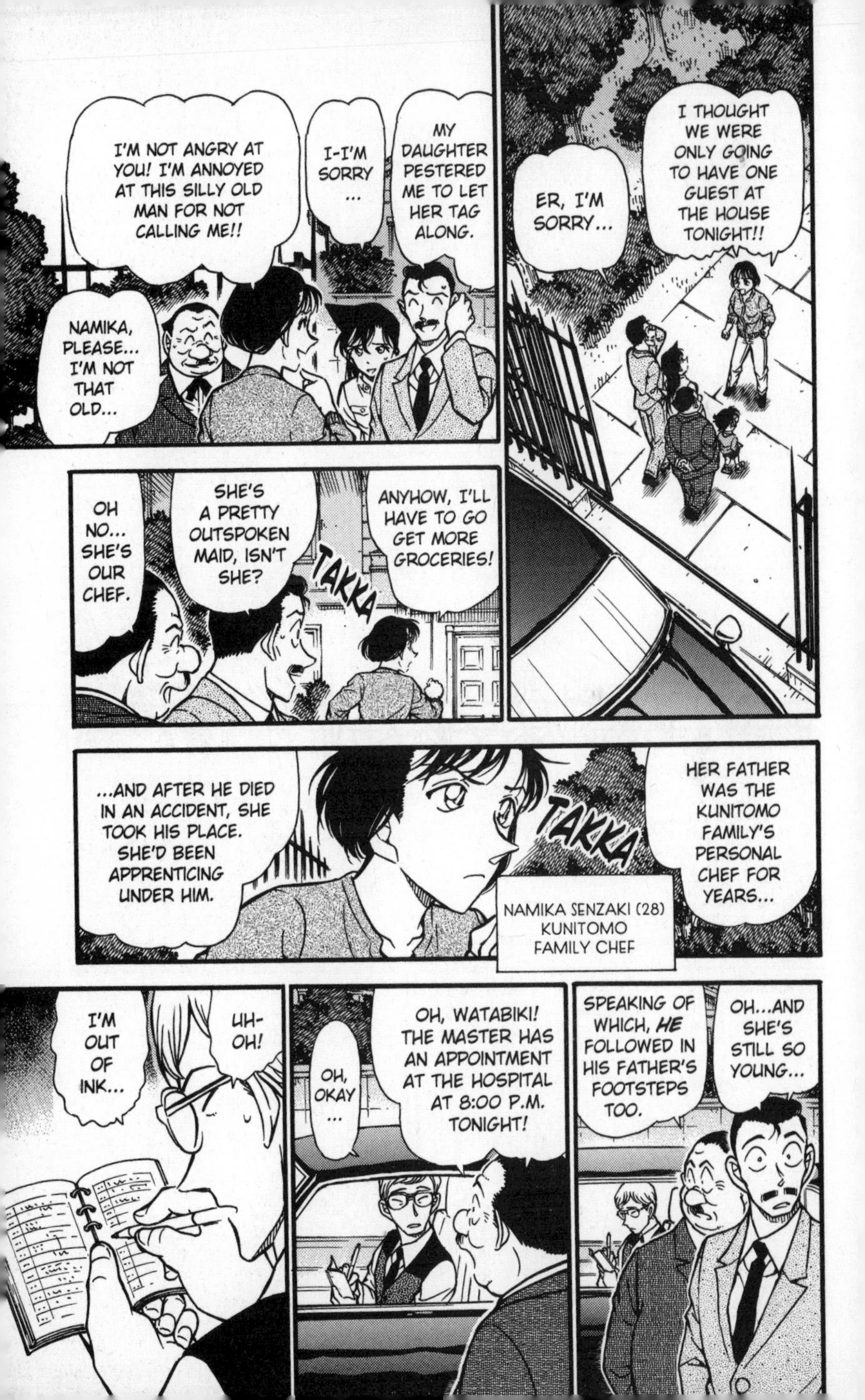
I THOUGHT WE WERE ONLY GOING TO HAVE ONE GUEST AT THE HOUSE TONIGHT!!
ER, I'M SORRY...
MY DAUGHTER PESTERED ME TO LET HER TAG ALONG.
I-I'M SORRY ...
I'M NOT ANGRY AT YOU! I'M ANNOYED AT THIS SILLY OLD MAN FOR NOT CALLING ME!!
NAMIKA, PLEASE... I'M NOT THAT OLD...
ANYHOW, I'LL HAVE TO GO GET MORE GROCERIES!
TAKKA
SHE'S A PRETTY OUTSPOKEN MAID, ISN'T SHE?
OH NO... SHE'S OUR CHEF.
HER FATHER WAS THE KUNITOMO FAMILY'S PERSONAL CHEF FOR YEARS...
TAKKA
NAMIKA SENZAKI (28) KUNITOMO FAMILY CHEF
...AND AFTER HE DIED IN AN ACCIDENT, SHE TOOK HIS PLACE. SHE'D BEEN APPRENTICING UNDER HIM.
OH...AND SHE'S STILL SO YOUNG...
SPEAKING OF WHICH, *HE* FOLLOWED IN HIS FATHER'S FOOTSTEPS TOO.
OH, WATABIKI! THE MASTER HAS AN APPOINTMENT AT THE HOSPITAL AT 8:00 P.M. TONIGHT!
OH, OKAY ...
UH-OH!
I'M OUT OF INK...

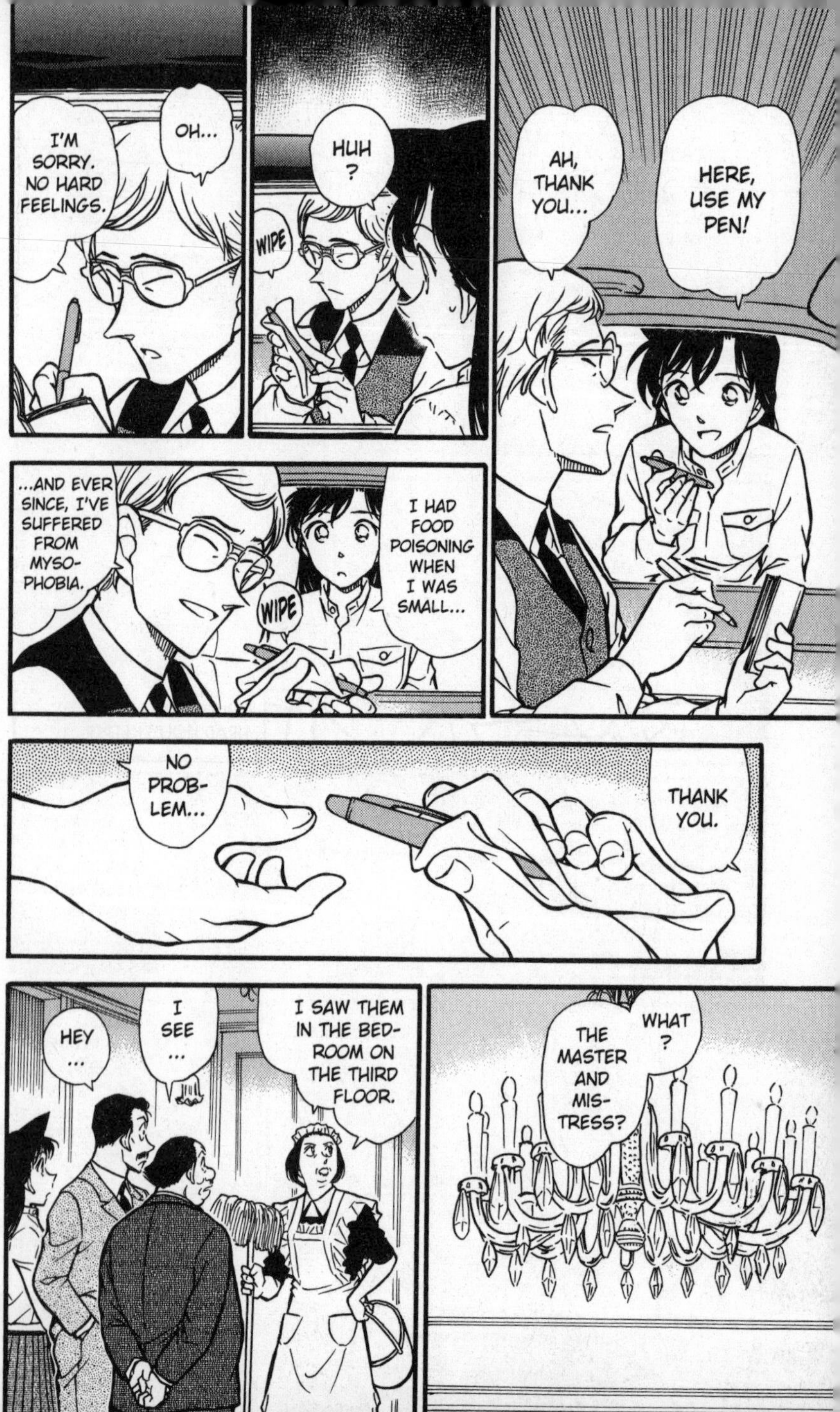
HERE, USE MY PEN!
AH, THANK YOU...
HUH ?
WIPE
OH...
I'M SORRY. NO HARD FEELINGS.
I HAD FOOD POISONING WHEN I WAS SMALL...
WIPE
...AND EVER SINCE, I'VE SUFFERED FROM MYSO-PHOBIA.
THANK YOU.
NO PROB-LEM...
WHAT ?
THE MASTER AND MIS-TRESS?
I SAW THEM IN THE BED-ROOM ON THE THIRD FLOOR.
I SEE ...
HEY ...

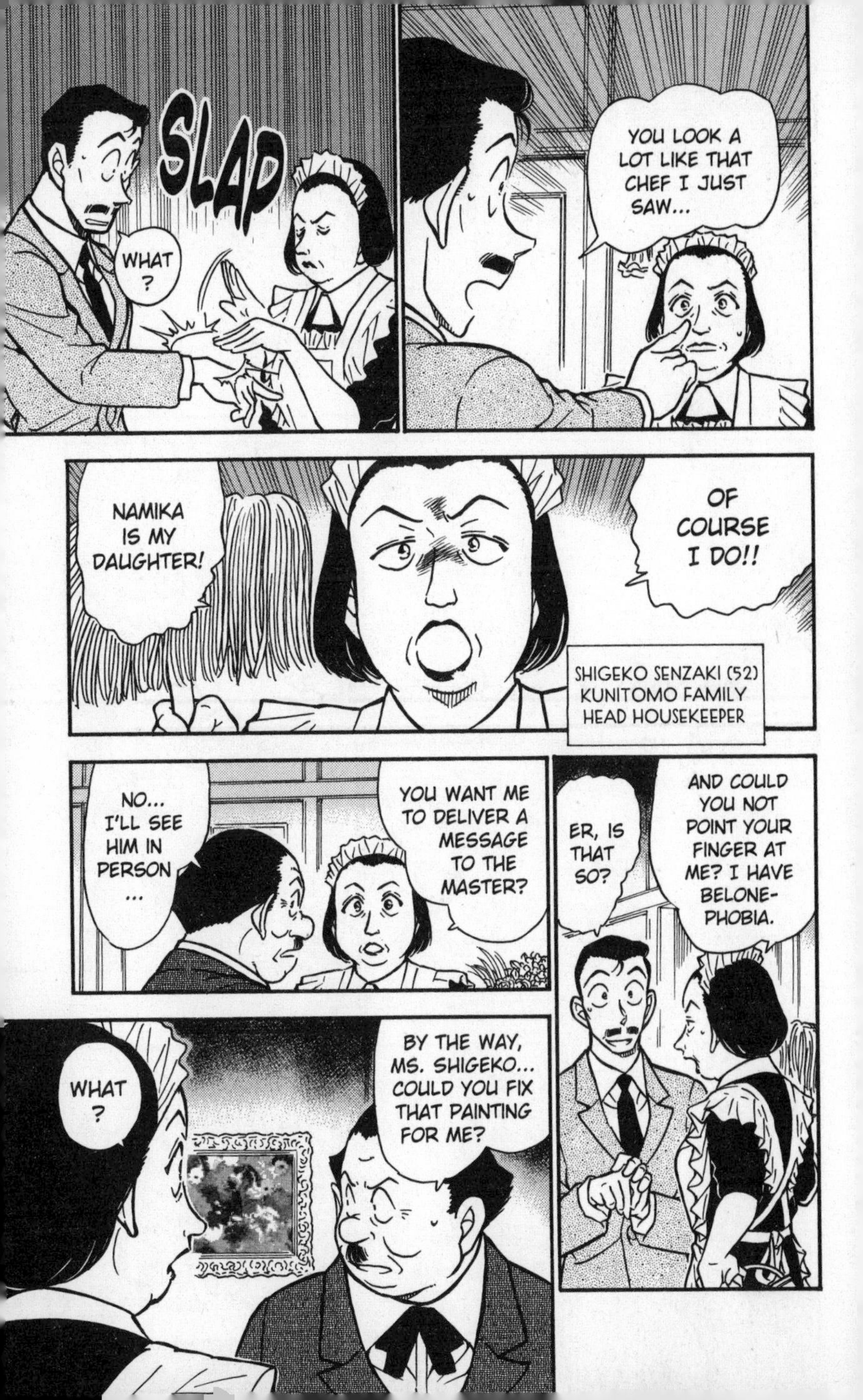
YOU LOOK A LOT LIKE THAT CHEF I JUST SAW...
SLAP
WHAT?
OF COURSE I DO!!
NAMIKA IS MY DAUGHTER!
SHIGEKO SENZAKI (52) KUNITOMO FAMILY HEAD HOUSEKEEPER
AND COULD YOU NOT POINT YOUR FINGER AT ME? I HAVE BELONE-PHOBIA.
ER, IS THAT SO?
YOU WANT ME TO DELIVER A MESSAGE TO THE MASTER?
NO... I'LL SEE HIM IN PERSON...
BY THE WAY, MS. SHIGEKO... COULD YOU FIX THAT PAINTING FOR ME?
WHAT?

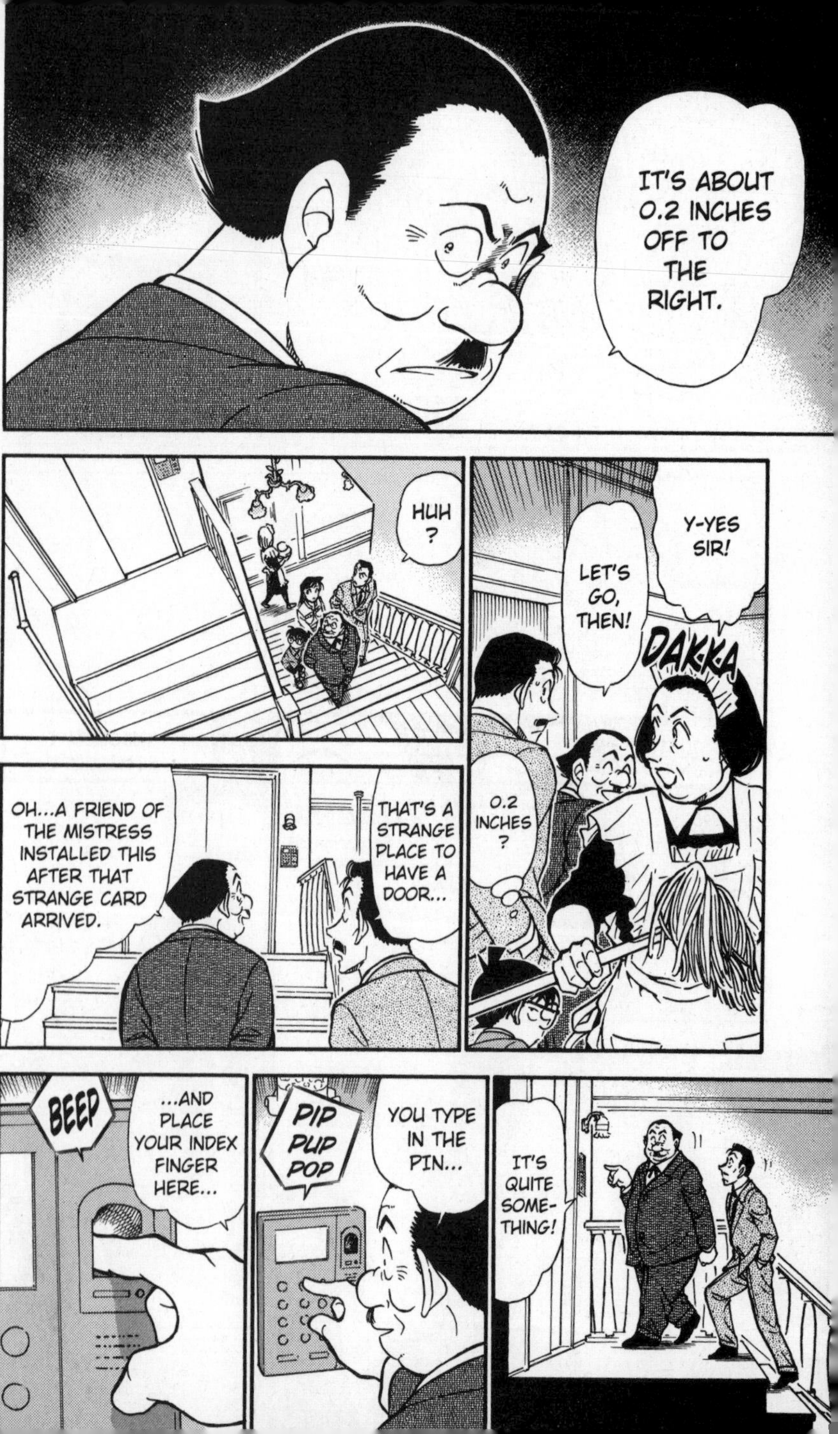
IT'S ABOUT 0.2 INCHES OFF TO THE RIGHT.
Y-YES SIR!
LET'S GO, THEN!
DAKKA
0.2 INCHES?
HUH?
THAT'S A STRANGE PLACE TO HAVE A DOOR...
OH...A FRIEND OF THE MISTRESS INSTALLED THIS AFTER THAT STRANGE CARD ARRIVED.
IT'S QUITE SOME-THING!
YOU TYPE IN THE PIN...
PIP PUP POP
...AND PLACE YOUR INDEX FINGER HERE...
BEEP

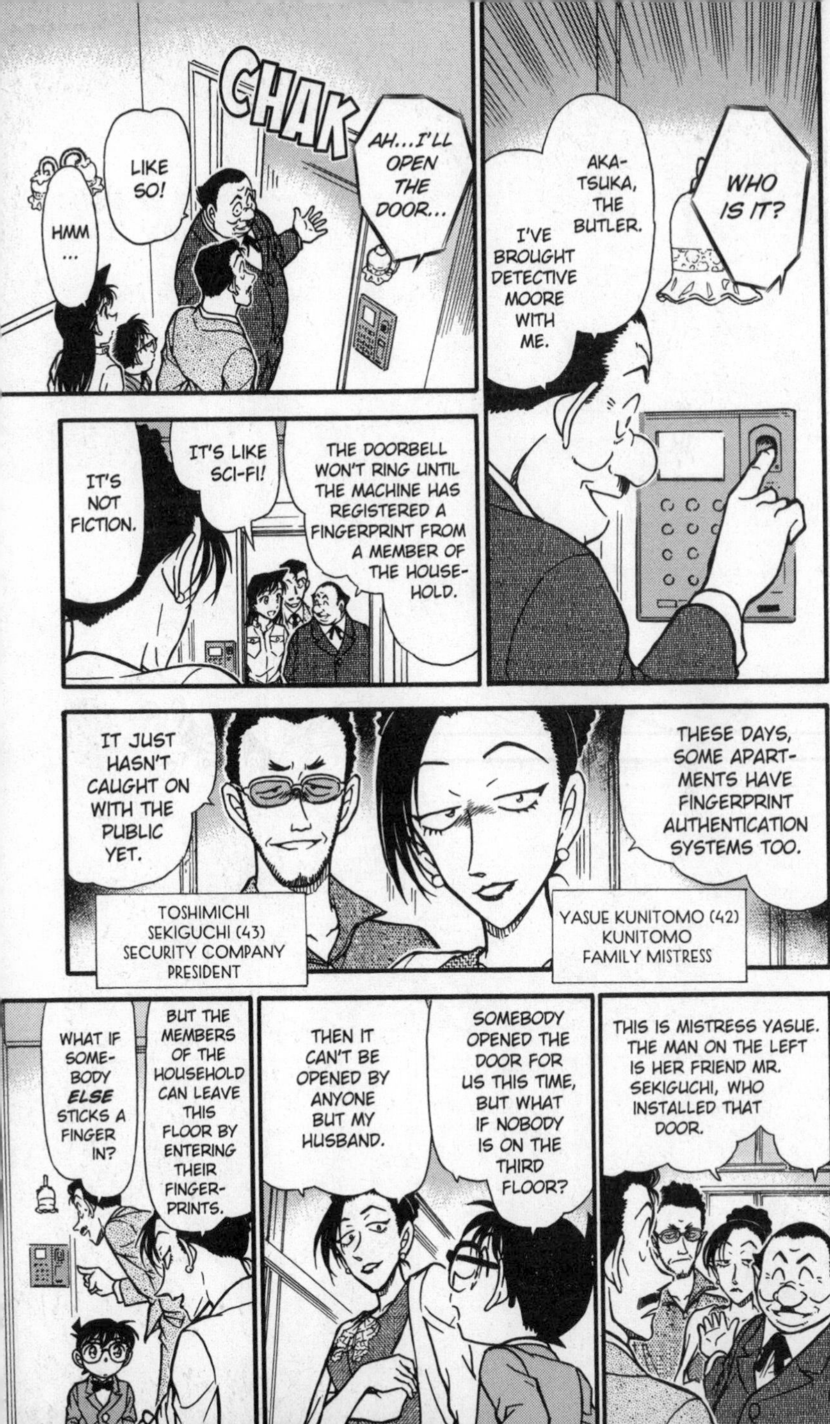
WHO IS IT?
AKA-TSUKA, THE BUTLER.
I'VE BROUGHT DETECTIVE MOORE WITH ME.
AH...I'LL OPEN THE DOOR...
CHAK
LIKE SO!
HMM ...
THE DOORBELL WON'T RING UNTIL THE MACHINE HAS REGISTERED A FINGERPRINT FROM A MEMBER OF THE HOUSE-HOLD.
IT'S LIKE SCI-FI!
IT'S NOT FICTION.
THESE DAYS, SOME APART-MENTS HAVE FINGERPRINT AUTHENTICATION SYSTEMS TOO.
IT JUST HASN'T CAUGHT ON WITH THE PUBLIC YET.
YASUE KUNITOMO (42) KUNITOMO FAMILY MISTRESS
TOSHIMICHI SEKIGUCHI (43) SECURITY COMPANY PRESIDENT
THIS IS MISTRESS YASUE. THE MAN ON THE LEFT IS HER FRIEND MR. SEKIGUCHI, WHO INSTALLED THAT DOOR.
SOMEBODY OPENED THE DOOR FOR US THIS TIME, BUT WHAT IF NOBODY IS ON THE THIRD FLOOR?
THEN IT CAN'T BE OPENED BY ANYONE BUT MY HUSBAND.
BUT THE MEMBERS OF THE HOUSEHOLD CAN LEAVE THIS FLOOR BY ENTERING THEIR FINGER-PRINTS.
WHAT IF SOME-BODY *ELSE* STICKS A FINGER IN?

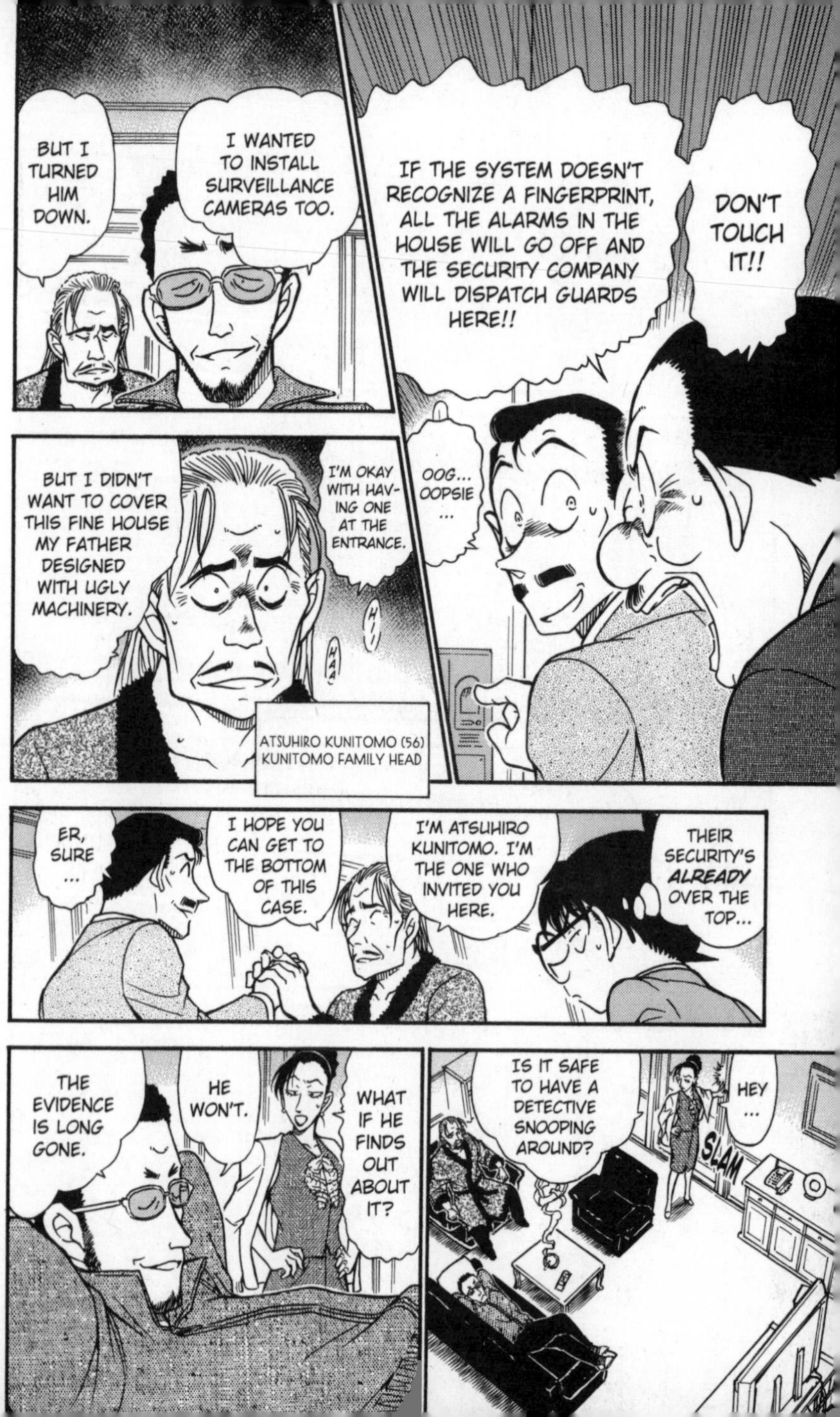
DON'T TOUCH IT!!
IF THE SYSTEM DOESN'T RECOGNIZE A FINGERPRINT, ALL THE ALARMS IN THE HOUSE WILL GO OFF AND THE SECURITY COMPANY WILL DISPATCH GUARDS HERE!!
OOG... OOPSIE ...
I WANTED TO INSTALL SURVEILLANCE CAMERAS TOO.
BUT I TURNED HIM DOWN.
I'M OKAY WITH HAV-ING ONE AT THE ENTRANCE.
BUT I DIDN'T WANT TO COVER THIS FINE HOUSE MY FATHER DESIGNED WITH UGLY MACHINERY.
ATSUHIRO KUNITOMO (56) KUNITOMO FAMILY HEAD
THEIR SECURITY'S *ALREADY* OVER THE TOP...
I'M ATSUHIRO KUNITOMO. I'M THE ONE WHO INVITED YOU HERE.
I HOPE YOU CAN GET TO THE BOTTOM OF THIS CASE.
ER, SURE ...
HEY ...
SLAM
IS IT SAFE TO HAVE A DETECTIVE SNOOPING AROUND?
WHAT IF HE FINDS OUT ABOUT IT?
HE WON'T.
THE EVIDENCE IS LONG GONE.

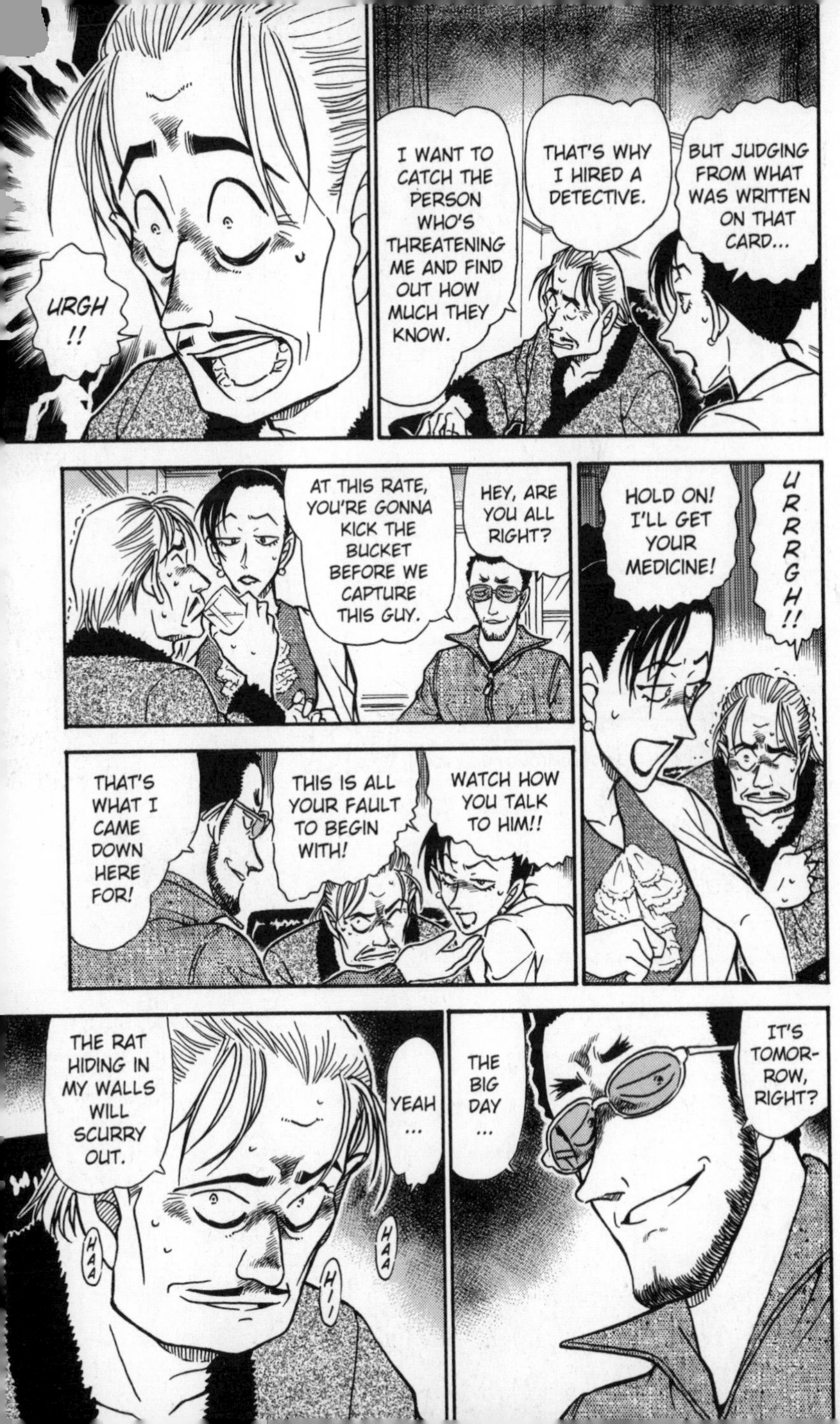
BUT JUDGING FROM WHAT WAS WRITTEN ON THAT CARD...
THAT'S WHY I HIRED A DETECTIVE.
I WANT TO CATCH THE PERSON WHO'S THREATENING ME AND FIND OUT HOW MUCH THEY KNOW.
URGH!!
URRRGH!!
HOLD ON! I'LL GET YOUR MEDICINE!
HEY, ARE YOU ALL RIGHT?
AT THIS RATE, YOU'RE GONNA KICK THE BUCKET BEFORE WE CAPTURE THIS GUY.
WATCH HOW YOU TALK TO HIM!!
THIS IS ALL YOUR FAULT TO BEGIN WITH!
THAT'S WHAT I CAME DOWN HERE FOR!
IT'S TOMORROW, RIGHT?
THE BIG DAY...
YEAH...
THE RAT HIDING IN MY WALLS WILL SCURRY OUT.
HAA
HI
HAA

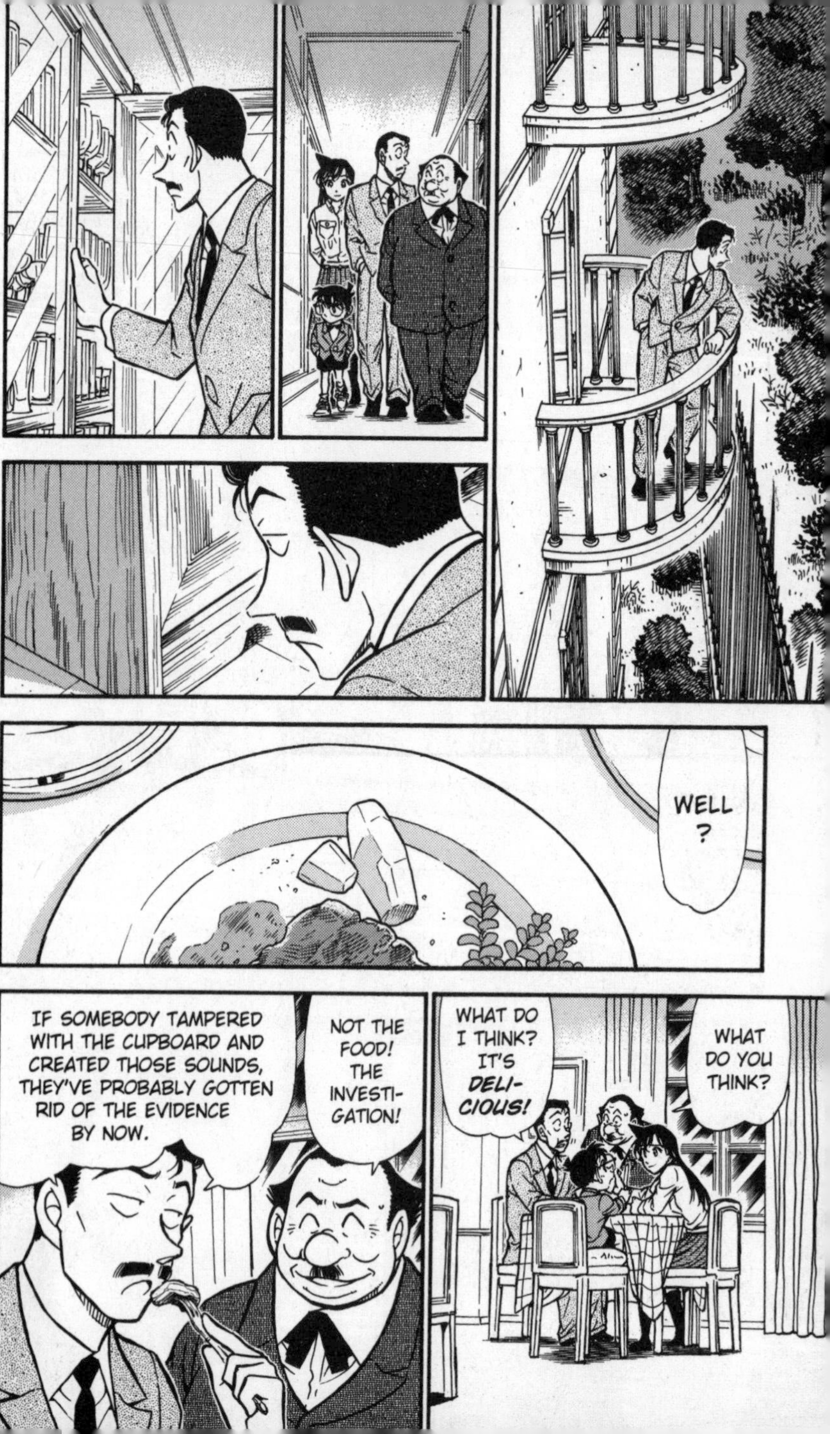
WELL ?
WHAT DO YOU THINK?
WHAT DO I THINK? IT'S DELICIOUS!
NOT THE FOOD! THE INVESTIGATION!
IF SOMEBODY TAMPERED WITH THE CUPBOARD AND CREATED THOSE SOUNDS, THEY'VE PROBABLY GOTTEN RID OF THE EVIDENCE BY NOW.

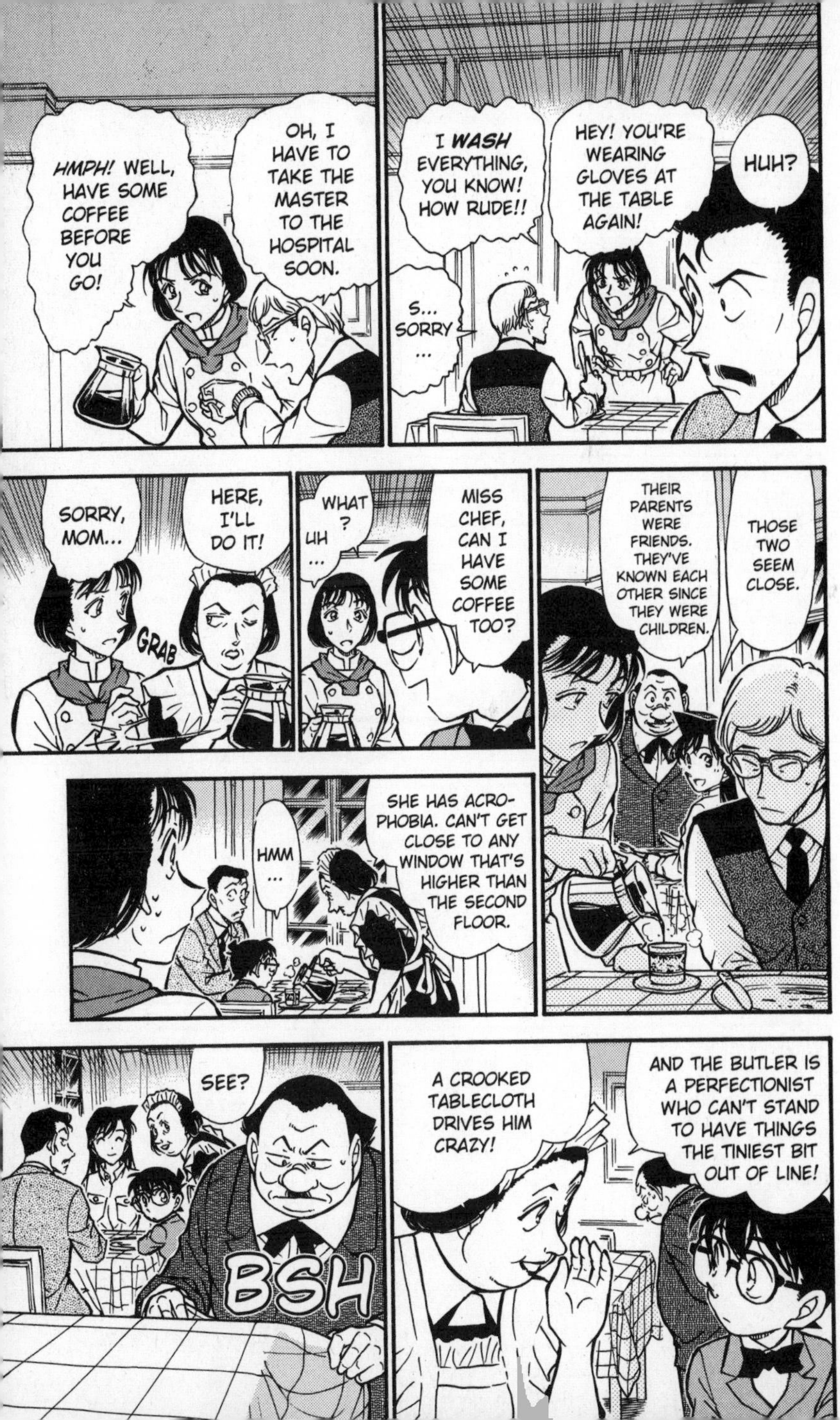
HUH?
HEY! YOU'RE WEARING GLOVES AT THE TABLE AGAIN!
I *WASH* EVERYTHING, YOU KNOW! HOW RUDE!!
S... SORRY ...
OH, I HAVE TO TAKE THE MASTER TO THE HOSPITAL SOON.
HMPH! WELL, HAVE SOME COFFEE BEFORE YOU GO!
THOSE TWO SEEM CLOSE.
THEIR PARENTS WERE FRIENDS. THEY'VE KNOWN EACH OTHER SINCE THEY WERE CHILDREN.
MISS CHEF, CAN I HAVE SOME COFFEE TOO?
WHAT ?
UH ...
HERE, I'LL DO IT!
SORRY, MOM...
GRAB
SHE HAS ACROPHOBIA. CAN'T GET CLOSE TO ANY WINDOW THAT'S HIGHER THAN THE SECOND FLOOR.
HMM ...
AND THE BUTLER IS A PERFECTIONIST WHO CAN'T STAND TO HAVE THINGS THE TINIEST BIT OUT OF LINE!
A CROOKED TABLECLOTH DRIVES HIM CRAZY!
SEE?
BSH

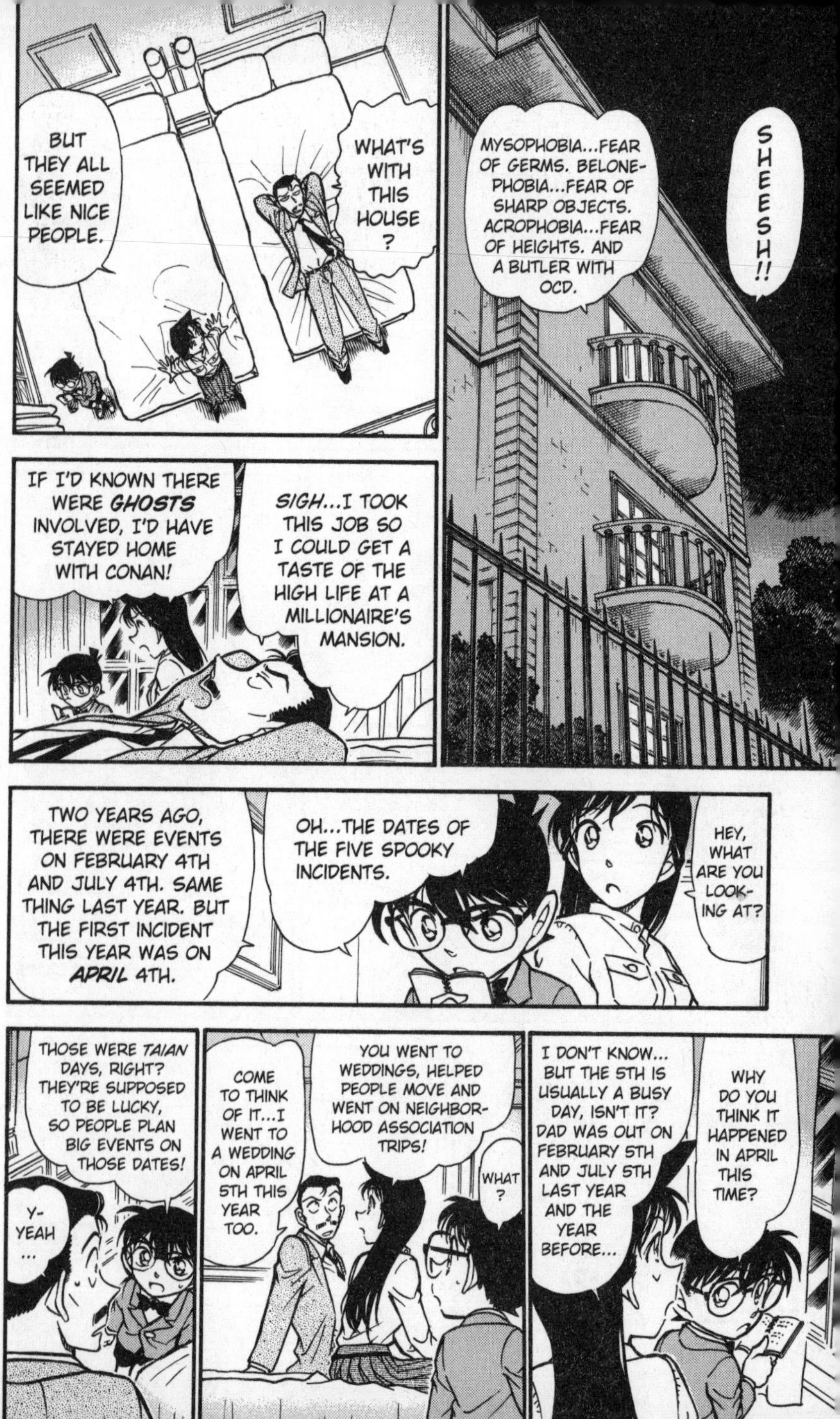
SHEESH!!
MYSOPHOBIA...FEAR OF GERMS. BELONE-PHOBIA...FEAR OF SHARP OBJECTS. ACROPHOBIA...FEAR OF HEIGHTS. AND A BUTLER WITH OCD.
WHAT'S WITH THIS HOUSE?
BUT THEY ALL SEEMED LIKE NICE PEOPLE.
SIGH...I TOOK THIS JOB SO I COULD GET A TASTE OF THE HIGH LIFE AT A MILLIONAIRE'S MANSION.
IF I'D KNOWN THERE WERE GHOSTS INVOLVED, I'D HAVE STAYED HOME WITH CONAN!
HEY, WHAT ARE YOU LOOK-ING AT?
OH...THE DATES OF THE FIVE SPOOKY INCIDENTS.
TWO YEARS AGO, THERE WERE EVENTS ON FEBRUARY 4TH AND JULY 4TH. SAME THING LAST YEAR. BUT THE FIRST INCIDENT THIS YEAR WAS ON APRIL 4TH.
WHY DO YOU THINK IT HAPPENED IN APRIL THIS TIME?
I DON'T KNOW... BUT THE 5TH IS USUALLY A BUSY DAY, ISN'T IT? DAD WAS OUT ON FEBRUARY 5TH AND JULY 5TH LAST YEAR AND THE YEAR BEFORE...
WHAT?
YOU WENT TO WEDDINGS, HELPED PEOPLE MOVE AND WENT ON NEIGHBOR-HOOD ASSOCIATION TRIPS!
COME TO THINK OF IT...I WENT TO A WEDDING ON APRIL 5TH THIS YEAR TOO.
THOSE WERE TAIAN DAYS, RIGHT? THEY'RE SUPPOSED TO BE LUCKY, SO PEOPLE PLAN BIG EVENTS ON THOSE DATES!
Y-YEAH...

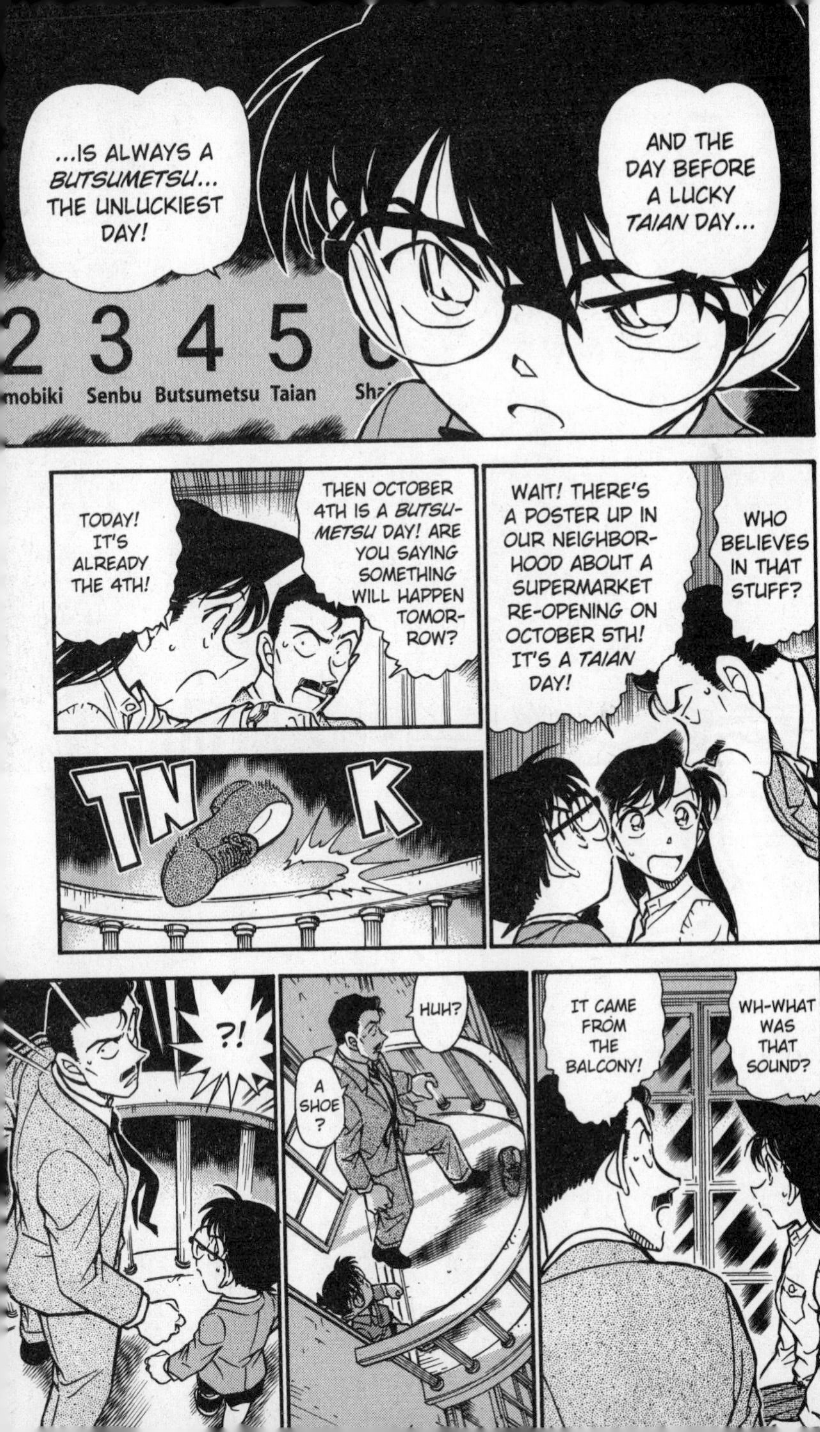
AND THE DAY BEFORE A LUCKY *TAIAN* DAY...
...IS ALWAYS A *BUTSUMETSU*... THE UNLUCKIEST DAY!
2 3 4 5
mobiki Senbu Butsumetsu Taian
WHO BELIEVES IN THAT STUFF?
WAIT! THERE'S A POSTER UP IN OUR NEIGHBORHOOD ABOUT A SUPERMARKET RE-OPENING ON OCTOBER 5TH! IT'S A *TAIAN* DAY!
THEN OCTOBER 4TH IS A *BUTSUMETSU* DAY! ARE YOU SAYING SOMETHING WILL HAPPEN TOMORROW?
TODAY! IT'S ALREADY THE 4TH!
TNK
WH-WHAT WAS THAT SOUND?
IT CAME FROM THE BALCONY!
HUH?
A SHOE?
?!

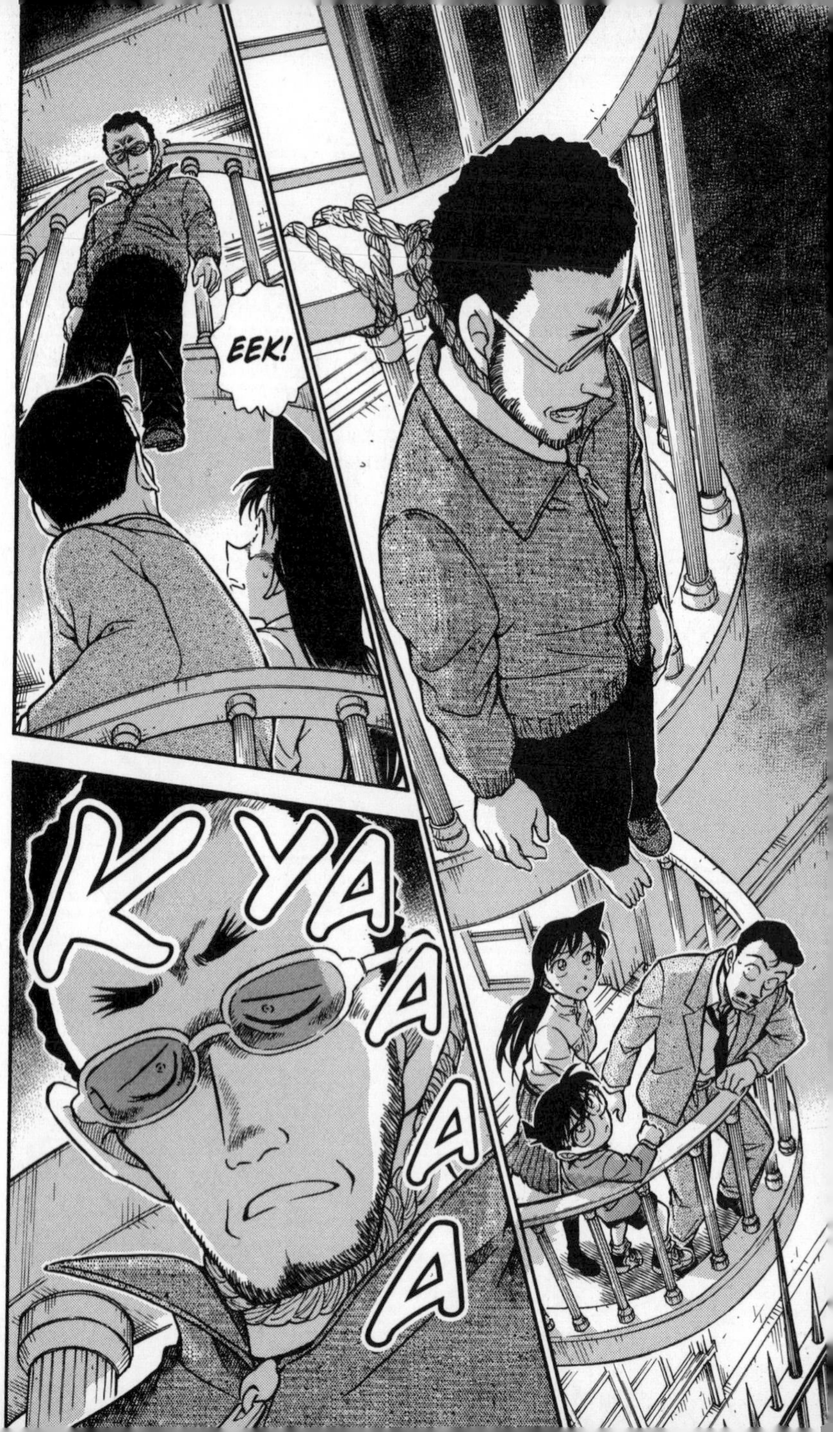
EEK!
KYAAAAAA

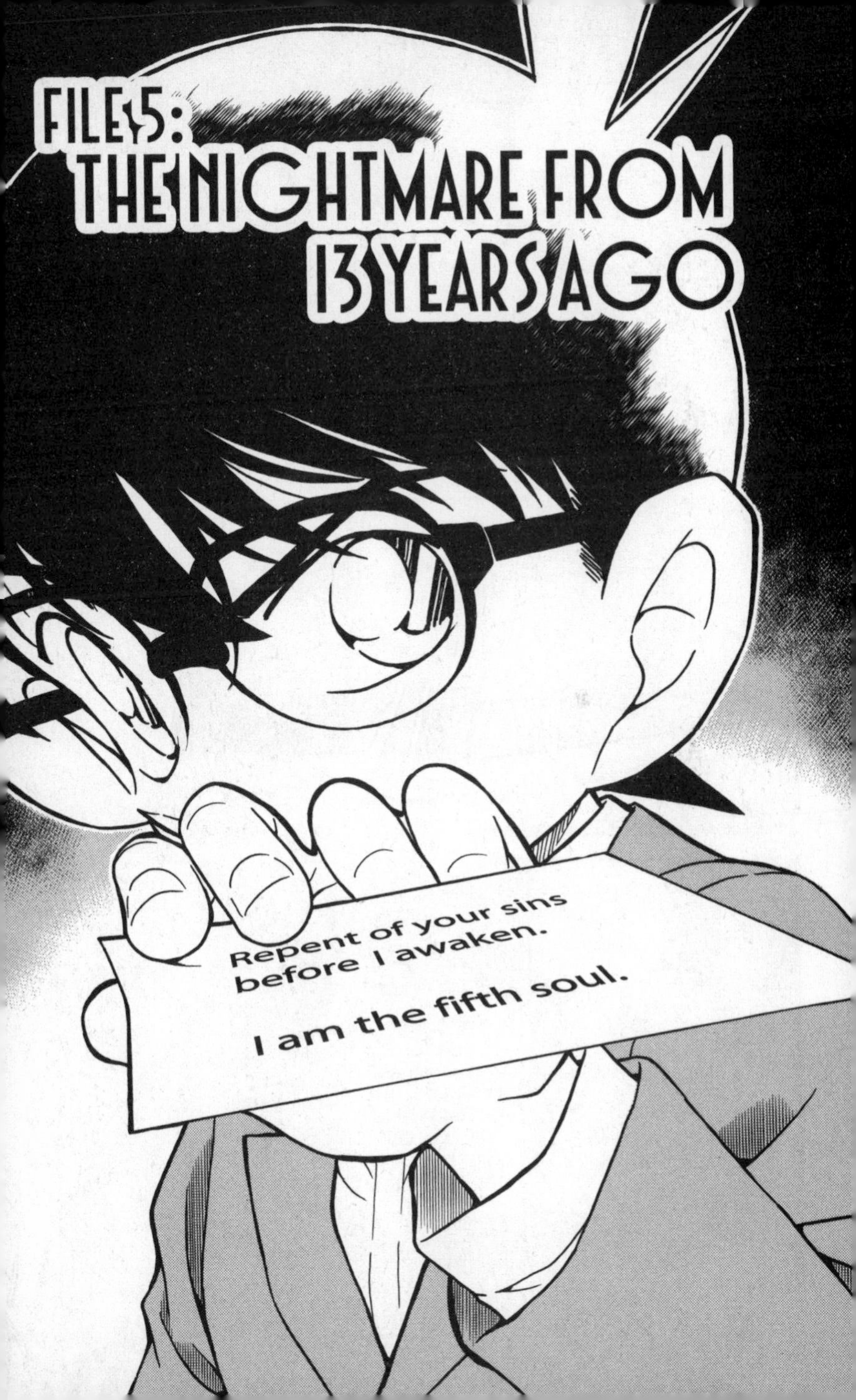
FILE 5:
THE NIGHTMARE FROM 13 YEARS AGO
Repent of your sins before I awaken.
I am the fifth soul.

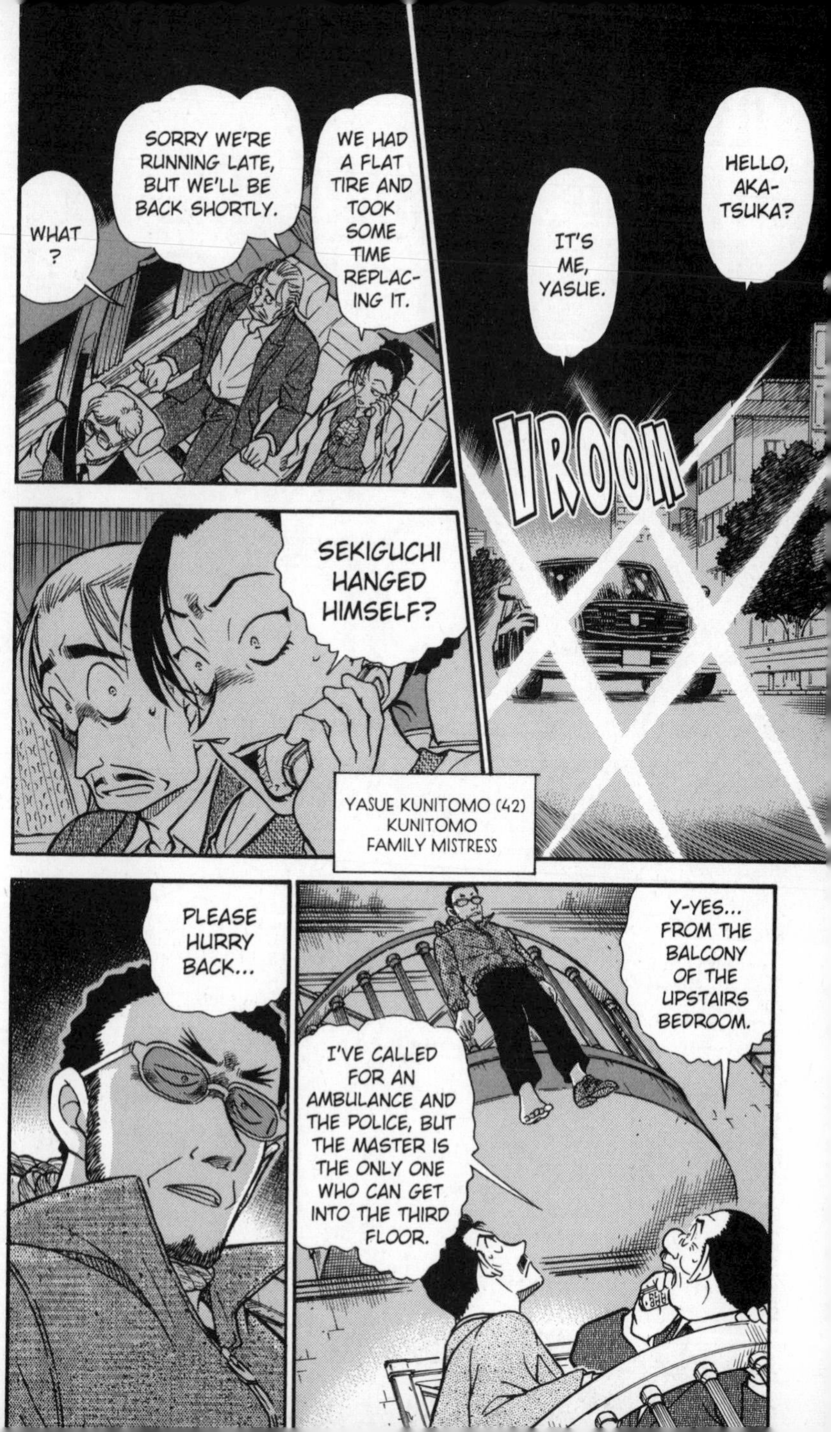
HELLO, AKA-TSUKA?
IT'S ME, YASUE.
VROOM
SORRY WE'RE RUNNING LATE, BUT WE'LL BE BACK SHORTLY.
WE HAD A FLAT TIRE AND TOOK SOME TIME REPLAC-ING IT.
WHAT ?
SEKIGUCHI HANGED HIMSELF?
YASUE KUNITOMO (42) KUNITOMO FAMILY MISTRESS
Y-YES... FROM THE BALCONY OF THE UPSTAIRS BEDROOM.
I'VE CALLED FOR AN AMBULANCE AND THE POLICE, BUT THE MASTER IS THE ONLY ONE WHO CAN GET INTO THE THIRD FLOOR.
PLEASE HURRY BACK...

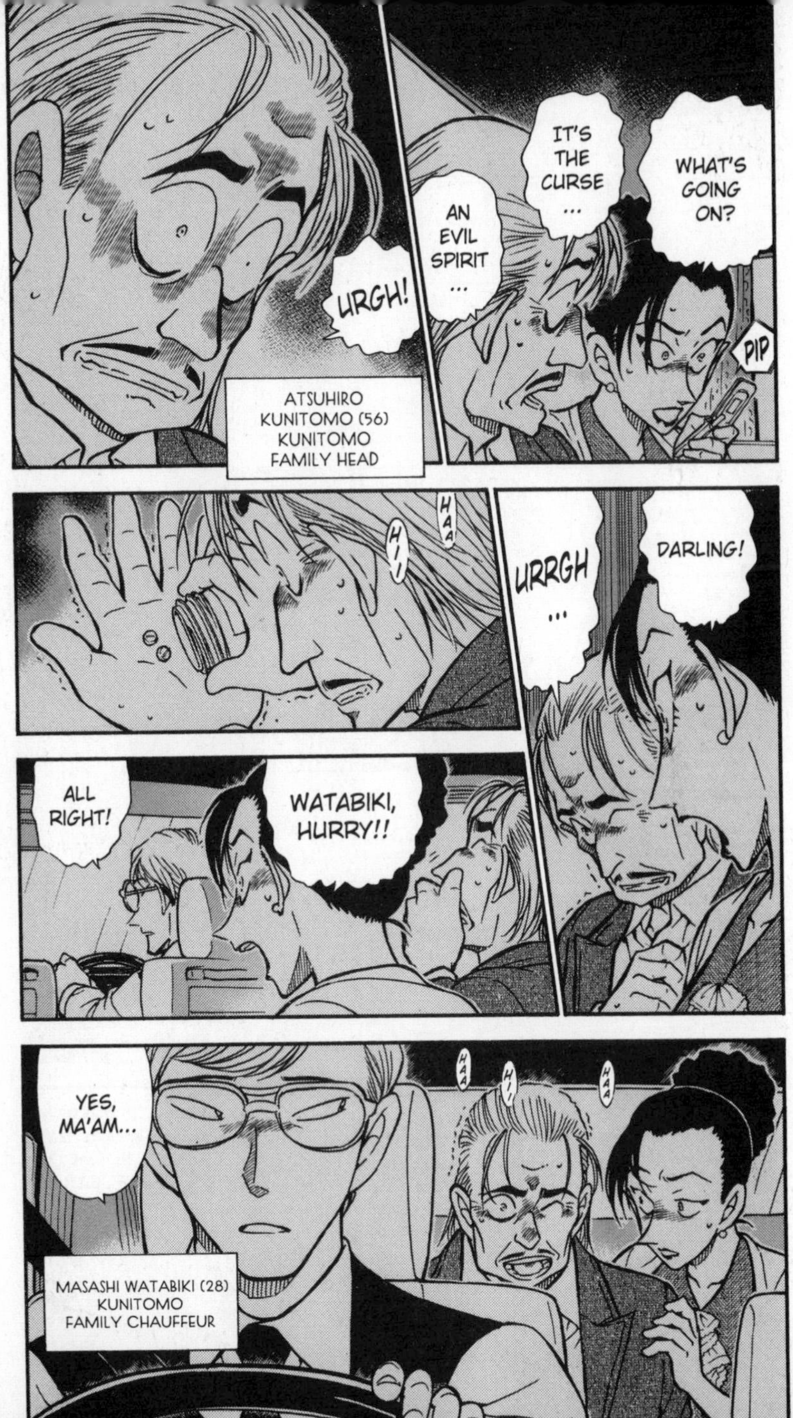
WHAT'S GOING ON?
IT'S THE CURSE...
AN EVIL SPIRIT...
URGH!
PIP
ATSUHIRO KUNITOMO (56) KUNITOMO FAMILY HEAD
DARLING!
URRGH...
HAA
HII
WATABIKI, HURRY!!
ALL RIGHT!
HAA
HII
HAA
YES, MA'AM...
MASASHI WATABIKI (28) KUNITOMO FAMILY CHAUFFEUR

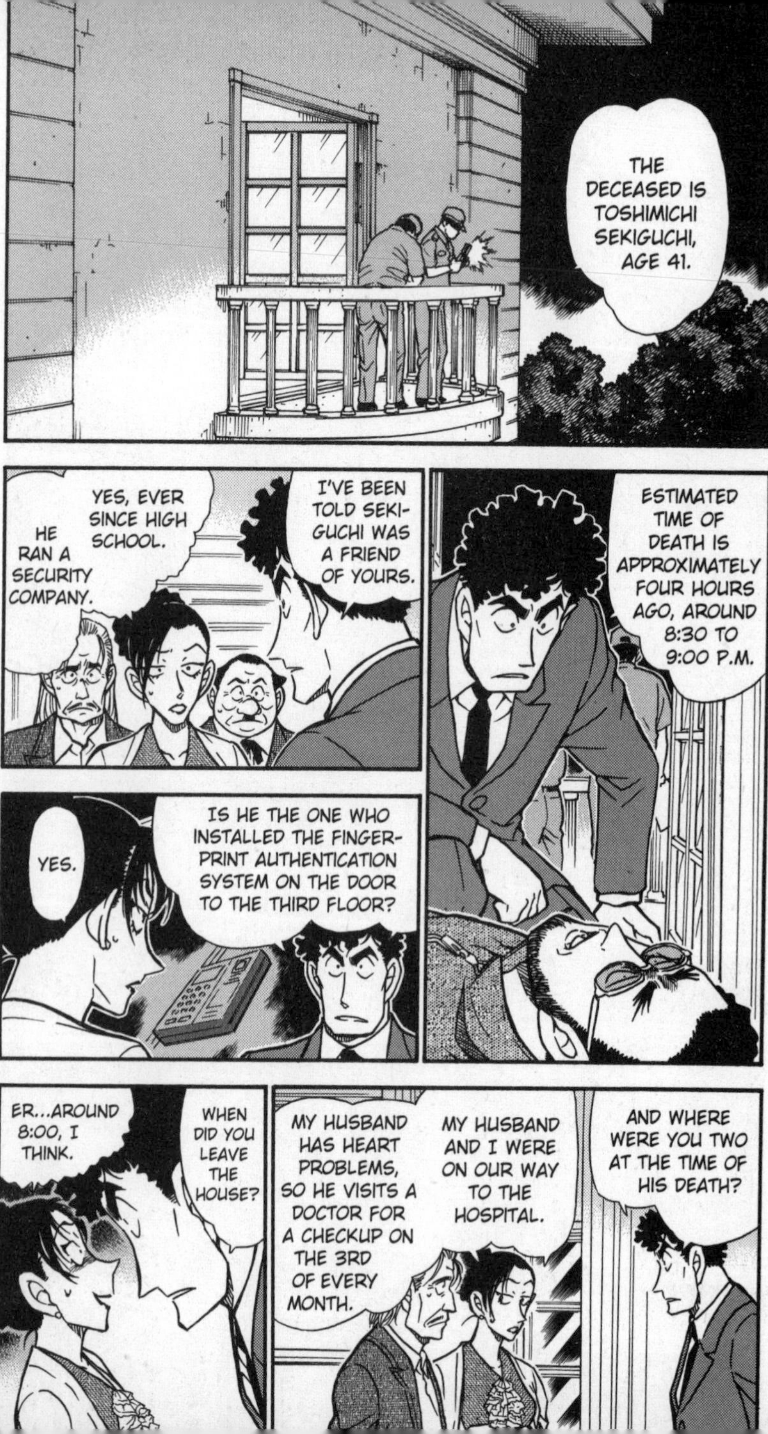
THE DECEASED IS TOSHIMICHI SEKIGUCHI, AGE 41.
ESTIMATED TIME OF DEATH IS APPROXIMATELY FOUR HOURS AGO, AROUND 8:30 TO 9:00 P.M.
I'VE BEEN TOLD SEKI-GUCHI WAS A FRIEND OF YOURS.
YES, EVER SINCE HIGH SCHOOL.
HE RAN A SECURITY COMPANY.
IS HE THE ONE WHO INSTALLED THE FINGER-PRINT AUTHENTICATION SYSTEM ON THE DOOR TO THE THIRD FLOOR?
YES.
AND WHERE WERE YOU TWO AT THE TIME OF HIS DEATH?
MY HUSBAND AND I WERE ON OUR WAY TO THE HOSPITAL.
MY HUSBAND HAS HEART PROBLEMS, SO HE VISITS A DOCTOR FOR A CHECKUP ON THE 3RD OF EVERY MONTH.
WHEN DID YOU LEAVE THE HOUSE?
ER...AROUND 8:00, I THINK.

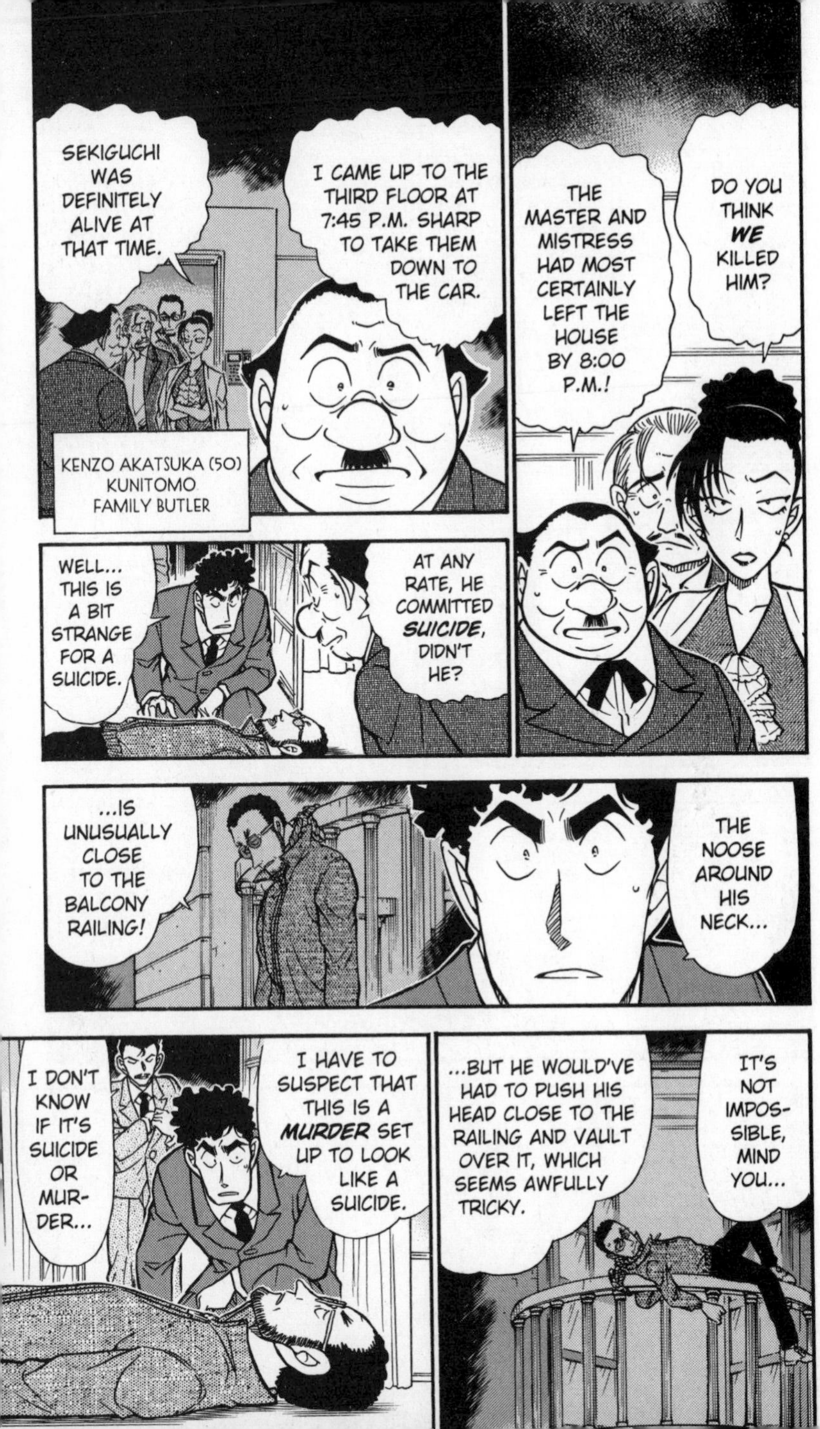
DO YOU THINK *WE* KILLED HIM?
THE MASTER AND MISTRESS HAD MOST CERTAINLY LEFT THE HOUSE BY 8:00 P.M.!
I CAME UP TO THE THIRD FLOOR AT 7:45 P.M. SHARP TO TAKE THEM DOWN TO THE CAR.
SEKIGUCHI WAS DEFINITELY ALIVE AT THAT TIME.
KENZO AKATSUKA (50) KUNITOMO FAMILY BUTLER
AT ANY RATE, HE COMMITTED *SUICIDE*, DIDN'T HE?
WELL... THIS IS A BIT STRANGE FOR A SUICIDE.
THE NOOSE AROUND HIS NECK...
...IS UNUSUALLY CLOSE TO THE BALCONY RAILING!
IT'S NOT IMPOSSIBLE, MIND YOU...
...BUT HE WOULD'VE HAD TO PUSH HIS HEAD CLOSE TO THE RAILING AND VAULT OVER IT, WHICH SEEMS AWFULLY TRICKY.
I HAVE TO SUSPECT THAT THIS IS A *MURDER* SET UP TO LOOK LIKE A SUICIDE.
I DON'T KNOW IF IT'S SUICIDE OR MUR-DER...

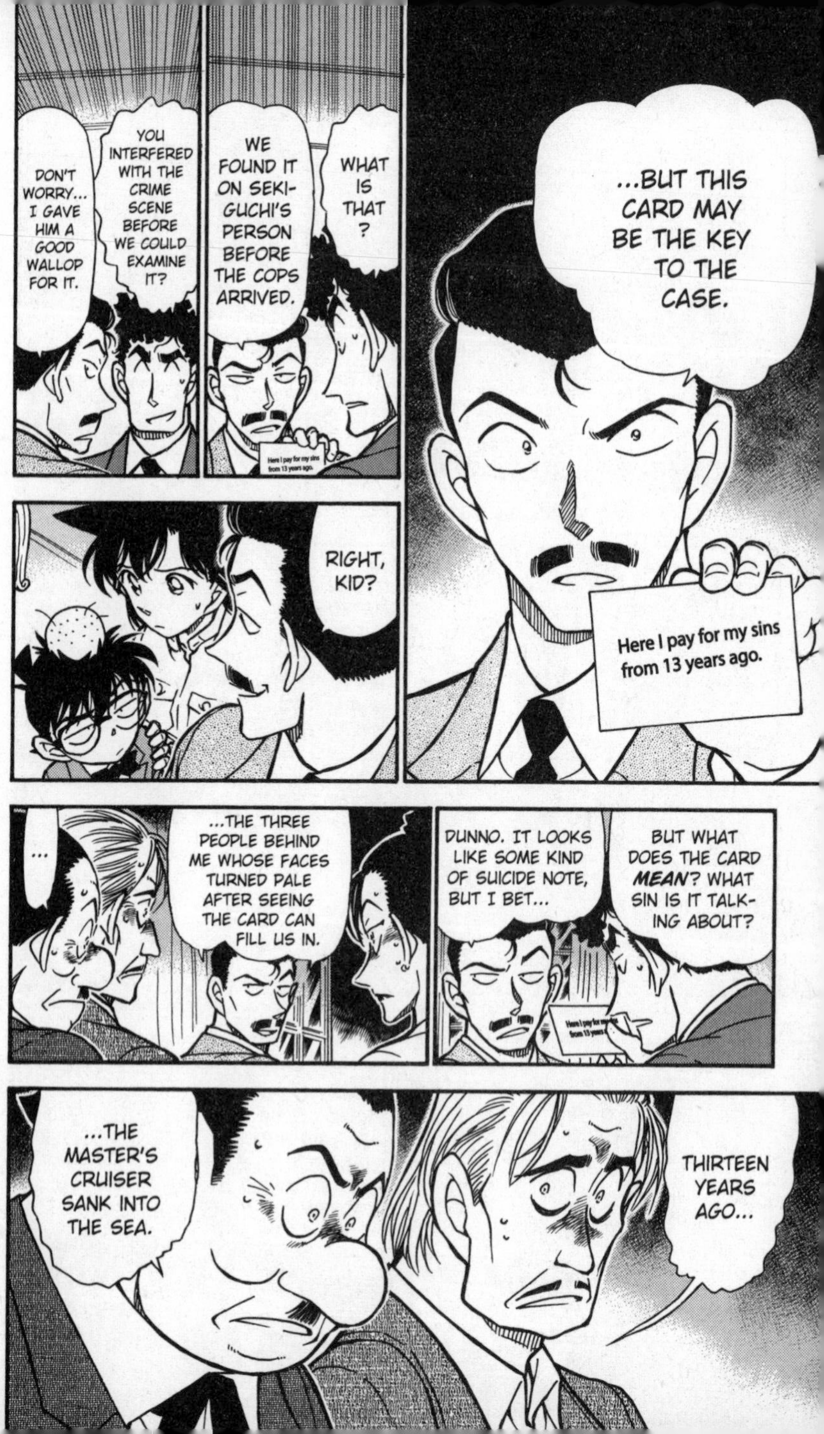
...BUT THIS CARD MAY BE THE KEY TO THE CASE.
Here I pay for my sins from 13 years ago.
WHAT IS THAT?
WE FOUND IT ON SEKI-GUCHI'S PERSON BEFORE THE COPS ARRIVED.
Here I pay for my sins from 13 years ago.
YOU INTERFERED WITH THE CRIME SCENE BEFORE WE COULD EXAMINE IT?
DON'T WORRY... I GAVE HIM A GOOD WALLOP FOR IT.
RIGHT, KID?
BUT WHAT DOES THE CARD *MEAN*? WHAT SIN IS IT TALK-ING ABOUT?
DUNNO. IT LOOKS LIKE SOME KIND OF SUICIDE NOTE, BUT I BET...
...THE THREE PEOPLE BEHIND ME WHOSE FACES TURNED PALE AFTER SEEING THE CARD CAN FILL US IN.
...
THIRTEEN YEARS AGO...
...THE MASTER'S CRUISER SANK INTO THE SEA.

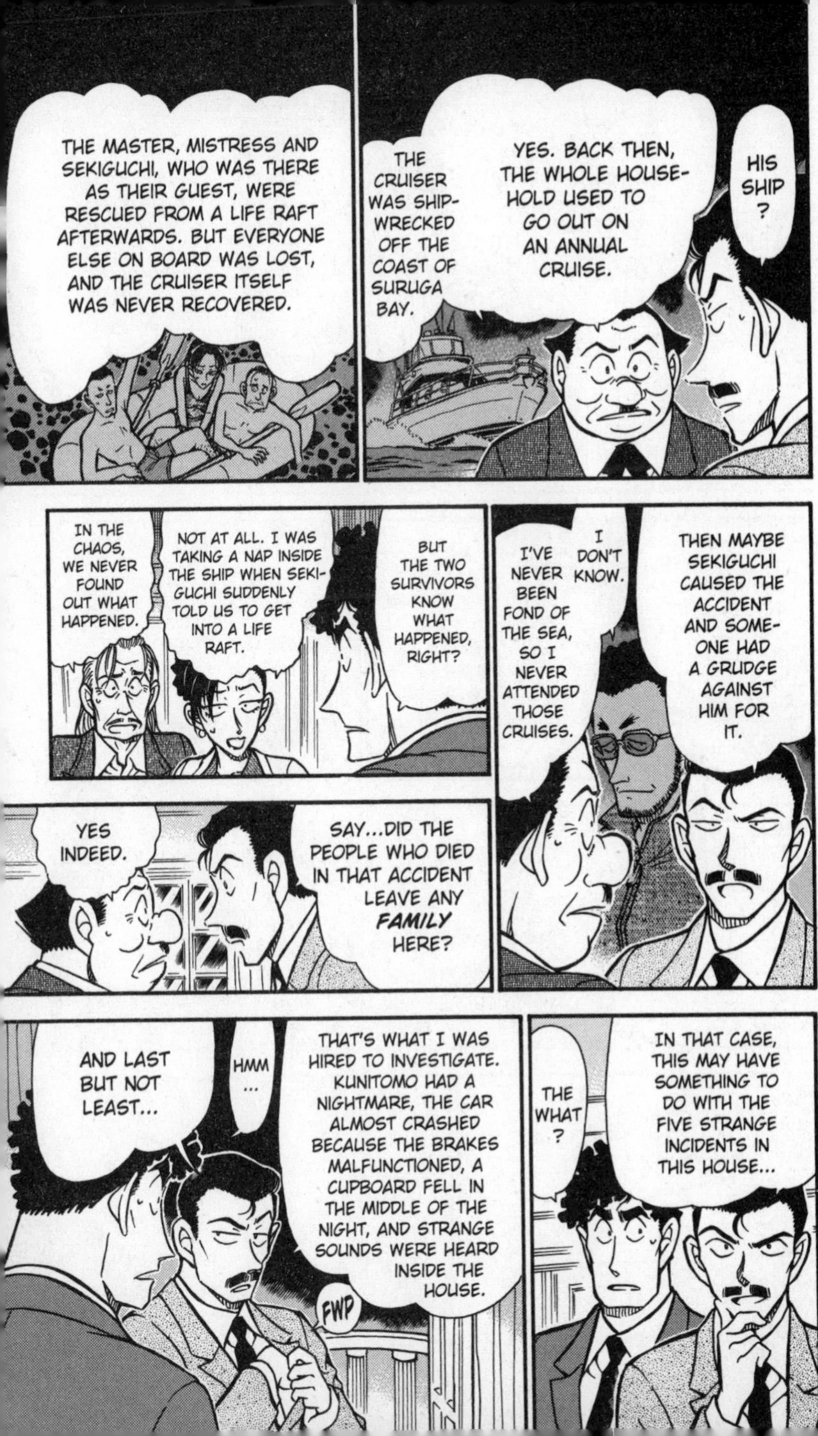
HIS SHIP?
YES. BACK THEN, THE WHOLE HOUSE-HOLD USED TO GO OUT ON AN ANNUAL CRUISE.
THE CRUISER WAS SHIP-WRECKED OFF THE COAST OF SURUGA BAY.
THE MASTER, MISTRESS AND SEKIGUCHI, WHO WAS THERE AS THEIR GUEST, WERE RESCUED FROM A LIFE RAFT AFTERWARDS. BUT EVERYONE ELSE ON BOARD WAS LOST, AND THE CRUISER ITSELF WAS NEVER RECOVERED.
THEN MAYBE SEKIGUCHI CAUSED THE ACCIDENT AND SOME-ONE HAD A GRUDGE AGAINST HIM FOR IT.
I DON'T KNOW.
I'VE NEVER BEEN FOND OF THE SEA, SO I NEVER ATTENDED THOSE CRUISES.
BUT THE TWO SURVIVORS KNOW WHAT HAPPENED, RIGHT?
NOT AT ALL. I WAS TAKING A NAP INSIDE THE SHIP WHEN SEKI-GUCHI SUDDENLY TOLD US TO GET INTO A LIFE RAFT.
IN THE CHAOS, WE NEVER FOUND OUT WHAT HAPPENED.
SAY...DID THE PEOPLE WHO DIED IN THAT ACCIDENT LEAVE ANY *FAMILY* HERE?
YES INDEED.
IN THAT CASE, THIS MAY HAVE SOMETHING TO DO WITH THE FIVE STRANGE INCIDENTS IN THIS HOUSE...
THE WHAT?
THAT'S WHAT I WAS HIRED TO INVESTIGATE. KUNITOMO HAD A NIGHTMARE, THE CAR ALMOST CRASHED BECAUSE THE BRAKES MALFUNCTIONED, A CUPBOARD FELL IN THE MIDDLE OF THE NIGHT, AND STRANGE SOUNDS WERE HEARD INSIDE THE HOUSE.
HMM...
AND LAST BUT NOT LEAST...
FWP

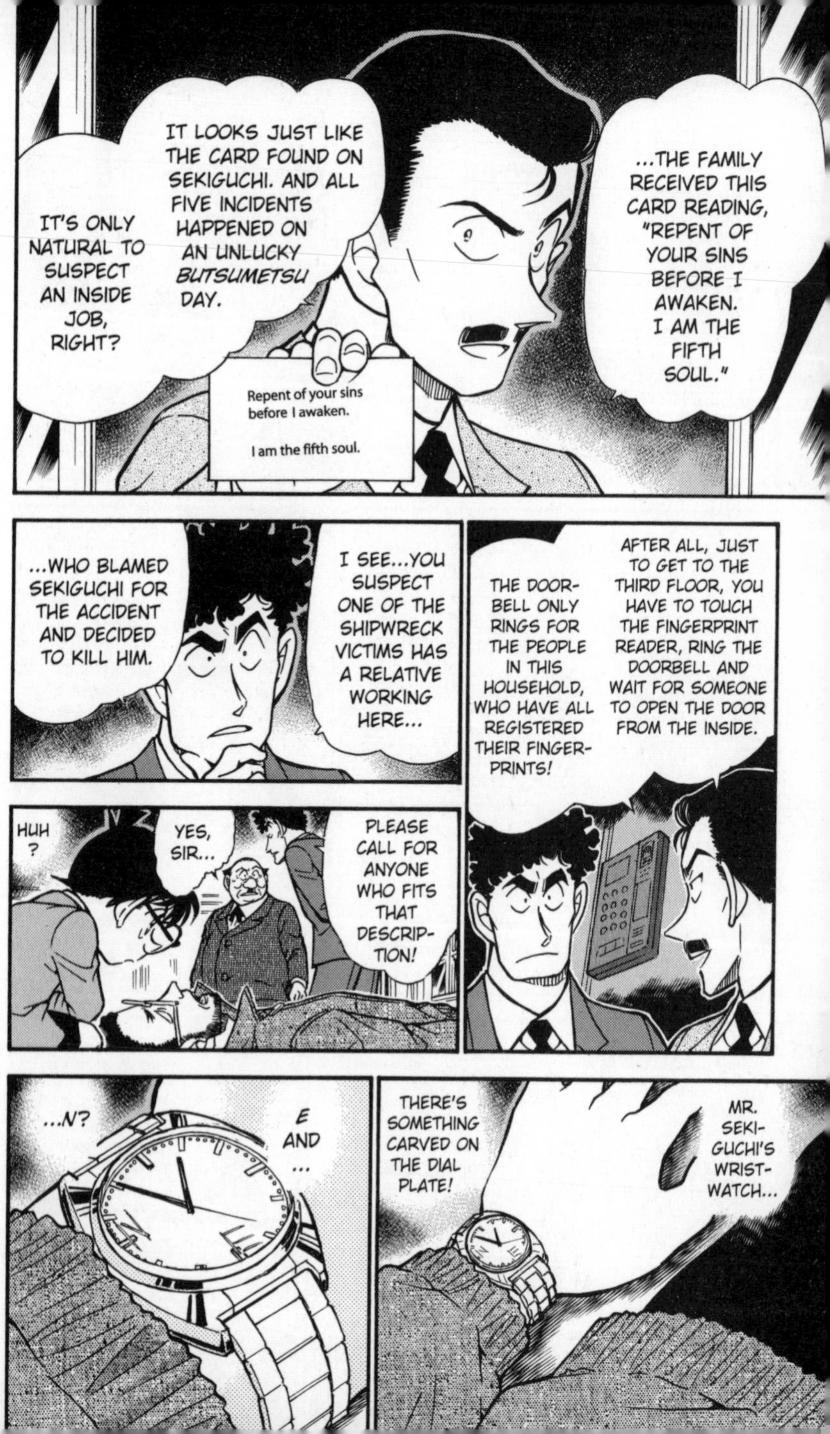
...THE FAMILY RECEIVED THIS CARD READING, "REPENT OF YOUR SINS BEFORE I AWAKEN. I AM THE FIFTH SOUL."
IT LOOKS JUST LIKE THE CARD FOUND ON SEKIGUCHI. AND ALL FIVE INCIDENTS HAPPENED ON AN UNLUCKY *BUTSUMETSU* DAY.
IT'S ONLY NATURAL TO SUSPECT AN INSIDE JOB, RIGHT?
Repent of your sins before I awaken.
I am the fifth soul.
AFTER ALL, JUST TO GET TO THE THIRD FLOOR, YOU HAVE TO TOUCH THE FINGERPRINT READER, RING THE DOORBELL AND WAIT FOR SOMEONE TO OPEN THE DOOR FROM THE INSIDE.
THE DOOR-BELL ONLY RINGS FOR THE PEOPLE IN THIS HOUSEHOLD, WHO HAVE ALL REGISTERED THEIR FINGER-PRINTS!
I SEE...YOU SUSPECT ONE OF THE SHIPWRECK VICTIMS HAS A RELATIVE WORKING HERE...
...WHO BLAMED SEKIGUCHI FOR THE ACCIDENT AND DECIDED TO KILL HIM.
PLEASE CALL FOR ANYONE WHO FITS THAT DESCRIP-TION!
YES, SIR...
HUH ?
MR. SEKI-GUCHI'S WRIST-WATCH...
THERE'S SOMETHING CARVED ON THE DIAL PLATE!
E AND ...
...N?

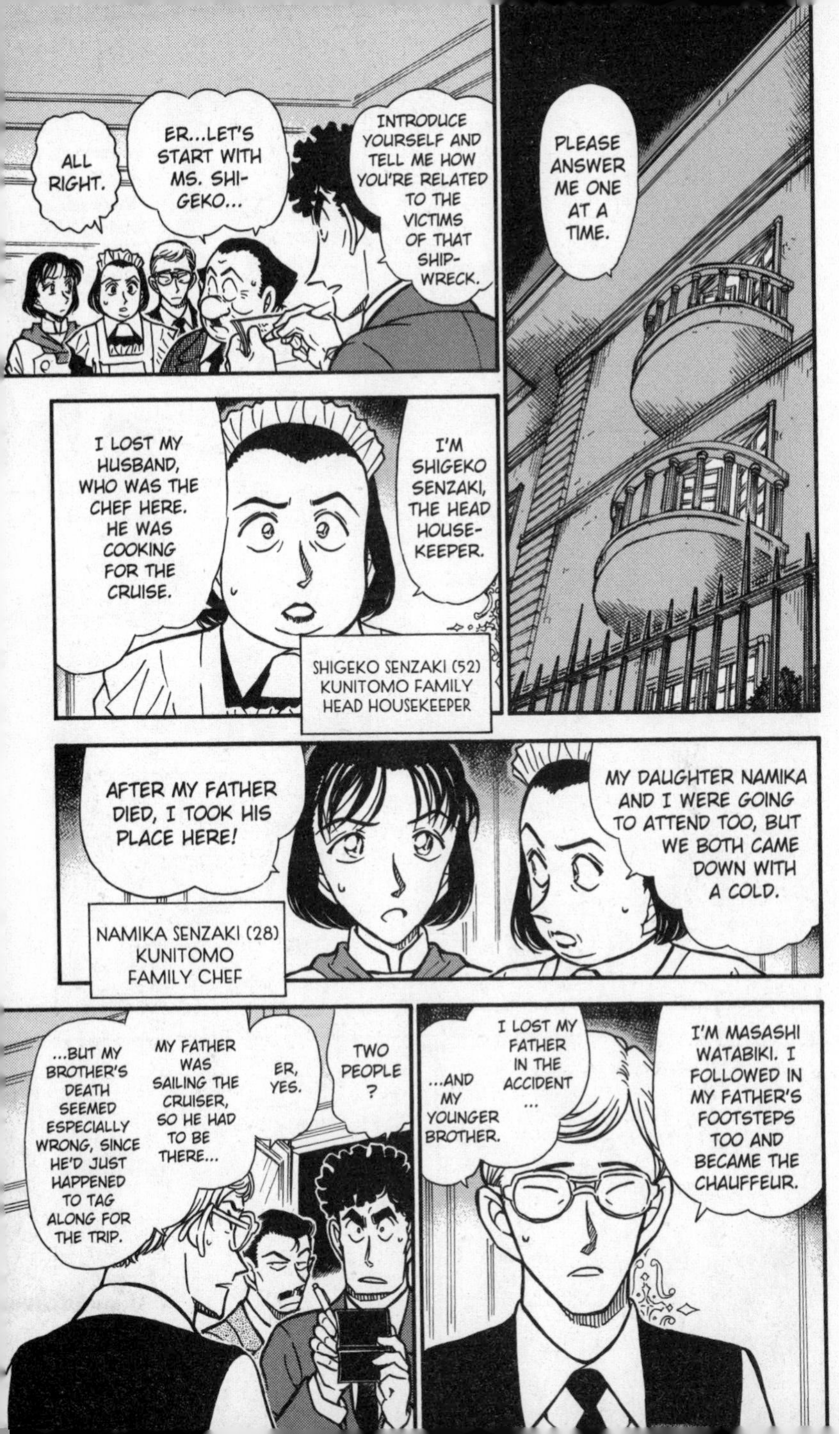
PLEASE ANSWER ME ONE AT A TIME.
INTRODUCE YOURSELF AND TELL ME HOW YOU'RE RELATED TO THE VICTIMS OF THAT SHIP-WRECK.
ER...LET'S START WITH MS. SHI-GEKO...
ALL RIGHT.
I'M SHIGEKO SENZAKI, THE HEAD HOUSE-KEEPER.
I LOST MY HUSBAND, WHO WAS THE CHEF HERE. HE WAS COOKING FOR THE CRUISE.
SHIGEKO SENZAKI (52) KUNITOMO FAMILY HEAD HOUSEKEEPER
MY DAUGHTER NAMIKA AND I WERE GOING TO ATTEND TOO, BUT WE BOTH CAME DOWN WITH A COLD.
AFTER MY FATHER DIED, I TOOK HIS PLACE HERE!
NAMIKA SENZAKI (28) KUNITOMO FAMILY CHEF
I'M MASASHI WATABIKI. I FOLLOWED IN MY FATHER'S FOOTSTEPS TOO AND BECAME THE CHAUFFEUR.
I LOST MY FATHER IN THE ACCIDENT...
...AND MY YOUNGER BROTHER.
TWO PEOPLE?
ER, YES.
MY FATHER WAS SAILING THE CRUISER, SO HE HAD TO BE THERE...
...BUT MY BROTHER'S DEATH SEEMED ESPECIALLY WRONG, SINCE HE'D JUST HAPPENED TO TAG ALONG FOR THE TRIP.

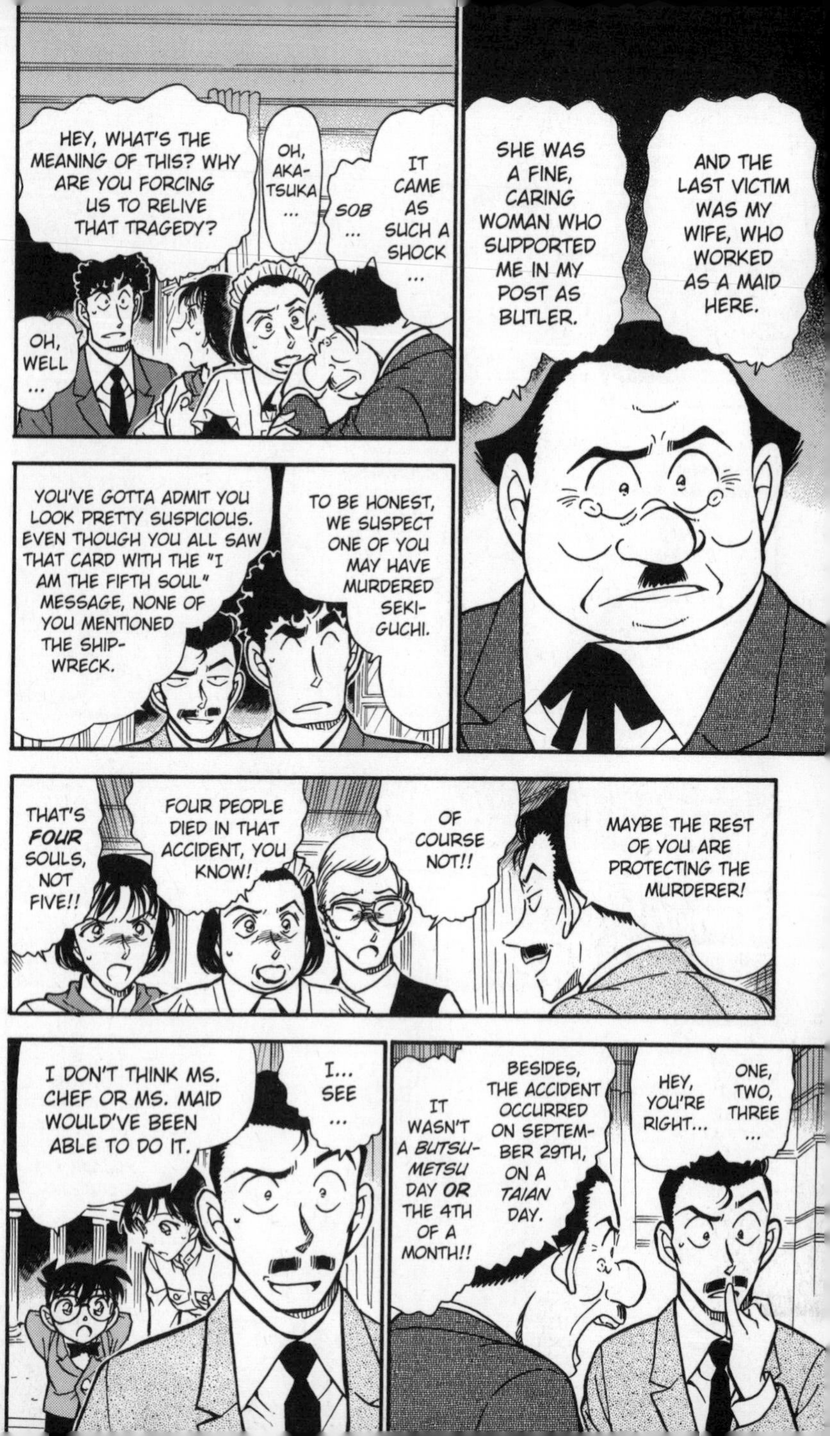
AND THE LAST VICTIM WAS MY WIFE, WHO WORKED AS A MAID HERE.
SHE WAS A FINE, CARING WOMAN WHO SUPPORTED ME IN MY POST AS BUTLER.
IT CAME AS SUCH A SHOCK...
SOB...
OH, AKATSUKA...
HEY, WHAT'S THE MEANING OF THIS? WHY ARE YOU FORCING US TO RELIVE THAT TRAGEDY?
OH, WELL...
TO BE HONEST, WE SUSPECT ONE OF YOU MAY HAVE MURDERED SEKI-GUCHI.
YOU'VE GOTTA ADMIT YOU LOOK PRETTY SUSPICIOUS. EVEN THOUGH YOU ALL SAW THAT CARD WITH THE "I AM THE FIFTH SOUL" MESSAGE, NONE OF YOU MENTIONED THE SHIP-WRECK.
MAYBE THE REST OF YOU ARE PROTECTING THE MURDERER!
OF COURSE NOT!!
FOUR PEOPLE DIED IN THAT ACCIDENT, YOU KNOW!
THAT'S *FOUR* SOULS, NOT FIVE!!
ONE, TWO, THREE...
HEY, YOU'RE RIGHT...
BESIDES, THE ACCIDENT OCCURRED ON SEPTEM-BER 29TH, ON A *TAIAN* DAY.
IT WASN'T A *BUTSU-METSU* DAY **OR** THE 4TH OF A MONTH!!
I... SEE...
I DON'T THINK MS. CHEF OR MS. MAID WOULD'VE BEEN ABLE TO DO IT.

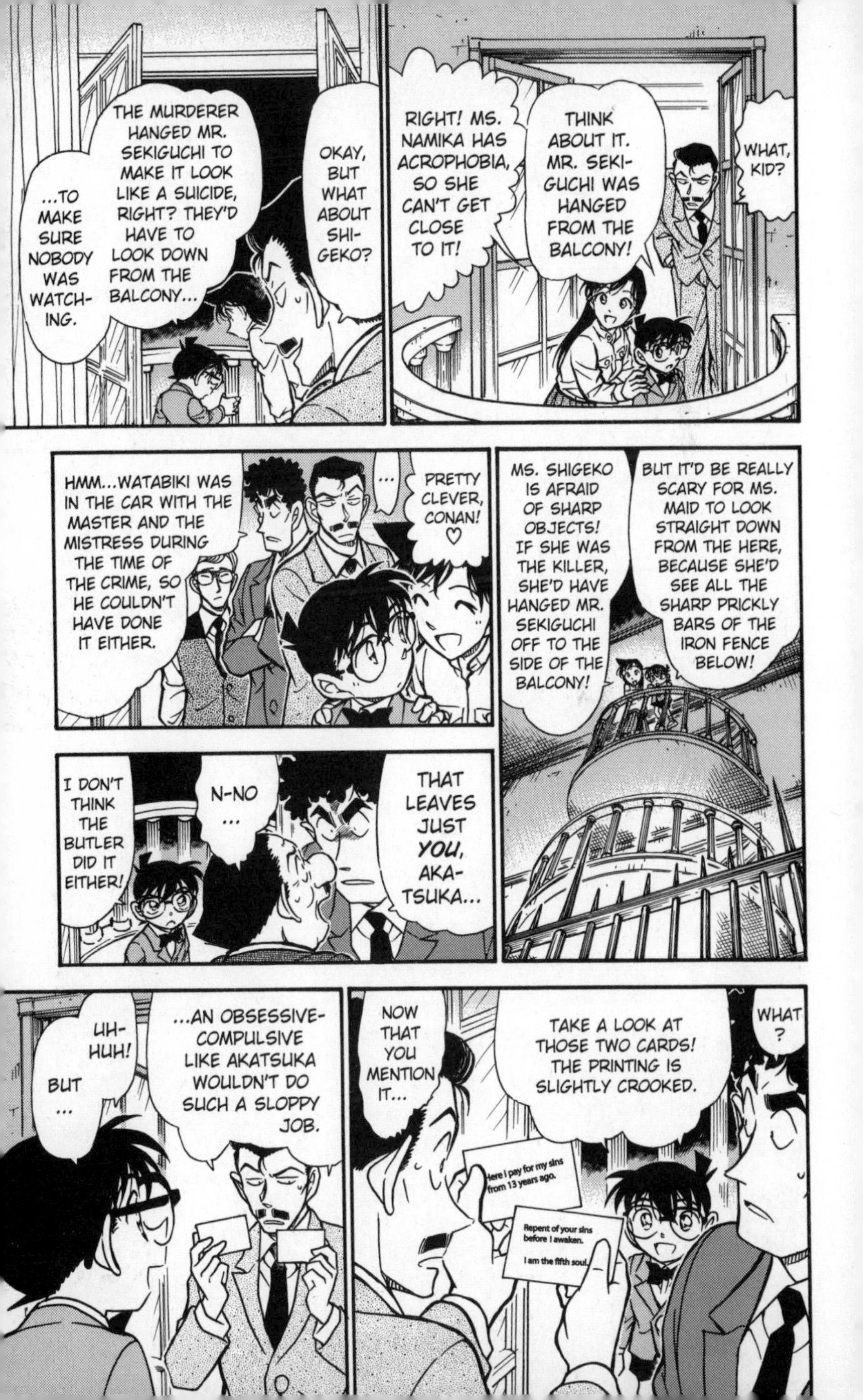
WHAT, KID?
THINK ABOUT IT. MR. SEKIGUCHI WAS HANGED FROM THE BALCONY!
RIGHT! MS. NAMIKA HAS ACROPHOBIA, SO SHE CAN'T GET CLOSE TO IT!
OKAY, BUT WHAT ABOUT SHIGEKO?
THE MURDERER HANGED MR. SEKIGUCHI TO MAKE IT LOOK LIKE A SUICIDE, RIGHT? THEY'D HAVE TO LOOK DOWN FROM THE BALCONY...
...TO MAKE SURE NOBODY WAS WATCHING.
BUT IT'D BE REALLY SCARY FOR MS. MAID TO LOOK STRAIGHT DOWN FROM THE HERE, BECAUSE SHE'D SEE ALL THE SHARP PRICKLY BARS OF THE IRON FENCE BELOW!
MS. SHIGEKO IS AFRAID OF SHARP OBJECTS! IF SHE WAS THE KILLER, SHE'D HAVE HANGED MR. SEKIGUCHI OFF TO THE SIDE OF THE BALCONY!
PRETTY CLEVER, CONAN! ♡
...
HMM...WATABIKI WAS IN THE CAR WITH THE MASTER AND THE MISTRESS DURING THE TIME OF THE CRIME, SO HE COULDN'T HAVE DONE IT EITHER.
THAT LEAVES JUST *YOU*, AKATSUKA...
N-NO ...
I DON'T THINK THE BUTLER DID IT EITHER!
WHAT ?
TAKE A LOOK AT THOSE TWO CARDS! THE PRINTING IS SLIGHTLY CROOKED.
NOW THAT YOU MENTION IT...
Here I pay for my sins from 13 years ago.
Repent of your sins before I awaken.
I am the fifth soul.
...AN OBSESSIVE-COMPULSIVE LIKE AKATSUKA WOULDN'T DO SUCH A SLOPPY JOB.
UH-HUH!
BUT ...

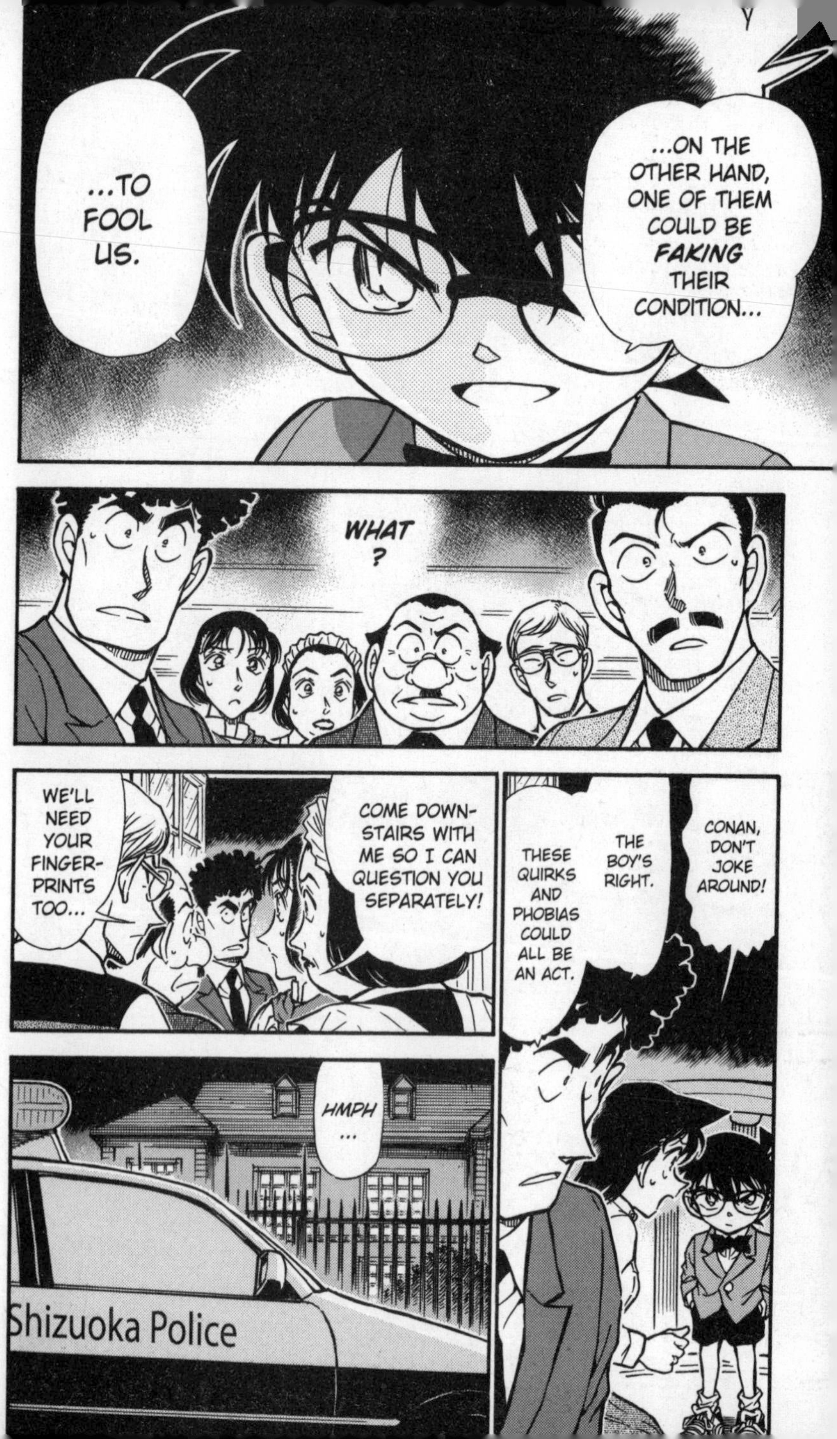
...ON THE OTHER HAND, ONE OF THEM COULD BE FAKING THEIR CONDITION...
...TO FOOL US.
WHAT?
CONAN, DON'T JOKE AROUND!
THE BOY'S RIGHT.
THESE QUIRKS AND PHOBIAS COULD ALL BE AN ACT.
COME DOWN-STAIRS WITH ME SO I CAN QUESTION YOU SEPARATELY!
WE'LL NEED YOUR FINGER-PRINTS TOO...
HMPH ...
Shizuoka Police

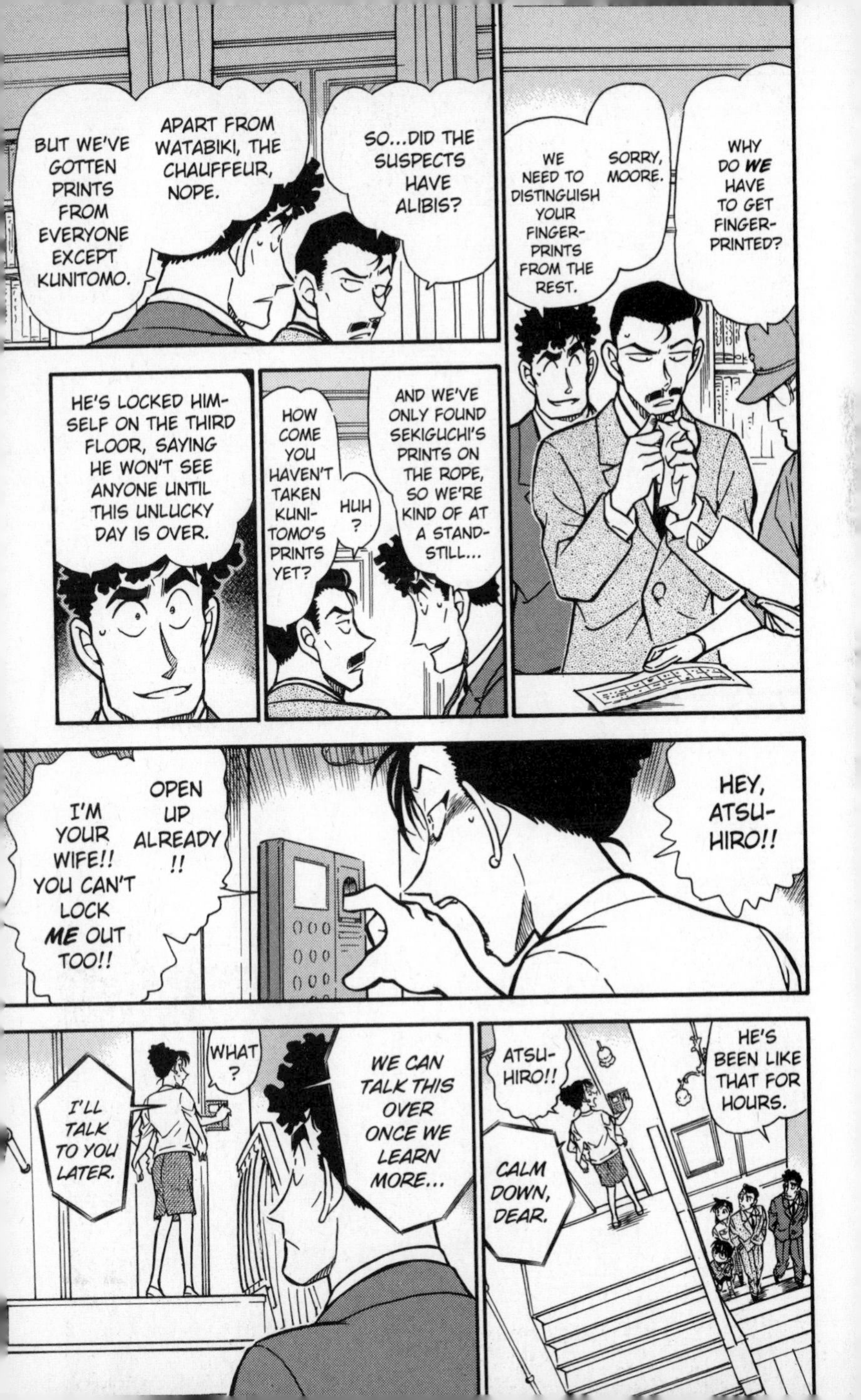
WHY DO WE HAVE TO GET FINGER-PRINTED?
SORRY, MOORE.
WE NEED TO DISTINGUISH YOUR FINGER-PRINTS FROM THE REST.
SO...DID THE SUSPECTS HAVE ALIBIS?
APART FROM WATABIKI, THE CHAUFFEUR, NOPE.
BUT WE'VE GOTTEN PRINTS FROM EVERYONE EXCEPT KUNITOMO.
AND WE'VE ONLY FOUND SEKIGUCHI'S PRINTS ON THE ROPE, SO WE'RE KIND OF AT A STAND-STILL...
HUH?
HOW COME YOU HAVEN'T TAKEN KUNI-TOMO'S PRINTS YET?
HE'S LOCKED HIM-SELF ON THE THIRD FLOOR, SAYING HE WON'T SEE ANYONE UNTIL THIS UNLUCKY DAY IS OVER.
HEY, ATSU-HIRO!!
OPEN UP ALREADY!!
I'M YOUR WIFE!! YOU CAN'T LOCK ME OUT TOO!!
HE'S BEEN LIKE THAT FOR HOURS.
ATSU-HIRO!!
CALM DOWN, DEAR.
WE CAN TALK THIS OVER ONCE WE LEARN MORE...
WHAT?
I'LL TALK TO YOU LATER.

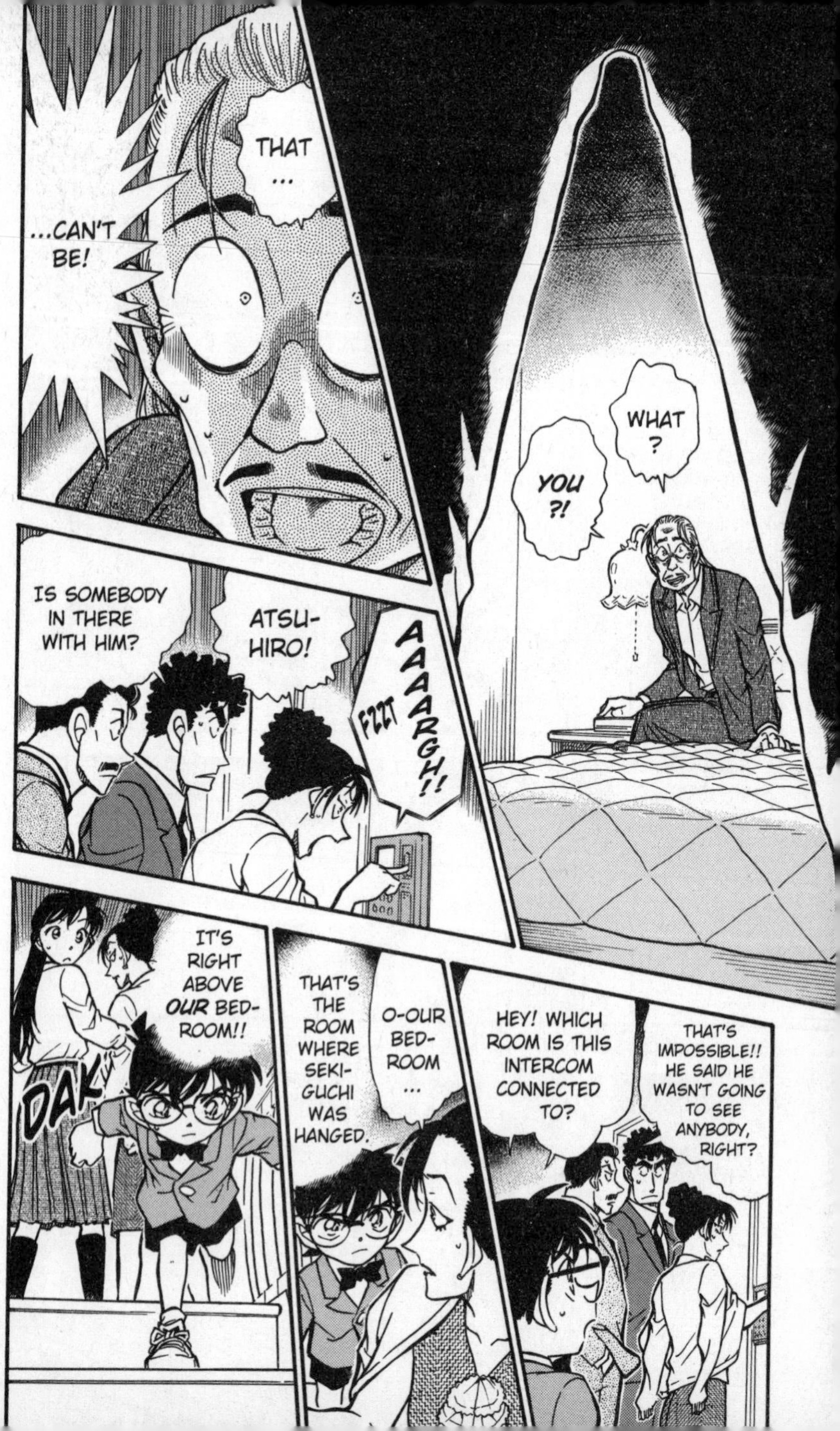
WHAT?
YOU?!
THAT...
...CAN'T BE!
AAAARGH!!
FZZT
ATSU-HIRO!
IS SOMEBODY IN THERE WITH HIM?
THAT'S IMPOSSIBLE!! HE SAID HE WASN'T GOING TO SEE ANYBODY, RIGHT?
HEY! WHICH ROOM IS THIS INTERCOM CONNECTED TO?
O-OUR BED-ROOM...
THAT'S THE ROOM WHERE SEKI-GUCHI WAS HANGED.
IT'S RIGHT ABOVE *OUR* BED-ROOM!!
DAK

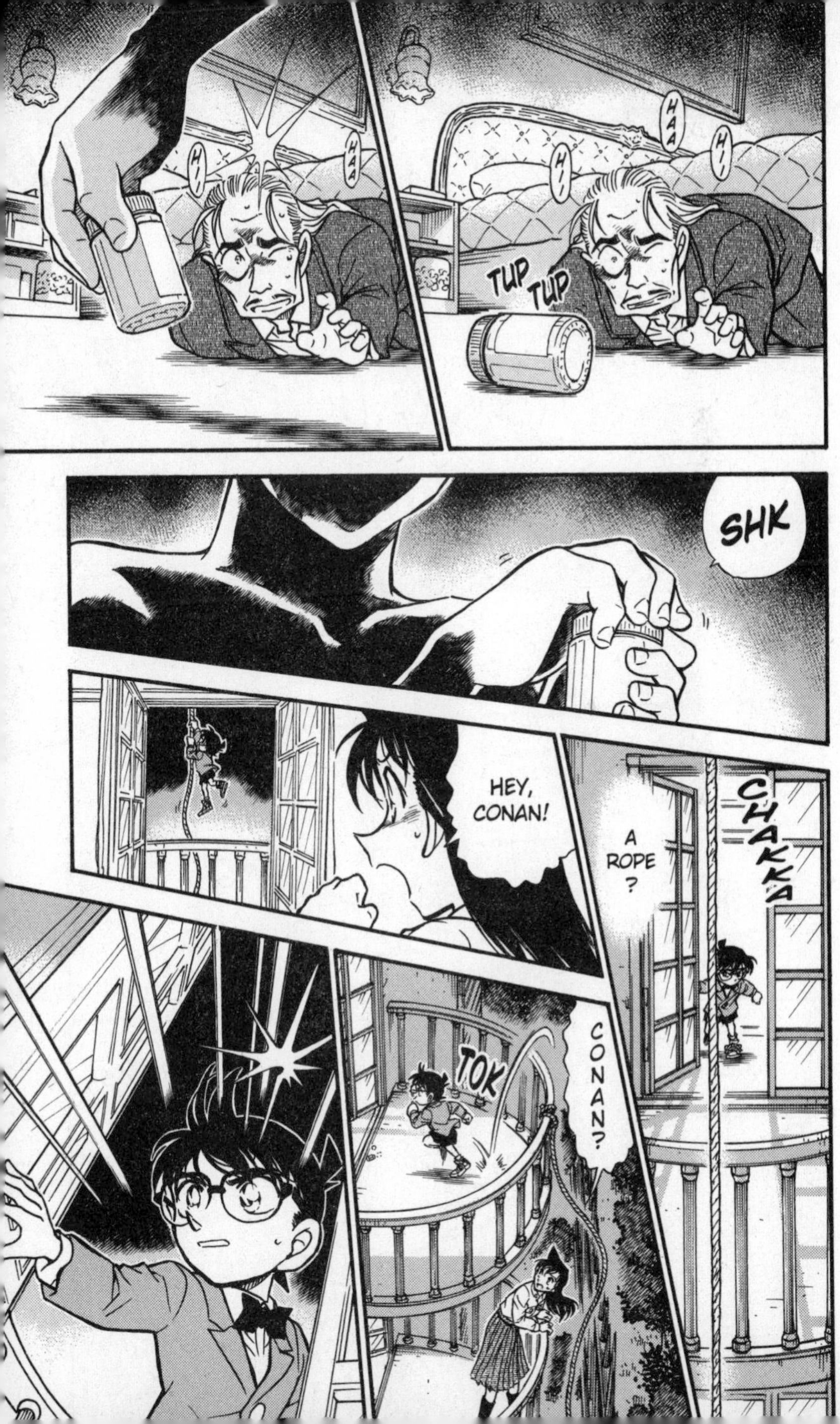
HAA
HI
HI
TUP TUP
HI
HAA
SHK
CHAKKA
A ROPE?
HEY, CONAN!
CONAN?
TOK

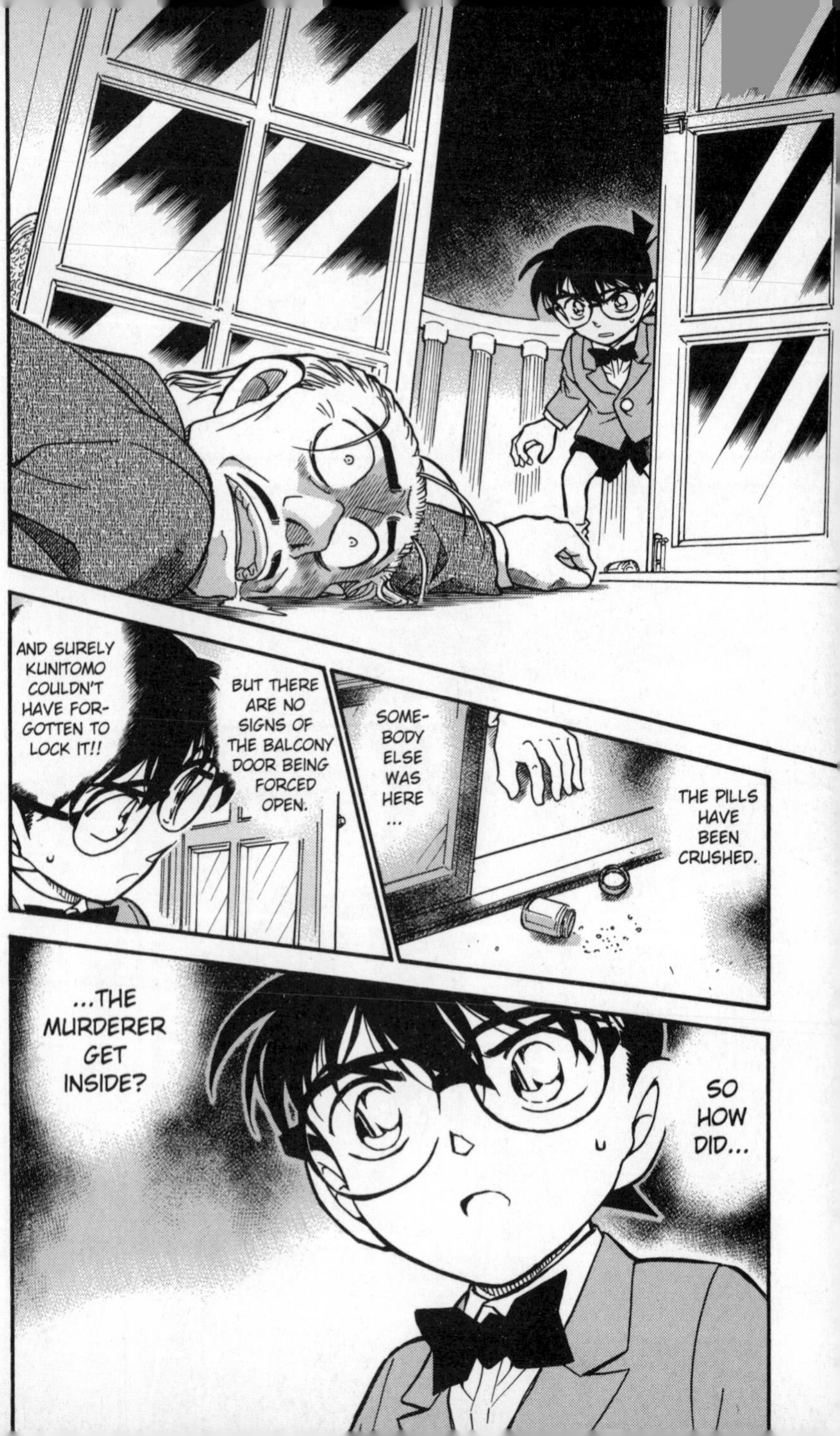
THE PILLS HAVE BEEN CRUSHED.
SOME-BODY ELSE WAS HERE ...
BUT THERE ARE NO SIGNS OF THE BALCONY DOOR BEING FORCED OPEN.
AND SURELY KUNITOMO COULDN'T HAVE FOR-GOTTEN TO LOCK IT!!
SO HOW DID...
...THE MURDERER GET INSIDE?

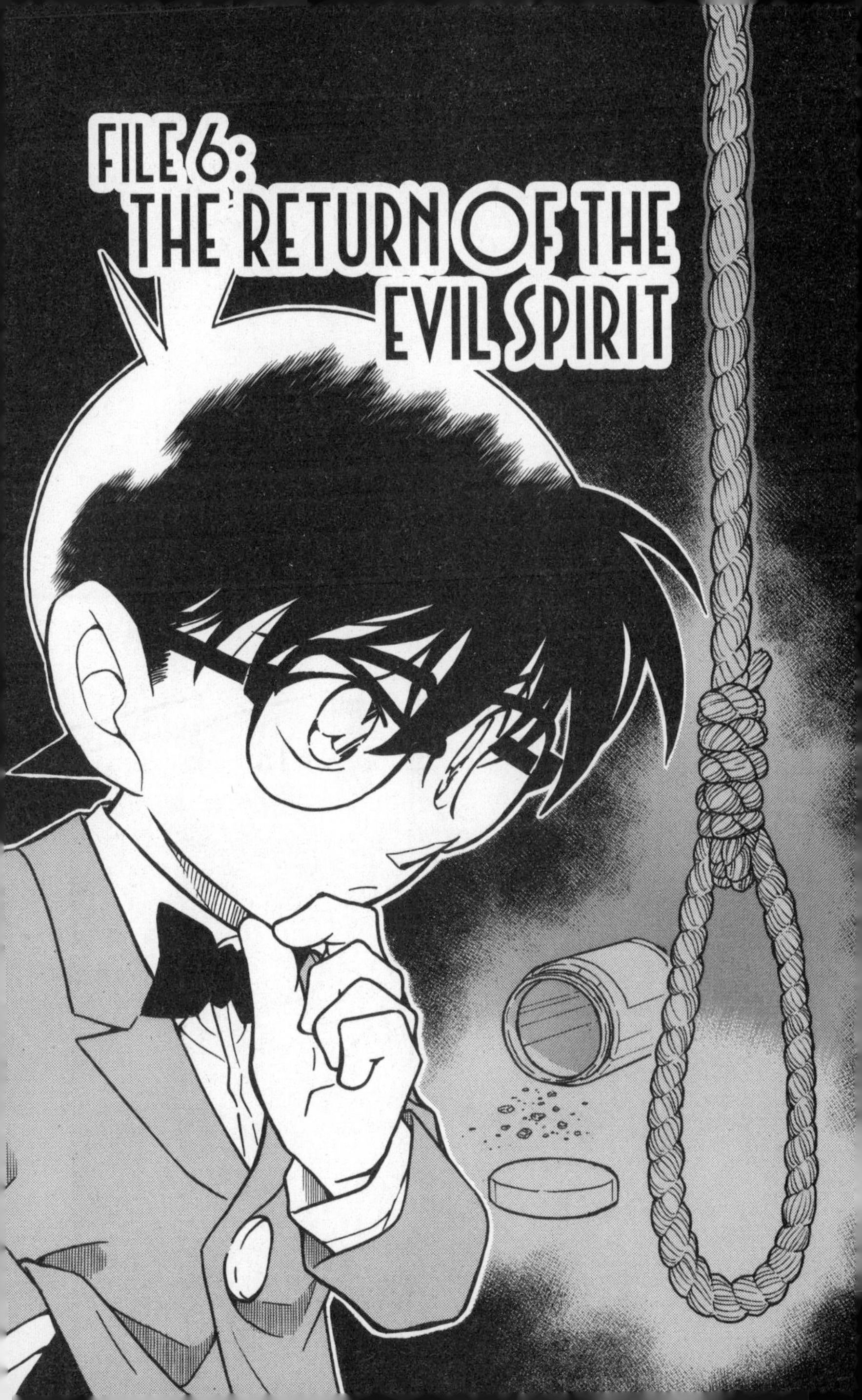
FILE 6:
THE RETURN OF THE EVIL SPIRIT

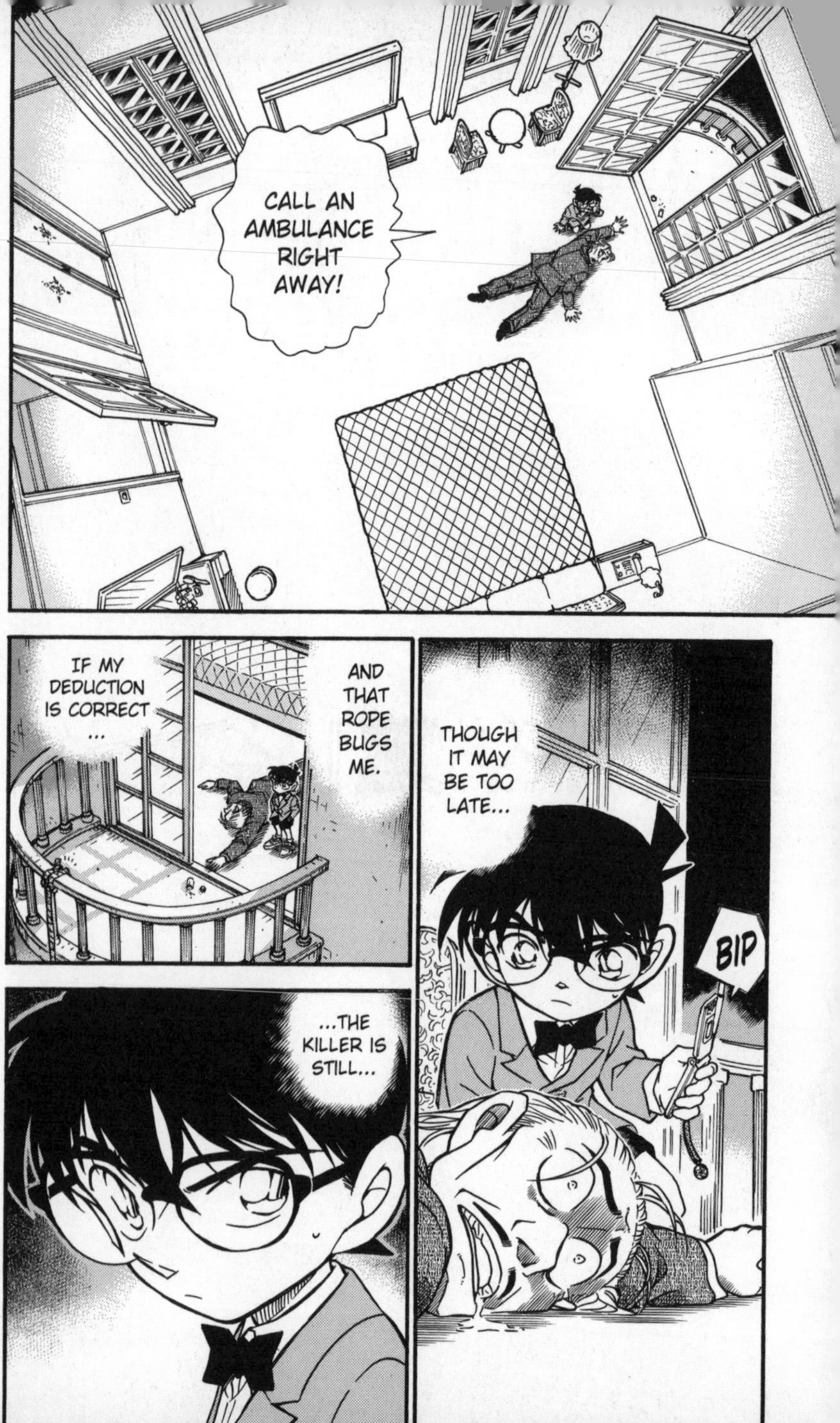
CALL AN AMBULANCE RIGHT AWAY!
THOUGH IT MAY BE TOO LATE...
BIP
AND THAT ROPE BUGS ME.
IF MY DEDUCTION IS CORRECT...
...THE KILLER IS STILL...

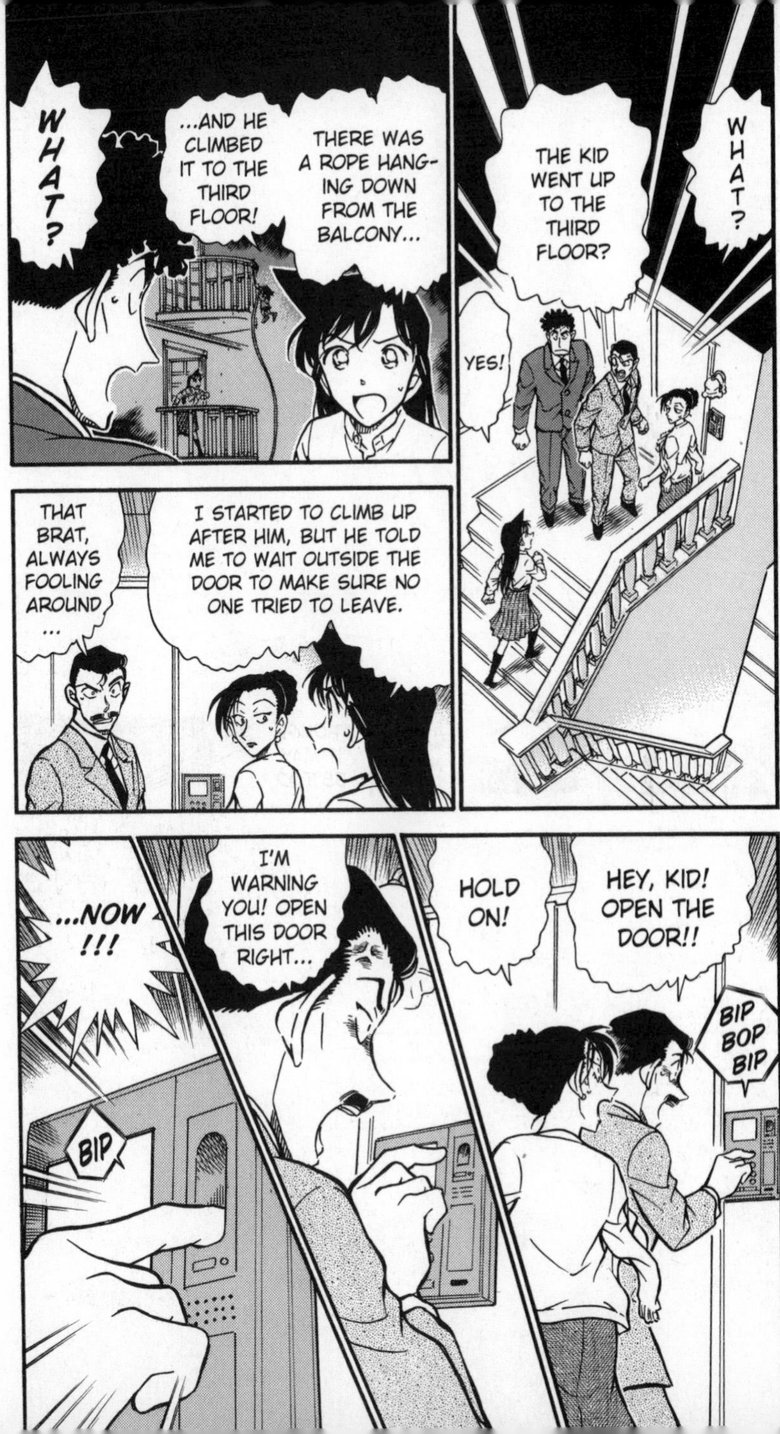
WHAT?
THE KID WENT UP TO THE THIRD FLOOR?
YES!
THERE WAS A ROPE HANG-ING DOWN FROM THE BALCONY...
...AND HE CLIMBED IT TO THE THIRD FLOOR!
WHAT?
I STARTED TO CLIMB UP AFTER HIM, BUT HE TOLD ME TO WAIT OUTSIDE THE DOOR TO MAKE SURE NO ONE TRIED TO LEAVE.
THAT BRAT, ALWAYS FOOLING AROUND...
HEY, KID! OPEN THE DOOR!!
HOLD ON!
BIP BOP BIP
I'M WARNING YOU! OPEN THIS DOOR RIGHT...
...NOW!!!
BIP

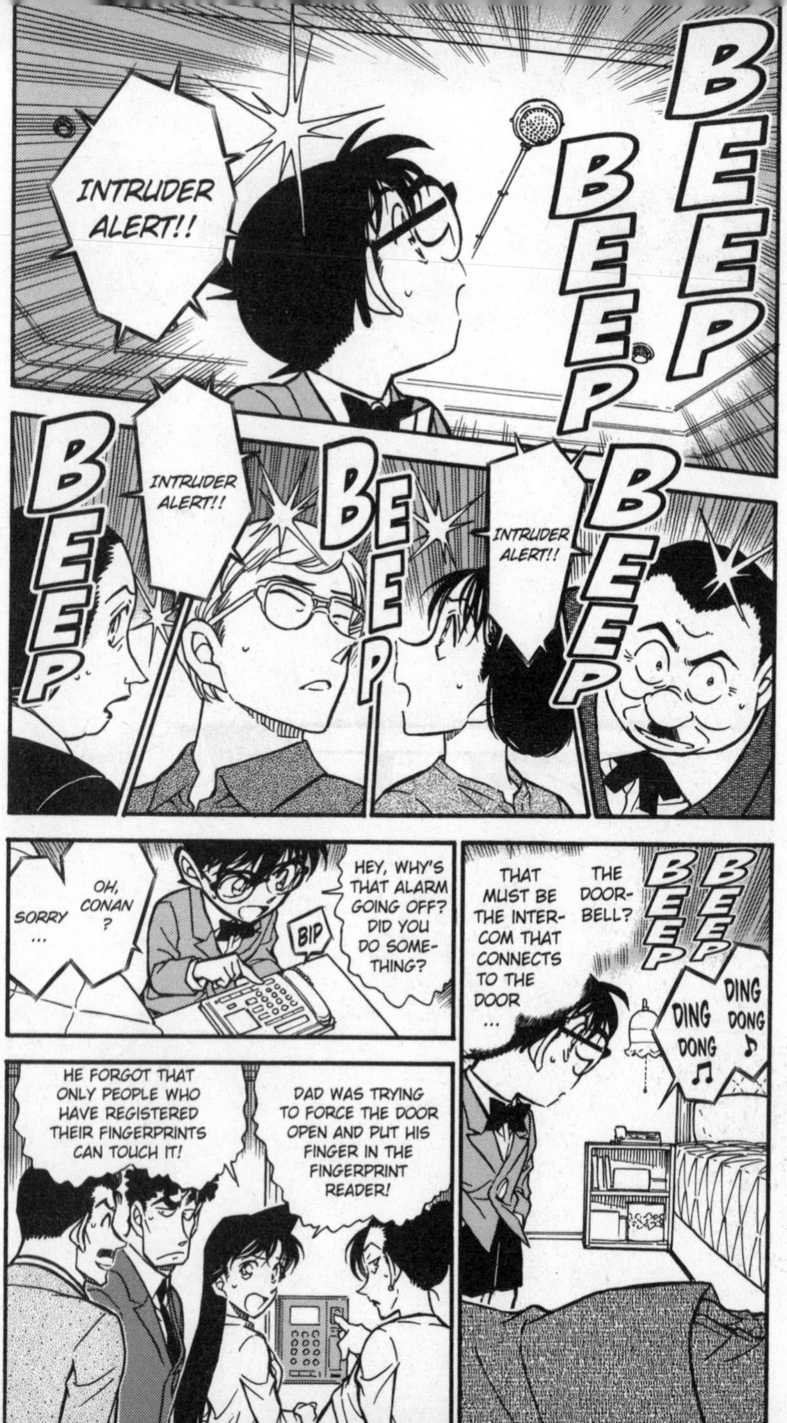
BEEP
BEEP
INTRUDER ALERT!!
BEEP
INTRUDER ALERT!!
BEEP
INTRUDER ALERT!!
BEEP
BEEP
BEEP
THE DOOR-BELL?
THAT MUST BE THE INTER-COM THAT CONNECTS TO THE DOOR ...
DING DONG ♪
DING DONG ♫
HEY, WHY'S THAT ALARM GOING OFF? DID YOU DO SOME-THING?
BIP
OH, CONAN ?
SORRY ...
DAD WAS TRYING TO FORCE THE DOOR OPEN AND PUT HIS FINGER IN THE FINGERPRINT READER!
HE FORGOT THAT ONLY PEOPLE WHO HAVE REGISTERED THEIR FINGERPRINTS CAN TOUCH IT!

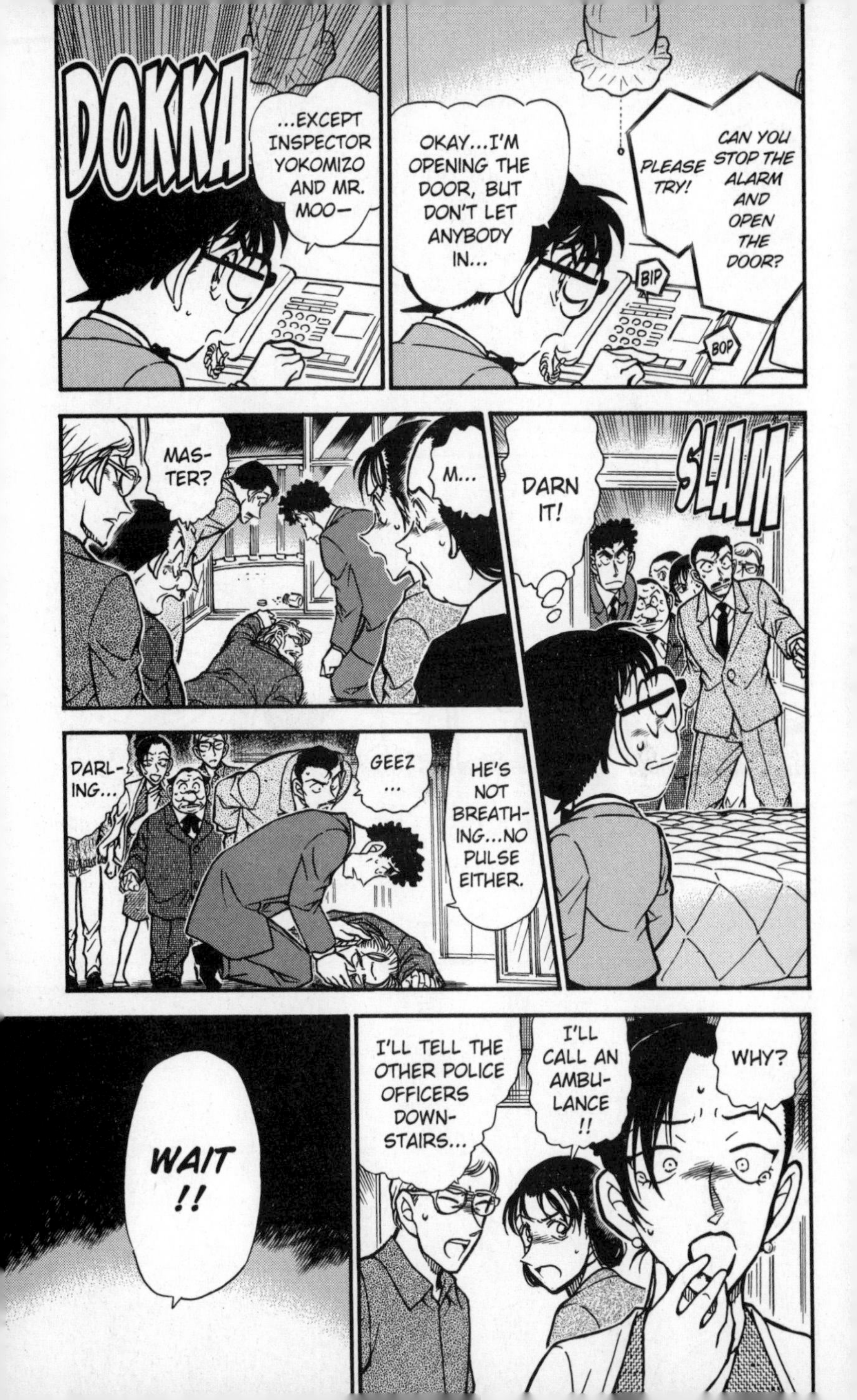
CAN YOU STOP THE ALARM AND OPEN THE DOOR?
PLEASE TRY!
BIP
BOP
OKAY...I'M OPENING THE DOOR, BUT DON'T LET ANYBODY IN...
...EXCEPT INSPECTOR YOKOMIZO AND MR. MOO—
DOKKA
SLAM
DARN IT!
M...
MAS-TER?
HE'S NOT BREATH-ING...NO PULSE EITHER.
GEEZ ...
DARL-ING...
WHY?
I'LL CALL AN AMBU-LANCE !!
I'LL TELL THE OTHER POLICE OFFICERS DOWN-STAIRS...
WAIT !!

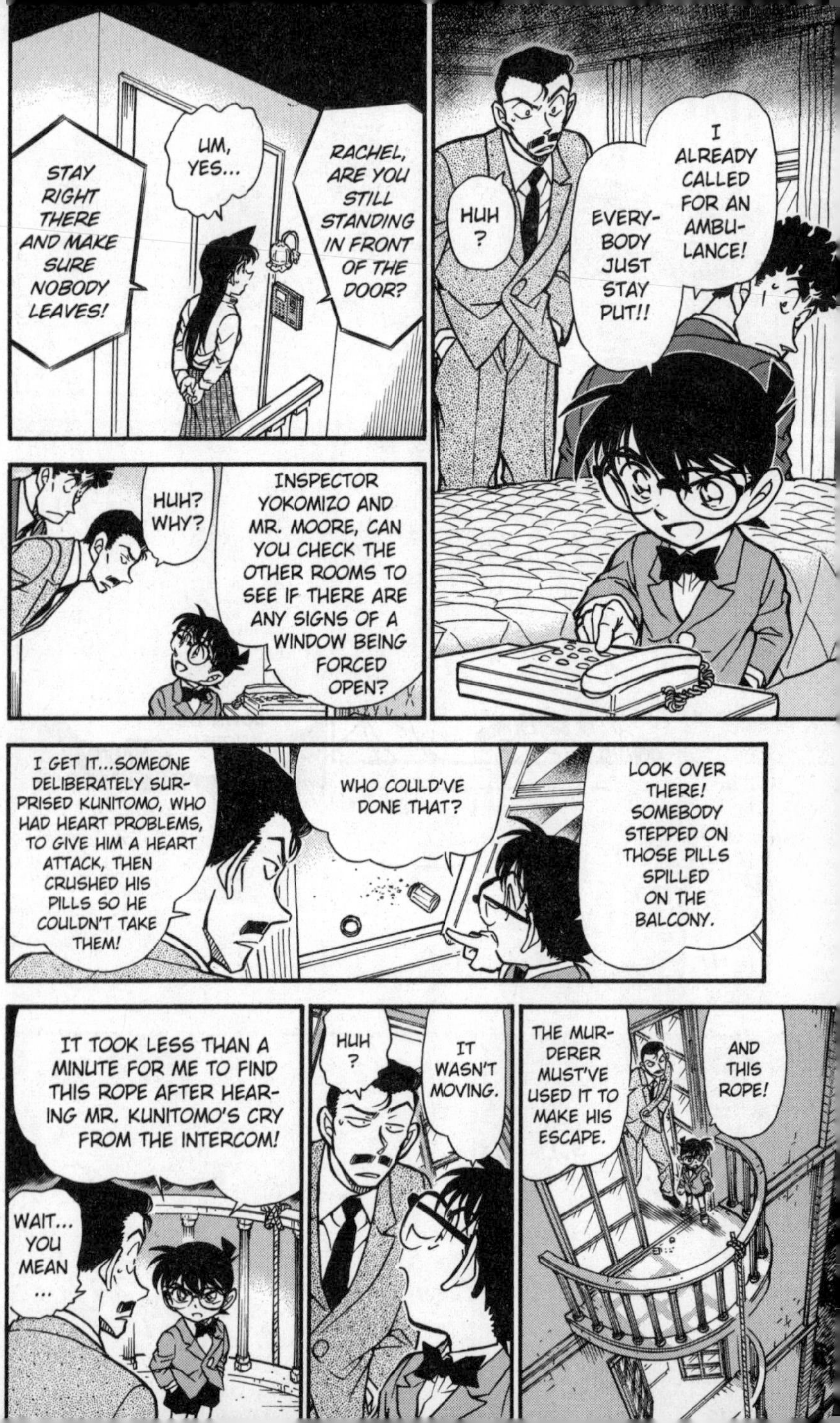

I ALREADY CALLED FOR AN AMBULANCE!
EVERYBODY JUST STAY PUT!!
HUH?
RACHEL, ARE YOU STILL STANDING IN FRONT OF THE DOOR?
UM, YES...
STAY RIGHT THERE AND MAKE SURE NOBODY LEAVES!
INSPECTOR YOKOMIZO AND MR. MOORE, CAN YOU CHECK THE OTHER ROOMS TO SEE IF THERE ARE ANY SIGNS OF A WINDOW BEING FORCED OPEN?
HUH? WHY?
LOOK OVER THERE! SOMEBODY STEPPED ON THOSE PILLS SPILLED ON THE BALCONY.
WHO COULD'VE DONE THAT?
I GET IT...SOMEONE DELIBERATELY SURPRISED KUNITOMO, WHO HAD HEART PROBLEMS, TO GIVE HIM A HEART ATTACK, THEN CRUSHED HIS PILLS SO HE COULDN'T TAKE THEM!
AND THIS ROPE!
THE MURDERER MUST'VE USED IT TO MAKE HIS ESCAPE.
IT WASN'T MOVING.
HUH?
IT TOOK LESS THAN A MINUTE FOR ME TO FIND THIS ROPE AFTER HEARING MR. KUNITOMO'S CRY FROM THE INTERCOM!
WAIT... YOU MEAN...

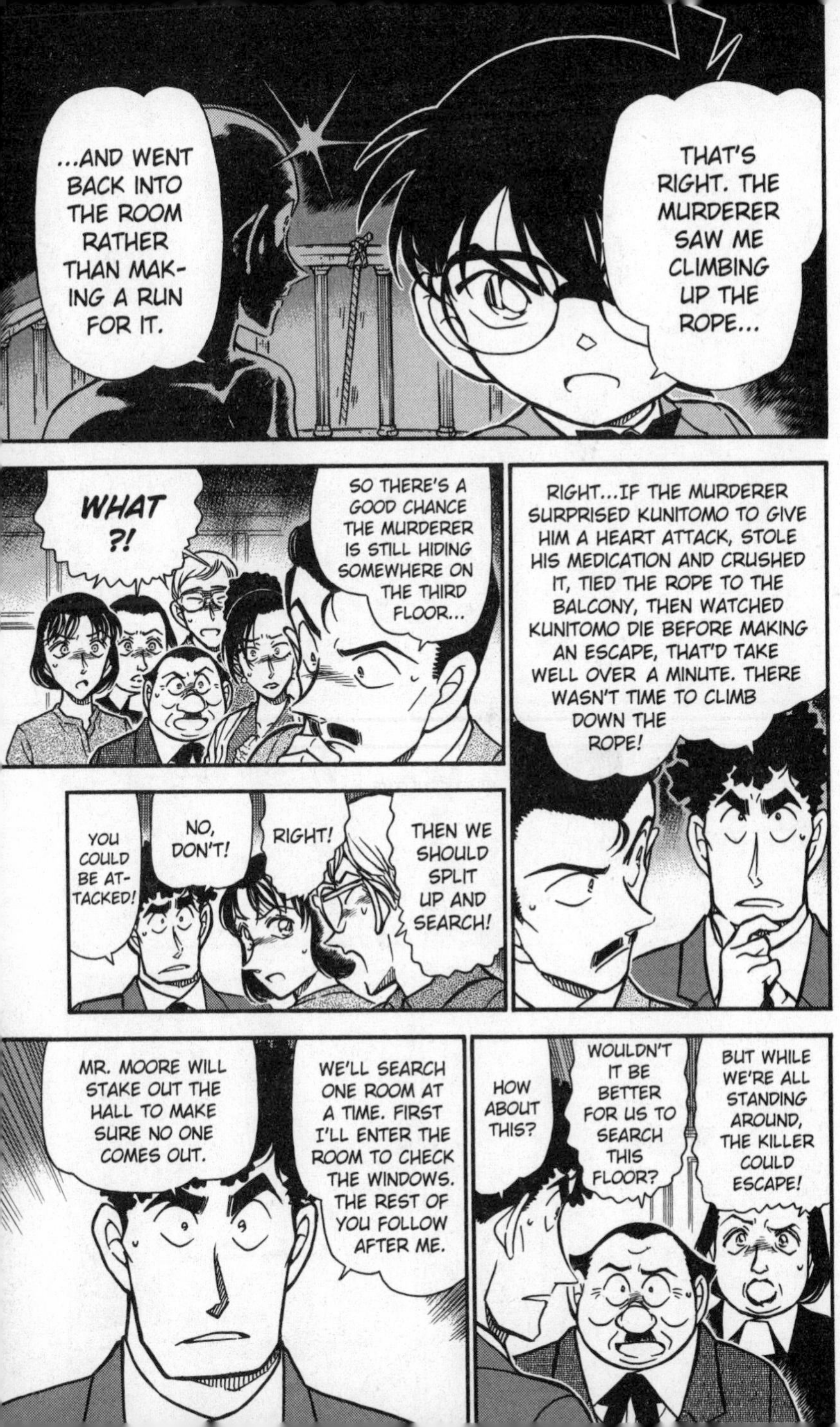
THAT'S RIGHT. THE MURDERER SAW ME CLIMBING UP THE ROPE...
...AND WENT BACK INTO THE ROOM RATHER THAN MAK-ING A RUN FOR IT.
RIGHT...IF THE MURDERER SURPRISED KUNITOMO TO GIVE HIM A HEART ATTACK, STOLE HIS MEDICATION AND CRUSHED IT, TIED THE ROPE TO THE BALCONY, THEN WATCHED KUNITOMO DIE BEFORE MAKING AN ESCAPE, THAT'D TAKE WELL OVER A MINUTE. THERE WASN'T TIME TO CLIMB DOWN THE ROPE!
SO THERE'S A GOOD CHANCE THE MURDERER IS STILL HIDING SOMEWHERE ON THE THIRD FLOOR...
WHAT ?!
THEN WE SHOULD SPLIT UP AND SEARCH!
RIGHT!
NO, DON'T!
YOU COULD BE AT-TACKED!
BUT WHILE WE'RE ALL STANDING AROUND, THE KILLER COULD ESCAPE!
WOULDN'T IT BE BETTER FOR US TO SEARCH THIS FLOOR?
HOW ABOUT THIS?
WE'LL SEARCH ONE ROOM AT A TIME. FIRST I'LL ENTER THE ROOM TO CHECK THE WINDOWS. THE REST OF YOU FOLLOW AFTER ME.
MR. MOORE WILL STAKE OUT THE HALL TO MAKE SURE NO ONE COMES OUT.

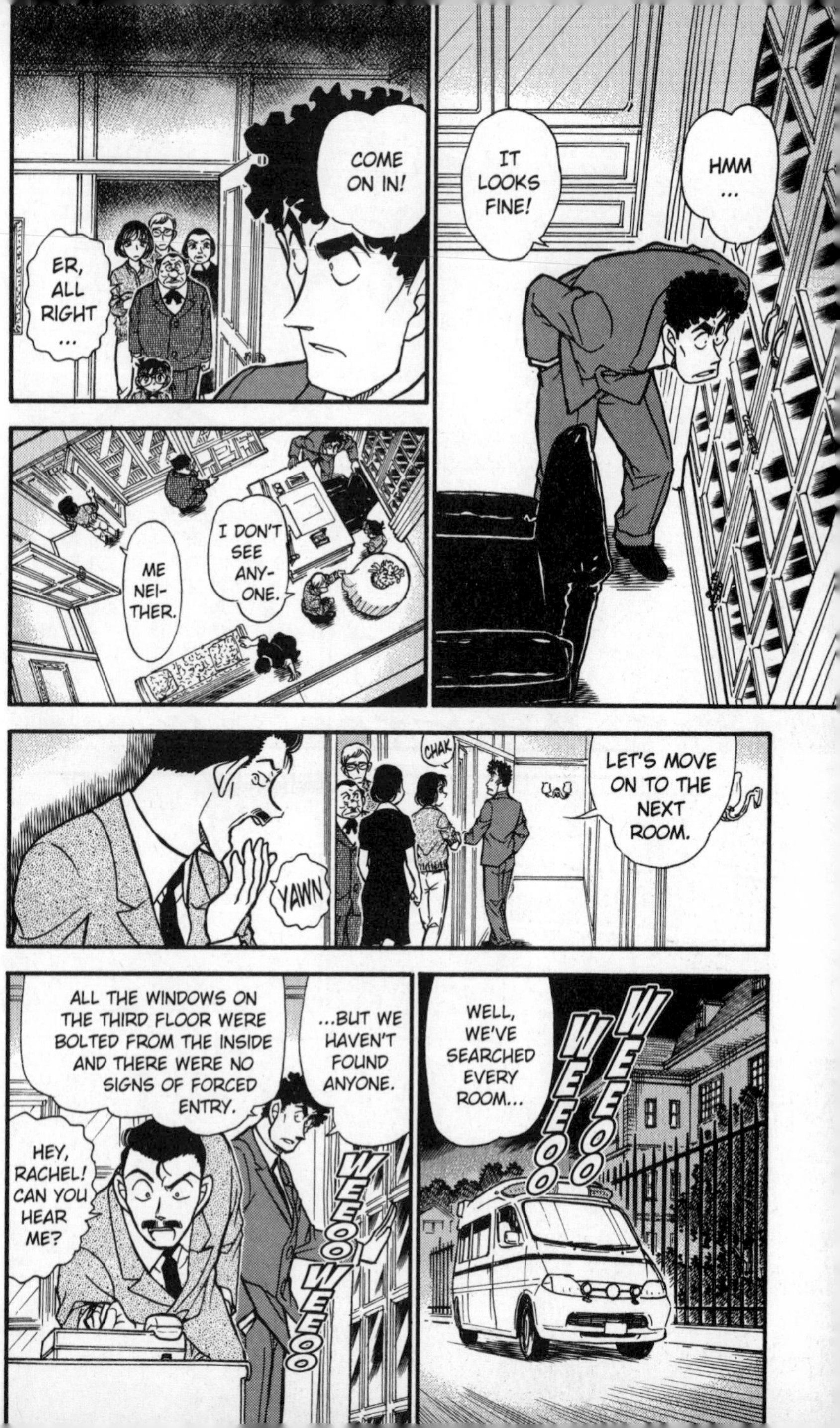
HMM ...
IT LOOKS FINE!
COME ON IN!
ER, ALL RIGHT ...
I DON'T SEE ANY-ONE.
ME NEI-THER.
LET'S MOVE ON TO THE NEXT ROOM.
CHAK
YAWN
WEEEOO
WEEEOO
WELL, WE'VE SEARCHED EVERY ROOM...
...BUT WE HAVEN'T FOUND ANYONE.
ALL THE WINDOWS ON THE THIRD FLOOR WERE BOLTED FROM THE INSIDE AND THERE WERE NO SIGNS OF FORCED ENTRY.
WEEOO WEEOO
HEY, RACHEL! CAN YOU HEAR ME?

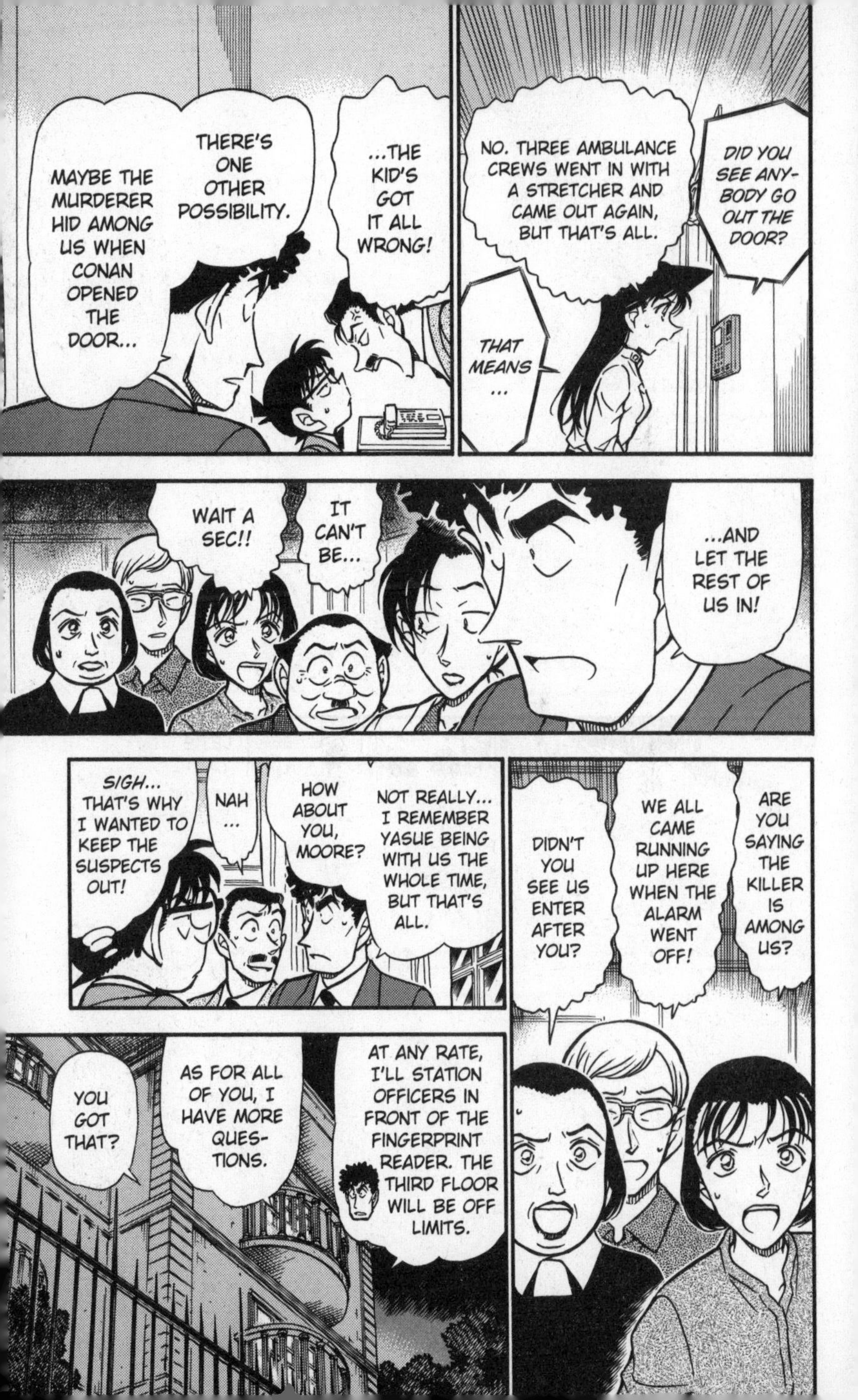
DID YOU SEE ANY-BODY GO OUT THE DOOR?
NO. THREE AMBULANCE CREWS WENT IN WITH A STRETCHER AND CAME OUT AGAIN, BUT THAT'S ALL.
THAT MEANS ...
...THE KID'S GOT IT ALL WRONG!
THERE'S ONE OTHER POSSIBILITY.
MAYBE THE MURDERER HID AMONG US WHEN CONAN OPENED THE DOOR...
...AND LET THE REST OF US IN!
IT CAN'T BE...
WAIT A SEC!!
ARE YOU SAYING THE KILLER IS AMONG US?
WE ALL CAME RUNNING UP HERE WHEN THE ALARM WENT OFF!
DIDN'T YOU SEE US ENTER AFTER YOU?
NOT REALLY... I REMEMBER YASUE BEING WITH US THE WHOLE TIME, BUT THAT'S ALL.
HOW ABOUT YOU, MOORE?
NAH ...
SIGH... THAT'S WHY I WANTED TO KEEP THE SUSPECTS OUT!
AT ANY RATE, I'LL STATION OFFICERS IN FRONT OF THE FINGERPRINT READER. THE THIRD FLOOR WILL BE OFF LIMITS.
AS FOR ALL OF YOU, I HAVE MORE QUES-TIONS.
YOU GOT THAT?

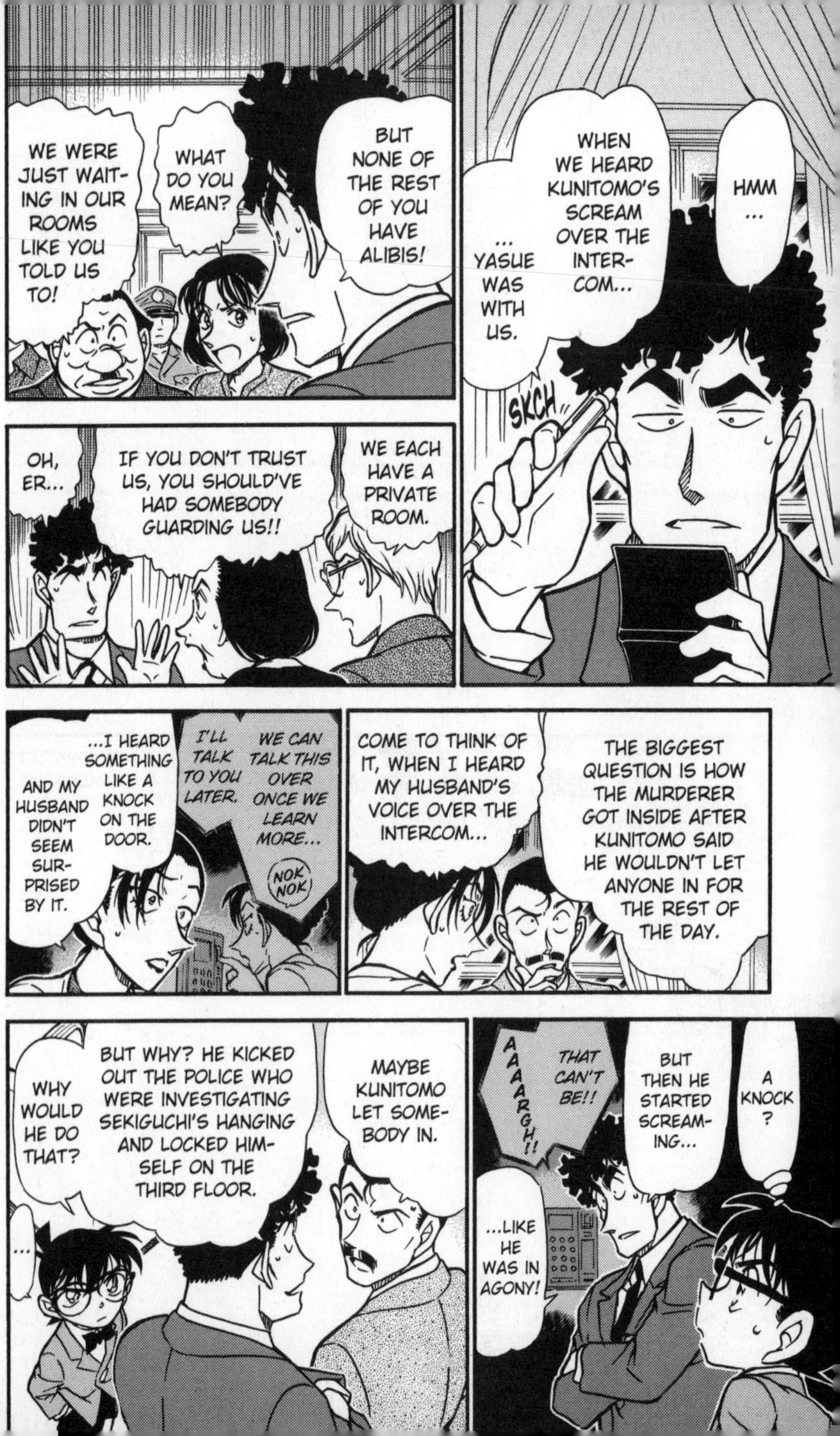
HMM ...
WHEN WE HEARD KUNITOMO'S SCREAM OVER THE INTER-COM...
... YASUE WAS WITH US.
SKCH
BUT NONE OF THE REST OF YOU HAVE ALIBIS!
WHAT DO YOU MEAN?
WE WERE JUST WAIT-ING IN OUR ROOMS LIKE YOU TOLD US TO!
WE EACH HAVE A PRIVATE ROOM.
IF YOU DON'T TRUST US, YOU SHOULD'VE HAD SOMEBODY GUARDING US!!
OH, ER...
THE BIGGEST QUESTION IS HOW THE MURDERER GOT INSIDE AFTER KUNITOMO SAID HE WOULDN'T LET ANYONE IN FOR THE REST OF THE DAY.
COME TO THINK OF IT, WHEN I HEARD MY HUSBAND'S VOICE OVER THE INTERCOM...
WE CAN TALK THIS OVER ONCE WE LEARN MORE...
I'LL TALK TO YOU LATER.
...I HEARD SOMETHING LIKE A KNOCK ON THE DOOR.
AND MY HUSBAND DIDN'T SEEM SUR-PRISED BY IT.
NOK NOK
A KNOCK?
BUT THEN HE STARTED SCREAM-ING...
THAT CAN'T BE!!
AAAAARGH!!
...LIKE HE WAS IN AGONY!
MAYBE KUNITOMO LET SOME-BODY IN.
BUT WHY? HE KICKED OUT THE POLICE WHO WERE INVESTIGATING SEKIGUCHI'S HANGING AND LOCKED HIM-SELF ON THE THIRD FLOOR.
WHY WOULD HE DO THAT?
...

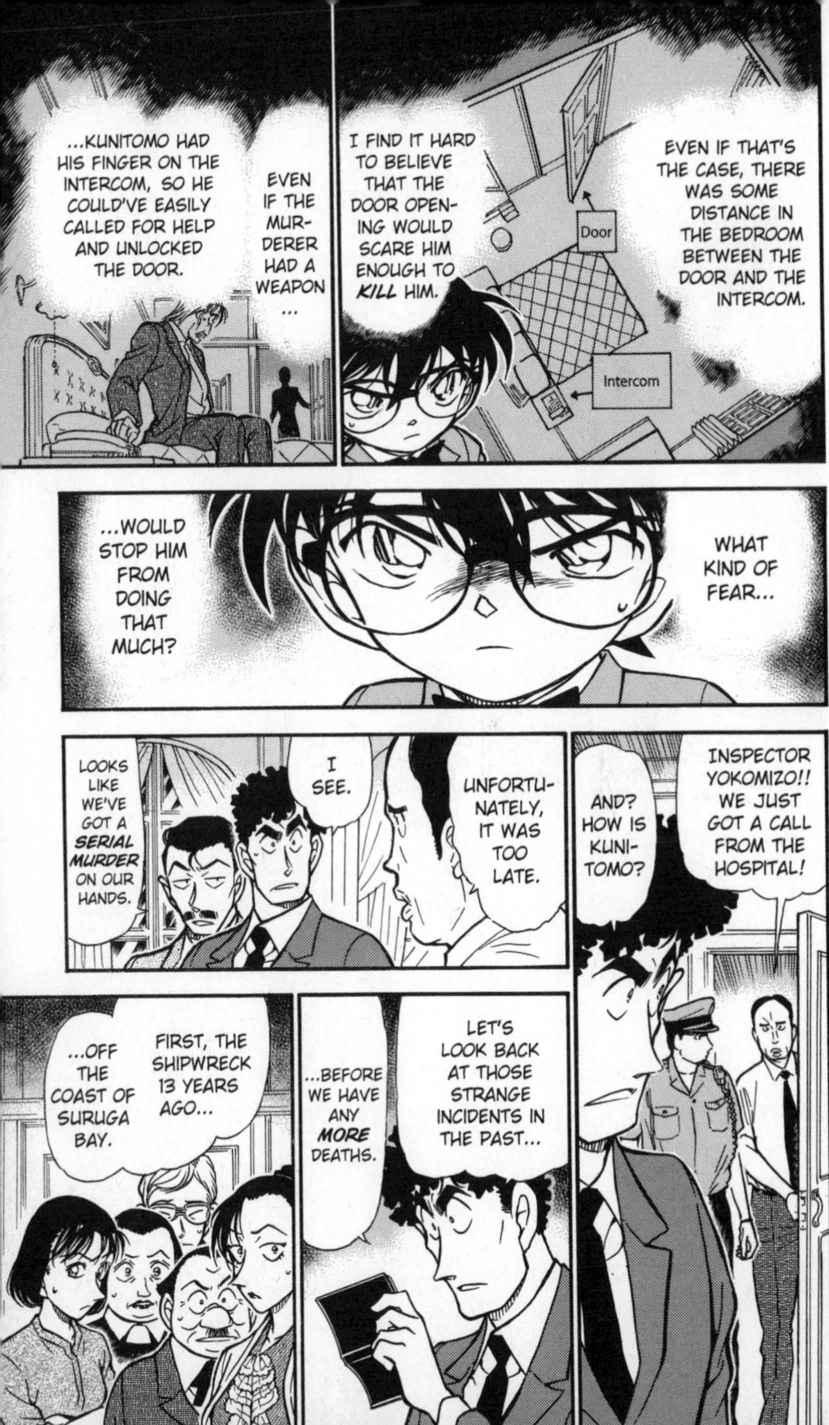
EVEN IF THAT'S THE CASE, THERE WAS SOME DISTANCE IN THE BEDROOM BETWEEN THE DOOR AND THE INTERCOM.
Door
Intercom
I FIND IT HARD TO BELIEVE THAT THE DOOR OPENING WOULD SCARE HIM ENOUGH TO ***KILL*** HIM.
EVEN IF THE MURDERER HAD A WEAPON...
...KUNITOMO HAD HIS FINGER ON THE INTERCOM, SO HE COULD'VE EASILY CALLED FOR HELP AND UNLOCKED THE DOOR.
WHAT KIND OF FEAR...
...WOULD STOP HIM FROM DOING THAT MUCH?
INSPECTOR YOKOMIZO!! WE JUST GOT A CALL FROM THE HOSPITAL!
AND? HOW IS KUNITOMO?
UNFORTUNATELY, IT WAS TOO LATE.
I SEE.
LOOKS LIKE WE'VE GOT A ***SERIAL MURDER*** ON OUR HANDS.
LET'S LOOK BACK AT THOSE STRANGE INCIDENTS IN THE PAST...
...BEFORE WE HAVE ANY ***MORE*** DEATHS.
FIRST, THE SHIPWRECK 13 YEARS AGO...
...OFF THE COAST OF SURUGA BAY.

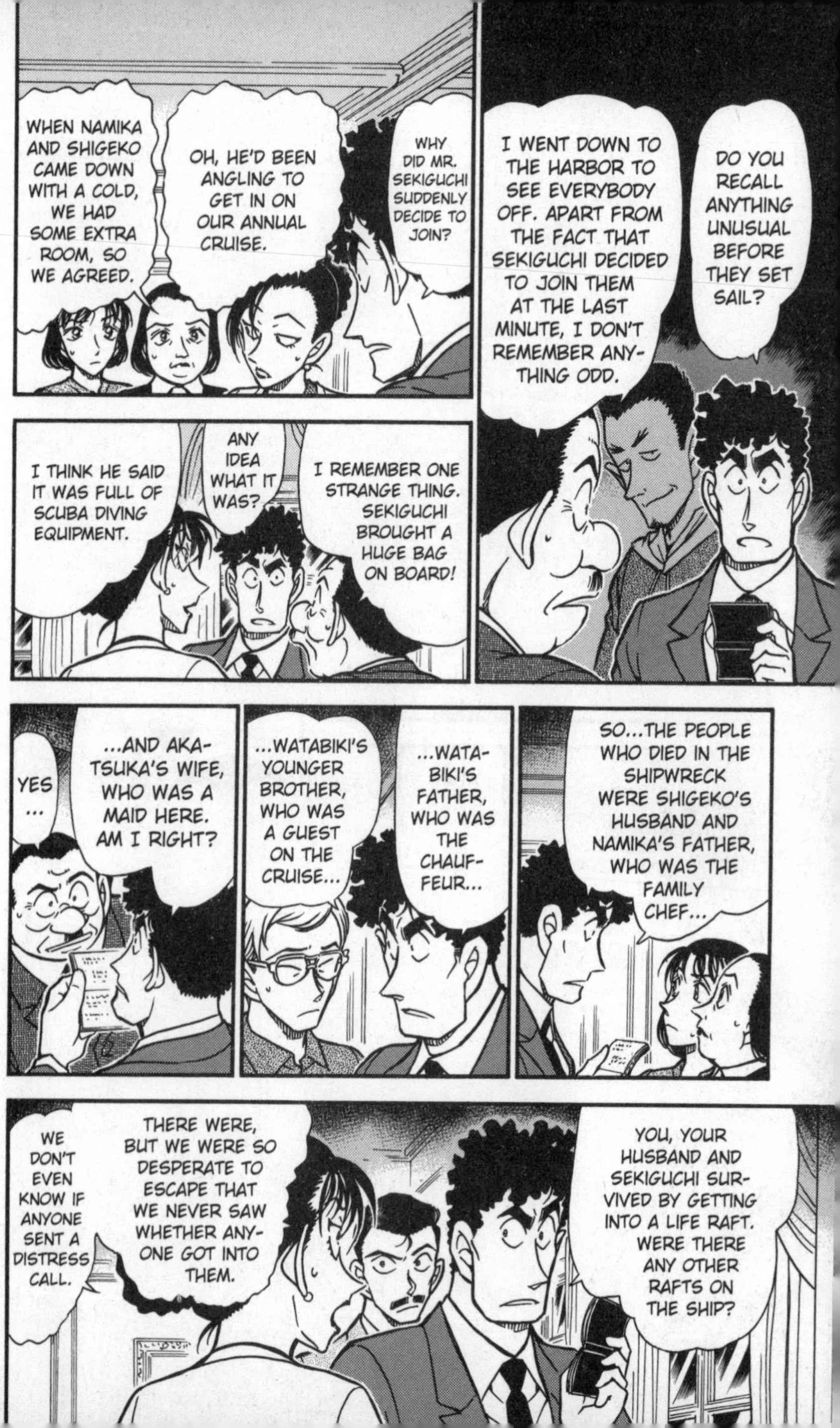

DO YOU RECALL ANYTHING UNUSUAL BEFORE THEY SET SAIL?
I WENT DOWN TO THE HARBOR TO SEE EVERYBODY OFF. APART FROM THE FACT THAT SEKIGUCHI DECIDED TO JOIN THEM AT THE LAST MINUTE, I DON'T REMEMBER ANYTHING ODD.
WHY DID MR. SEKIGUCHI SUDDENLY DECIDE TO JOIN?
OH, HE'D BEEN ANGLING TO GET IN ON OUR ANNUAL CRUISE.
WHEN NAMIKA AND SHIGEKO CAME DOWN WITH A COLD, WE HAD SOME EXTRA ROOM, SO WE AGREED.
I REMEMBER ONE STRANGE THING. SEKIGUCHI BROUGHT A HUGE BAG ON BOARD!
ANY IDEA WHAT IT WAS?
I THINK HE SAID IT WAS FULL OF SCUBA DIVING EQUIPMENT.
SO...THE PEOPLE WHO DIED IN THE SHIPWRECK WERE SHIGEKO'S HUSBAND AND NAMIKA'S FATHER, WHO WAS THE FAMILY CHEF...
...WATABIKI'S FATHER, WHO WAS THE CHAUFFEUR...
...WATABIKI'S YOUNGER BROTHER, WHO WAS A GUEST ON THE CRUISE...
...AND AKATSUKA'S WIFE, WHO WAS A MAID HERE. AM I RIGHT?
YES ...
YOU, YOUR HUSBAND AND SEKIGUCHI SURVIVED BY GETTING INTO A LIFE RAFT. WERE THERE ANY OTHER RAFTS ON THE SHIP?
THERE WERE, BUT WE WERE SO DESPERATE TO ESCAPE THAT WE NEVER SAW WHETHER ANYONE GOT INTO THEM.
WE DON'T EVEN KNOW IF ANYONE SENT A DISTRESS CALL.

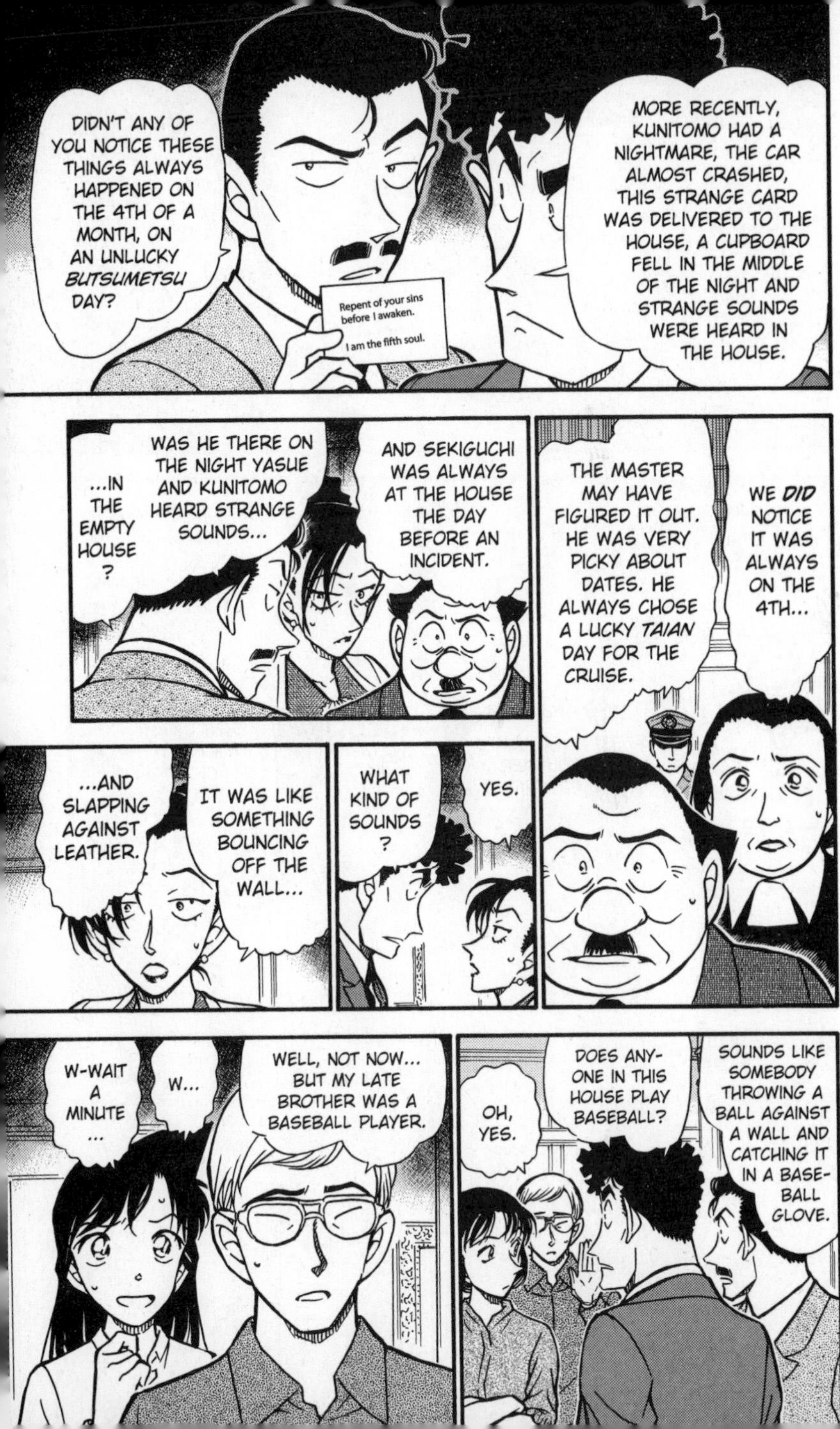
MORE RECENTLY, KUNITOMO HAD A NIGHTMARE, THE CAR ALMOST CRASHED, THIS STRANGE CARD WAS DELIVERED TO THE HOUSE, A CUPBOARD FELL IN THE MIDDLE OF THE NIGHT AND STRANGE SOUNDS WERE HEARD IN THE HOUSE.
Repent of your sins before I awaken.
I am the fifth soul.
DIDN'T ANY OF YOU NOTICE THESE THINGS ALWAYS HAPPENED ON THE 4TH OF A MONTH, ON AN UNLUCKY *BUTSUMETSU* DAY?
WE *DID* NOTICE IT WAS ALWAYS ON THE 4TH...
THE MASTER MAY HAVE FIGURED IT OUT. HE WAS VERY PICKY ABOUT DATES. HE ALWAYS CHOSE A LUCKY *TAIAN* DAY FOR THE CRUISE.
AND SEKIGUCHI WAS ALWAYS AT THE HOUSE THE DAY BEFORE AN INCIDENT.
WAS HE THERE ON THE NIGHT YASUE AND KUNITOMO HEARD STRANGE SOUNDS...
...IN THE EMPTY HOUSE?
YES.
WHAT KIND OF SOUNDS?
IT WAS LIKE SOMETHING BOUNCING OFF THE WALL...
...AND SLAPPING AGAINST LEATHER.
SOUNDS LIKE SOMEBODY THROWING A BALL AGAINST A WALL AND CATCHING IT IN A BASEBALL GLOVE.
DOES ANYONE IN THIS HOUSE PLAY BASEBALL?
OH, YES.
WELL, NOT NOW... BUT MY LATE BROTHER WAS A BASEBALL PLAYER.
W...
W-WAIT A MINUTE...

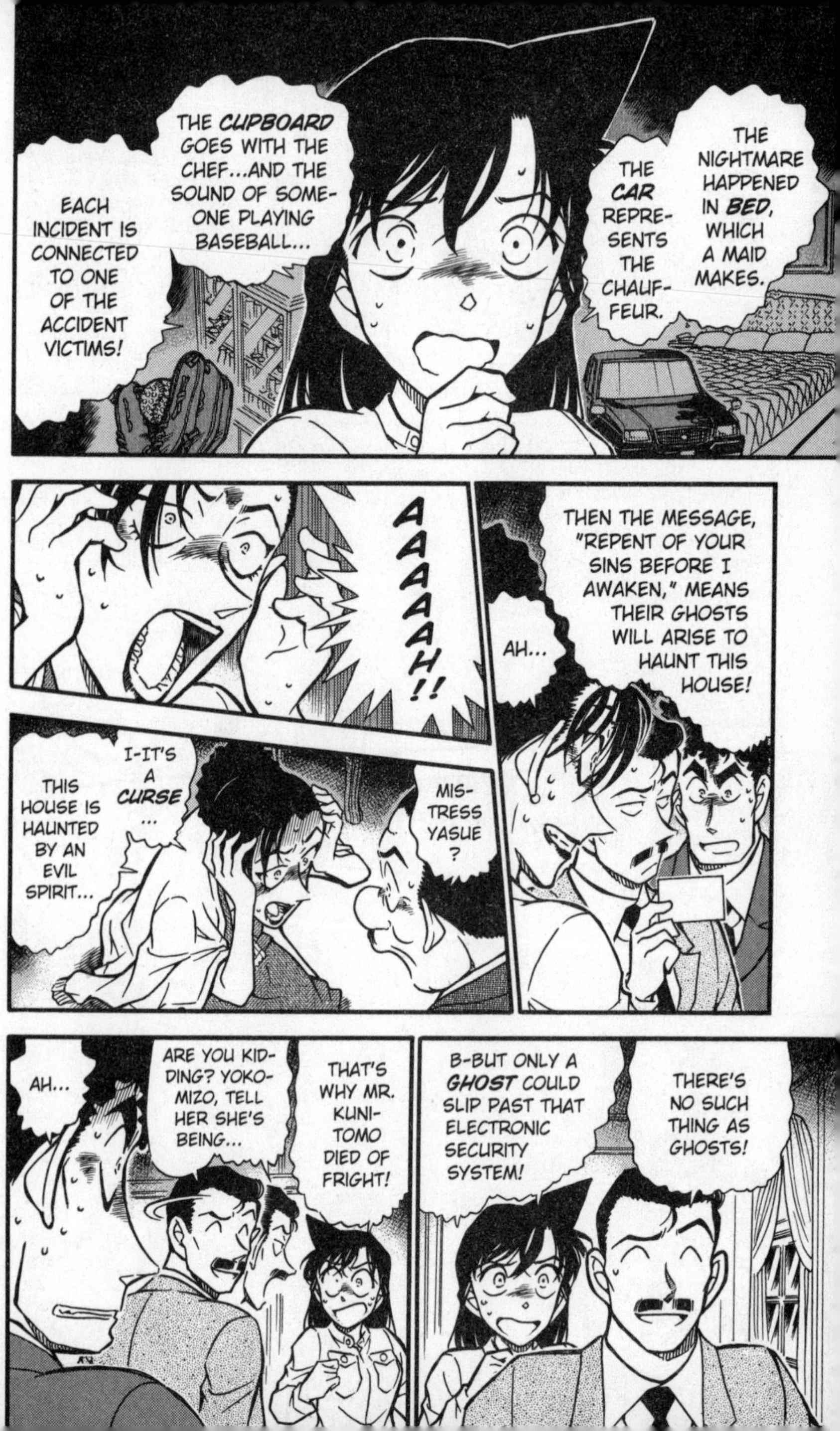
THE NIGHTMARE HAPPENED IN BED, WHICH A MAID MAKES.
THE CAR REPRESENTS THE CHAUFFEUR.
THE CUPBOARD GOES WITH THE CHEF...AND THE SOUND OF SOMEONE PLAYING BASEBALL...
EACH INCIDENT IS CONNECTED TO ONE OF THE ACCIDENT VICTIMS!
THEN THE MESSAGE, "REPENT OF YOUR SINS BEFORE I AWAKEN," MEANS THEIR GHOSTS WILL ARISE TO HAUNT THIS HOUSE!
AH...
AAAAAAH!!
MISTRESS YASUE?
I-IT'S A CURSE...
THIS HOUSE IS HAUNTED BY AN EVIL SPIRIT...
THERE'S NO SUCH THING AS GHOSTS!
B-BUT ONLY A GHOST COULD SLIP PAST THAT ELECTRONIC SECURITY SYSTEM!
THAT'S WHY MR. KUNITOMO DIED OF FRIGHT!
ARE YOU KIDDING? YOKOMIZO, TELL HER SHE'S BEING...
AH...

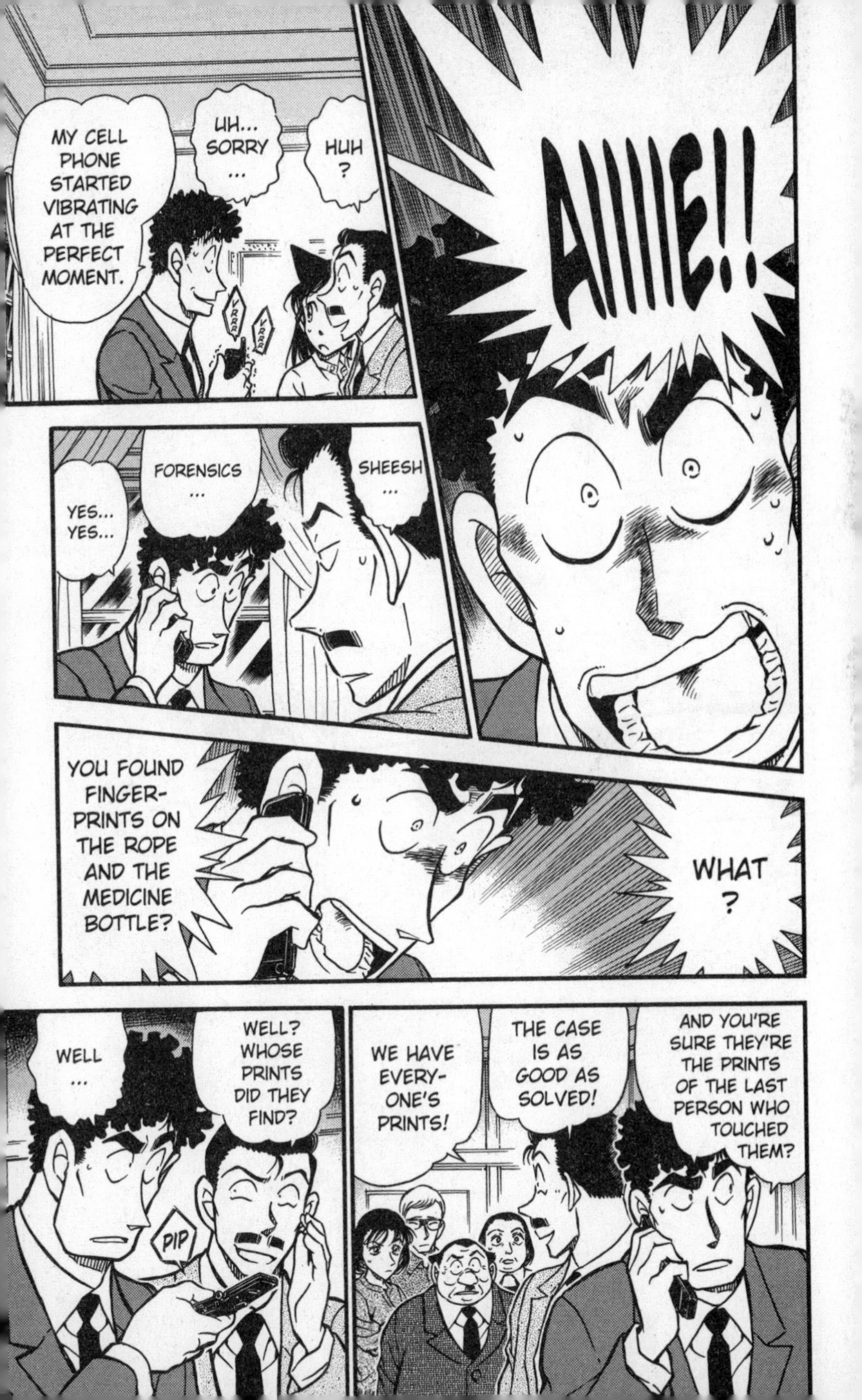
AIIIIE!!
HUH ?
UH... SORRY ...
MY CELL PHONE STARTED VIBRATING AT THE PERFECT MOMENT.
VRRR
VRRR
SHEESH ...
FORENSICS ...
YES... YES...
WHAT ?
YOU FOUND FINGER-PRINTS ON THE ROPE AND THE MEDICINE BOTTLE?
AND YOU'RE SURE THEY'RE THE PRINTS OF THE LAST PERSON WHO TOUCHED THEM?
THE CASE IS AS GOOD AS SOLVED!
WE HAVE EVERY-ONE'S PRINTS!
WELL? WHOSE PRINTS DID THEY FIND?
PIP
WELL ...

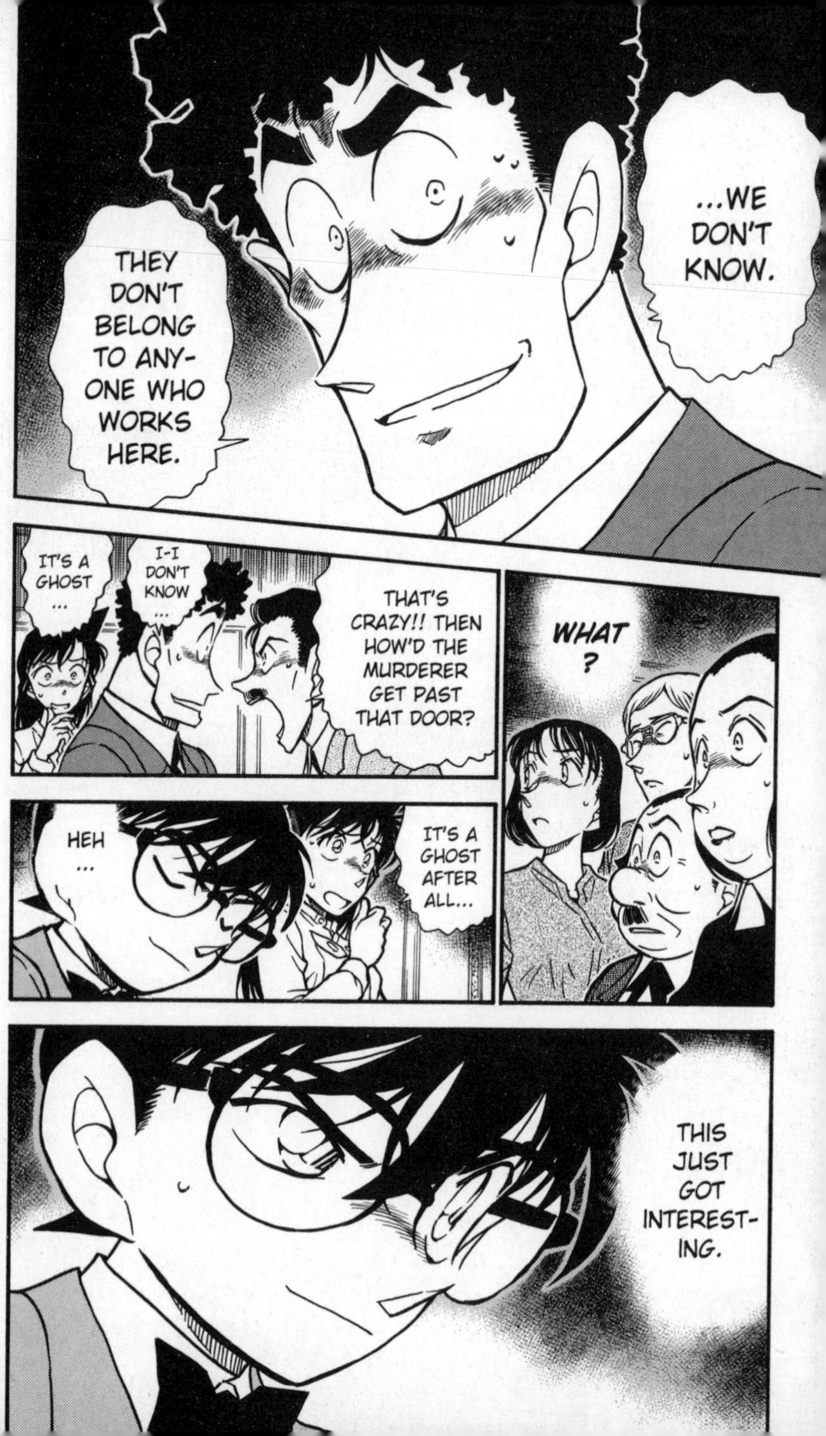
...WE DON'T KNOW.
THEY DON'T BELONG TO ANYONE WHO WORKS HERE.
WHAT?
THAT'S CRAZY!! THEN HOW'D THE MURDERER GET PAST THAT DOOR?
I-I DON'T KNOW...
IT'S A GHOST...
IT'S A GHOST AFTER ALL...
HEH...
THIS JUST GOT INTERESTING.

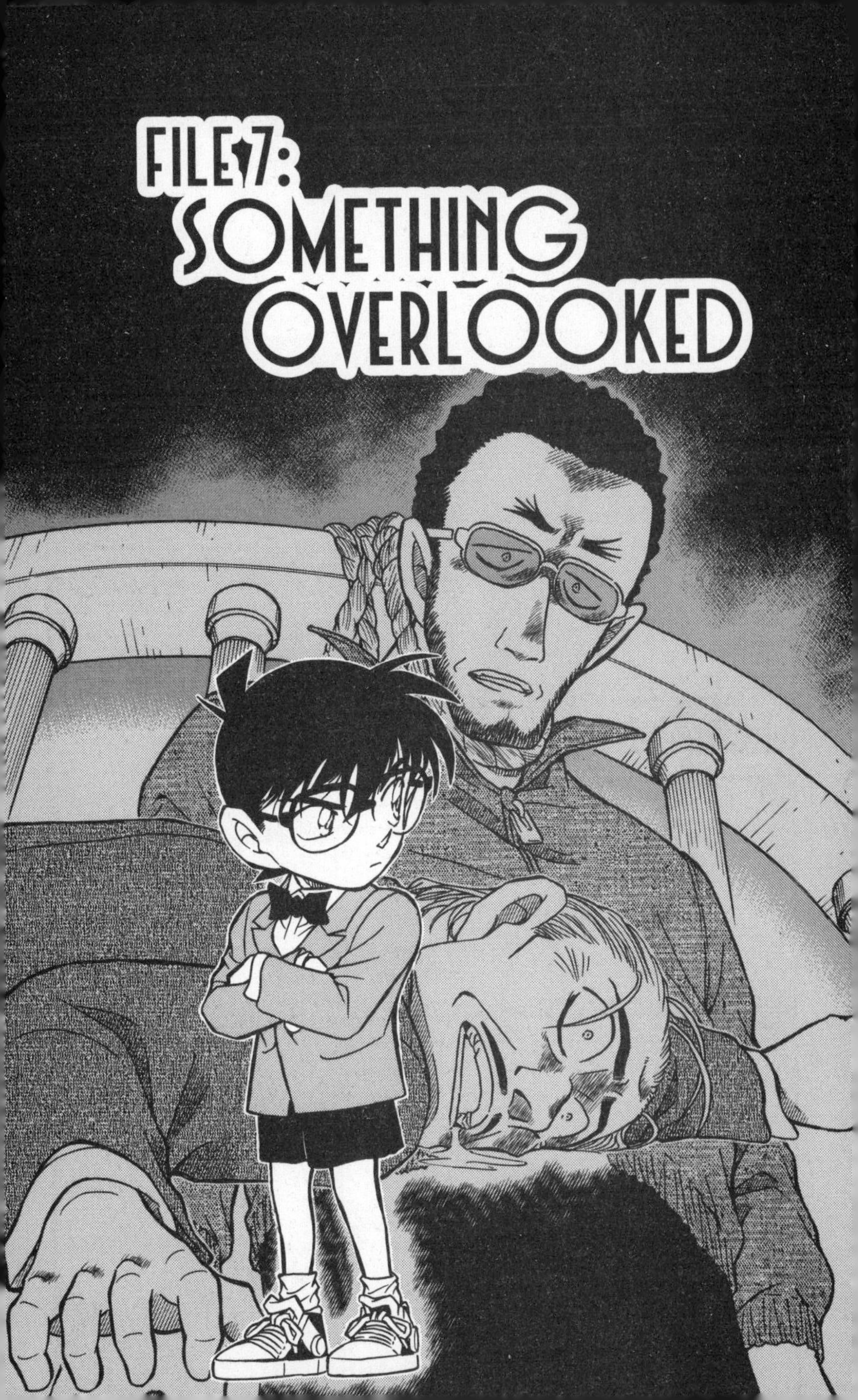
FILE 7:
SOMETHING OVERLOOKED

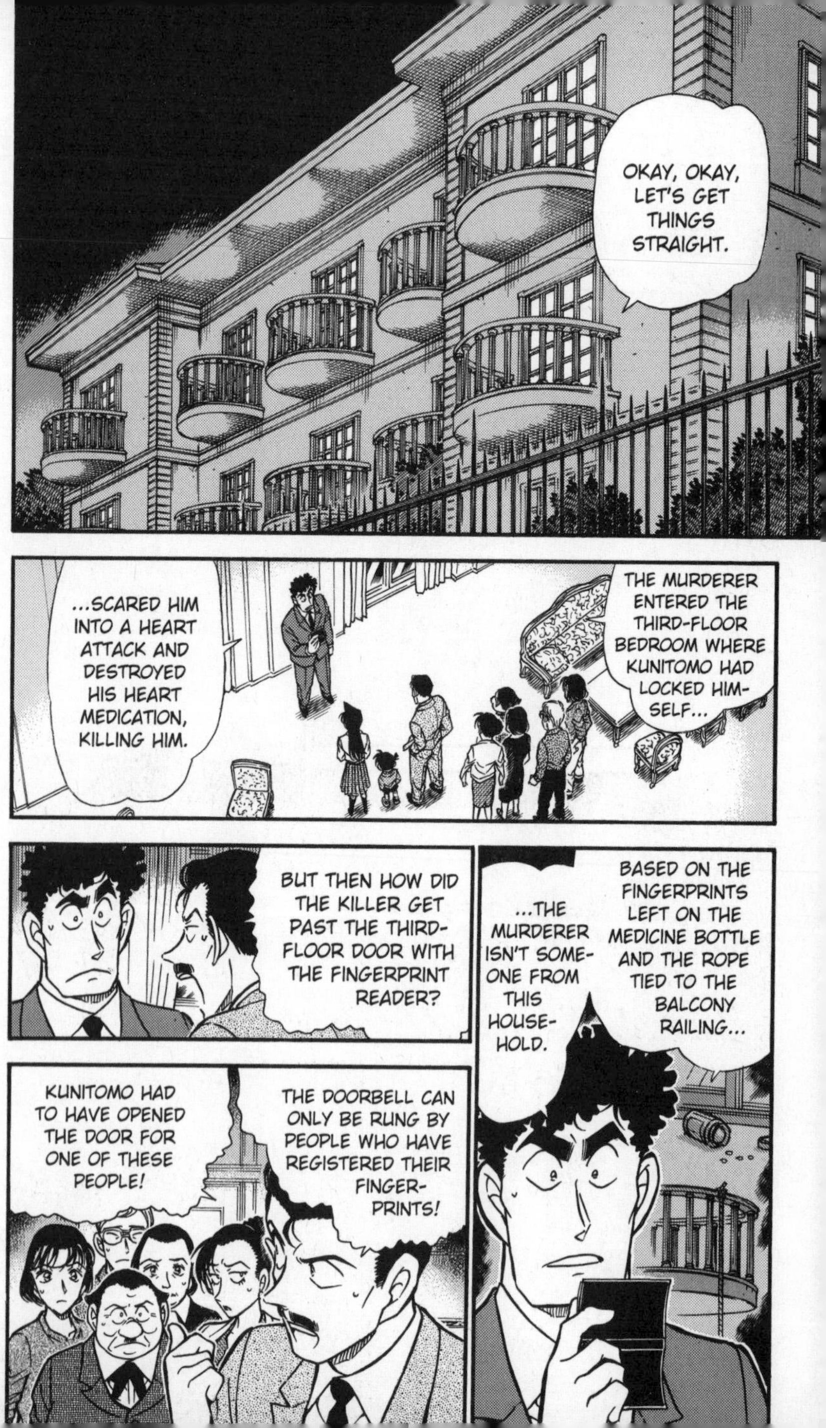
OKAY, OKAY, LET'S GET THINGS STRAIGHT.
THE MURDERER ENTERED THE THIRD-FLOOR BEDROOM WHERE KUNITOMO HAD LOCKED HIM-SELF...
...SCARED HIM INTO A HEART ATTACK AND DESTROYED HIS HEART MEDICATION, KILLING HIM.
BASED ON THE FINGERPRINTS LEFT ON THE MEDICINE BOTTLE AND THE ROPE TIED TO THE BALCONY RAILING...
...THE MURDERER ISN'T SOME-ONE FROM THIS HOUSE-HOLD.
BUT THEN HOW DID THE KILLER GET PAST THE THIRD-FLOOR DOOR WITH THE FINGERPRINT READER?
THE DOORBELL CAN ONLY BE RUNG BY PEOPLE WHO HAVE REGISTERED THEIR FINGER-PRINTS!
KUNITOMO HAD TO HAVE OPENED THE DOOR FOR ONE OF THESE PEOPLE!

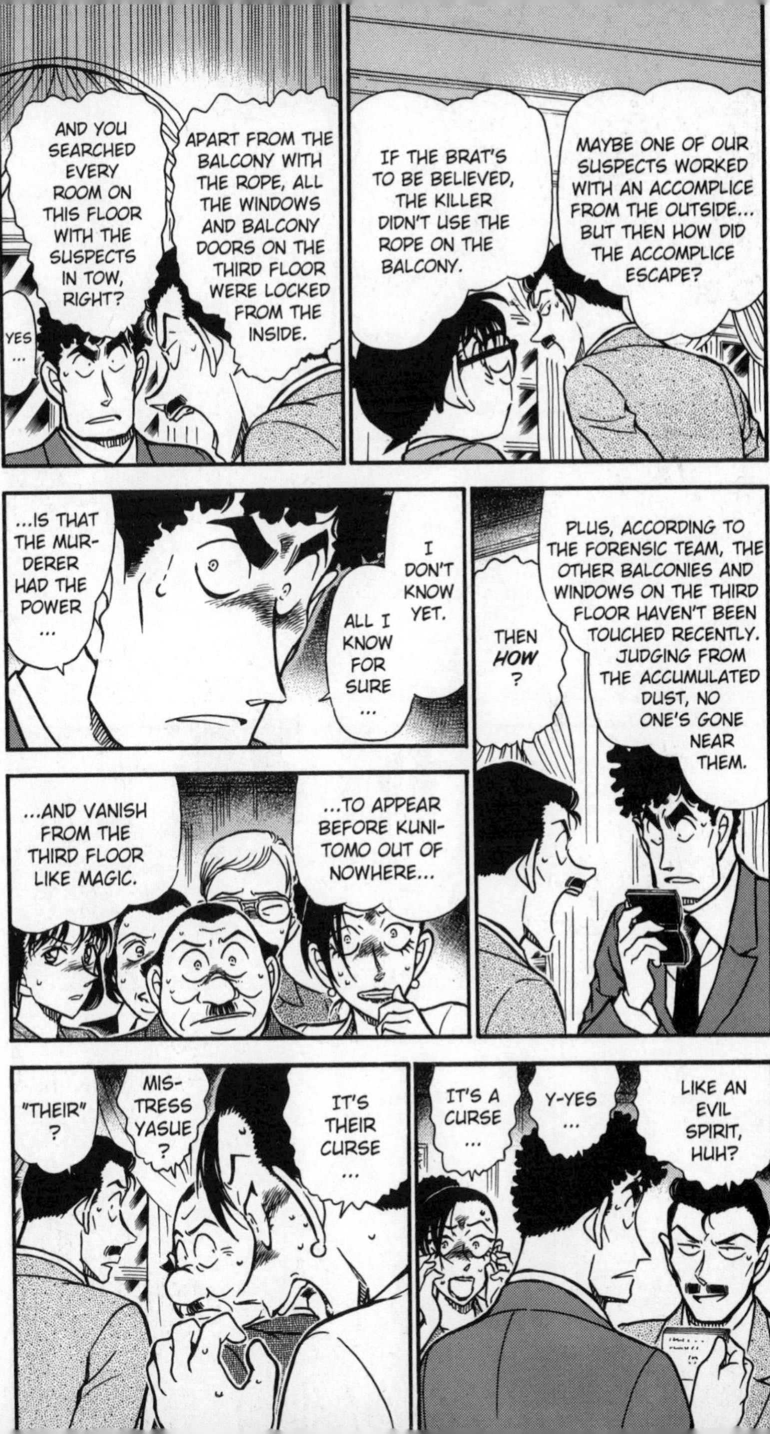
MAYBE ONE OF OUR SUSPECTS WORKED WITH AN ACCOMPLICE FROM THE OUTSIDE... BUT THEN HOW DID THE ACCOMPLICE ESCAPE?
IF THE BRAT'S TO BE BELIEVED, THE KILLER DIDN'T USE THE ROPE ON THE BALCONY.
APART FROM THE BALCONY WITH THE ROPE, ALL THE WINDOWS AND BALCONY DOORS ON THE THIRD FLOOR WERE LOCKED FROM THE INSIDE.
AND YOU SEARCHED EVERY ROOM ON THIS FLOOR WITH THE SUSPECTS IN TOW, RIGHT?
YES...
PLUS, ACCORDING TO THE FORENSIC TEAM, THE OTHER BALCONIES AND WINDOWS ON THE THIRD FLOOR HAVEN'T BEEN TOUCHED RECENTLY. JUDGING FROM THE ACCUMULATED DUST, NO ONE'S GONE NEAR THEM.
THEN *HOW*?
I DON'T KNOW YET.
ALL I KNOW FOR SURE...
...IS THAT THE MURDERER HAD THE POWER...
...TO APPEAR BEFORE KUNITOMO OUT OF NOWHERE...
...AND VANISH FROM THE THIRD FLOOR LIKE MAGIC.
LIKE AN EVIL SPIRIT, HUH?
Y-YES...
IT'S A CURSE...
IT'S THEIR CURSE...
MISTRESS YASUE?
"THEIR"?

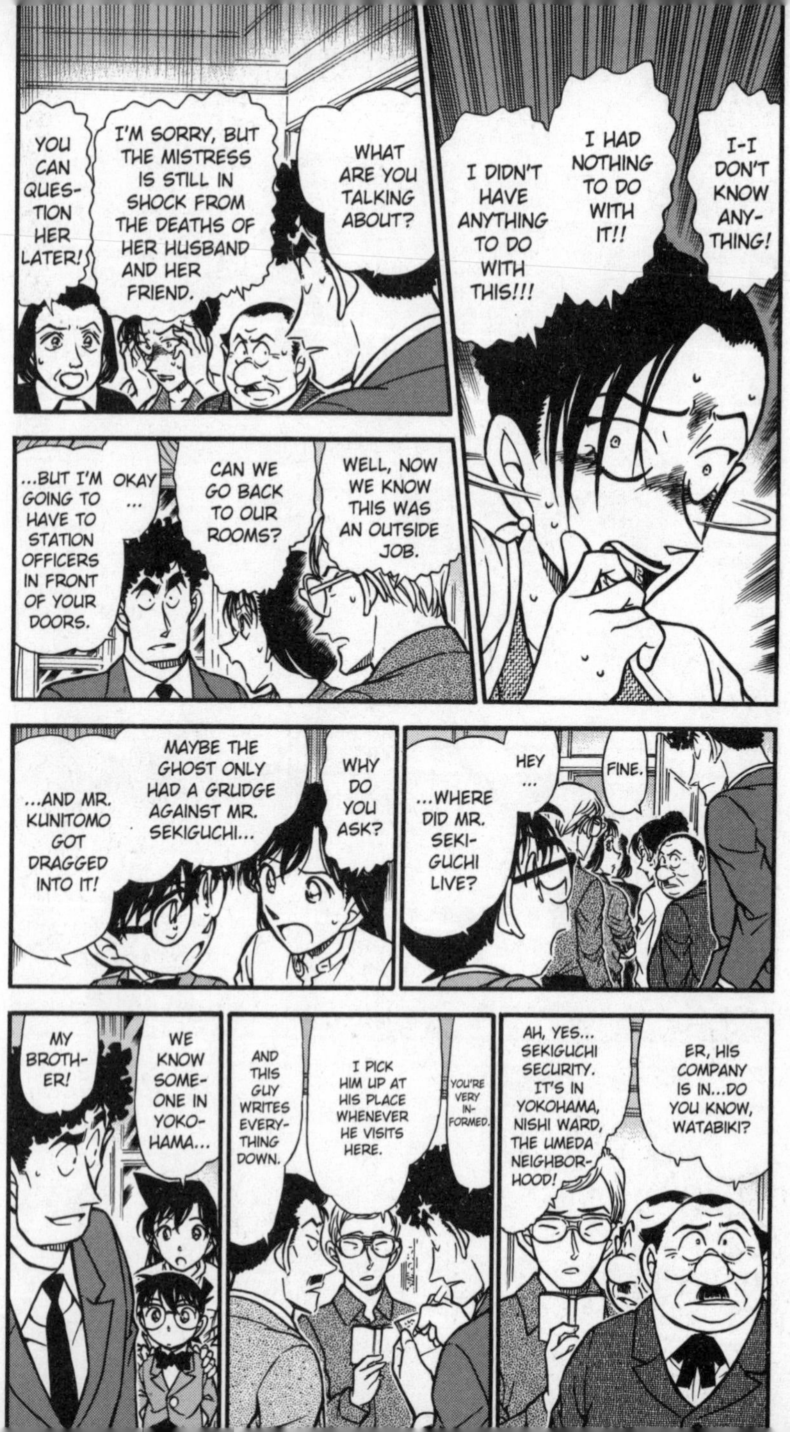
I-I DON'T KNOW ANYTHING!
I HAD NOTHING TO DO WITH IT!!
I DIDN'T HAVE ANYTHING TO DO WITH THIS!!!
WHAT ARE YOU TALKING ABOUT?
I'M SORRY, BUT THE MISTRESS IS STILL IN SHOCK FROM THE DEATHS OF HER HUSBAND AND HER FRIEND.
YOU CAN QUESTION HER LATER!
WELL, NOW WE KNOW THIS WAS AN OUTSIDE JOB.
CAN WE GO BACK TO OUR ROOMS?
OKAY...
...BUT I'M GOING TO HAVE TO STATION OFFICERS IN FRONT OF YOUR DOORS.
FINE.
HEY...
...WHERE DID MR. SEKIGUCHI LIVE?
WHY DO YOU ASK?
MAYBE THE GHOST ONLY HAD A GRUDGE AGAINST MR. SEKIGUCHI...
...AND MR. KUNITOMO GOT DRAGGED INTO IT!
ER, HIS COMPANY IS IN...DO YOU KNOW, WATABIKI?
AH, YES... SEKIGUCHI SECURITY. IT'S IN YOKOHAMA, NISHI WARD, THE UMEDA NEIGHBORHOOD!
YOU'RE VERY INFORMED.
I PICK HIM UP AT HIS PLACE WHENEVER HE VISITS HERE.
AND THIS GUY WRITES EVERYTHING DOWN.
WE KNOW SOMEONE IN YOKOHAMA...
MY BROTHER!

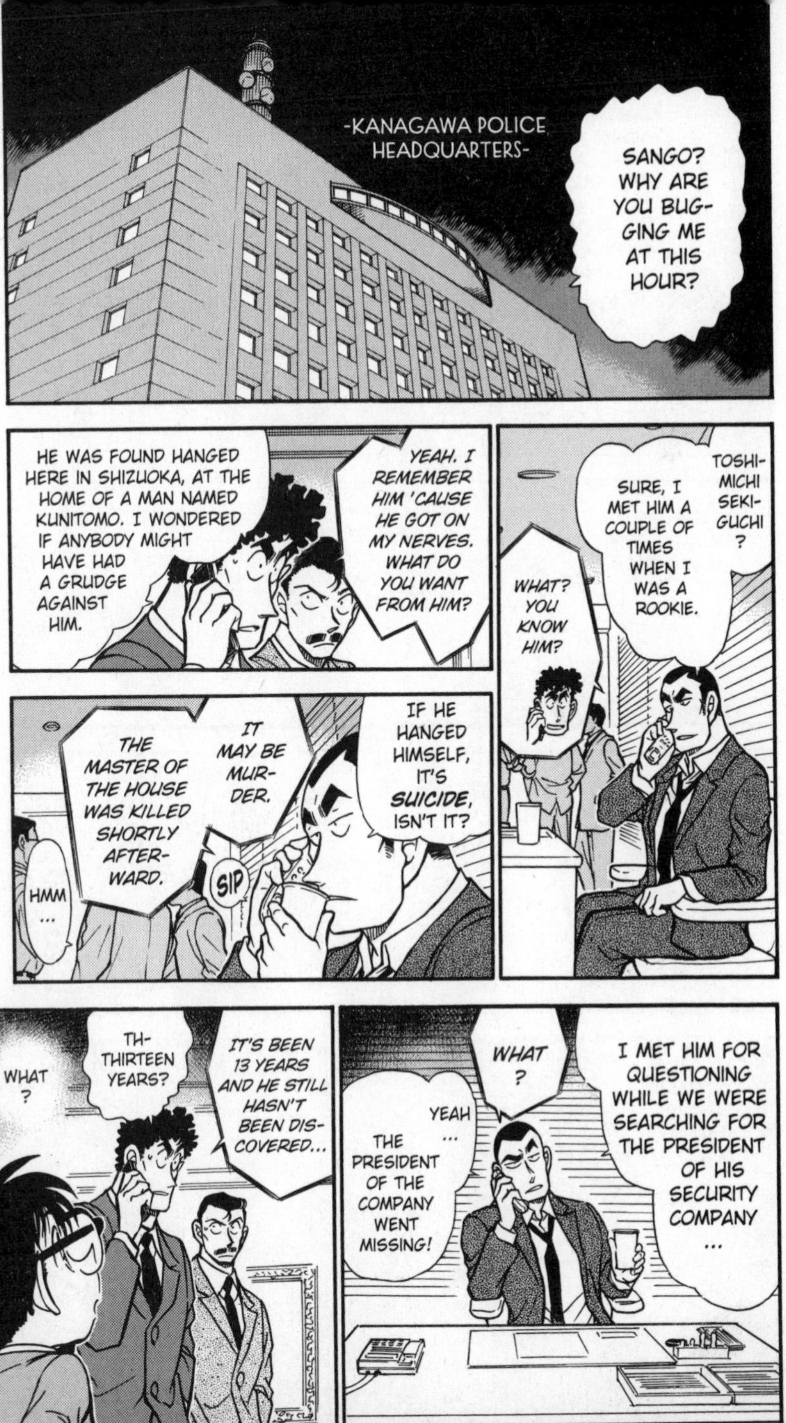
SANGO? WHY ARE YOU BUG-GING ME AT THIS HOUR?
-KANAGAWA POLICE HEADQUARTERS-
TOSHI-MICHI SEKI-GUCHI?
SURE, I MET HIM A COUPLE OF TIMES WHEN I WAS A ROOKIE.
WHAT? YOU KNOW HIM?
YEAH. I REMEMBER HIM 'CAUSE HE GOT ON MY NERVES. WHAT DO YOU WANT FROM HIM?
HE WAS FOUND HANGED HERE IN SHIZUOKA, AT THE HOME OF A MAN NAMED KUNITOMO. I WONDERED IF ANYBODY MIGHT HAVE HAD A GRUDGE AGAINST HIM.
IF HE HANGED HIMSELF, IT'S SUICIDE, ISN'T IT?
IT MAY BE MUR-DER.
THE MASTER OF THE HOUSE WAS KILLED SHORTLY AFTER-WARD.
SIP
HMM ...
I MET HIM FOR QUESTIONING WHILE WE WERE SEARCHING FOR THE PRESIDENT OF HIS SECURITY COMPANY ...
WHAT ?
YEAH ...
THE PRESIDENT OF THE COMPANY WENT MISSING!
IT'S BEEN 13 YEARS AND HE STILL HASN'T BEEN DIS-COVERED...
TH-THIRTEEN YEARS?
WHAT ?

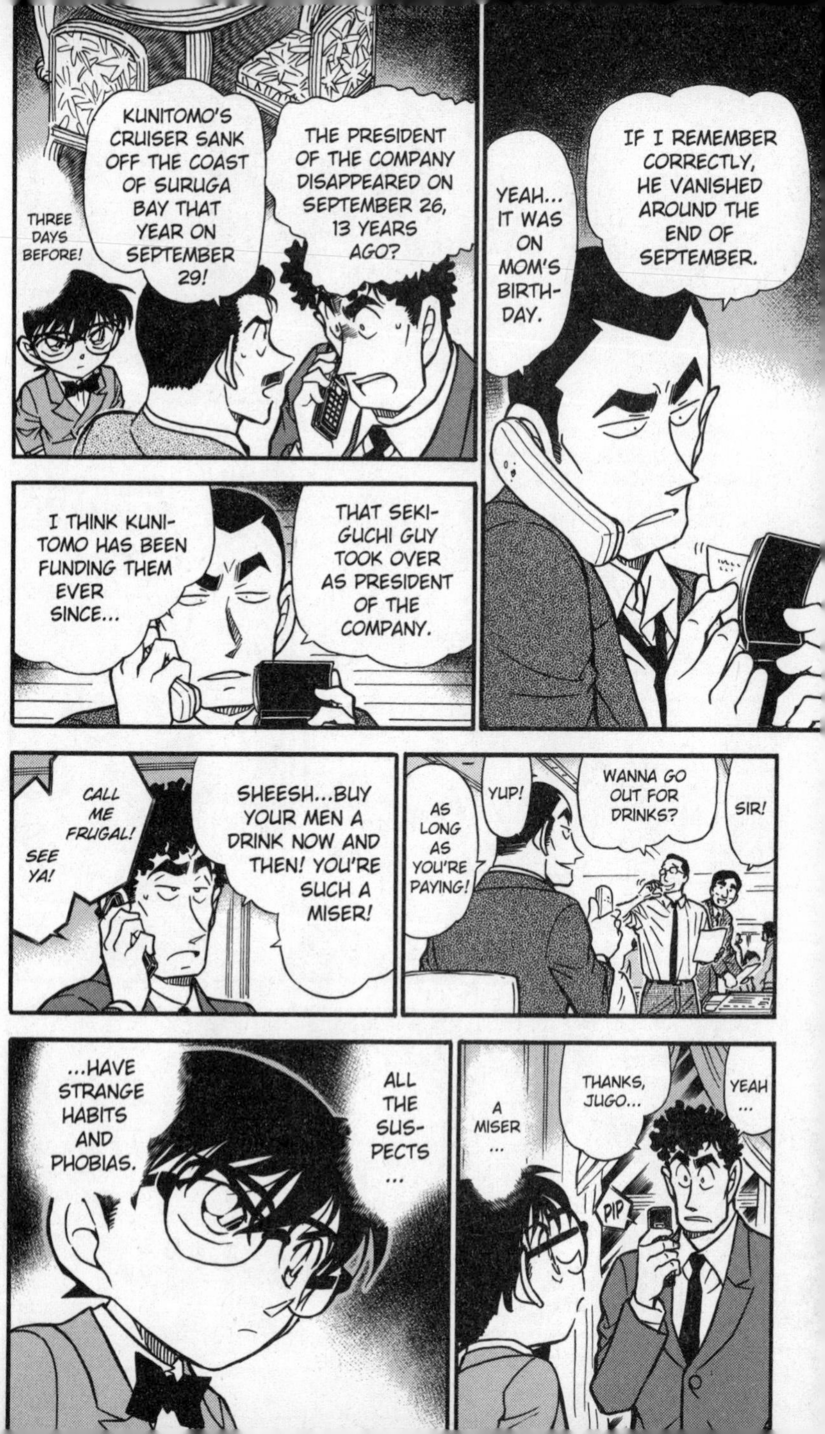
IF I REMEMBER CORRECTLY, HE VANISHED AROUND THE END OF SEPTEMBER.
YEAH... IT WAS ON MOM'S BIRTH-DAY.
THE PRESIDENT OF THE COMPANY DISAPPEARED ON SEPTEMBER 26, 13 YEARS AGO?
KUNITOMO'S CRUISER SANK OFF THE COAST OF SURUGA BAY THAT YEAR ON SEPTEMBER 29!
THREE DAYS BEFORE!
THAT SEKI-GUCHI GUY TOOK OVER AS PRESIDENT OF THE COMPANY.
I THINK KUNI-TOMO HAS BEEN FUNDING THEM EVER SINCE...
SIR!
WANNA GO OUT FOR DRINKS?
YUP!
AS LONG AS YOU'RE PAYING!
SHEESH...BUY YOUR MEN A DRINK NOW AND THEN! YOU'RE SUCH A MISER!
CALL ME FRUGAL!
SEE YA!
YEAH ...
THANKS, JUGO...
PIP
A MISER ...
ALL THE SUS-PECTS ...
...HAVE STRANGE HABITS AND PHOBIAS.

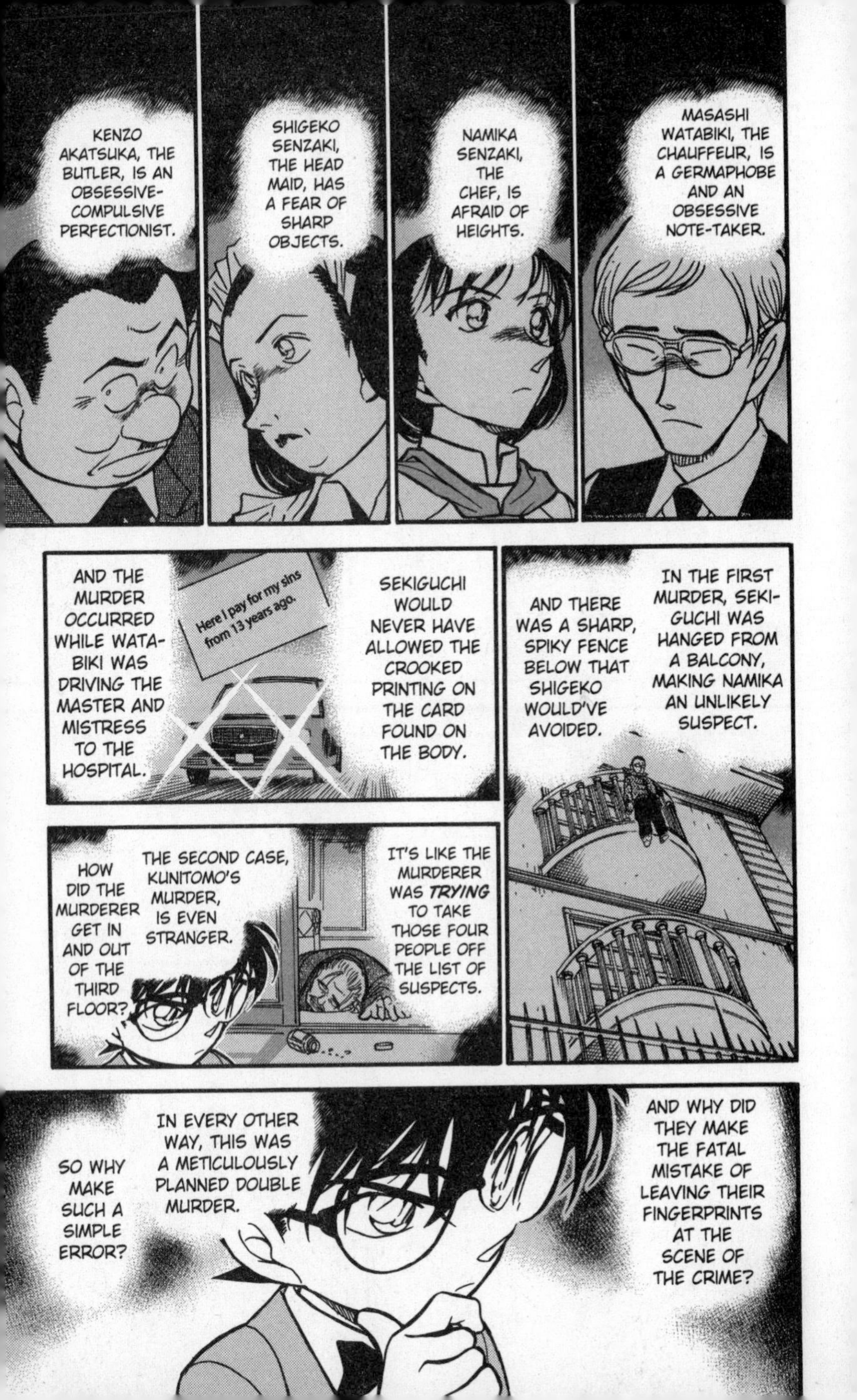
MASASHI WATABIKI, THE CHAUFFEUR, IS A GERMAPHOBE AND AN OBSESSIVE NOTE-TAKER.
NAMIKA SENZAKI, THE CHEF, IS AFRAID OF HEIGHTS.
SHIGEKO SENZAKI, THE HEAD MAID, HAS A FEAR OF SHARP OBJECTS.
KENZO AKATSUKA, THE BUTLER, IS AN OBSESSIVE-COMPULSIVE PERFECTIONIST.
IN THE FIRST MURDER, SEKI-GUCHI WAS HANGED FROM A BALCONY, MAKING NAMIKA AN UNLIKELY SUSPECT.
AND THERE WAS A SHARP, SPIKY FENCE BELOW THAT SHIGEKO WOULD'VE AVOIDED.
SEKIGUCHI WOULD NEVER HAVE ALLOWED THE CROOKED PRINTING ON THE CARD FOUND ON THE BODY.
Here I pay for my sins from 13 years ago.
AND THE MURDER OCCURRED WHILE WATA-BIKI WAS DRIVING THE MASTER AND MISTRESS TO THE HOSPITAL.
IT'S LIKE THE MURDERER WAS *TRYING* TO TAKE THOSE FOUR PEOPLE OFF THE LIST OF SUSPECTS.
THE SECOND CASE, KUNITOMO'S MURDER, IS EVEN STRANGER.
HOW DID THE MURDERER GET IN AND OUT OF THE THIRD FLOOR?
AND WHY DID THEY MAKE THE FATAL MISTAKE OF LEAVING THEIR FINGERPRINTS AT THE SCENE OF THE CRIME?
IN EVERY OTHER WAY, THIS WAS A METICULOUSLY PLANNED DOUBLE MURDER.
SO WHY MAKE SUCH A SIMPLE ERROR?

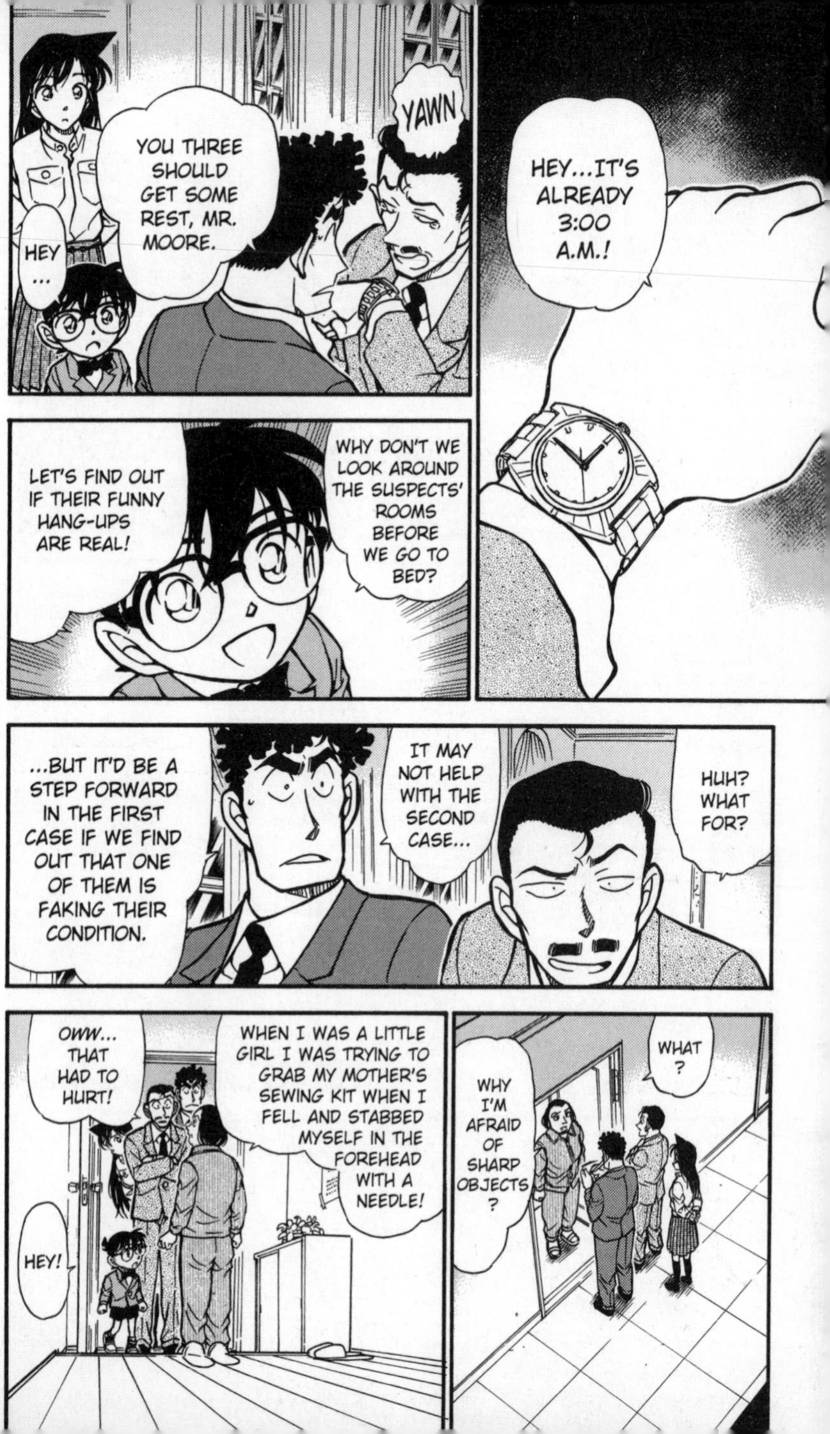
HEY...IT'S ALREADY 3:00 A.M.!
YAWN
YOU THREE SHOULD GET SOME REST, MR. MOORE.
HEY...
WHY DON'T WE LOOK AROUND THE SUSPECTS' ROOMS BEFORE WE GO TO BED?
LET'S FIND OUT IF THEIR FUNNY HANG-UPS ARE REAL!
HUH? WHAT FOR?
IT MAY NOT HELP WITH THE SECOND CASE...
...BUT IT'D BE A STEP FORWARD IN THE FIRST CASE IF WE FIND OUT THAT ONE OF THEM IS FAKING THEIR CONDITION.
WHAT?
WHY I'M AFRAID OF SHARP OBJECTS?
WHEN I WAS A LITTLE GIRL I WAS TRYING TO GRAB MY MOTHER'S SEWING KIT WHEN I FELL AND STABBED MYSELF IN THE FOREHEAD WITH A NEEDLE!
OWW... THAT HAD TO HURT!
HEY!

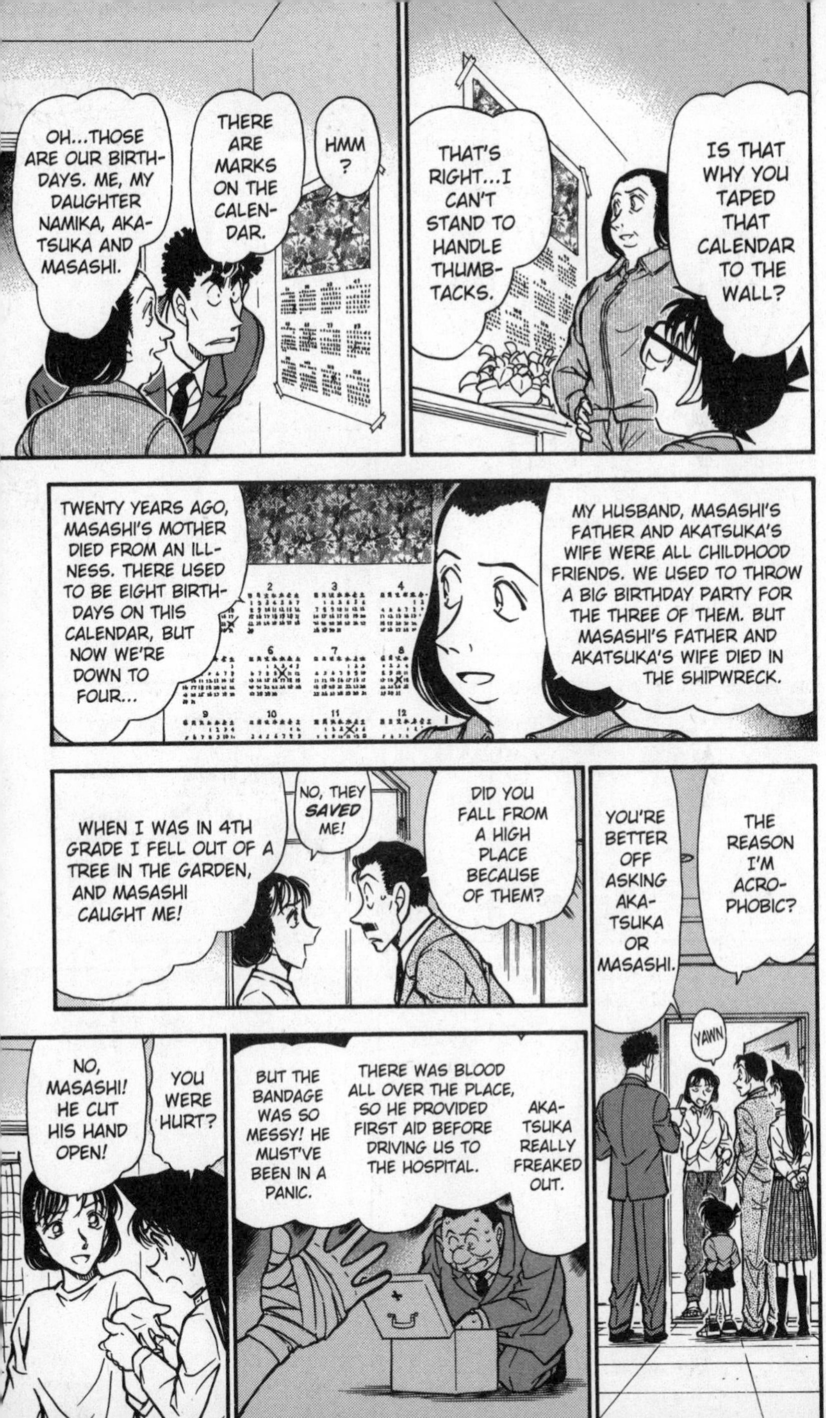
IS THAT WHY YOU TAPED THAT CALENDAR TO THE WALL?
THAT'S RIGHT...I CAN'T STAND TO HANDLE THUMBTACKS.
HMM?
THERE ARE MARKS ON THE CALENDAR.
OH...THOSE ARE OUR BIRTHDAYS. ME, MY DAUGHTER NAMIKA, AKATSUKA AND MASASHI.
MY HUSBAND, MASASHI'S FATHER AND AKATSUKA'S WIFE WERE ALL CHILDHOOD FRIENDS. WE USED TO THROW A BIG BIRTHDAY PARTY FOR THE THREE OF THEM. BUT MASASHI'S FATHER AND AKATSUKA'S WIFE DIED IN THE SHIPWRECK.
TWENTY YEARS AGO, MASASHI'S MOTHER DIED FROM AN ILLNESS. THERE USED TO BE EIGHT BIRTHDAYS ON THIS CALENDAR, BUT NOW WE'RE DOWN TO FOUR...
THE REASON I'M ACROPHOBIC?
YOU'RE BETTER OFF ASKING AKATSUKA OR MASASHI.
YAWN
DID YOU FALL FROM A HIGH PLACE BECAUSE OF THEM?
NO, THEY *SAVED* ME!
WHEN I WAS IN 4TH GRADE I FELL OUT OF A TREE IN THE GARDEN, AND MASASHI CAUGHT ME!
AKATSUKA REALLY FREAKED OUT.
THERE WAS BLOOD ALL OVER THE PLACE, SO HE PROVIDED FIRST AID BEFORE DRIVING US TO THE HOSPITAL.
BUT THE BANDAGE WAS SO MESSY! HE MUST'VE BEEN IN A PANIC.
YOU WERE HURT?
NO, MASASHI! HE CUT HIS HAND OPEN!

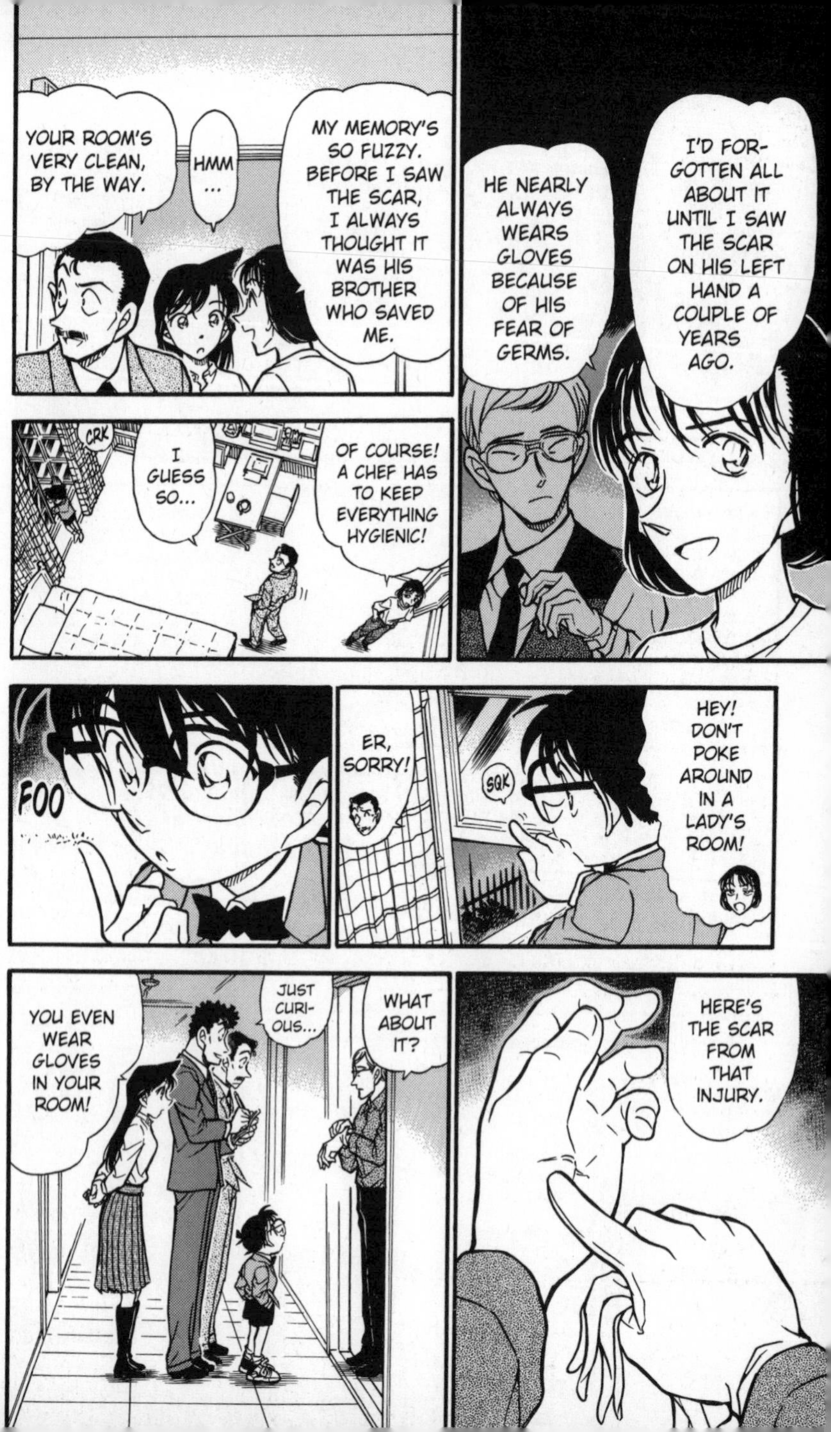
I'D FOR-GOTTEN ALL ABOUT IT UNTIL I SAW THE SCAR ON HIS LEFT HAND A COUPLE OF YEARS AGO.
HE NEARLY ALWAYS WEARS GLOVES BECAUSE OF HIS FEAR OF GERMS.
MY MEMORY'S SO FUZZY. BEFORE I SAW THE SCAR, I ALWAYS THOUGHT IT WAS HIS BROTHER WHO SAVED ME.
HMM ...
YOUR ROOM'S VERY CLEAN, BY THE WAY.
OF COURSE! A CHEF HAS TO KEEP EVERYTHING HYGIENIC!
I GUESS SO...
CRK
HEY! DON'T POKE AROUND IN A LADY'S ROOM!
SQK
ER, SORRY!
FOO
HERE'S THE SCAR FROM THAT INJURY.
WHAT ABOUT IT?
JUST CURI-OUS...
YOU EVEN WEAR GLOVES IN YOUR ROOM!

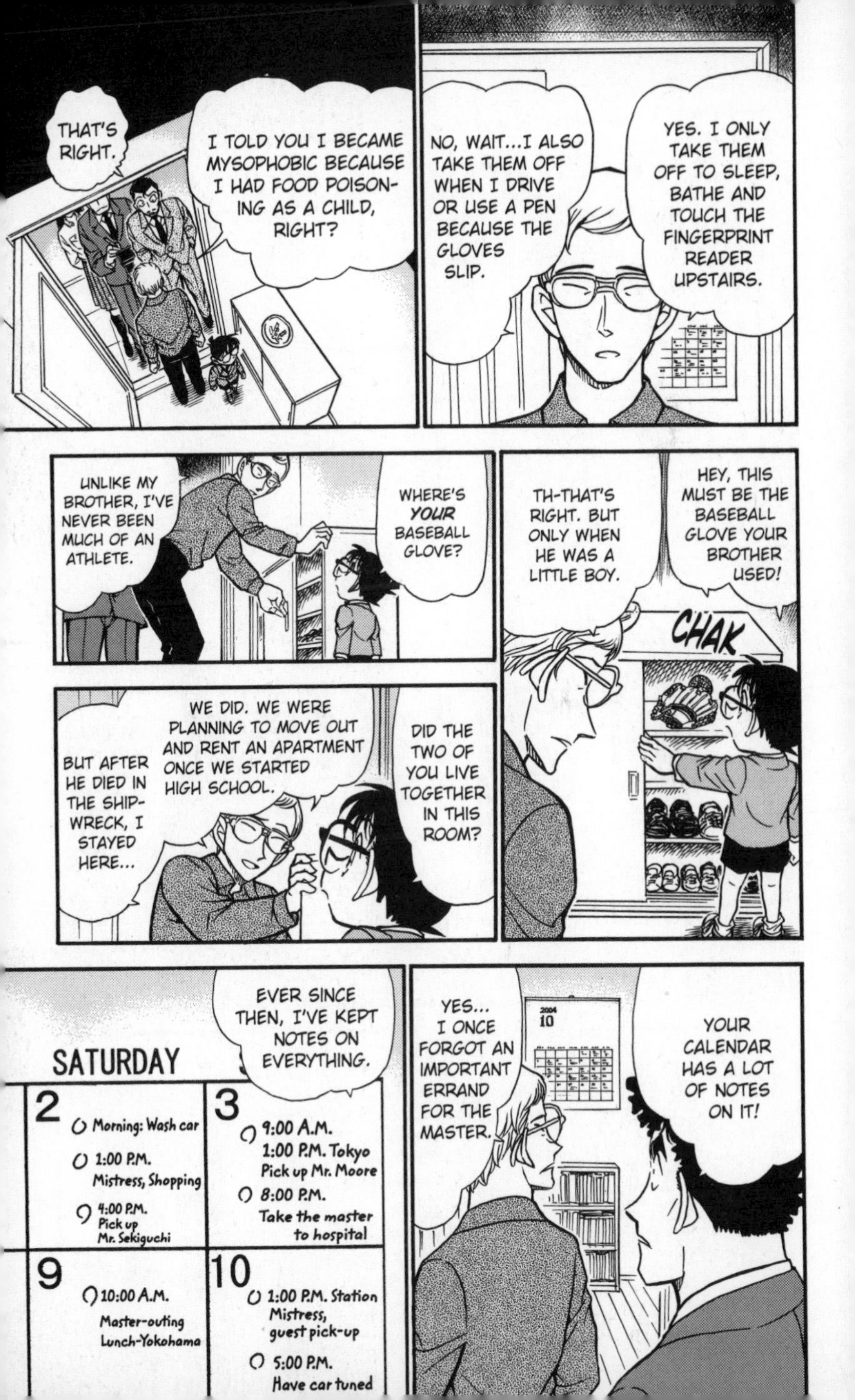

YES. I ONLY TAKE THEM OFF TO SLEEP, BATHE AND TOUCH THE FINGERPRINT READER UPSTAIRS.
NO, WAIT...I ALSO TAKE THEM OFF WHEN I DRIVE OR USE A PEN BECAUSE THE GLOVES SLIP.
I TOLD YOU I BECAME MYSOPHOBIC BECAUSE I HAD FOOD POISONING AS A CHILD, RIGHT?
THAT'S RIGHT.
HEY, THIS MUST BE THE BASEBALL GLOVE YOUR BROTHER USED!
CHAK
TH-THAT'S RIGHT. BUT ONLY WHEN HE WAS A LITTLE BOY.
WHERE'S *YOUR* BASEBALL GLOVE?
UNLIKE MY BROTHER, I'VE NEVER BEEN MUCH OF AN ATHLETE.
DID THE TWO OF YOU LIVE TOGETHER IN THIS ROOM?
WE DID. WE WERE PLANNING TO MOVE OUT AND RENT AN APARTMENT ONCE WE STARTED HIGH SCHOOL.
BUT AFTER HE DIED IN THE SHIPWRECK, I STAYED HERE...
YOUR CALENDAR HAS A LOT OF NOTES ON IT!
2004
10
YES... I ONCE FORGOT AN IMPORTANT ERRAND FOR THE MASTER.
EVER SINCE THEN, I'VE KEPT NOTES ON EVERYTHING.
SATURDAY
2
Morning: Wash car
1:00 P.M. Mistress, Shopping
4:00 P.M. Pick up Mr. Sekiguchi
3
9:00 A.M. 1:00 P.M. Tokyo Pick up Mr. Moore
8:00 P.M. Take the master to hospital
9
10:00 A.M. Master-outing Lunch-Yokohama
10
1:00 P.M. Station Mistress, guest pick-up
5:00 P.M. Have car tuned

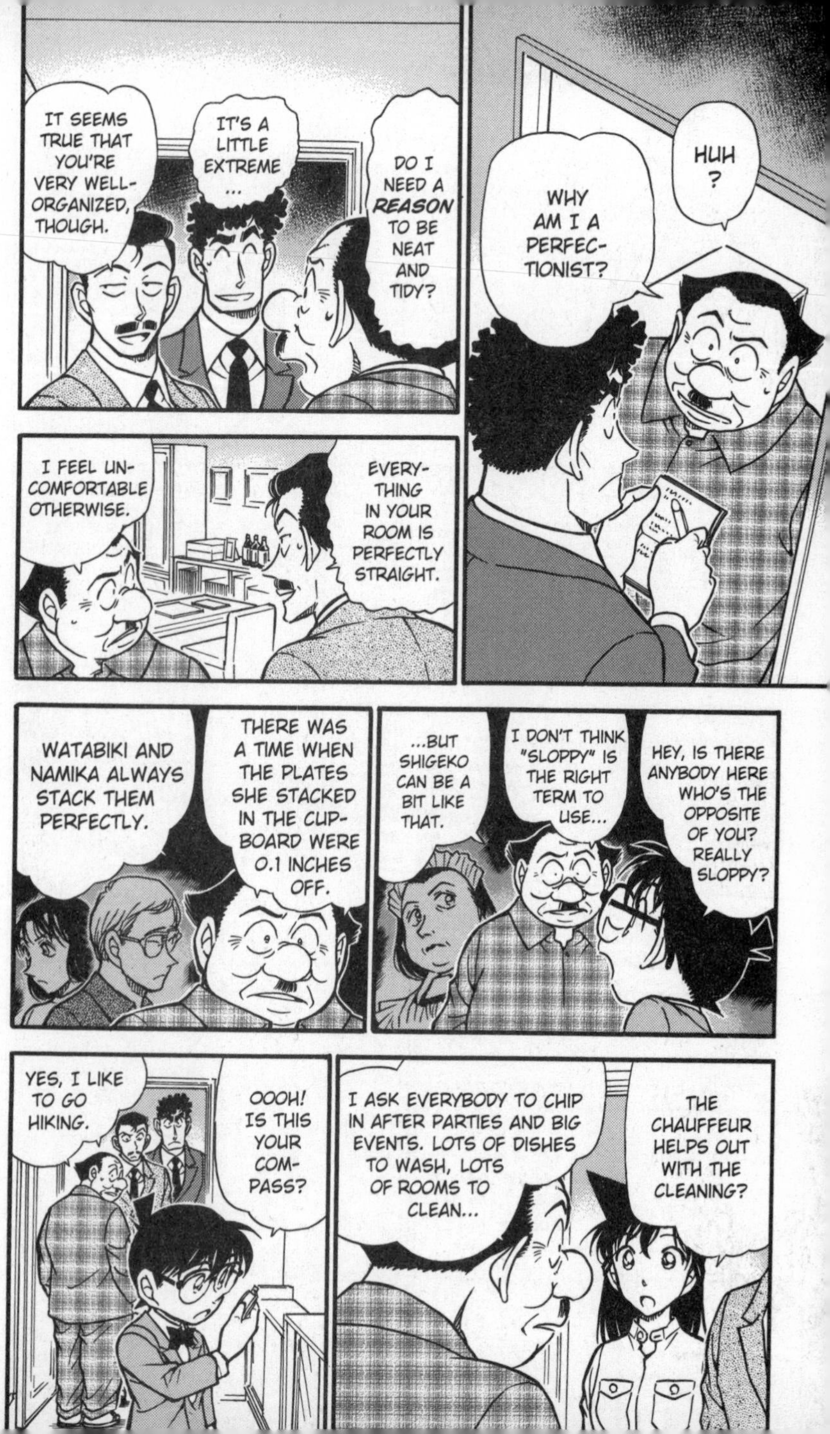
HUH?
WHY AM I A PERFECTIONIST?
DO I NEED A REASON TO BE NEAT AND TIDY?
IT'S A LITTLE EXTREME...
IT SEEMS TRUE THAT YOU'RE VERY WELL-ORGANIZED, THOUGH.
EVERYTHING IN YOUR ROOM IS PERFECTLY STRAIGHT.
I FEEL UNCOMFORTABLE OTHERWISE.
HEY, IS THERE ANYBODY HERE WHO'S THE OPPOSITE OF YOU? REALLY SLOPPY?
I DON'T THINK "SLOPPY" IS THE RIGHT TERM TO USE...
...BUT SHIGEKO CAN BE A BIT LIKE THAT.
THERE WAS A TIME WHEN THE PLATES SHE STACKED IN THE CUPBOARD WERE 0.1 INCHES OFF.
WATABIKI AND NAMIKA ALWAYS STACK THEM PERFECTLY.
THE CHAUFFEUR HELPS OUT WITH THE CLEANING?
I ASK EVERYBODY TO CHIP IN AFTER PARTIES AND BIG EVENTS. LOTS OF DISHES TO WASH, LOTS OF ROOMS TO CLEAN...
OOOH! IS THIS YOUR COMPASS?
YES, I LIKE TO GO HIKING.

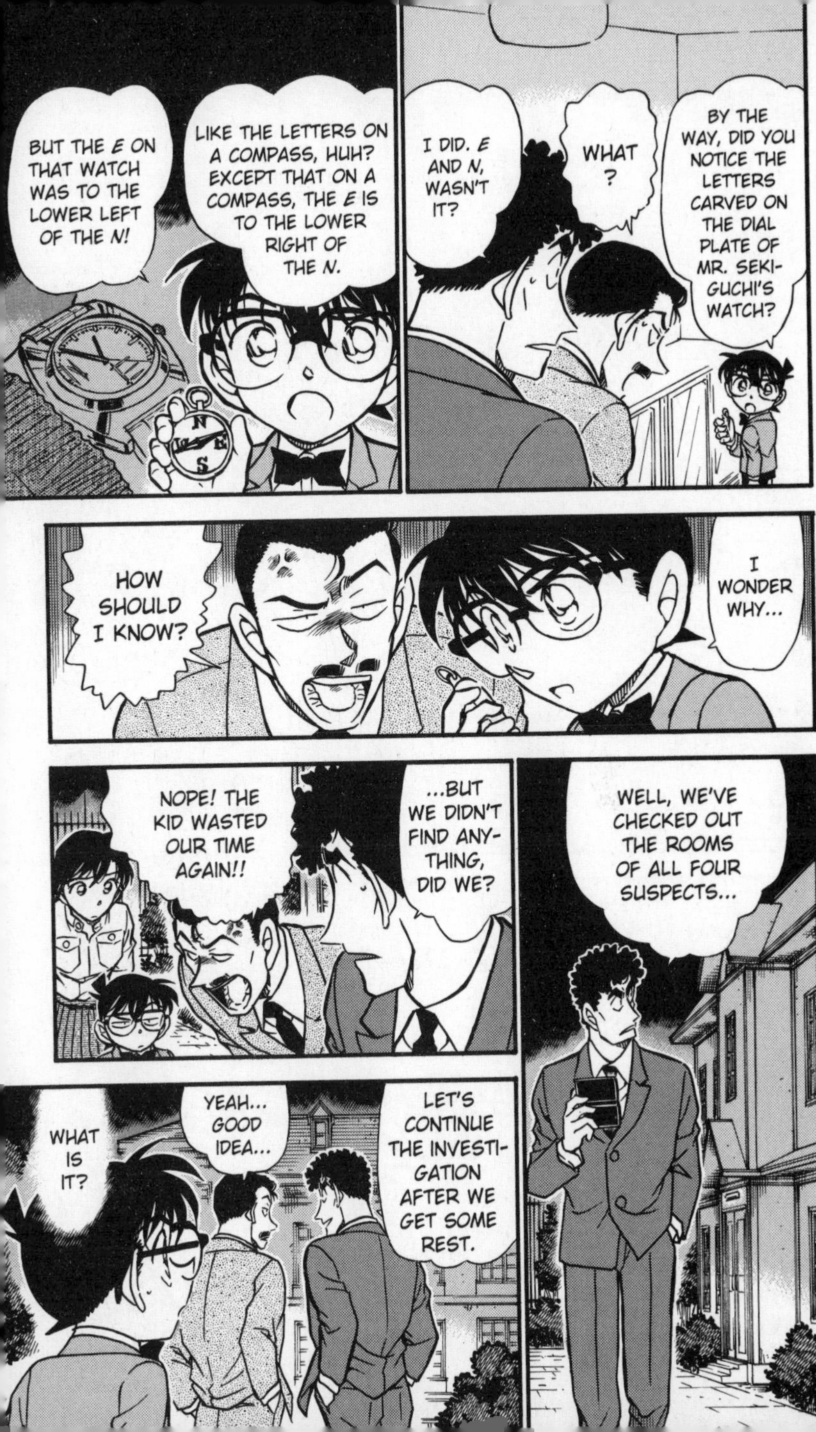
BY THE WAY, DID YOU NOTICE THE LETTERS CARVED ON THE DIAL PLATE OF MR. SEKI-GUCHI'S WATCH?
WHAT?
I DID. *E* AND *N*, WASN'T IT?
LIKE THE LETTERS ON A COMPASS, HUH? EXCEPT THAT ON A COMPASS, THE *E* IS TO THE LOWER RIGHT OF THE *N*.
BUT THE *E* ON THAT WATCH WAS TO THE LOWER LEFT OF THE *N*!
I WONDER WHY...
HOW SHOULD I KNOW?
WELL, WE'VE CHECKED OUT THE ROOMS OF ALL FOUR SUSPECTS...
...BUT WE DIDN'T FIND ANY-THING, DID WE?
NOPE! THE KID WASTED OUR TIME AGAIN!!
LET'S CONTINUE THE INVESTI-GATION AFTER WE GET SOME REST.
YEAH... GOOD IDEA...
WHAT IS IT?

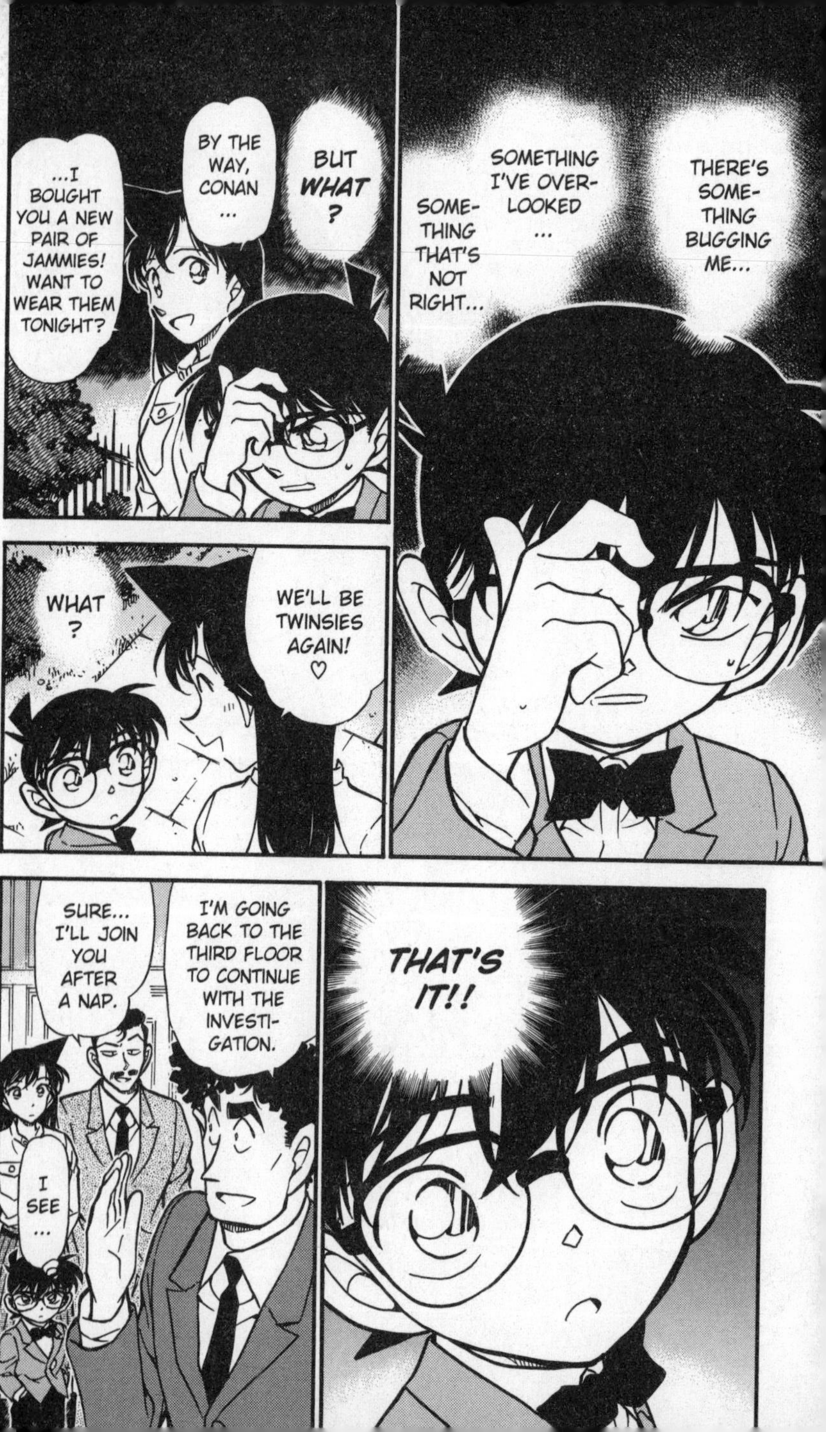
THERE'S SOMETHING BUGGING ME...
SOMETHING I'VE OVERLOOKED...
SOMETHING THAT'S NOT RIGHT...
BUT *WHAT*?
BY THE WAY, CONAN...
...I BOUGHT YOU A NEW PAIR OF JAMMIES! WANT TO WEAR THEM TONIGHT?
WE'LL BE TWINSIES AGAIN! ♡
WHAT?
THAT'S IT!!
I'M GOING BACK TO THE THIRD FLOOR TO CONTINUE WITH THE INVESTIGATION.
SURE... I'LL JOIN YOU AFTER A NAP.
I SEE...

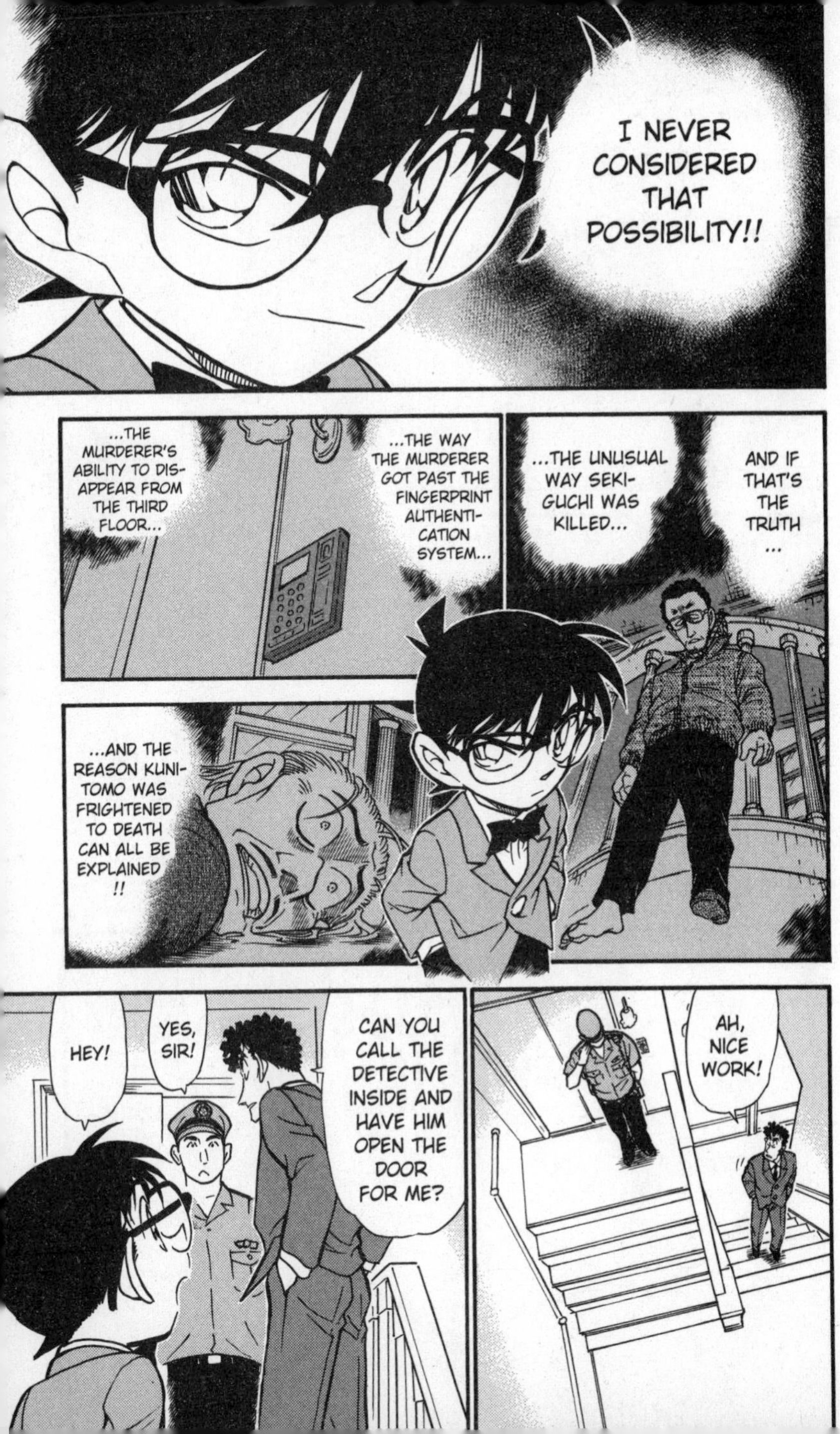
I NEVER CONSIDERED THAT POSSIBILITY!!
AND IF THAT'S THE TRUTH ...
...THE UNUSUAL WAY SEKI-GUCHI WAS KILLED...
...THE WAY THE MURDERER GOT PAST THE FINGERPRINT AUTHENTI-CATION SYSTEM...
...THE MURDERER'S ABILITY TO DIS-APPEAR FROM THE THIRD FLOOR...
...AND THE REASON KUNI-TOMO WAS FRIGHTENED TO DEATH CAN ALL BE EXPLAINED !!
AH, NICE WORK!
CAN YOU CALL THE DETECTIVE INSIDE AND HAVE HIM OPEN THE DOOR FOR ME?
YES, SIR!
HEY!

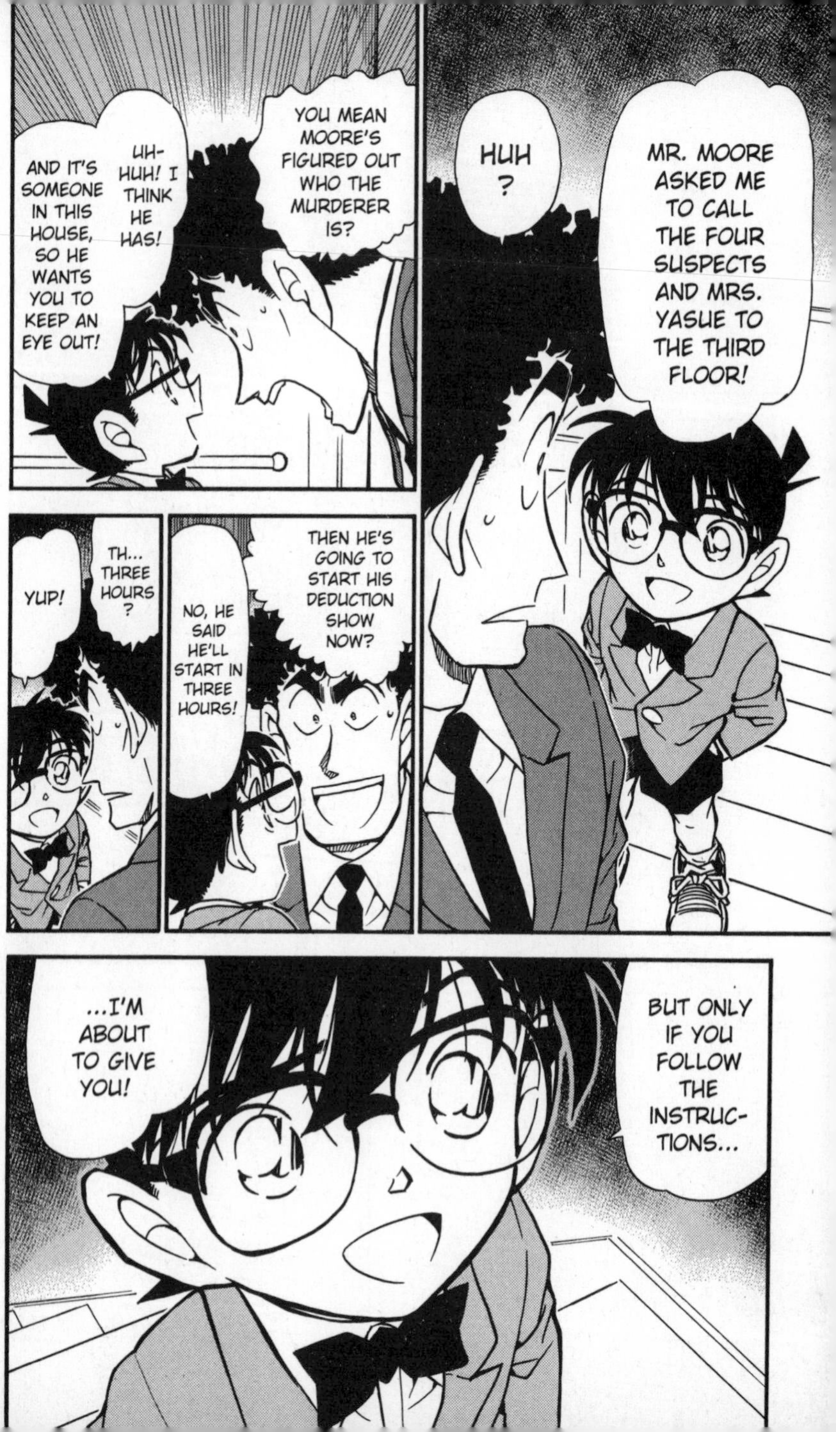
MR. MOORE ASKED ME TO CALL THE FOUR SUSPECTS AND MRS. YASUE TO THE THIRD FLOOR!
HUH?
YOU MEAN MOORE'S FIGURED OUT WHO THE MURDERER IS?
UH-HUH! I THINK HE HAS!
AND IT'S SOMEONE IN THIS HOUSE, SO HE WANTS YOU TO KEEP AN EYE OUT!
THEN HE'S GOING TO START HIS DEDUCTION SHOW NOW?
NO, HE SAID HE'LL START IN THREE HOURS!
TH... THREE HOURS?
YUP!
BUT ONLY IF YOU FOLLOW THE INSTRUCTIONS...
...I'M ABOUT TO GIVE YOU!

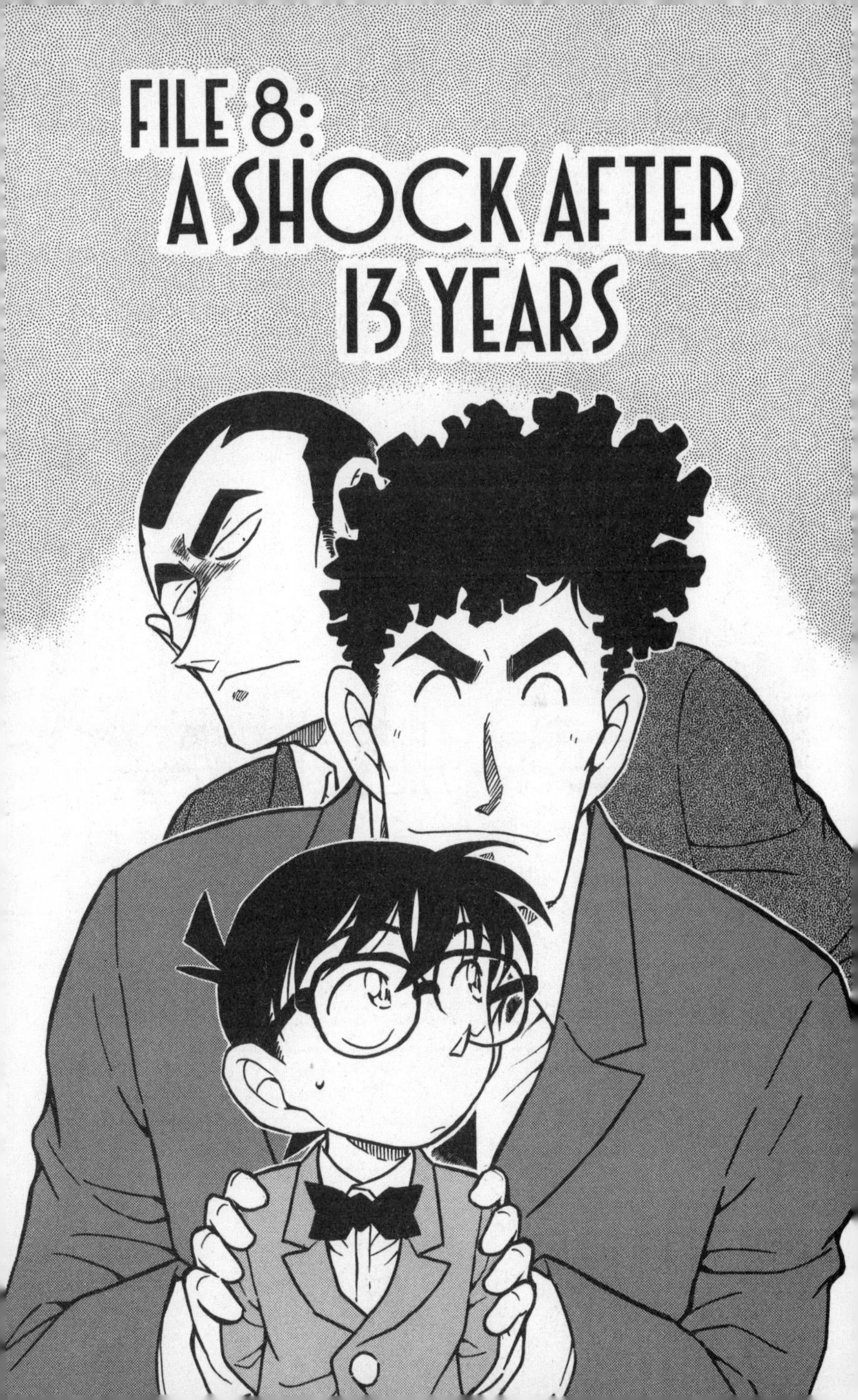
FILE 8:
A SHOCK AFTER
13 YEARS

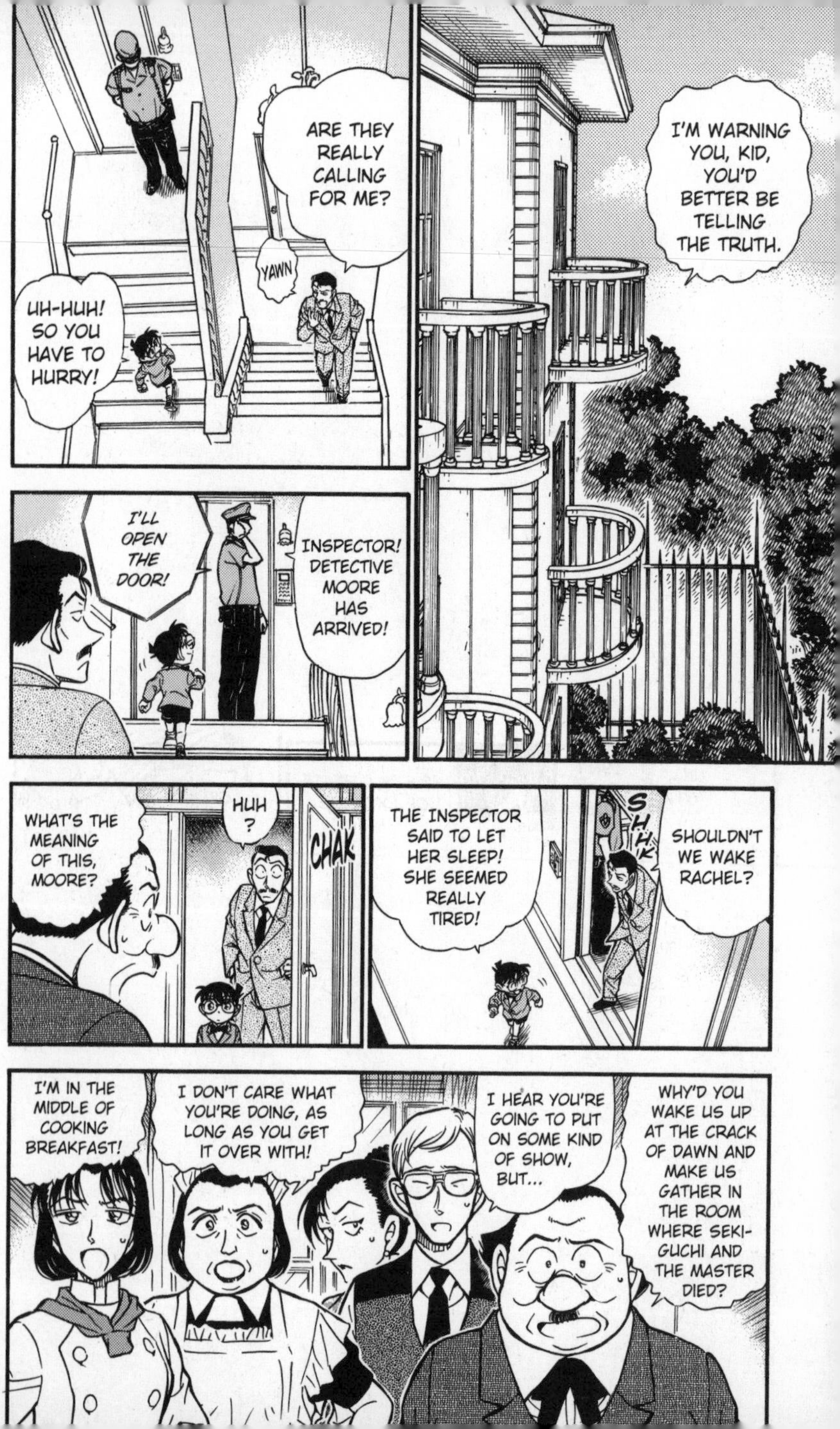
I'M WARNING YOU, KID, YOU'D BETTER BE TELLING THE TRUTH.
ARE THEY REALLY CALLING FOR ME?
YAWN
UH-HUH! SO YOU HAVE TO HURRY!
INSPECTOR! DETECTIVE MOORE HAS ARRIVED!
I'LL OPEN THE DOOR!
SHOULDN'T WE WAKE RACHEL?
SHHK
THE INSPECTOR SAID TO LET HER SLEEP! SHE SEEMED REALLY TIRED!
CHAK
HUH?
WHAT'S THE MEANING OF THIS, MOORE?
WHY'D YOU WAKE US UP AT THE CRACK OF DAWN AND MAKE US GATHER IN THE ROOM WHERE SEKI-GUCHI AND THE MASTER DIED?
I HEAR YOU'RE GOING TO PUT ON SOME KIND OF SHOW, BUT...
I DON'T CARE WHAT YOU'RE DOING, AS LONG AS YOU GET IT OVER WITH!
I'M IN THE MIDDLE OF COOKING BREAKFAST!

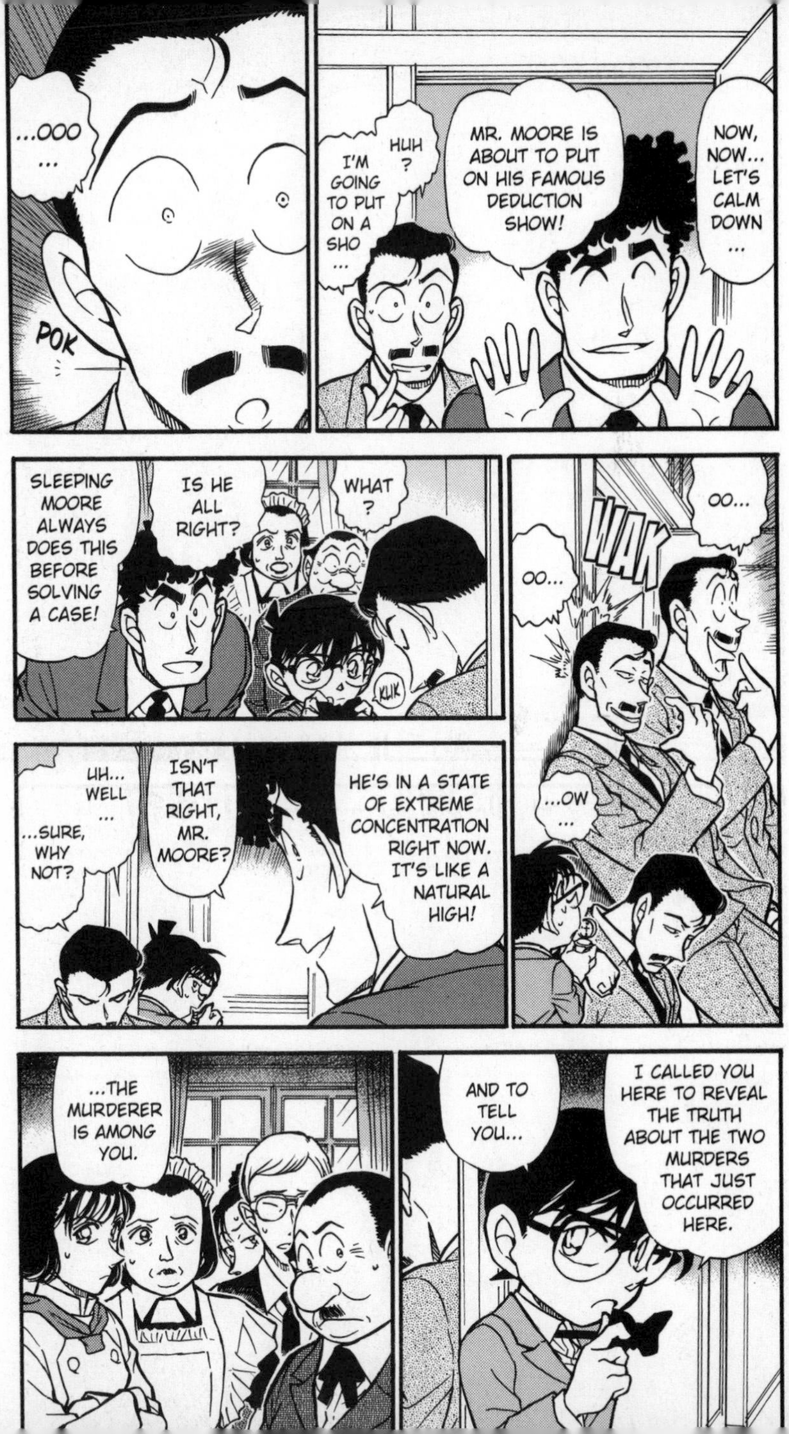
NOW, NOW... LET'S CALM DOWN...
MR. MOORE IS ABOUT TO PUT ON HIS FAMOUS DEDUCTION SHOW!
HUH?
I'M GOING TO PUT ON A SHO...
POK
...OOO...
OO...
WAK
OO...
...OW...
WHAT?
IS HE ALL RIGHT?
SLEEPING MOORE ALWAYS DOES THIS BEFORE SOLVING A CASE!
KLIK
HE'S IN A STATE OF EXTREME CONCENTRATION RIGHT NOW. IT'S LIKE A NATURAL HIGH!
ISN'T THAT RIGHT, MR. MOORE?
UH... WELL...
...SURE, WHY NOT?
I CALLED YOU HERE TO REVEAL THE TRUTH ABOUT THE TWO MURDERS THAT JUST OCCURRED HERE.
AND TO TELL YOU...
...THE MURDERER IS AMONG YOU.

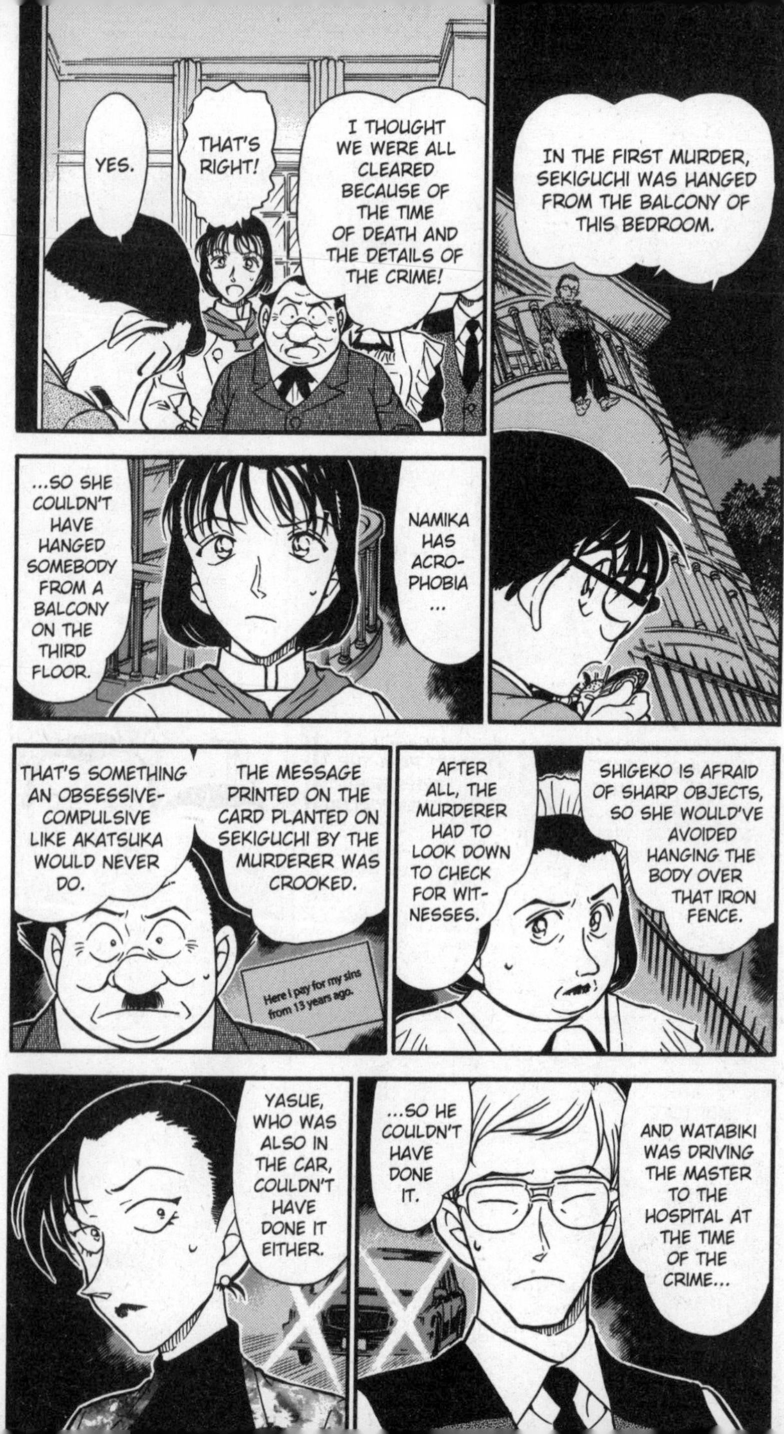
IN THE FIRST MURDER, SEKIGUCHI WAS HANGED FROM THE BALCONY OF THIS BEDROOM.
I THOUGHT WE WERE ALL CLEARED BECAUSE OF THE TIME OF DEATH AND THE DETAILS OF THE CRIME!
THAT'S RIGHT!
YES.
NAMIKA HAS ACROPHOBIA...
...SO SHE COULDN'T HAVE HANGED SOMEBODY FROM A BALCONY ON THE THIRD FLOOR.
SHIGEKO IS AFRAID OF SHARP OBJECTS, SO SHE WOULD'VE AVOIDED HANGING THE BODY OVER THAT IRON FENCE.
AFTER ALL, THE MURDERER HAD TO LOOK DOWN TO CHECK FOR WITNESSES.
THE MESSAGE PRINTED ON THE CARD PLANTED ON SEKIGUCHI BY THE MURDERER WAS CROOKED.
THAT'S SOMETHING AN OBSESSIVE-COMPULSIVE LIKE AKATSUKA WOULD NEVER DO.
Here I pay for my sins from 13 years ago.
AND WATABIKI WAS DRIVING THE MASTER TO THE HOSPITAL AT THE TIME OF THE CRIME...
...SO HE COULDN'T HAVE DONE IT.
YASUE, WHO WAS ALSO IN THE CAR, COULDN'T HAVE DONE IT EITHER.

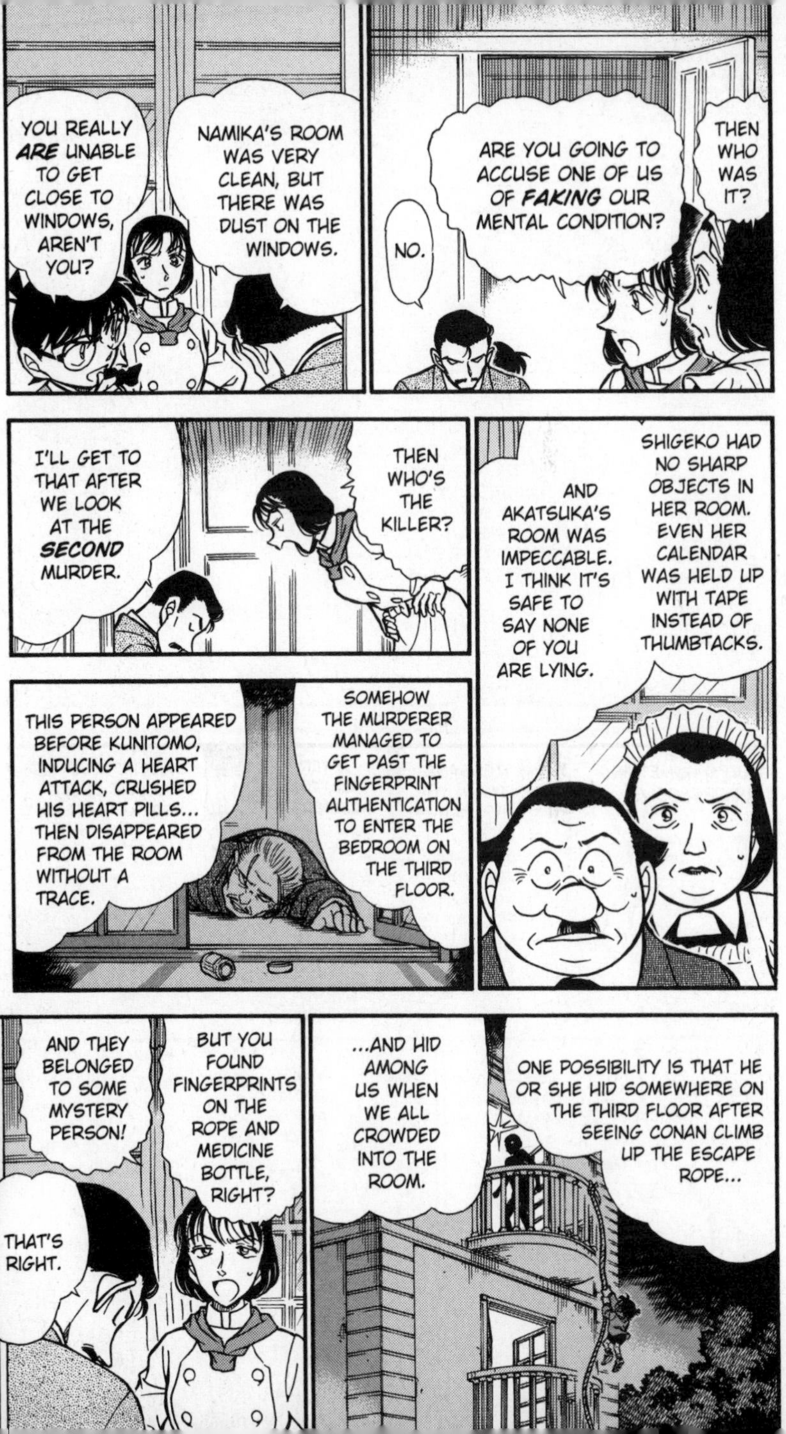
THEN WHO WAS IT?
ARE YOU GOING TO ACCUSE ONE OF US OF FAKING OUR MENTAL CONDITION?
NO.
NAMIKA'S ROOM WAS VERY CLEAN, BUT THERE WAS DUST ON THE WINDOWS.
YOU REALLY ARE UNABLE TO GET CLOSE TO WINDOWS, AREN'T YOU?
SHIGEKO HAD NO SHARP OBJECTS IN HER ROOM. EVEN HER CALENDAR WAS HELD UP WITH TAPE INSTEAD OF THUMBTACKS.
AND AKATSUKA'S ROOM WAS IMPECCABLE. I THINK IT'S SAFE TO SAY NONE OF YOU ARE LYING.
THEN WHO'S THE KILLER?
I'LL GET TO THAT AFTER WE LOOK AT THE SECOND MURDER.
SOMEHOW THE MURDERER MANAGED TO GET PAST THE FINGERPRINT AUTHENTICATION TO ENTER THE BEDROOM ON THE THIRD FLOOR.
THIS PERSON APPEARED BEFORE KUNITOMO, INDUCING A HEART ATTACK, CRUSHED HIS HEART PILLS... THEN DISAPPEARED FROM THE ROOM WITHOUT A TRACE.
ONE POSSIBILITY IS THAT HE OR SHE HID SOMEWHERE ON THE THIRD FLOOR AFTER SEEING CONAN CLIMB UP THE ESCAPE ROPE...
...AND HID AMONG US WHEN WE ALL CROWDED INTO THE ROOM.
BUT YOU FOUND FINGERPRINTS ON THE ROPE AND MEDICINE BOTTLE, RIGHT?
AND THEY BELONGED TO SOME MYSTERY PERSON!
THAT'S RIGHT.

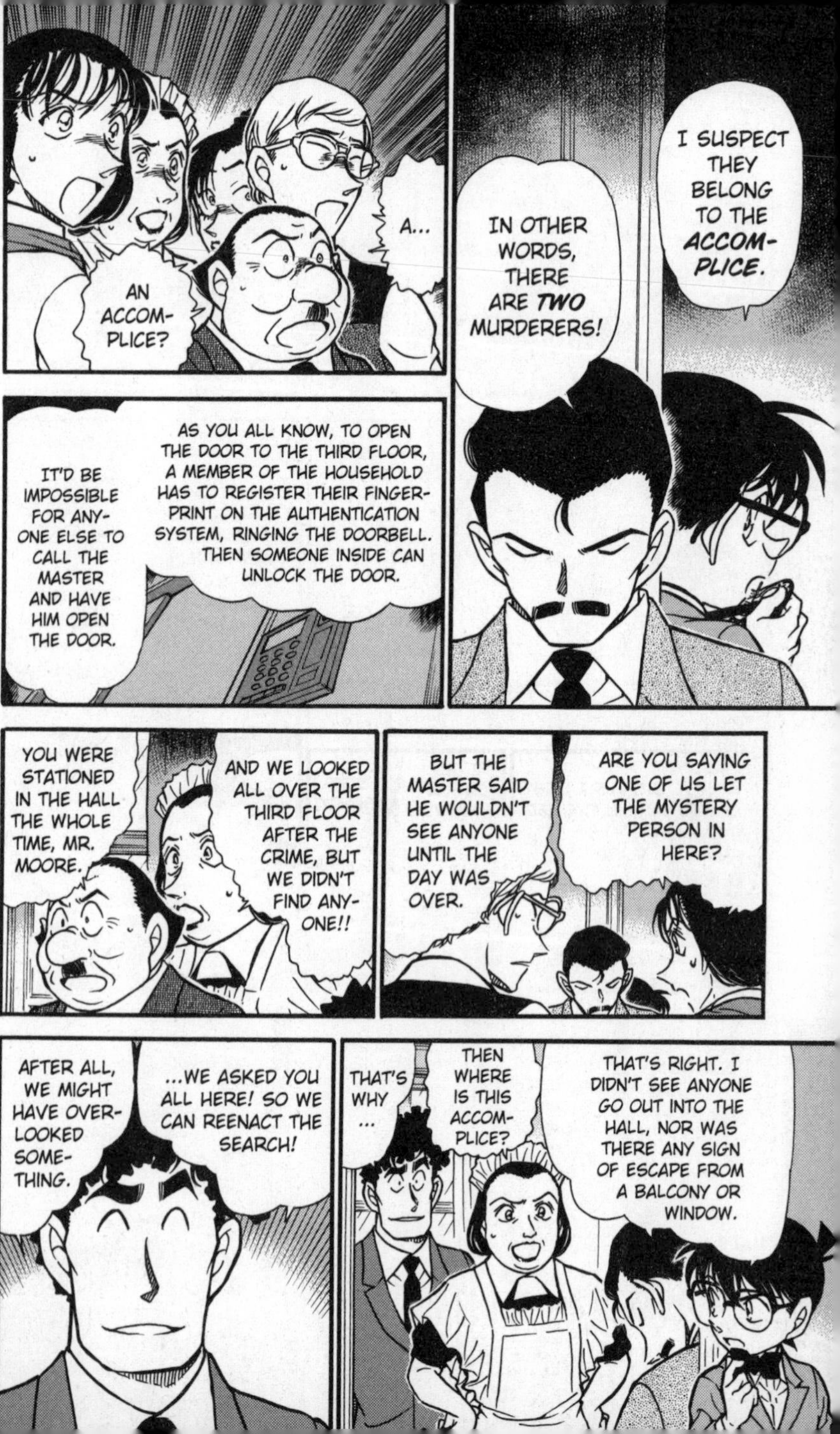

I SUSPECT THEY BELONG TO THE *ACCOMPLICE*.
IN OTHER WORDS, THERE ARE *TWO* MURDERERS!
A...
AN ACCOMPLICE?
AS YOU ALL KNOW, TO OPEN THE DOOR TO THE THIRD FLOOR, A MEMBER OF THE HOUSEHOLD HAS TO REGISTER THEIR FINGERPRINT ON THE AUTHENTICATION SYSTEM, RINGING THE DOORBELL. THEN SOMEONE INSIDE CAN UNLOCK THE DOOR.
IT'D BE IMPOSSIBLE FOR ANYONE ELSE TO CALL THE MASTER AND HAVE HIM OPEN THE DOOR.
ARE YOU SAYING ONE OF US LET THE MYSTERY PERSON IN HERE?
BUT THE MASTER SAID HE WOULDN'T SEE ANYONE UNTIL THE DAY WAS OVER.
AND WE LOOKED ALL OVER THE THIRD FLOOR AFTER THE CRIME, BUT WE DIDN'T FIND ANYONE!!
YOU WERE STATIONED IN THE HALL THE WHOLE TIME, MR. MOORE.
THAT'S RIGHT. I DIDN'T SEE ANYONE GO OUT INTO THE HALL, NOR WAS THERE ANY SIGN OF ESCAPE FROM A BALCONY OR WINDOW.
THEN WHERE IS THIS ACCOMPLICE?
THAT'S WHY ...
...WE ASKED YOU ALL HERE! SO WE CAN REENACT THE SEARCH!
AFTER ALL, WE MIGHT HAVE OVERLOOKED SOMETHING.

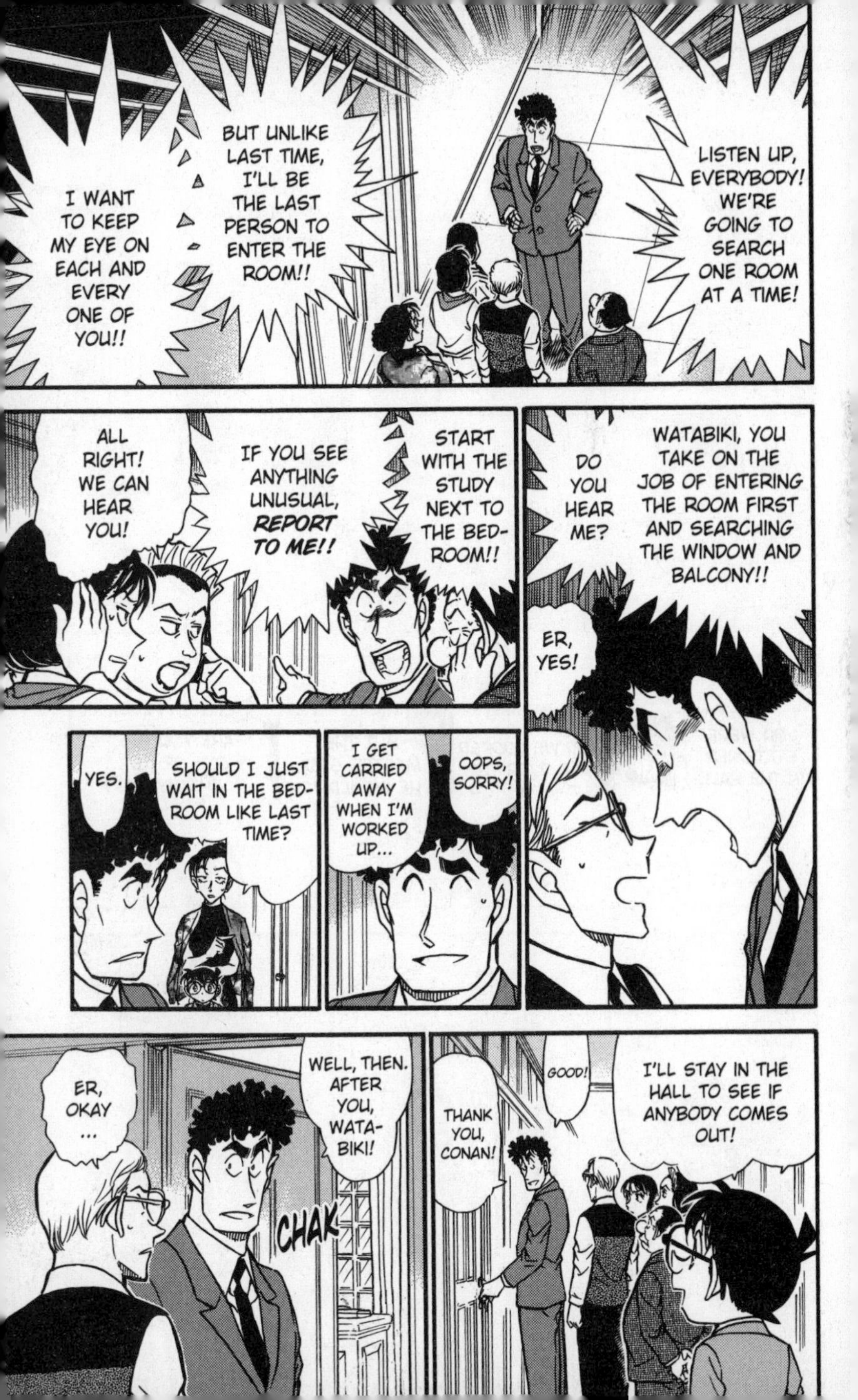
LISTEN UP, EVERYBODY! WE'RE GOING TO SEARCH ONE ROOM AT A TIME!
BUT UNLIKE LAST TIME, I'LL BE THE LAST PERSON TO ENTER THE ROOM!!
I WANT TO KEEP MY EYE ON EACH AND EVERY ONE OF YOU!!
WATABIKI, YOU TAKE ON THE JOB OF ENTERING THE ROOM FIRST AND SEARCHING THE WINDOW AND BALCONY!!
DO YOU HEAR ME?
ER, YES!
START WITH THE STUDY NEXT TO THE BED-ROOM!!
IF YOU SEE ANYTHING UNUSUAL, ***REPORT TO ME!!***
ALL RIGHT! WE CAN HEAR YOU!
OOPS, SORRY!
I GET CARRIED AWAY WHEN I'M WORKED UP...
SHOULD I JUST WAIT IN THE BED-ROOM LIKE LAST TIME?
YES.
I'LL STAY IN THE HALL TO SEE IF ANYBODY COMES OUT!
GOOD!
THANK YOU, CONAN!
WELL, THEN. AFTER YOU, WATA-BIKI!
CHAK
ER, OKAY ...

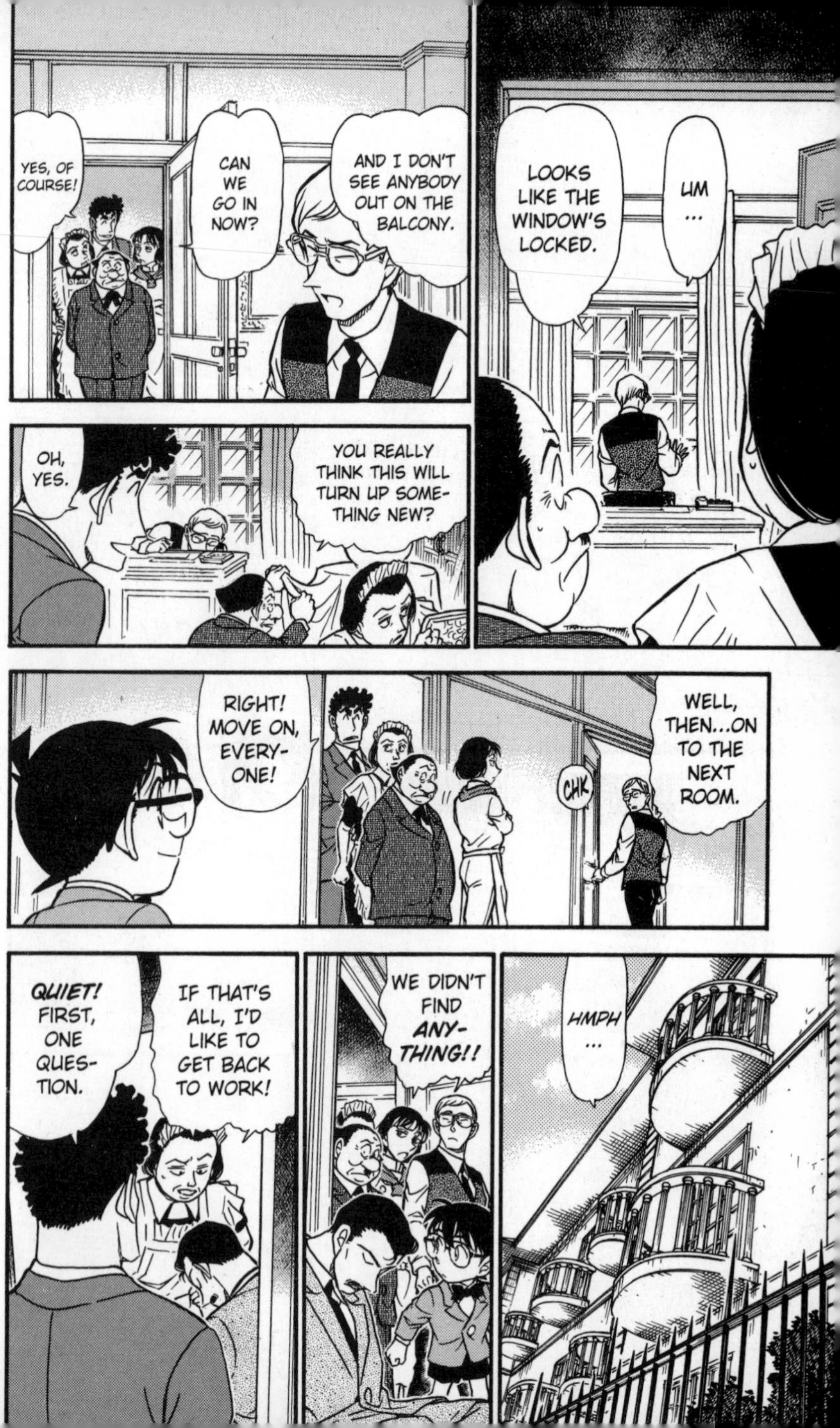
UM ...
LOOKS LIKE THE WINDOW'S LOCKED.
AND I DON'T SEE ANYBODY OUT ON THE BALCONY.
CAN WE GO IN NOW?
YES, OF COURSE!
YOU REALLY THINK THIS WILL TURN UP SOMETHING NEW?
OH, YES.
WELL, THEN...ON TO THE NEXT ROOM.
CHK
RIGHT! MOVE ON, EVERYONE!
HMPH ...
WE DIDN'T FIND *ANYTHING!!*
IF THAT'S ALL, I'D LIKE TO GET BACK TO WORK!
QUIET! FIRST, ONE QUESTION.

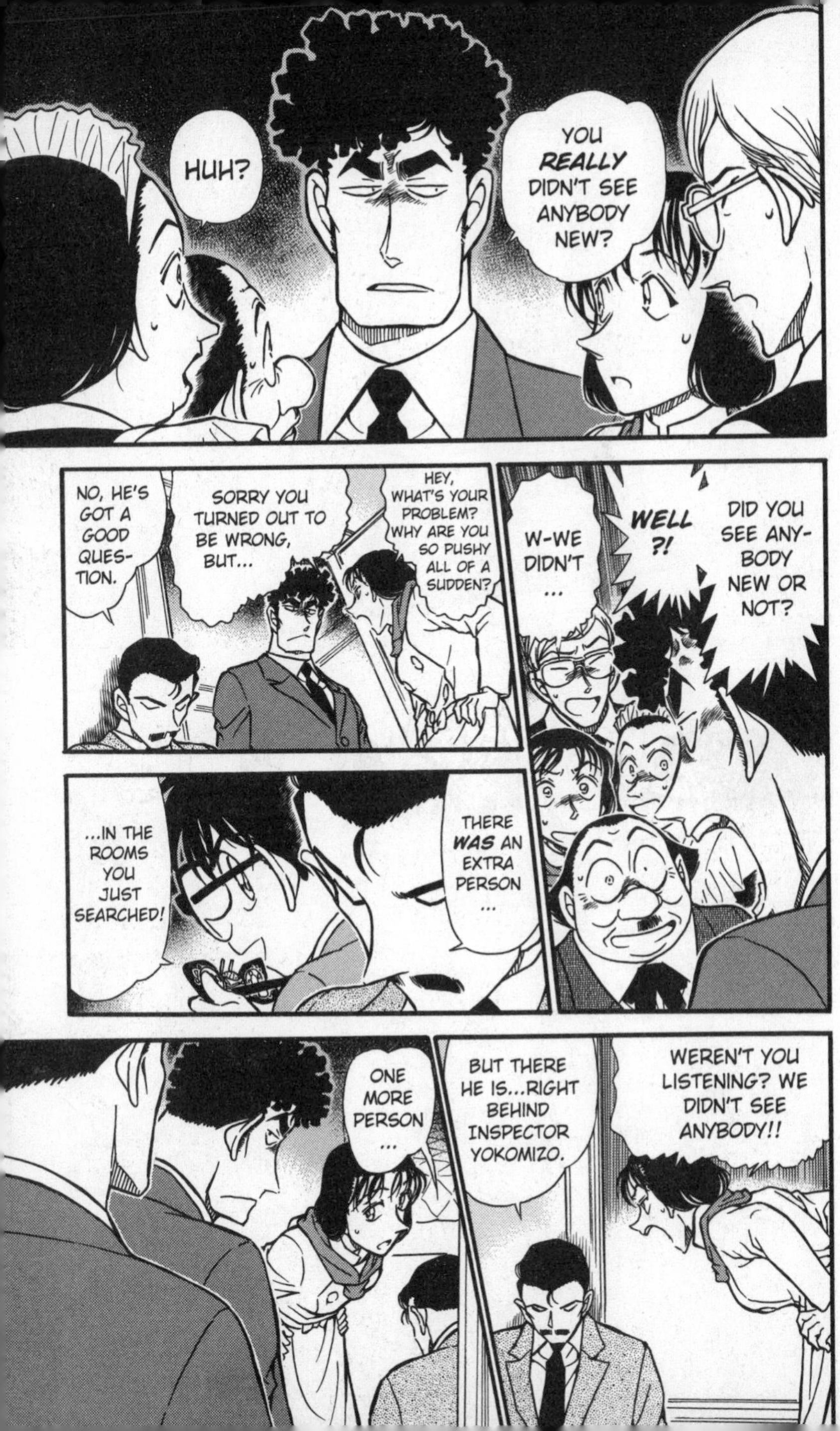
YOU REALLY DIDN'T SEE ANYBODY NEW?
HUH?
DID YOU SEE ANY-BODY NEW OR NOT?
WELL ?!
W-WE DIDN'T ...
HEY, WHAT'S YOUR PROBLEM? WHY ARE YOU SO PUSHY ALL OF A SUDDEN?
SORRY YOU TURNED OUT TO BE WRONG, BUT...
NO, HE'S GOT A GOOD QUES-TION.
THERE WAS AN EXTRA PERSON ...
...IN THE ROOMS YOU JUST SEARCHED!
WEREN'T YOU LISTENING? WE DIDN'T SEE ANYBODY!!
BUT THERE HE IS...RIGHT BEHIND INSPECTOR YOKOMIZO.
ONE MORE PERSON ...

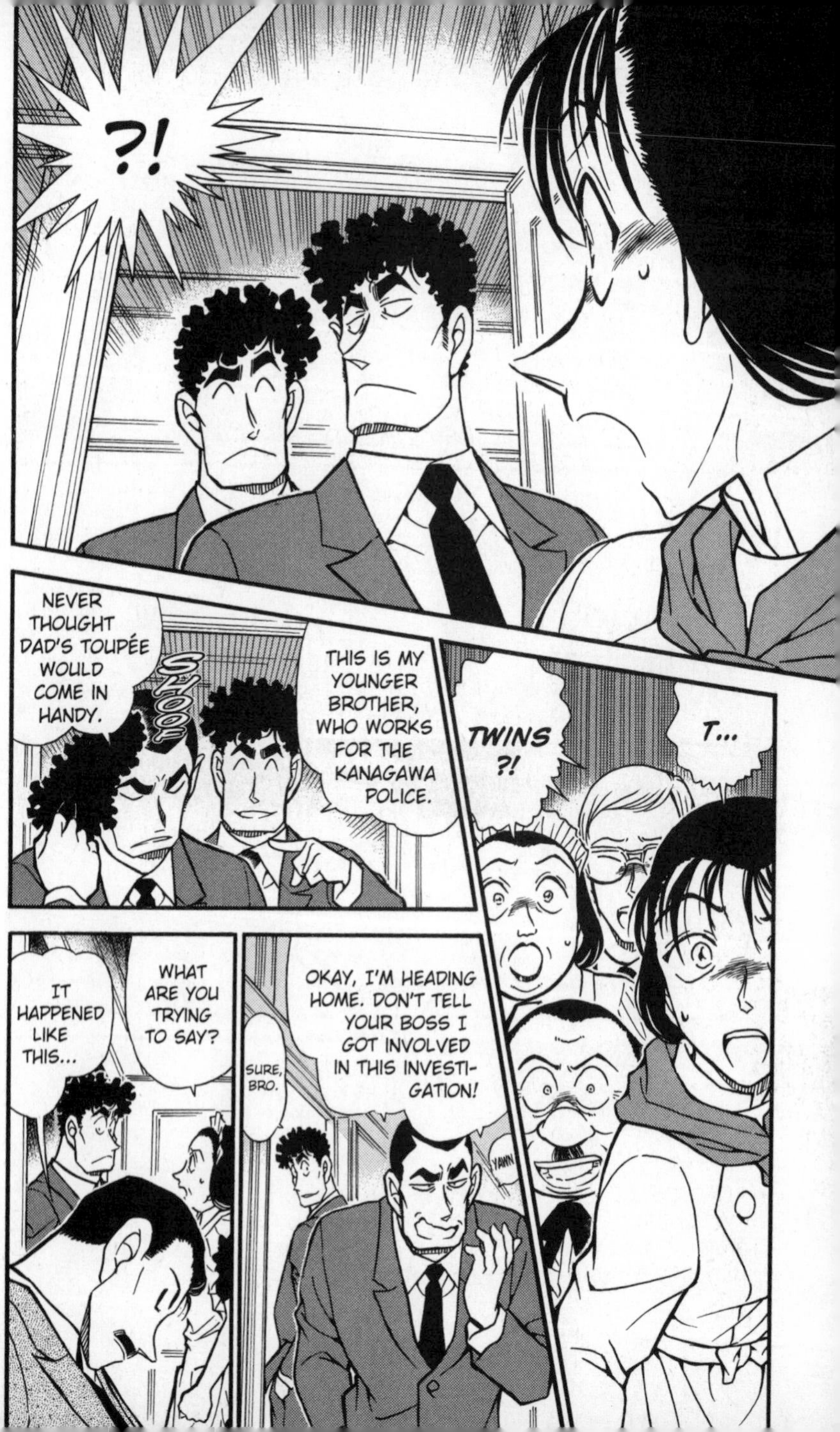
?!
T...
TWINS ?!
YAWN
THIS IS MY YOUNGER BROTHER, WHO WORKS FOR THE KANAGAWA POLICE.
SHOOP
NEVER THOUGHT DAD'S TOUPÉE WOULD COME IN HANDY.
OKAY, I'M HEADING HOME. DON'T TELL YOUR BOSS I GOT INVOLVED IN THIS INVESTIGATION!
SURE, BRO.
WHAT ARE YOU TRYING TO SAY?
IT HAPPENED LIKE THIS...

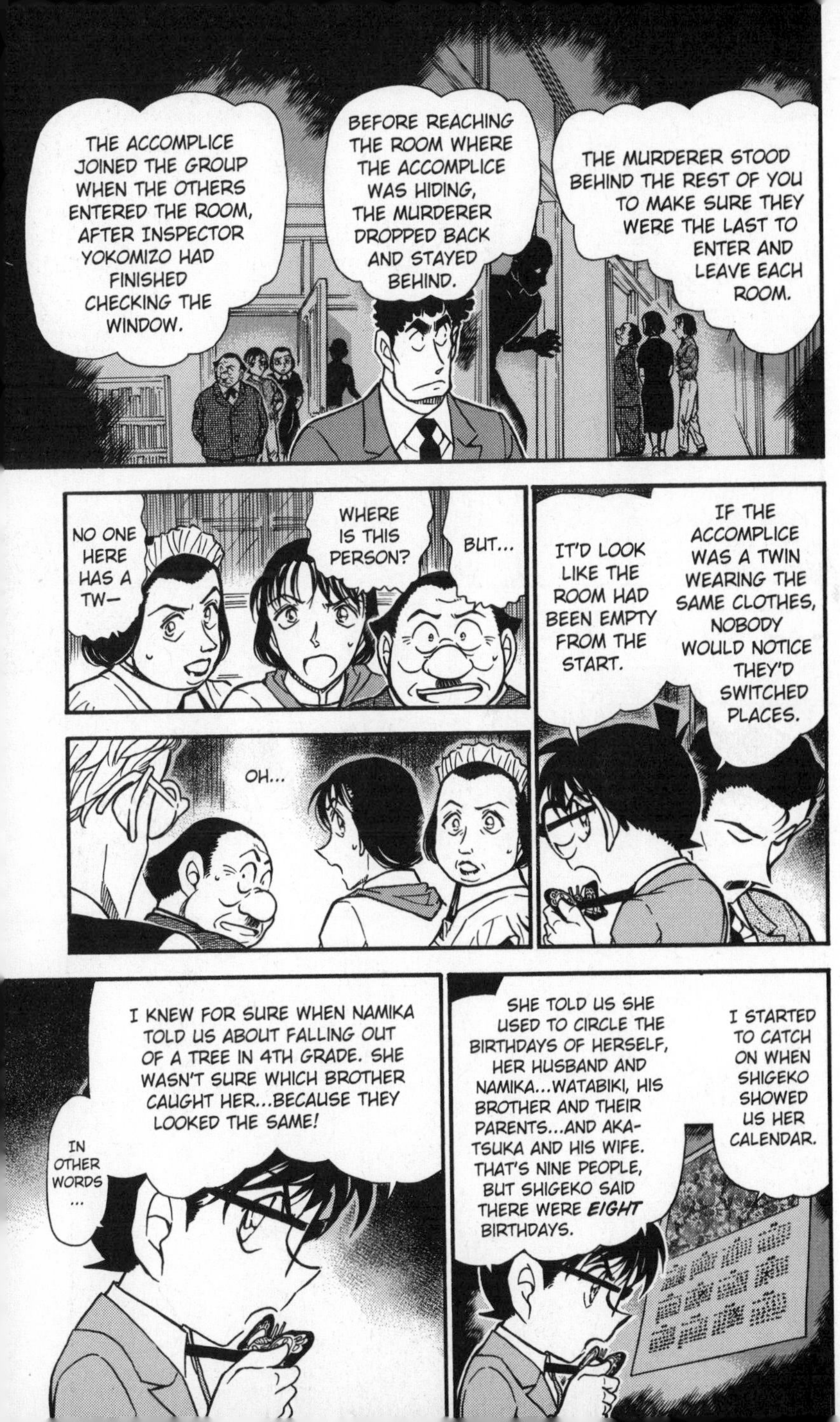
THE MURDERER STOOD BEHIND THE REST OF YOU TO MAKE SURE THEY WERE THE LAST TO ENTER AND LEAVE EACH ROOM.
BEFORE REACHING THE ROOM WHERE THE ACCOMPLICE WAS HIDING, THE MURDERER DROPPED BACK AND STAYED BEHIND.
THE ACCOMPLICE JOINED THE GROUP WHEN THE OTHERS ENTERED THE ROOM, AFTER INSPECTOR YOKOMIZO HAD FINISHED CHECKING THE WINDOW.
IF THE ACCOMPLICE WAS A TWIN WEARING THE SAME CLOTHES, NOBODY WOULD NOTICE THEY'D SWITCHED PLACES.
IT'D LOOK LIKE THE ROOM HAD BEEN EMPTY FROM THE START.
BUT...
WHERE IS THIS PERSON?
NO ONE HERE HAS A TW—
OH...
I STARTED TO CATCH ON WHEN SHIGEKO SHOWED US HER CALENDAR.
SHE TOLD US SHE USED TO CIRCLE THE BIRTHDAYS OF HERSELF, HER HUSBAND AND NAMIKA...WATABIKI, HIS BROTHER AND THEIR PARENTS...AND AKA-TSUKA AND HIS WIFE. THAT'S NINE PEOPLE, BUT SHIGEKO SAID THERE WERE *EIGHT* BIRTHDAYS.
I KNEW FOR SURE WHEN NAMIKA TOLD US ABOUT FALLING OUT OF A TREE IN 4TH GRADE. SHE WASN'T SURE WHICH BROTHER CAUGHT HER...BECAUSE THEY LOOKED THE SAME!
IN OTHER WORDS...

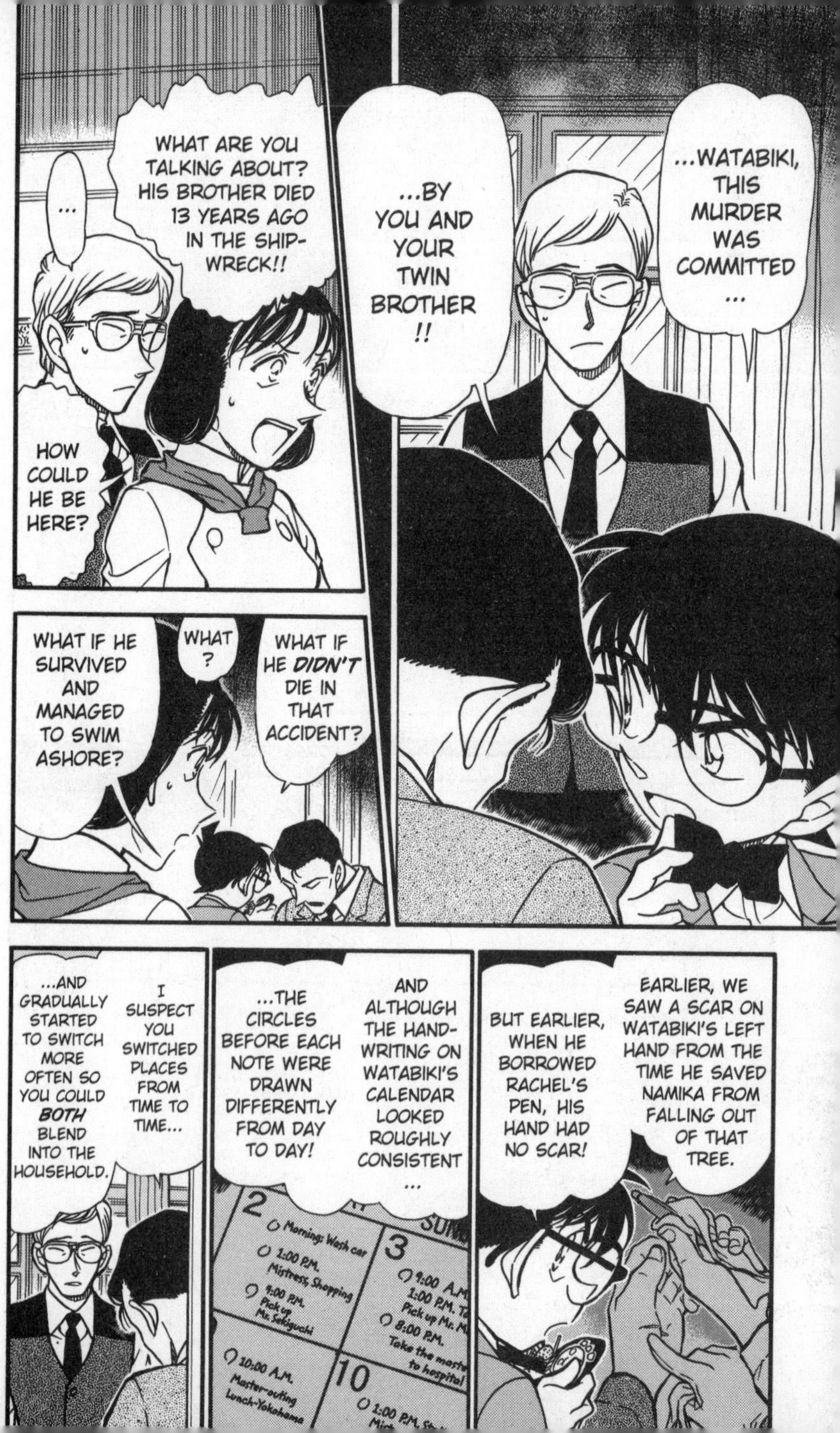
...WATABIKI, THIS MURDER WAS COMMITTED...
...BY YOU AND YOUR TWIN BROTHER!!
WHAT ARE YOU TALKING ABOUT? HIS BROTHER DIED 13 YEARS AGO IN THE SHIP-WRECK!!
...
HOW COULD HE BE HERE?
WHAT IF HE DIDN'T DIE IN THAT ACCIDENT?
WHAT?
WHAT IF HE SURVIVED AND MANAGED TO SWIM ASHORE?
EARLIER, WE SAW A SCAR ON WATABIKI'S LEFT HAND FROM THE TIME HE SAVED NAMIKA FROM FALLING OUT OF THAT TREE.
BUT EARLIER, WHEN HE BORROWED RACHEL'S PEN, HIS HAND HAD NO SCAR!
AND ALTHOUGH THE HAND-WRITING ON WATABIKI'S CALENDAR LOOKED ROUGHLY CONSISTENT...
...THE CIRCLES BEFORE EACH NOTE WERE DRAWN DIFFERENTLY FROM DAY TO DAY!
2
Morning: Wash car
1:00 P.M. Mistress, Shopping
4:00 P.M. Pick up Mr. Sekiguchi
3
9:00 A.M.
8:00 P.M. Take the master to hospital
10
10:00 A.M. Master-outing Lunch-Yokohama
I SUSPECT YOU SWITCHED PLACES FROM TIME TO TIME...
...AND GRADUALLY STARTED TO SWITCH MORE OFTEN SO YOU COULD BOTH BLEND INTO THE HOUSEHOLD.

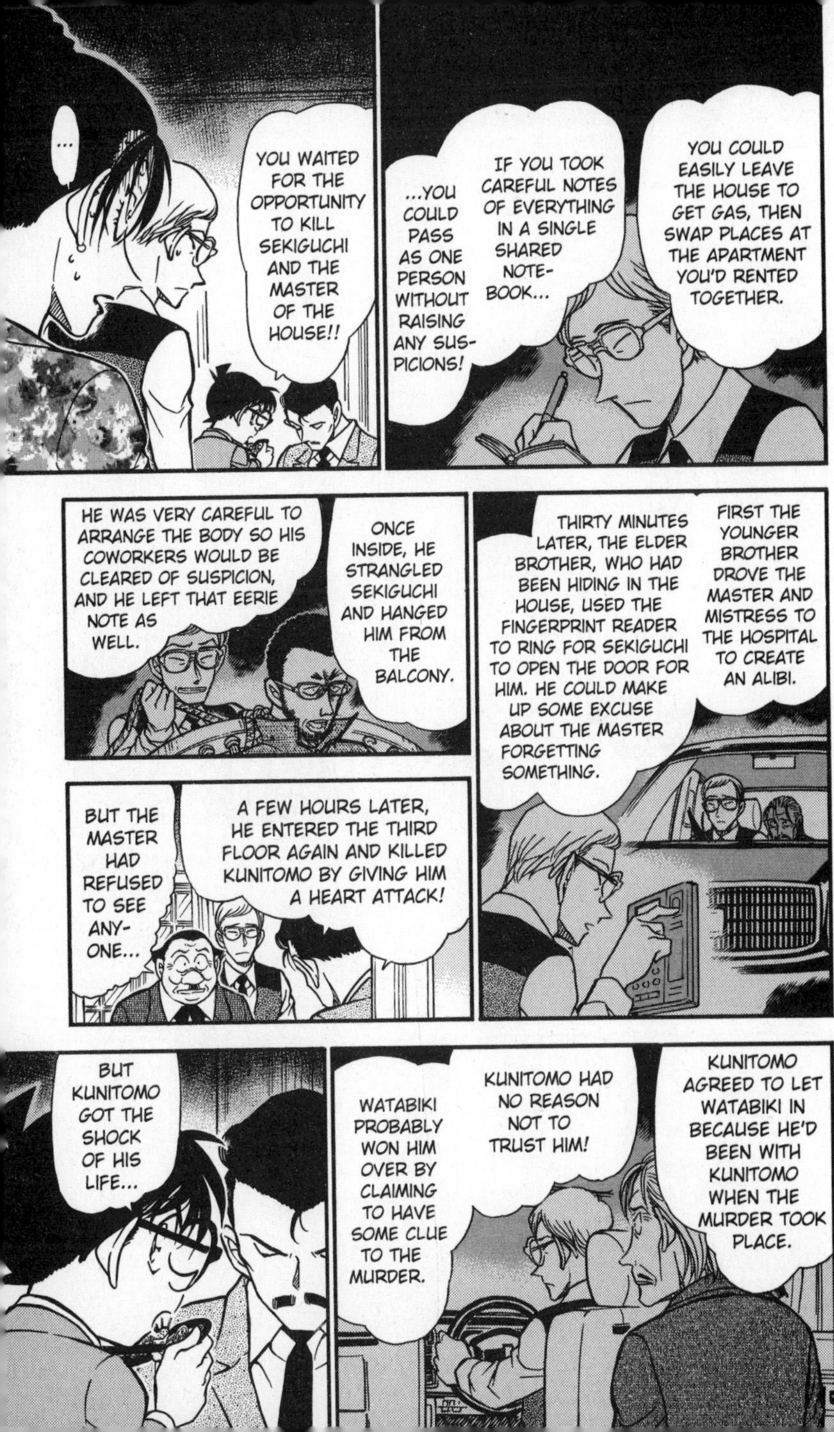
YOU COULD EASILY LEAVE THE HOUSE TO GET GAS, THEN SWAP PLACES AT THE APARTMENT YOU'D RENTED TOGETHER.
IF YOU TOOK CAREFUL NOTES OF EVERYTHING IN A SINGLE SHARED NOTE-BOOK...
...YOU COULD PASS AS ONE PERSON WITHOUT RAISING ANY SUS-PICIONS!
YOU WAITED FOR THE OPPORTUNITY TO KILL SEKIGUCHI AND THE MASTER OF THE HOUSE!!
...
FIRST THE YOUNGER BROTHER DROVE THE MASTER AND MISTRESS TO THE HOSPITAL TO CREATE AN ALIBI.
THIRTY MINUTES LATER, THE ELDER BROTHER, WHO HAD BEEN HIDING IN THE HOUSE, USED THE FINGERPRINT READER TO RING FOR SEKIGUCHI TO OPEN THE DOOR FOR HIM. HE COULD MAKE UP SOME EXCUSE ABOUT THE MASTER FORGETTING SOMETHING.
ONCE INSIDE, HE STRANGLED SEKIGUCHI AND HANGED HIM FROM THE BALCONY.
HE WAS VERY CAREFUL TO ARRANGE THE BODY SO HIS COWORKERS WOULD BE CLEARED OF SUSPICION, AND HE LEFT THAT EERIE NOTE AS WELL.
A FEW HOURS LATER, HE ENTERED THE THIRD FLOOR AGAIN AND KILLED KUNITOMO BY GIVING HIM A HEART ATTACK!
BUT THE MASTER HAD REFUSED TO SEE ANY-ONE...
KUNITOMO AGREED TO LET WATABIKI IN BECAUSE HE'D BEEN WITH KUNITOMO WHEN THE MURDER TOOK PLACE.
KUNITOMO HAD NO REASON NOT TO TRUST HIM!
WATABIKI PROBABLY WON HIM OVER BY CLAIMING TO HAVE SOME CLUE TO THE MURDER.
BUT KUNITOMO GOT THE SHOCK OF HIS LIFE...

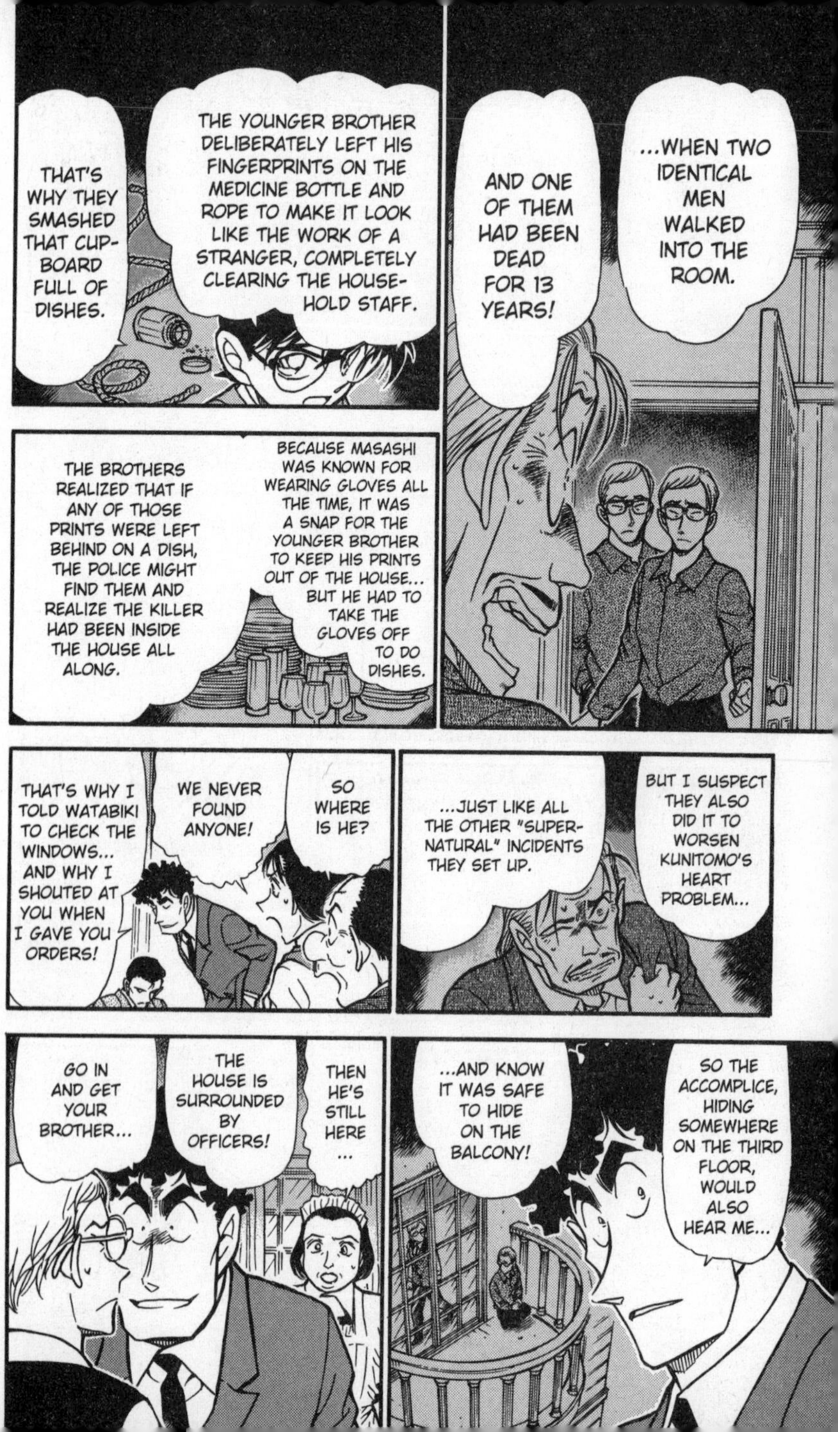
...WHEN TWO IDENTICAL MEN WALKED INTO THE ROOM.
AND ONE OF THEM HAD BEEN DEAD FOR 13 YEARS!
THE YOUNGER BROTHER DELIBERATELY LEFT HIS FINGERPRINTS ON THE MEDICINE BOTTLE AND ROPE TO MAKE IT LOOK LIKE THE WORK OF A STRANGER, COMPLETELY CLEARING THE HOUSE-HOLD STAFF.
THAT'S WHY THEY SMASHED THAT CUP-BOARD FULL OF DISHES.
BECAUSE MASASHI WAS KNOWN FOR WEARING GLOVES ALL THE TIME, IT WAS A SNAP FOR THE YOUNGER BROTHER TO KEEP HIS PRINTS OUT OF THE HOUSE... BUT HE HAD TO TAKE THE GLOVES OFF TO DO DISHES.
THE BROTHERS REALIZED THAT IF ANY OF THOSE PRINTS WERE LEFT BEHIND ON A DISH, THE POLICE MIGHT FIND THEM AND REALIZE THE KILLER HAD BEEN INSIDE THE HOUSE ALL ALONG.
BUT I SUSPECT THEY ALSO DID IT TO WORSEN KUNITOMO'S HEART PROBLEM...
...JUST LIKE ALL THE OTHER "SUPER-NATURAL" INCIDENTS THEY SET UP.
SO WHERE IS HE?
WE NEVER FOUND ANYONE!
THAT'S WHY I TOLD WATABIKI TO CHECK THE WINDOWS... AND WHY I SHOUTED AT YOU WHEN I GAVE YOU ORDERS!
SO THE ACCOMPLICE, HIDING SOMEWHERE ON THE THIRD FLOOR, WOULD ALSO HEAR ME...
...AND KNOW IT WAS SAFE TO HIDE ON THE BALCONY!
THEN HE'S STILL HERE ...
THE HOUSE IS SURROUNDED BY OFFICERS!
GO IN AND GET YOUR BROTHER...

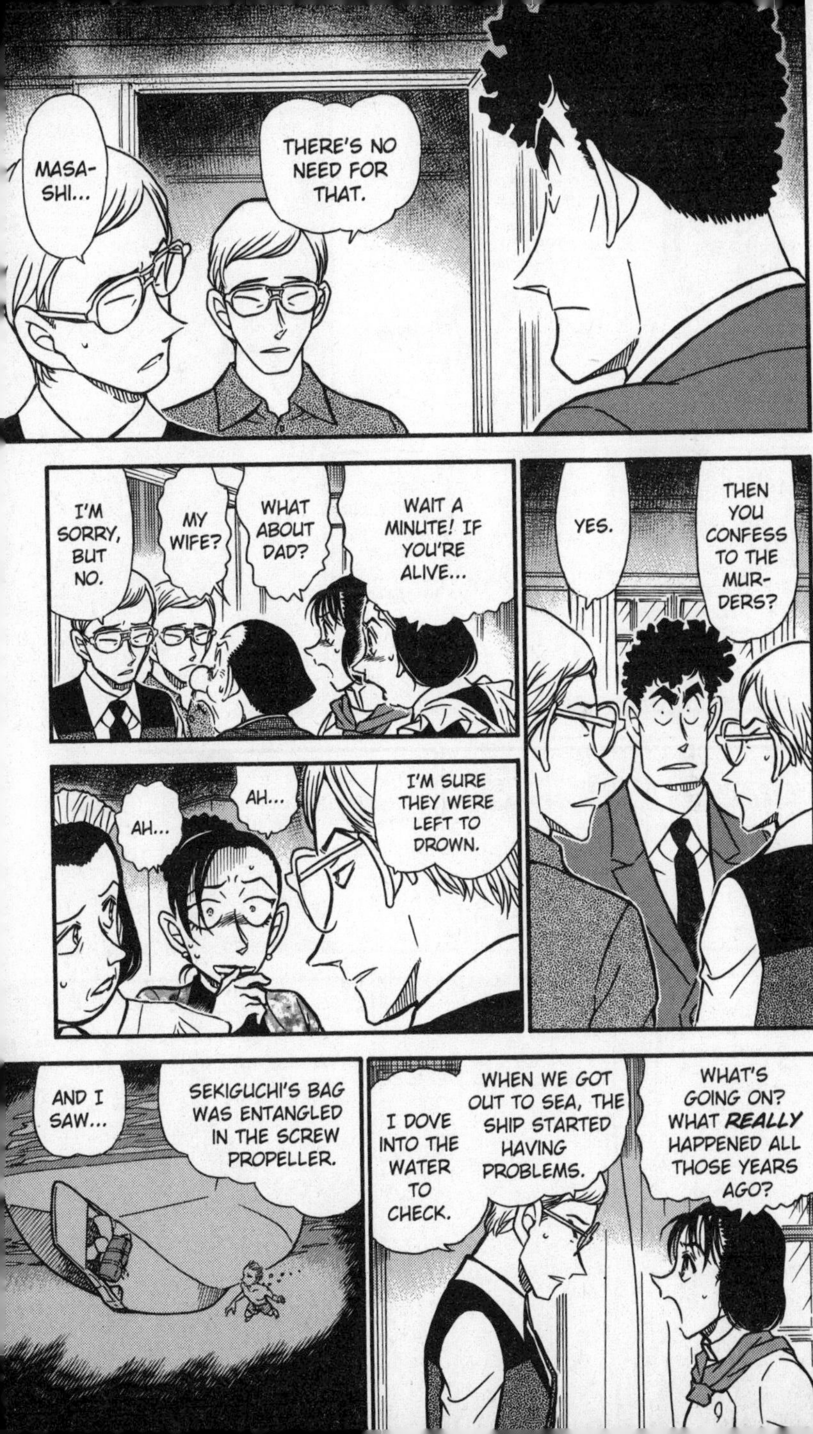
THERE'S NO NEED FOR THAT.
MASA-SHI...
THEN YOU CONFESS TO THE MUR-DERS?
YES.
WAIT A MINUTE! IF YOU'RE ALIVE...
WHAT ABOUT DAD?
MY WIFE?
I'M SORRY, BUT NO.
I'M SURE THEY WERE LEFT TO DROWN.
AH...
AH...
WHAT'S GOING ON? WHAT **REALLY** HAPPENED ALL THOSE YEARS AGO?
WHEN WE GOT OUT TO SEA, THE SHIP STARTED HAVING PROBLEMS.
I DOVE INTO THE WATER TO CHECK.
SEKIGUCHI'S BAG WAS ENTANGLED IN THE SCREW PROPELLER.
AND I SAW...

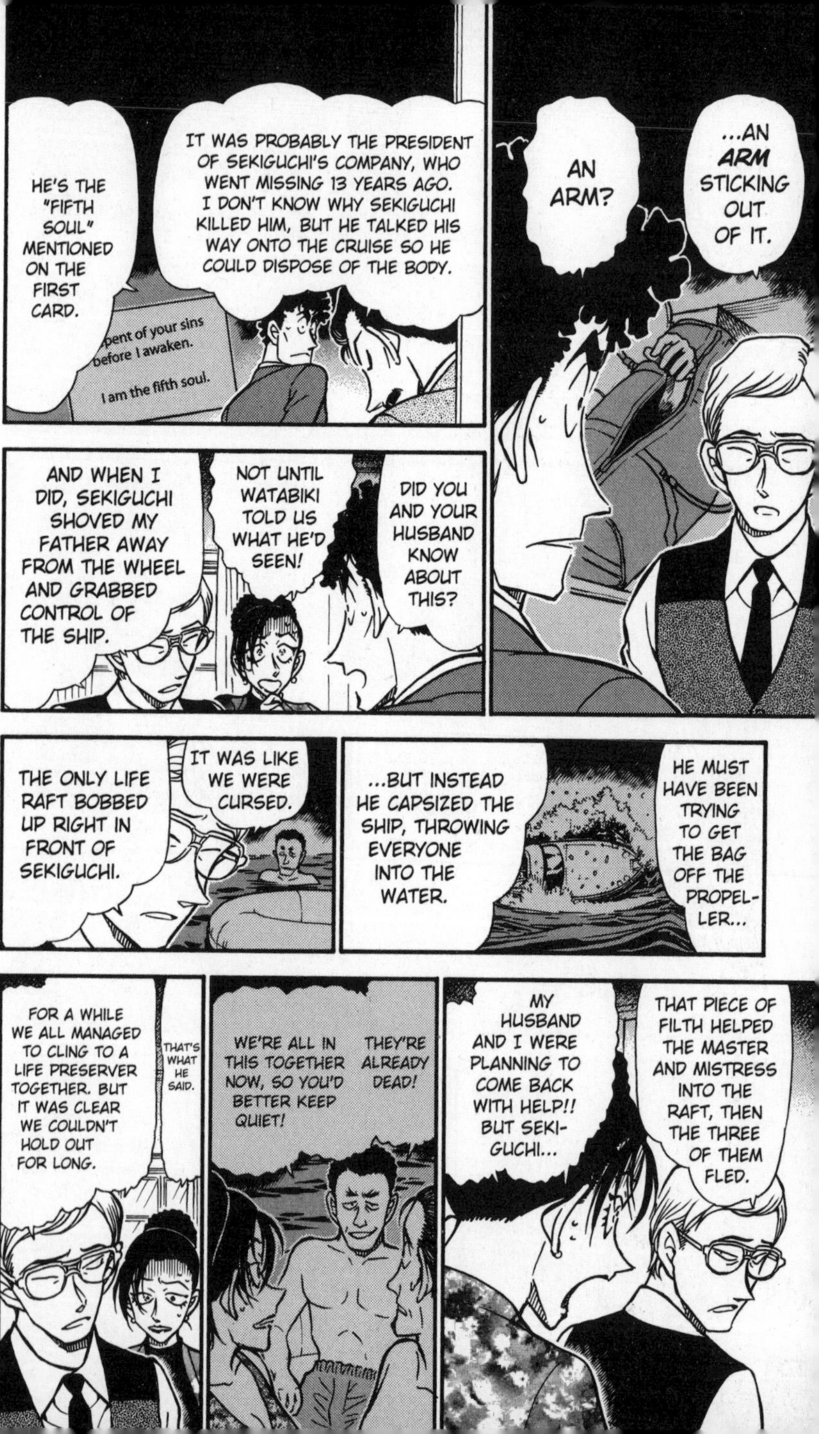
...AN ARM STICKING OUT OF IT.
AN ARM?
IT WAS PROBABLY THE PRESIDENT OF SEKIGUCHI'S COMPANY, WHO WENT MISSING 13 YEARS AGO. I DON'T KNOW WHY SEKIGUCHI KILLED HIM, BUT HE TALKED HIS WAY ONTO THE CRUISE SO HE COULD DISPOSE OF THE BODY.
HE'S THE "FIFTH SOUL" MENTIONED ON THE FIRST CARD.
pent of your sins before I awaken.
I am the fifth soul.
DID YOU AND YOUR HUSBAND KNOW ABOUT THIS?
NOT UNTIL WATABIKI TOLD US WHAT HE'D SEEN!
AND WHEN I DID, SEKIGUCHI SHOVED MY FATHER AWAY FROM THE WHEEL AND GRABBED CONTROL OF THE SHIP.
HE MUST HAVE BEEN TRYING TO GET THE BAG OFF THE PROPEL-LER...
...BUT INSTEAD HE CAPSIZED THE SHIP, THROWING EVERYONE INTO THE WATER.
IT WAS LIKE WE WERE CURSED.
THE ONLY LIFE RAFT BOBBED UP RIGHT IN FRONT OF SEKIGUCHI.
THAT PIECE OF FILTH HELPED THE MASTER AND MISTRESS INTO THE RAFT, THEN THE THREE OF THEM FLED.
MY HUSBAND AND I WERE PLANNING TO COME BACK WITH HELP!! BUT SEKI-GUCHI...
THEY'RE ALREADY DEAD!
WE'RE ALL IN THIS TOGETHER NOW, SO YOU'D BETTER KEEP QUIET!
THAT'S WHAT HE SAID.
FOR A WHILE WE ALL MANAGED TO CLING TO A LIFE PRESERVER TOGETHER. BUT IT WAS CLEAR WE COULDN'T HOLD OUT FOR LONG.

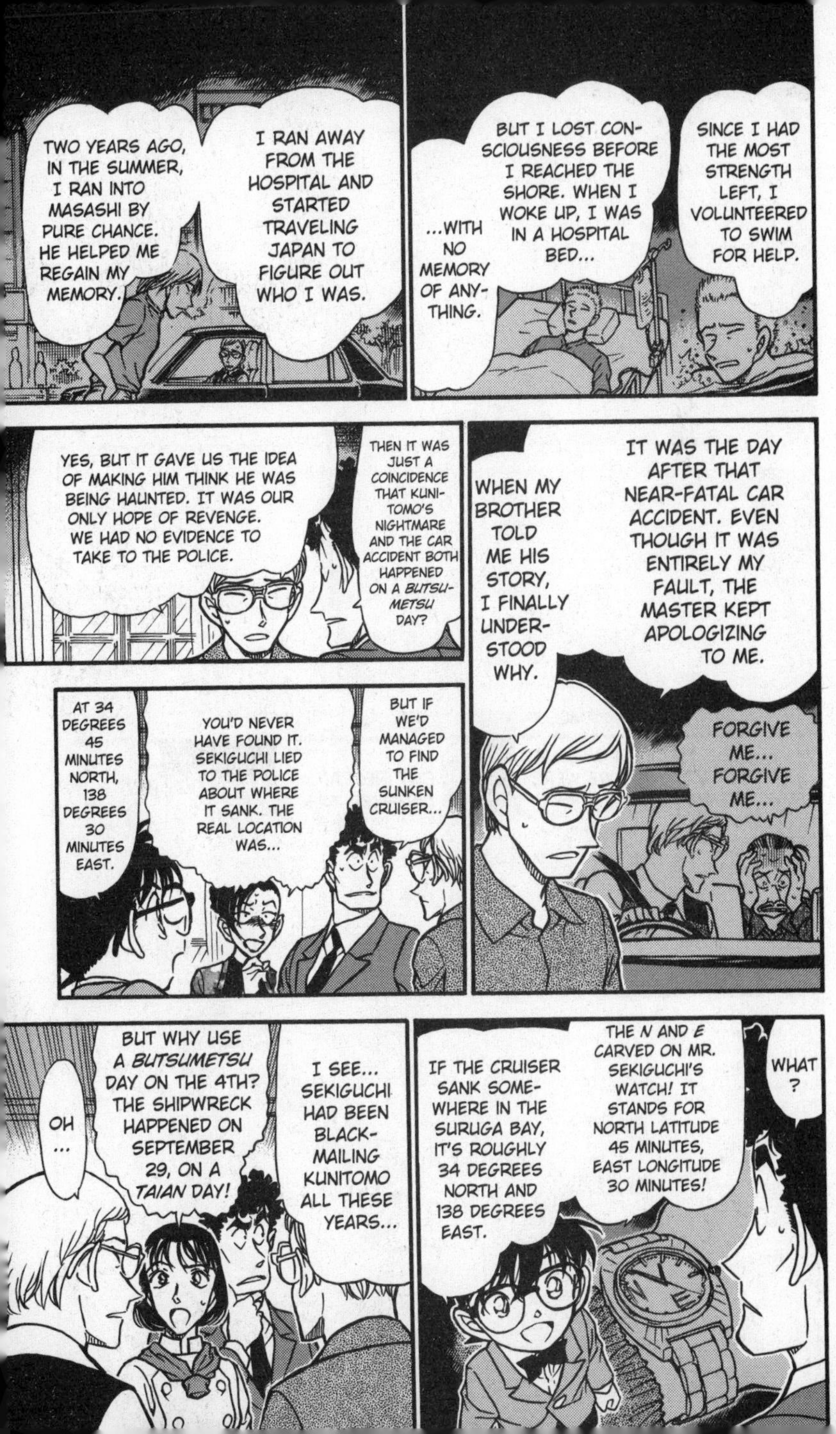
SINCE I HAD THE MOST STRENGTH LEFT, I VOLUNTEERED TO SWIM FOR HELP.
BUT I LOST CONSCIOUSNESS BEFORE I REACHED THE SHORE. WHEN I WOKE UP, I WAS IN A HOSPITAL BED...
...WITH NO MEMORY OF ANYTHING.
I RAN AWAY FROM THE HOSPITAL AND STARTED TRAVELING JAPAN TO FIGURE OUT WHO I WAS.
TWO YEARS AGO, IN THE SUMMER, I RAN INTO MASASHI BY PURE CHANCE. HE HELPED ME REGAIN MY MEMORY.
IT WAS THE DAY AFTER THAT NEAR-FATAL CAR ACCIDENT. EVEN THOUGH IT WAS ENTIRELY MY FAULT, THE MASTER KEPT APOLOGIZING TO ME.
WHEN MY BROTHER TOLD ME HIS STORY, I FINALLY UNDERSTOOD WHY.
FORGIVE ME... FORGIVE ME...
THEN IT WAS JUST A COINCIDENCE THAT KUNITOMO'S NIGHTMARE AND THE CAR ACCIDENT BOTH HAPPENED ON A *BUTSUMETSU* DAY?
YES, BUT IT GAVE US THE IDEA OF MAKING HIM THINK HE WAS BEING HAUNTED. IT WAS OUR ONLY HOPE OF REVENGE. WE HAD NO EVIDENCE TO TAKE TO THE POLICE.
BUT IF WE'D MANAGED TO FIND THE SUNKEN CRUISER...
YOU'D NEVER HAVE FOUND IT. SEKIGUCHI LIED TO THE POLICE ABOUT WHERE IT SANK. THE REAL LOCATION WAS...
AT 34 DEGREES 45 MINUTES NORTH, 138 DEGREES 30 MINUTES EAST.
WHAT?
THE *N* AND *E* CARVED ON MR. SEKIGUCHI'S WATCH! IT STANDS FOR NORTH LATITUDE 45 MINUTES, EAST LONGITUDE 30 MINUTES!
IF THE CRUISER SANK SOMEWHERE IN THE SURUGA BAY, IT'S ROUGHLY 34 DEGREES NORTH AND 138 DEGREES EAST.
I SEE... SEKIGUCHI HAD BEEN BLACKMAILING KUNITOMO ALL THESE YEARS...
BUT WHY USE A *BUTSUMETSU* DAY ON THE 4TH? THE SHIPWRECK HAPPENED ON SEPTEMBER 29, ON A *TAIAN* DAY!
OH...

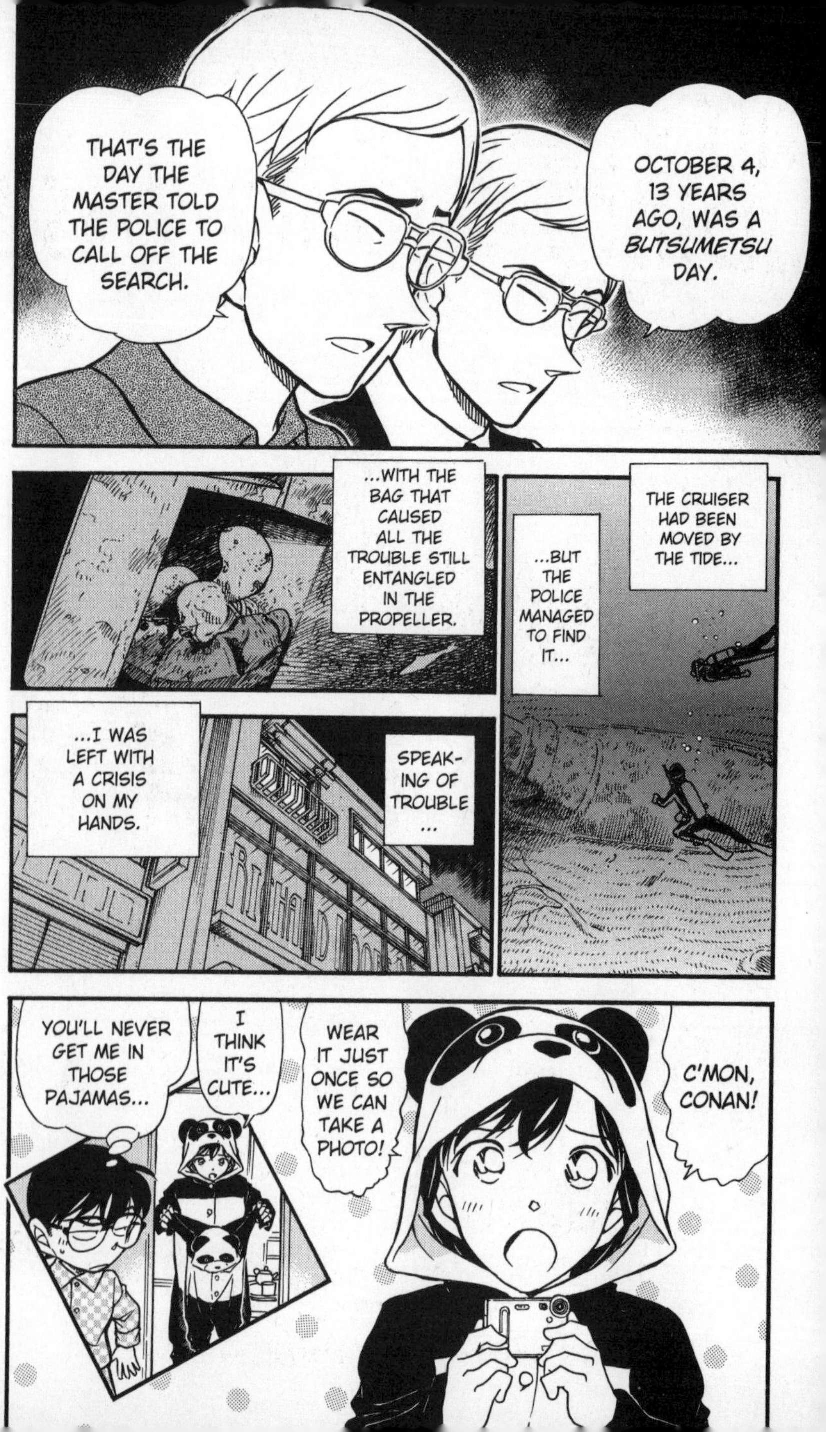
OCTOBER 4, 13 YEARS AGO, WAS A BUTSUMETSU DAY.
THAT'S THE DAY THE MASTER TOLD THE POLICE TO CALL OFF THE SEARCH.
THE CRUISER HAD BEEN MOVED BY THE TIDE...
...BUT THE POLICE MANAGED TO FIND IT...
...WITH THE BAG THAT CAUSED ALL THE TROUBLE STILL ENTANGLED IN THE PROPELLER.
SPEAK-ING OF TROUBLE...
...I WAS LEFT WITH A CRISIS ON MY HANDS.
C'MON, CONAN!
WEAR IT JUST ONCE SO WE CAN TAKE A PHOTO!
I THINK IT'S CUTE...
YOU'LL NEVER GET ME IN THOSE PAJAMAS...

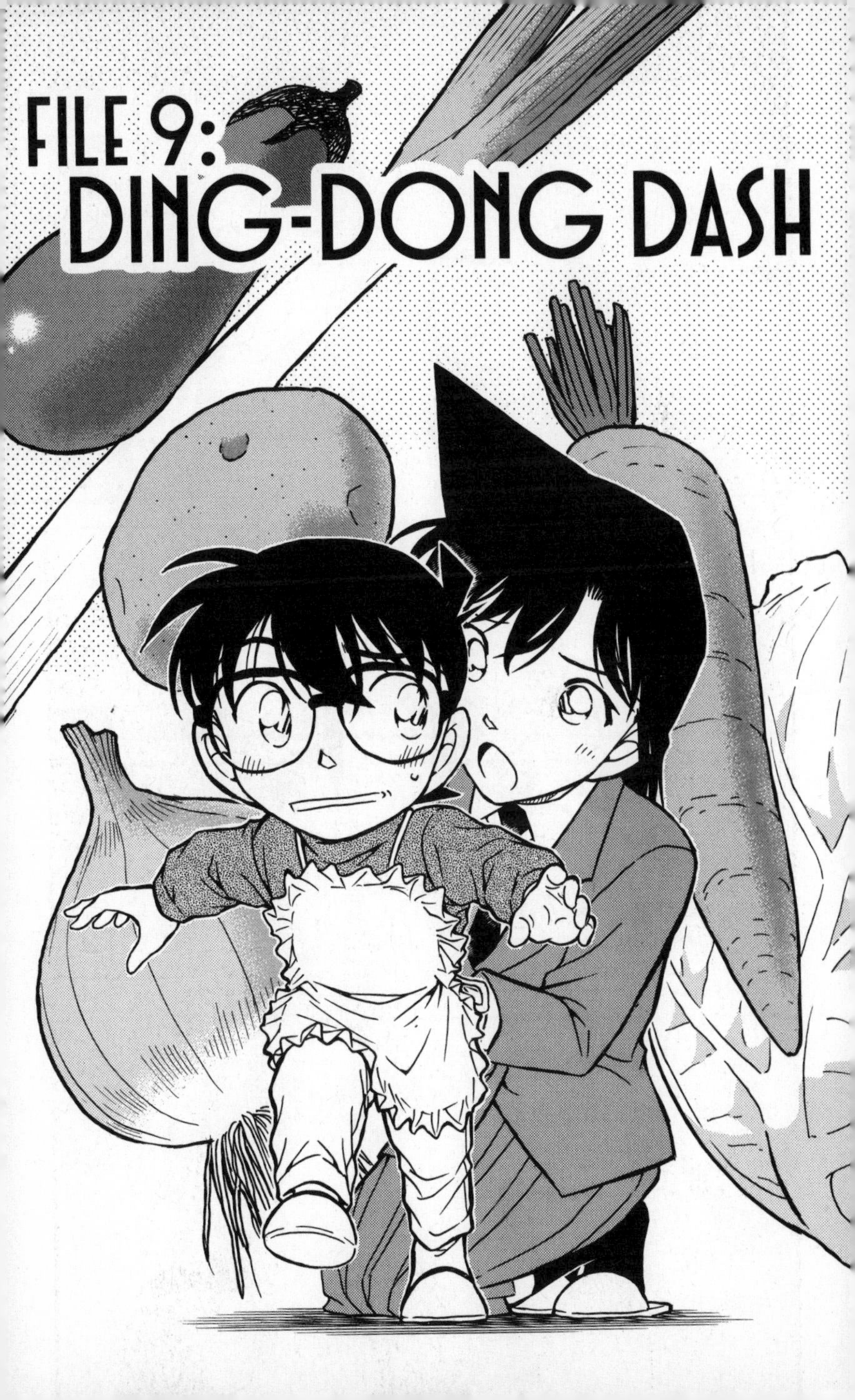
FILE 9:
DING-DONG DASH

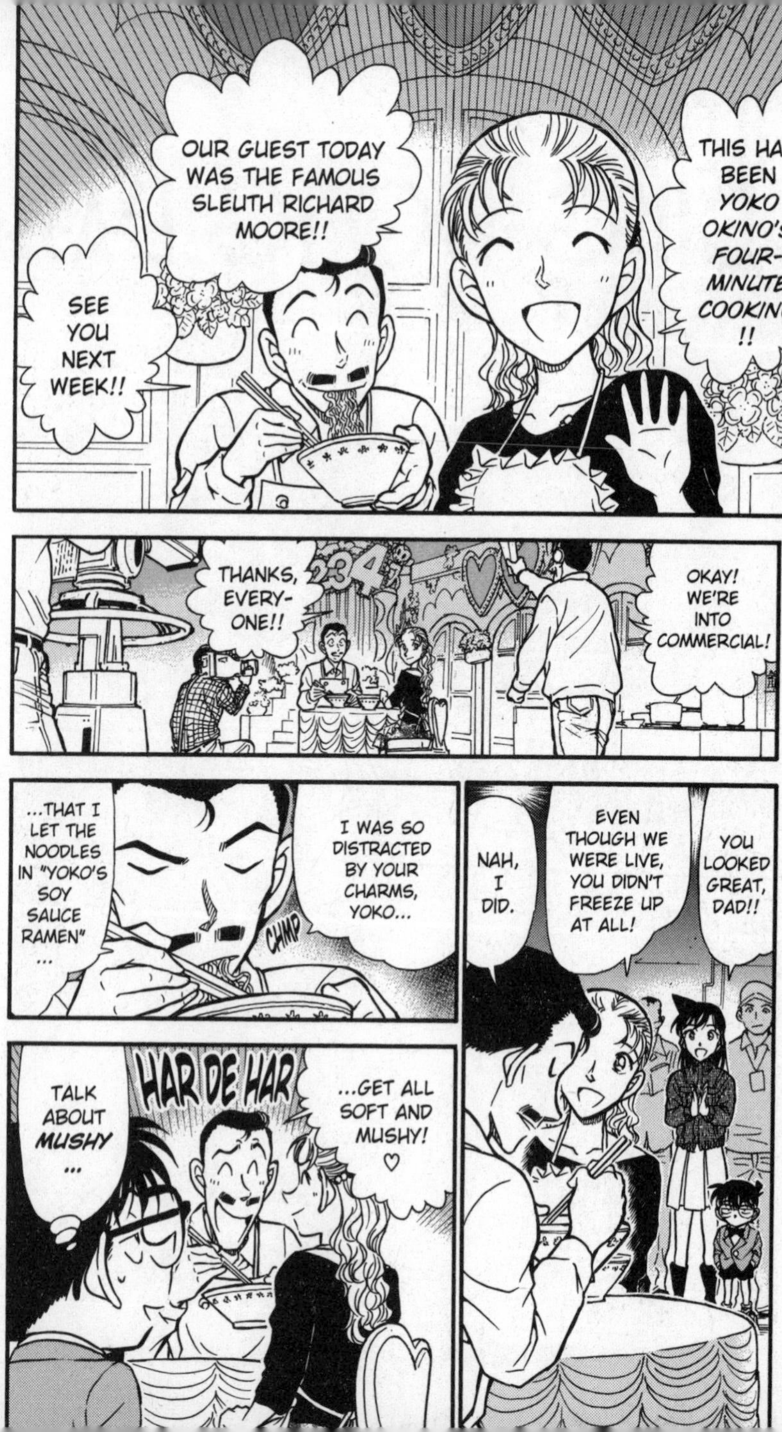
THIS HAS BEEN YOKO OKINO'S FOUR-MINUTE COOKING!!
OUR GUEST TODAY WAS THE FAMOUS SLEUTH RICHARD MOORE!!
SEE YOU NEXT WEEK!!
OKAY! WE'RE INTO COMMERCIAL!
THANKS, EVERYONE!!
YOU LOOKED GREAT, DAD!!
EVEN THOUGH WE WERE LIVE, YOU DIDN'T FREEZE UP AT ALL!
NAH, I DID.
I WAS SO DISTRACTED BY YOUR CHARMS, YOKO...
CHMP
...THAT I LET THE NOODLES IN "YOKO'S SOY SAUCE RAMEN"...
...GET ALL SOFT AND MUSHY! ♡
HAR DE HAR
TALK ABOUT MUSHY...

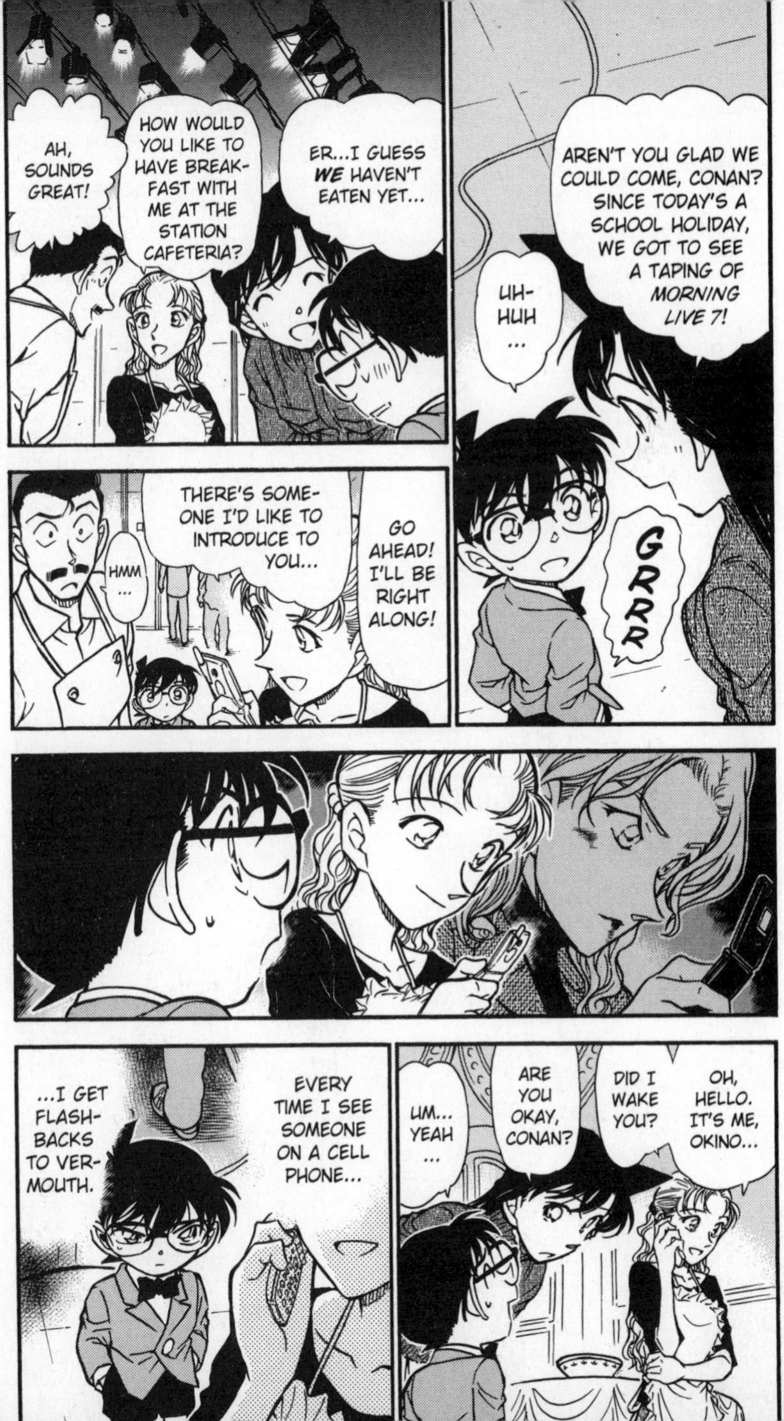
AREN'T YOU GLAD WE COULD COME, CONAN? SINCE TODAY'S A SCHOOL HOLIDAY, WE GOT TO SEE A TAPING OF *MORNING LIVE 7*!
UH-HUH...
GRRR
ER...I GUESS ***WE*** HAVEN'T EATEN YET...
HOW WOULD YOU LIKE TO HAVE BREAK-FAST WITH ME AT THE STATION CAFETERIA?
AH, SOUNDS GREAT!
GO AHEAD! I'LL BE RIGHT ALONG!
THERE'S SOME-ONE I'D LIKE TO INTRODUCE TO YOU...
HMM...
OH, HELLO. IT'S ME, OKINO...
DID I WAKE YOU?
ARE YOU OKAY, CONAN?
UM... YEAH...
EVERY TIME I SEE SOMEONE ON A CELL PHONE...
...I GET FLASH-BACKS TO VER-MOUTH.

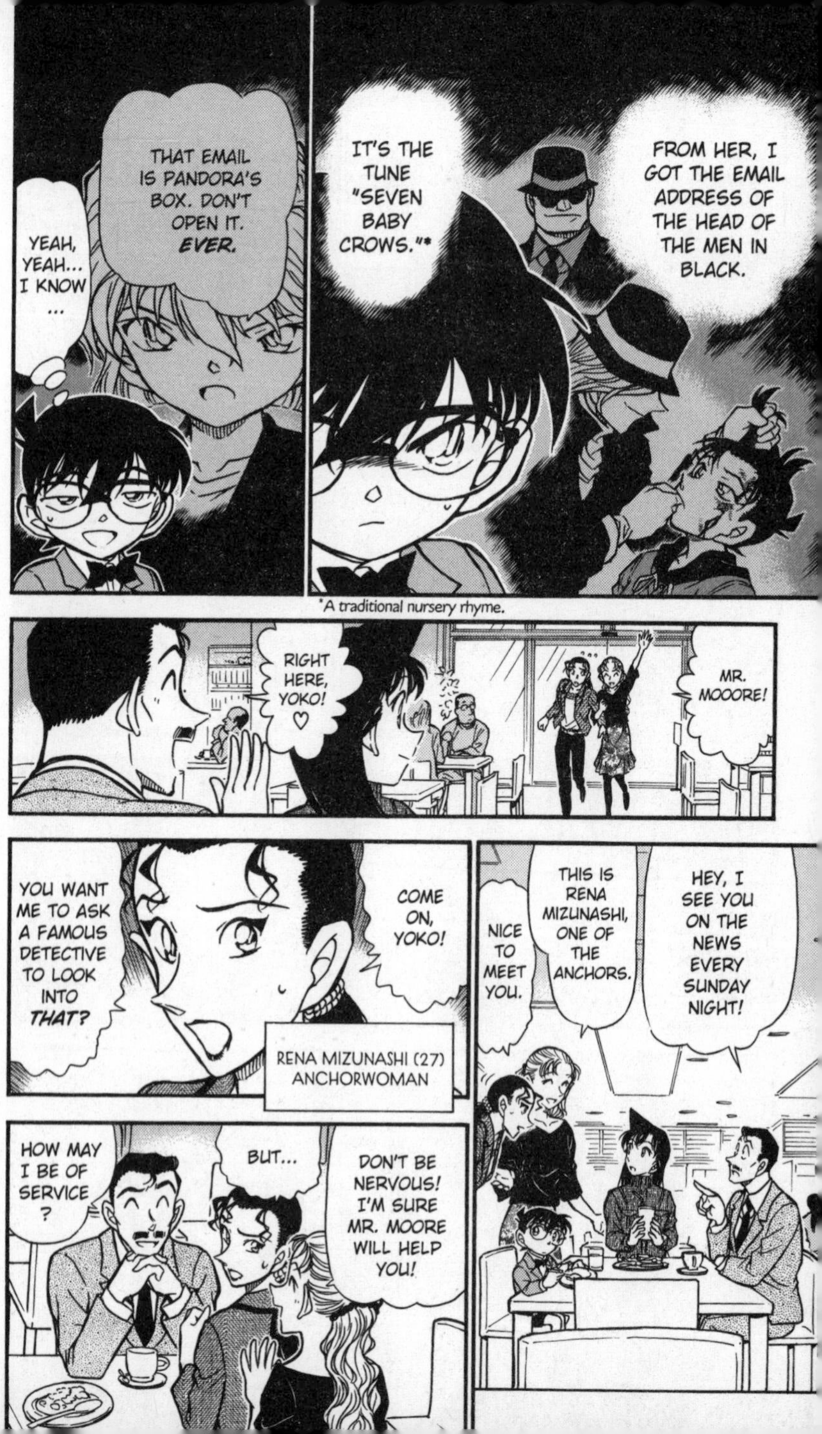
FROM HER, I GOT THE EMAIL ADDRESS OF THE HEAD OF THE MEN IN BLACK.
IT'S THE TUNE "SEVEN BABY CROWS."*
THAT EMAIL IS PANDORA'S BOX. DON'T OPEN IT. *EVER.*
YEAH, YEAH... I KNOW ...
*A traditional nursery rhyme.
MR. MOOORE!
RIGHT HERE, YOKO! ♡
HEY, I SEE YOU ON THE NEWS EVERY SUNDAY NIGHT!
THIS IS RENA MIZUNASHI, ONE OF THE ANCHORS.
NICE TO MEET YOU.
COME ON, YOKO!
YOU WANT ME TO ASK A FAMOUS DETECTIVE TO LOOK INTO *THAT?*
RENA MIZUNASHI (27) ANCHORWOMAN
DON'T BE NERVOUS! I'M SURE MR. MOORE WILL HELP YOU!
BUT...
HOW MAY I BE OF SERVICE?

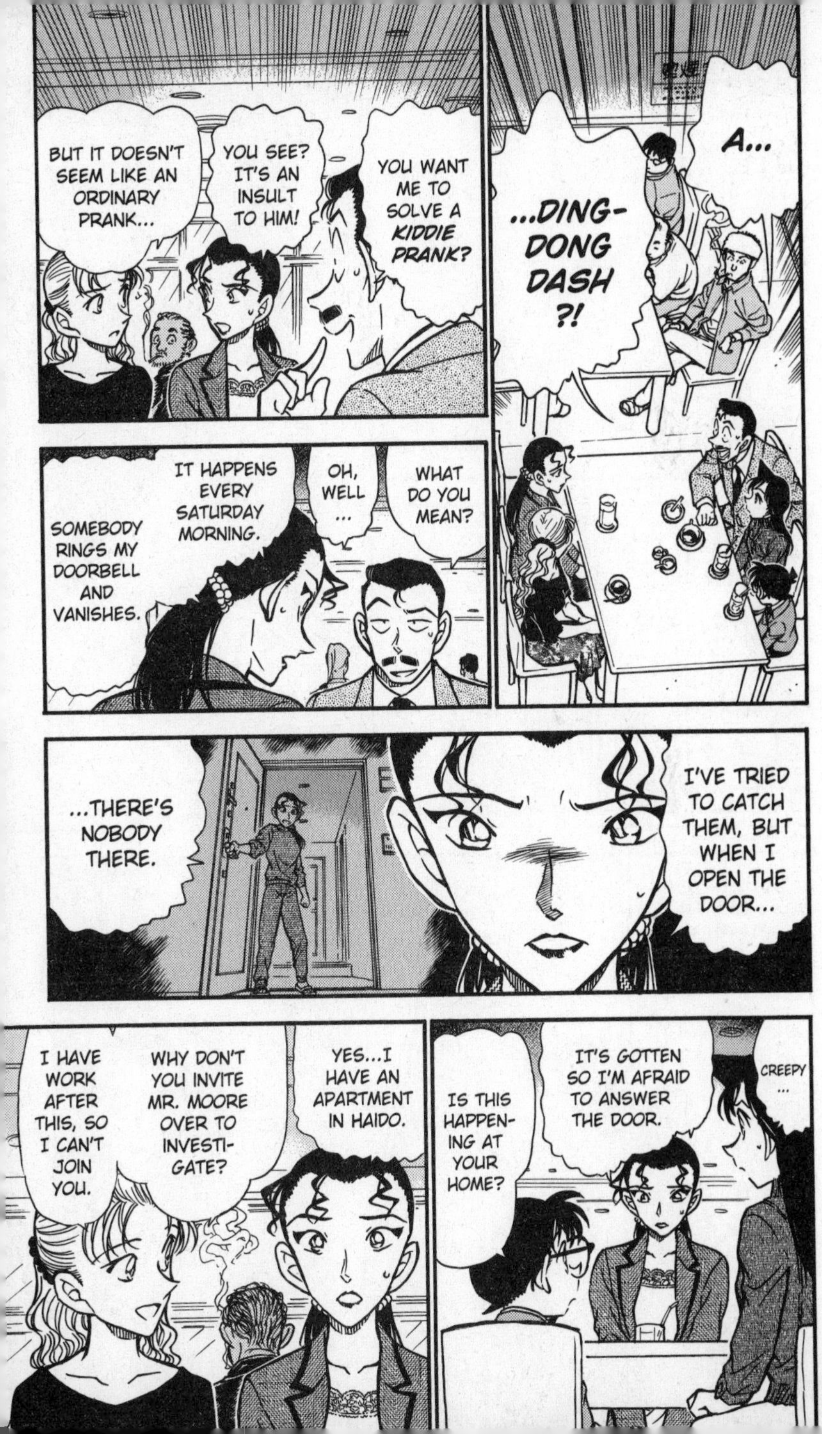
A...
...DING-DONG DASH ?!
YOU WANT ME TO SOLVE A *KIDDIE PRANK?*
YOU SEE? IT'S AN INSULT TO HIM!
BUT IT DOESN'T SEEM LIKE AN ORDINARY PRANK...
WHAT DO YOU MEAN?
OH, WELL ...
IT HAPPENS EVERY SATURDAY MORNING.
SOMEBODY RINGS MY DOORBELL AND VANISHES.
I'VE TRIED TO CATCH THEM, BUT WHEN I OPEN THE DOOR...
...THERE'S NOBODY THERE.
CREEPY ...
IT'S GOTTEN SO I'M AFRAID TO ANSWER THE DOOR.
IS THIS HAPPENING AT YOUR HOME?
YES...I HAVE AN APARTMENT IN HAIDO.
WHY DON'T YOU INVITE MR. MOORE OVER TO INVESTIGATE?
I HAVE WORK AFTER THIS, SO I CAN'T JOIN YOU.

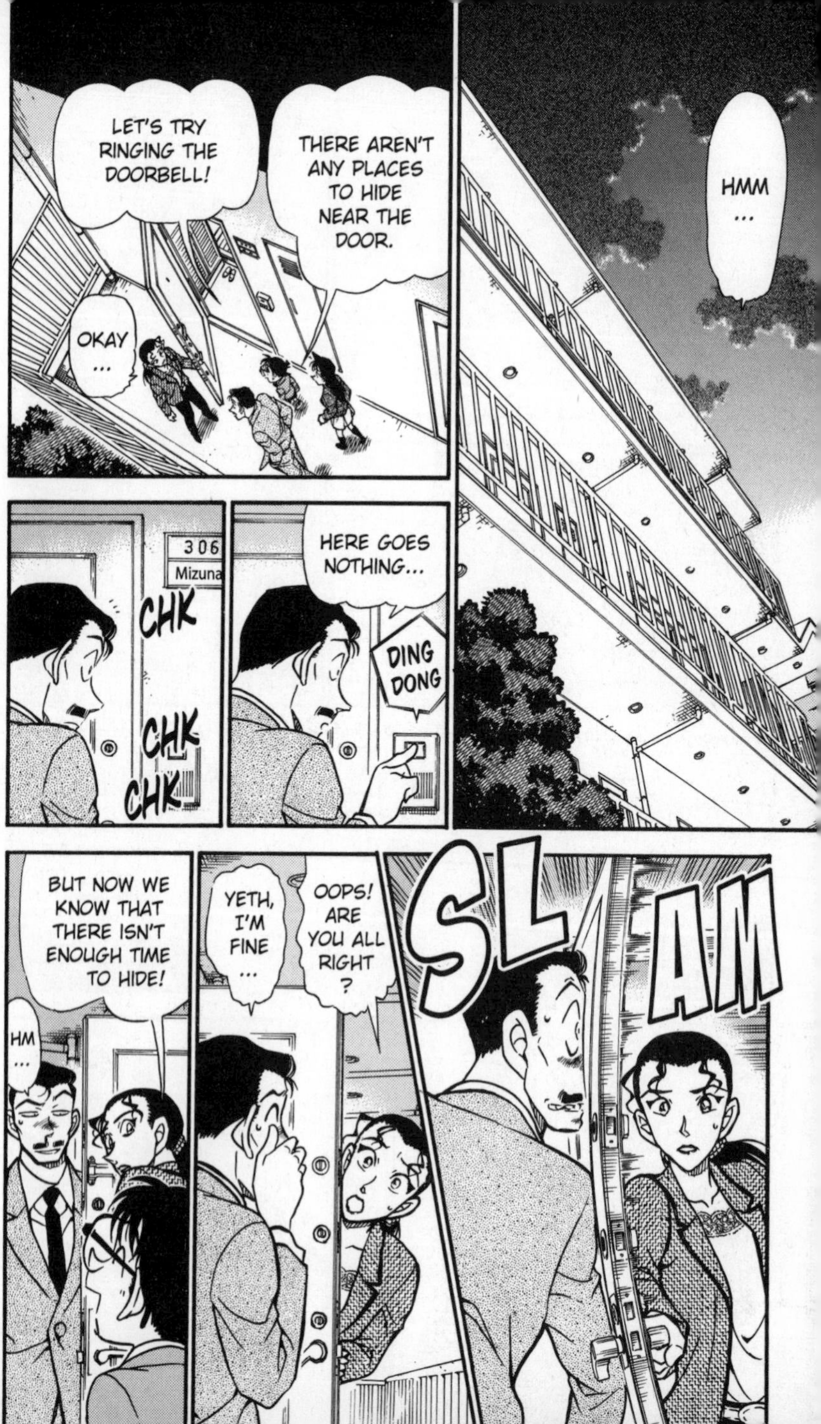
HMM ...
THERE AREN'T ANY PLACES TO HIDE NEAR THE DOOR.
LET'S TRY RINGING THE DOORBELL!
OKAY ...
HERE GOES NOTHING...
DING DONG
306
Mizuna
CHK
CHK
CHK
SLAM
OOPS! ARE YOU ALL RIGHT ?
YETH, I'M FINE ...
BUT NOW WE KNOW THAT THERE ISN'T ENOUGH TIME TO HIDE!
HM ...

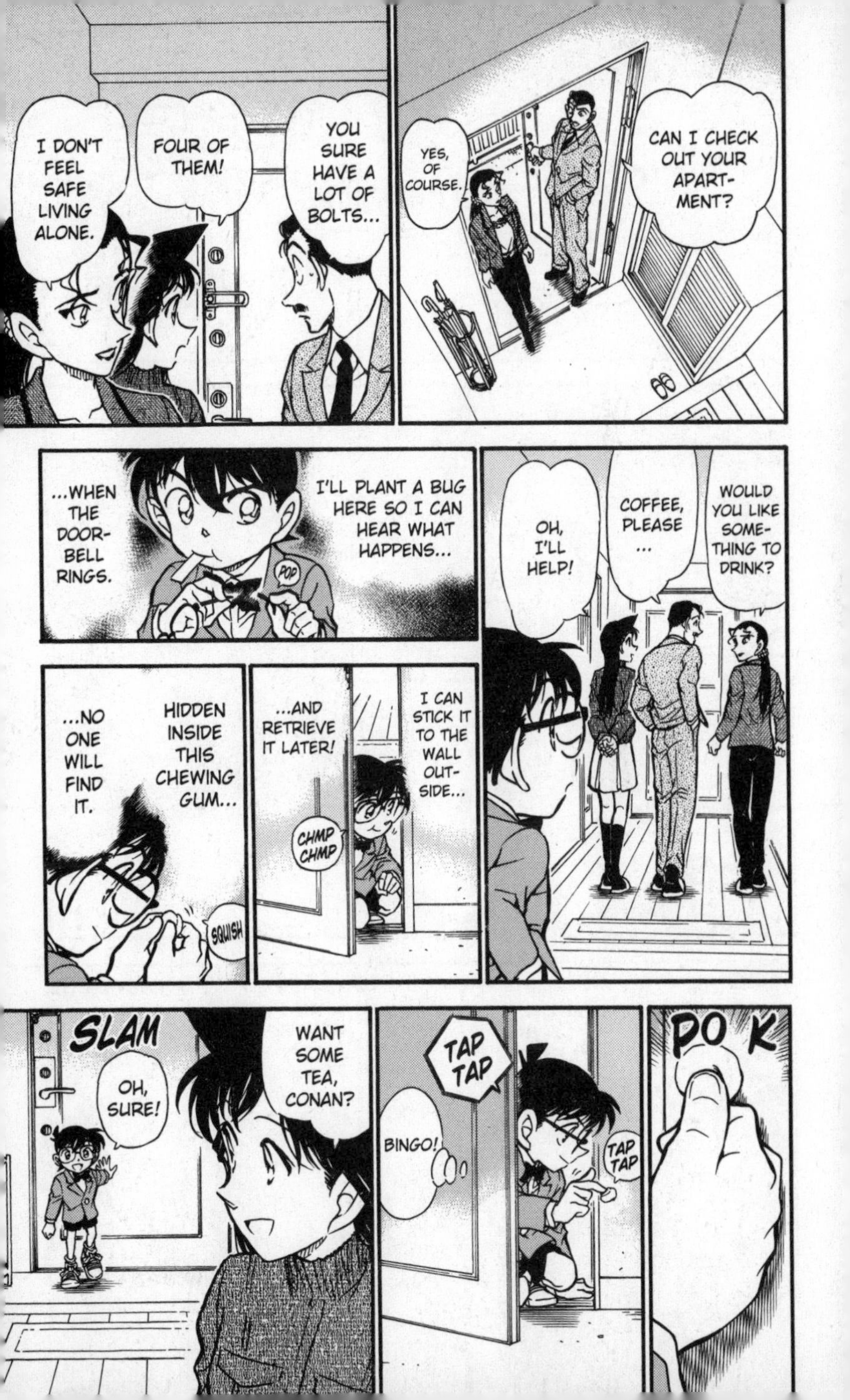
CAN I CHECK OUT YOUR APART-MENT?
YES, OF COURSE.
YOU SURE HAVE A LOT OF BOLTS...
FOUR OF THEM!
I DON'T FEEL SAFE LIVING ALONE.
WOULD YOU LIKE SOME-THING TO DRINK?
COFFEE, PLEASE...
OH, I'LL HELP!
I'LL PLANT A BUG HERE SO I CAN HEAR WHAT HAPPENS...
POP
...WHEN THE DOOR-BELL RINGS.
I CAN STICK IT TO THE WALL OUT-SIDE...
...AND RETRIEVE IT LATER!
CHMP CHMP
HIDDEN INSIDE THIS CHEWING GUM...
...NO ONE WILL FIND IT.
SQUISH
POK
TAP TAP
TAP TAP
BINGO!
WANT SOME TEA, CONAN?
SLAM
OH, SURE!

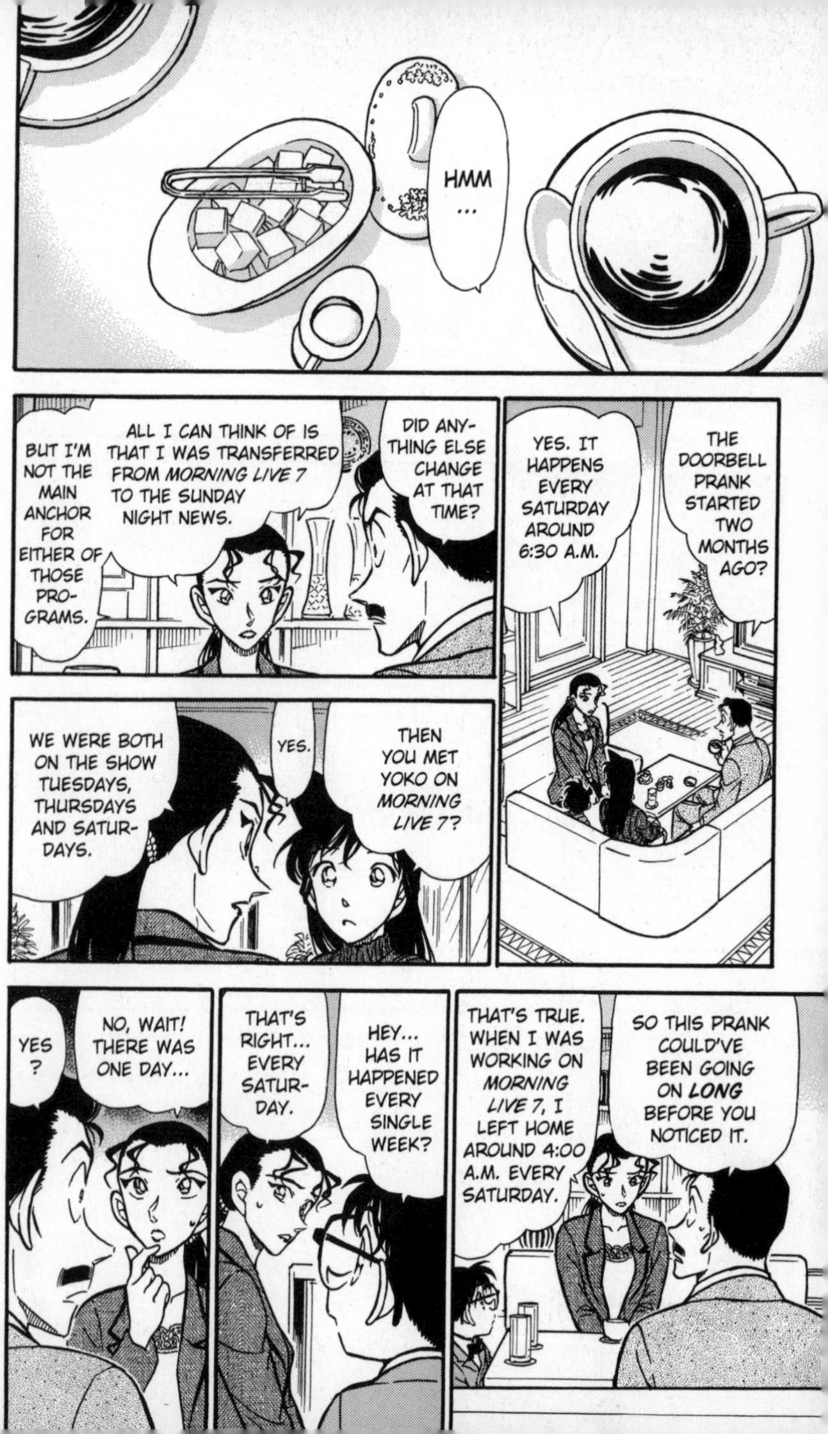
HMM ...
THE DOORBELL PRANK STARTED TWO MONTHS AGO?
YES. IT HAPPENS EVERY SATURDAY AROUND 6:30 A.M.
DID ANYTHING ELSE CHANGE AT THAT TIME?
ALL I CAN THINK OF IS THAT I WAS TRANSFERRED FROM *MORNING LIVE 7* TO THE SUNDAY NIGHT NEWS.
BUT I'M NOT THE MAIN ANCHOR FOR EITHER OF THOSE PROGRAMS.
THEN YOU MET YOKO ON *MORNING LIVE 7*?
YES.
WE WERE BOTH ON THE SHOW TUESDAYS, THURSDAYS AND SATURDAYS.
SO THIS PRANK COULD'VE BEEN GOING ON **LONG** BEFORE YOU NOTICED IT.
THAT'S TRUE. WHEN I WAS WORKING ON *MORNING LIVE 7*, I LEFT HOME AROUND 4:00 A.M. EVERY SATURDAY.
HEY... HAS IT HAPPENED EVERY SINGLE WEEK?
THAT'S RIGHT... EVERY SATURDAY.
NO, WAIT! THERE WAS ONE DAY...
YES?

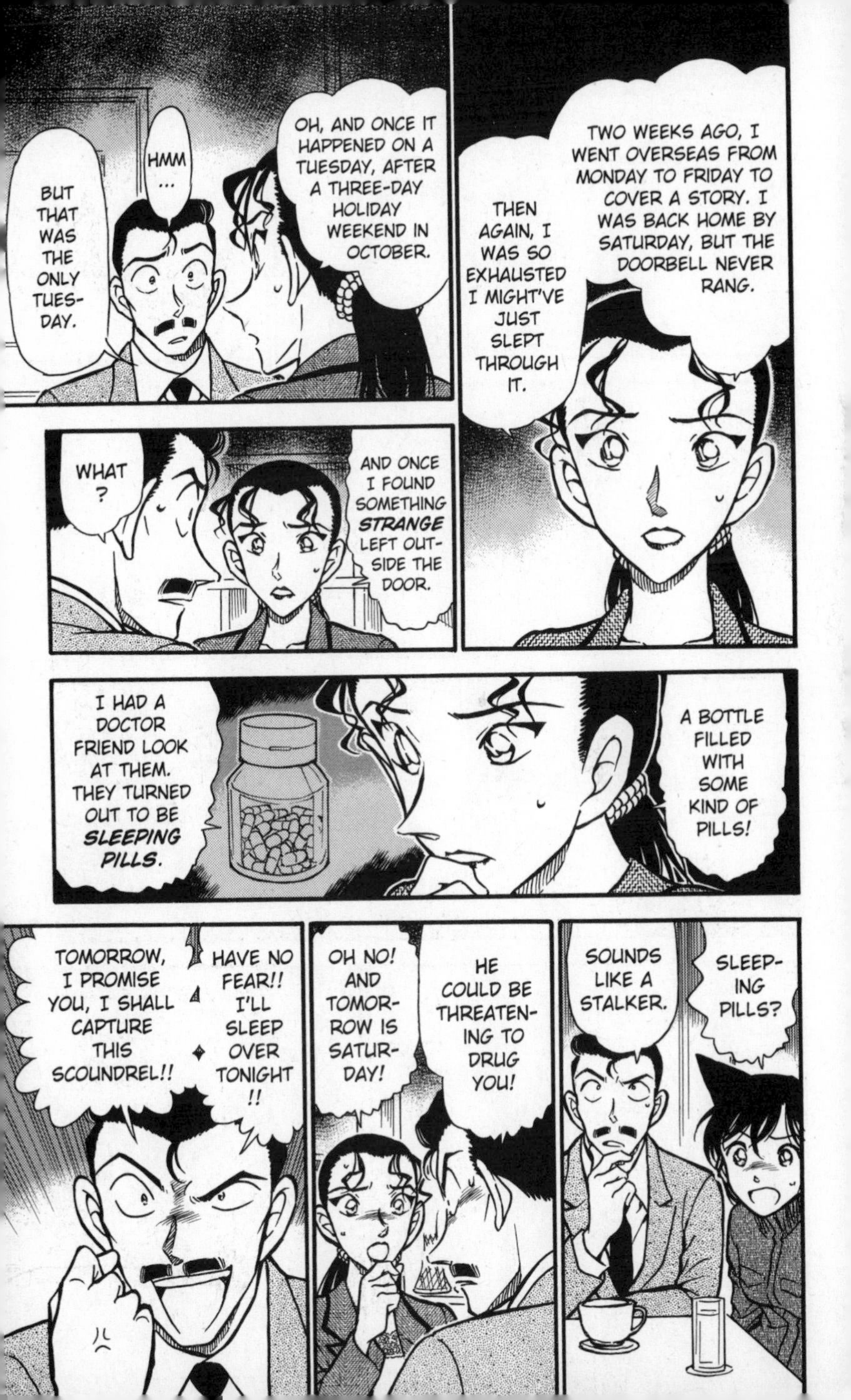
TWO WEEKS AGO, I WENT OVERSEAS FROM MONDAY TO FRIDAY TO COVER A STORY. I WAS BACK HOME BY SATURDAY, BUT THE DOORBELL NEVER RANG.
THEN AGAIN, I WAS SO EXHAUSTED I MIGHT'VE JUST SLEPT THROUGH IT.
OH, AND ONCE IT HAPPENED ON A TUESDAY, AFTER A THREE-DAY HOLIDAY WEEKEND IN OCTOBER.
HMM...
BUT THAT WAS THE ONLY TUES-DAY.
AND ONCE I FOUND SOMETHING **STRANGE** LEFT OUT-SIDE THE DOOR.
WHAT?
A BOTTLE FILLED WITH SOME KIND OF PILLS!
I HAD A DOCTOR FRIEND LOOK AT THEM. THEY TURNED OUT TO BE **SLEEPING PILLS**.
SLEEP-ING PILLS?
SOUNDS LIKE A STALKER.
HE COULD BE THREATEN-ING TO DRUG YOU!
OH NO! AND TOMOR-ROW IS SATUR-DAY!
HAVE NO FEAR!! I'LL SLEEP OVER TONIGHT!!
TOMORROW, I PROMISE YOU, I SHALL CAPTURE THIS SCOUNDREL!!

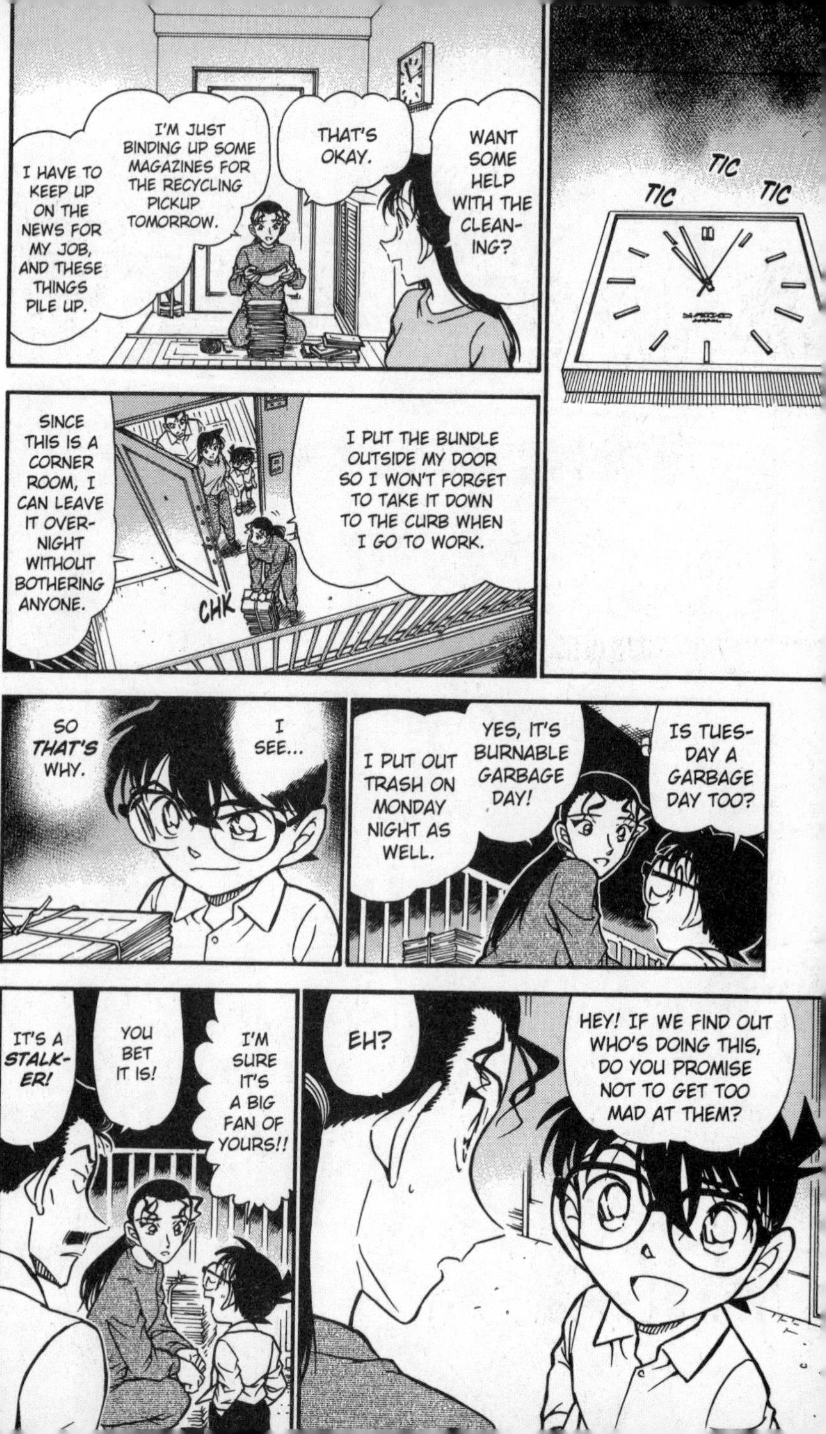
TIC TIC TIC
WANT SOME HELP WITH THE CLEANING?
THAT'S OKAY.
I'M JUST BINDING UP SOME MAGAZINES FOR THE RECYCLING PICKUP TOMORROW.
I HAVE TO KEEP UP ON THE NEWS FOR MY JOB, AND THESE THINGS PILE UP.
I PUT THE BUNDLE OUTSIDE MY DOOR SO I WON'T FORGET TO TAKE IT DOWN TO THE CURB WHEN I GO TO WORK.
SINCE THIS IS A CORNER ROOM, I CAN LEAVE IT OVERNIGHT WITHOUT BOTHERING ANYONE.
CHK
IS TUESDAY A GARBAGE DAY TOO?
YES, IT'S BURNABLE GARBAGE DAY!
I PUT OUT TRASH ON MONDAY NIGHT AS WELL.
I SEE...
SO *THAT'S* WHY.
HEY! IF WE FIND OUT WHO'S DOING THIS, DO YOU PROMISE NOT TO GET TOO MAD AT THEM?
EH?
I'M SURE IT'S A BIG FAN OF YOURS!!
YOU BET IT IS!
IT'S A *STALKER!*

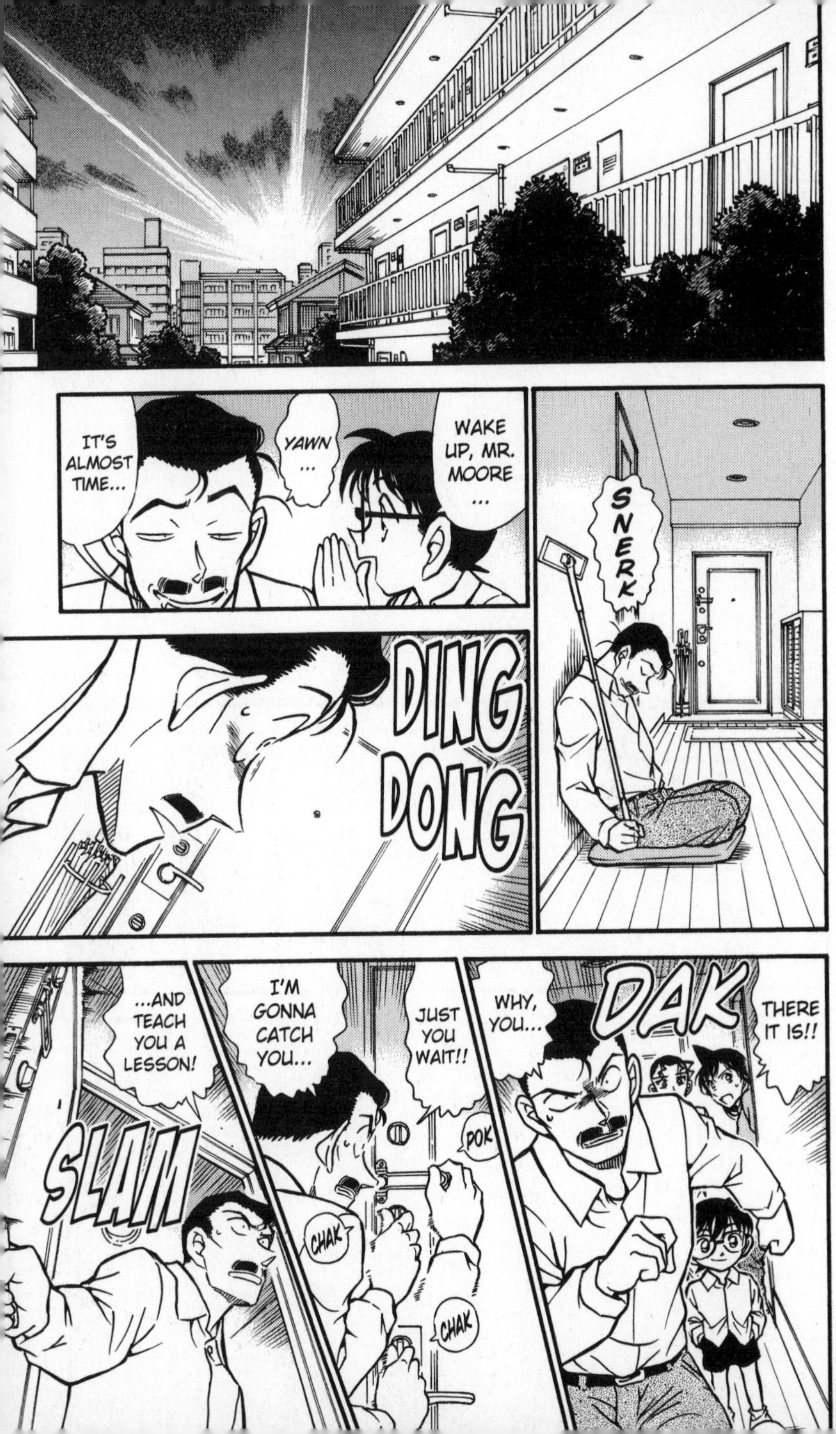
SNERK
WAKE UP, MR. MOORE...
YAWN...
IT'S ALMOST TIME...
DING DONG
THERE IT IS!!
DAK
WHY, YOU...
JUST YOU WAIT!!
I'M GONNA CATCH YOU...
POK
CHAK
CHAK
...AND TEACH YOU A LESSON!
SLAM

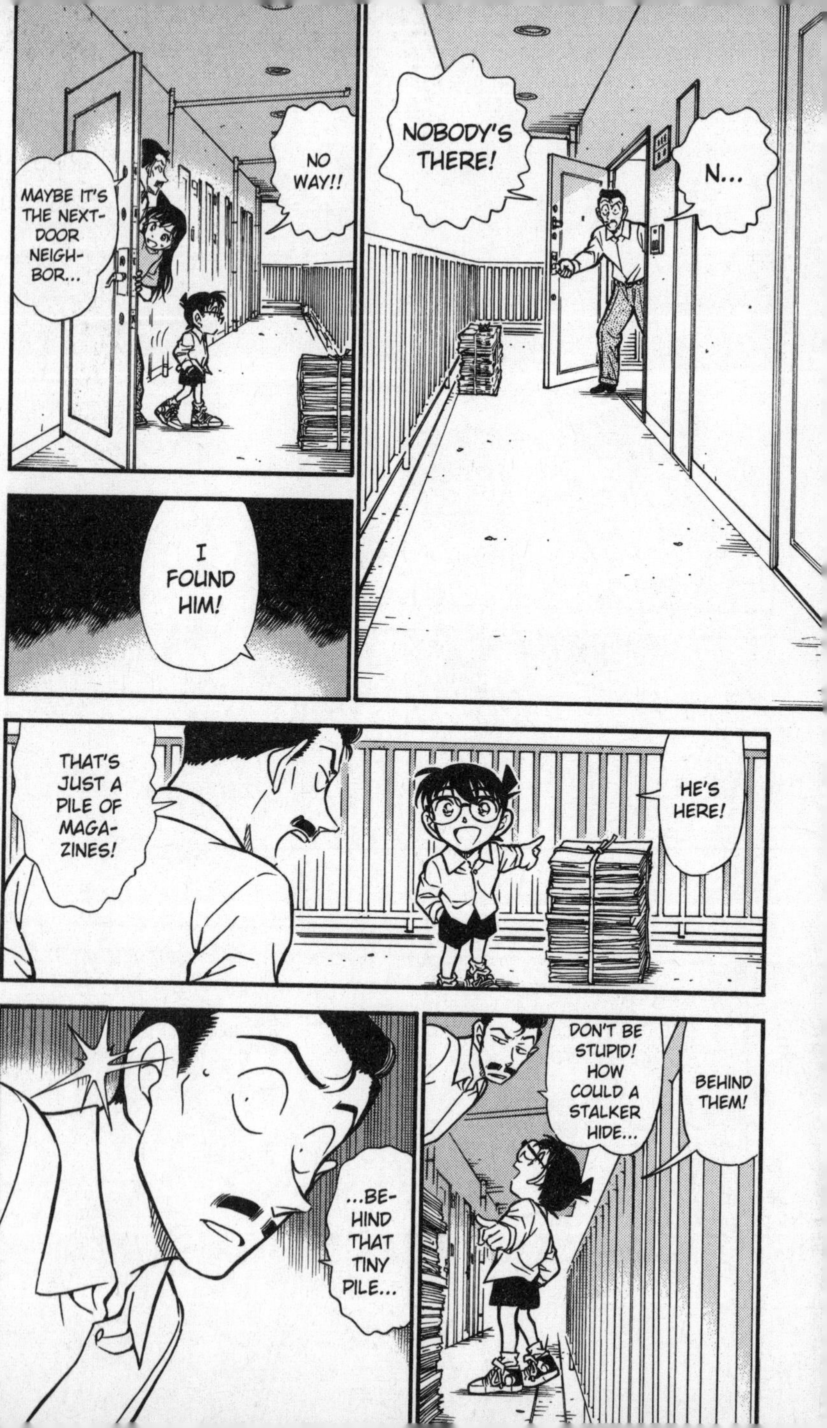
N...
NOBODY'S THERE!
NO WAY!!
MAYBE IT'S THE NEXT-DOOR NEIGHBOR...
I FOUND HIM!
HE'S HERE!
THAT'S JUST A PILE OF MAGAZINES!
BEHIND THEM!
DON'T BE STUPID! HOW COULD A STALKER HIDE...
...BEHIND THAT TINY PILE...

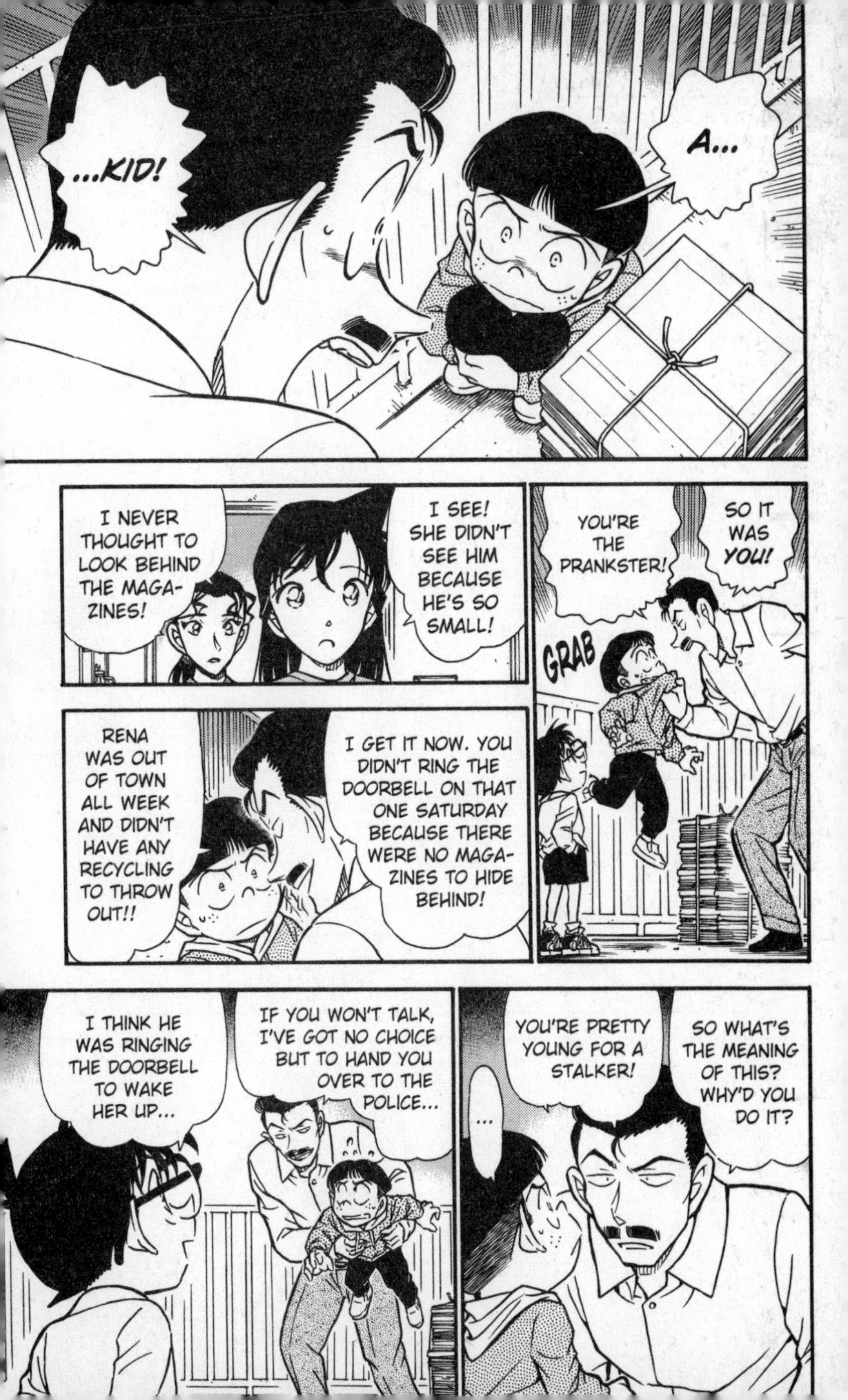
A...
...KID!
SO IT WAS YOU!
YOU'RE THE PRANKSTER!
GRAB
I SEE! SHE DIDN'T SEE HIM BECAUSE HE'S SO SMALL!
I NEVER THOUGHT TO LOOK BEHIND THE MAGAZINES!
I GET IT NOW. YOU DIDN'T RING THE DOORBELL ON THAT ONE SATURDAY BECAUSE THERE WERE NO MAGAZINES TO HIDE BEHIND!
RENA WAS OUT OF TOWN ALL WEEK AND DIDN'T HAVE ANY RECYCLING TO THROW OUT!!
SO WHAT'S THE MEANING OF THIS? WHY'D YOU DO IT?
YOU'RE PRETTY YOUNG FOR A STALKER!
...
IF YOU WON'T TALK, I'VE GOT NO CHOICE BUT TO HAND YOU OVER TO THE POLICE...
I THINK HE WAS RINGING THE DOORBELL TO WAKE HER UP...

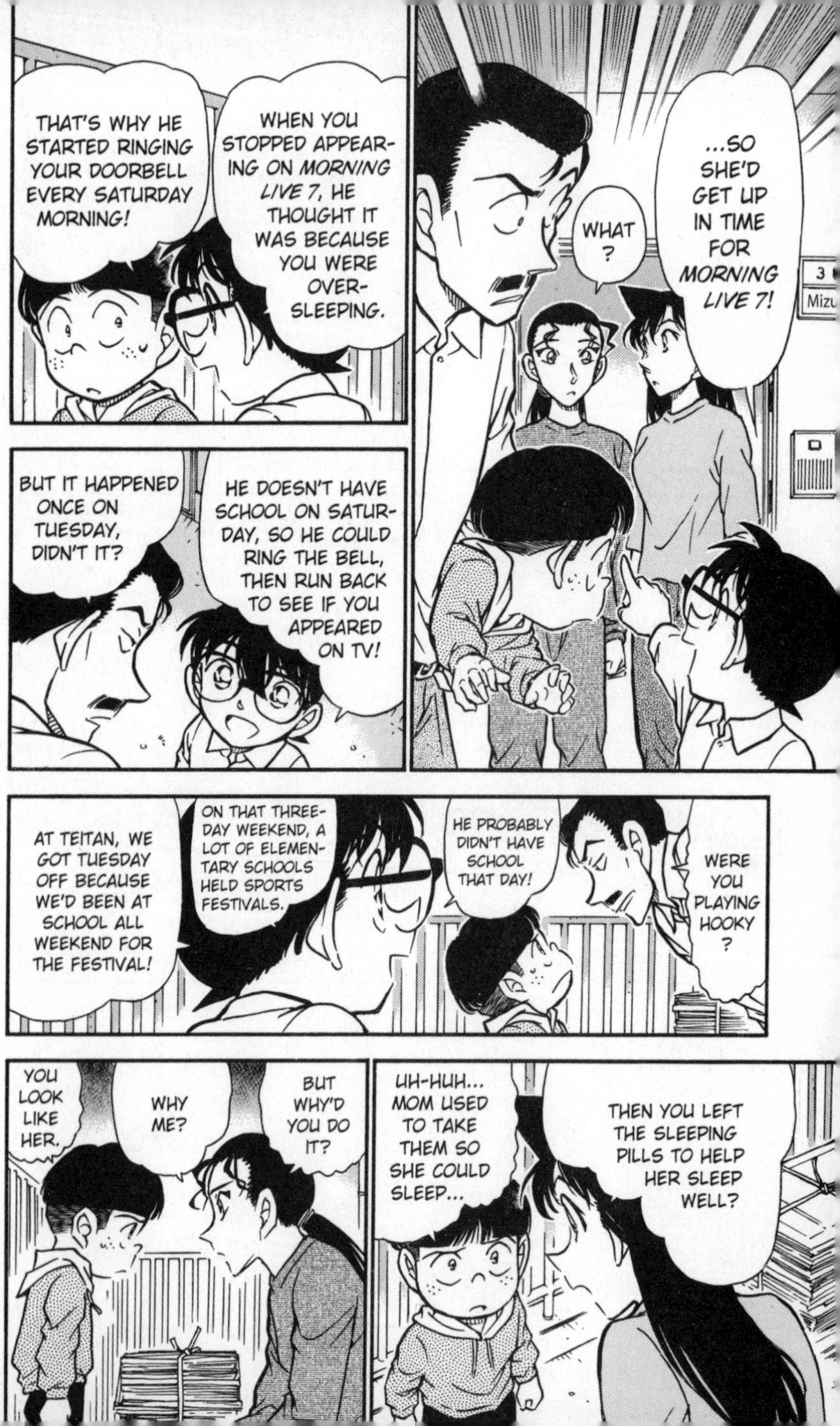
...SO SHE'D GET UP IN TIME FOR *MORNING LIVE 7*!
WHAT?
WHEN YOU STOPPED APPEARING ON *MORNING LIVE 7*, HE THOUGHT IT WAS BECAUSE YOU WERE OVERSLEEPING.
THAT'S WHY HE STARTED RINGING YOUR DOORBELL EVERY SATURDAY MORNING!
HE DOESN'T HAVE SCHOOL ON SATURDAY, SO HE COULD RING THE BELL, THEN RUN BACK TO SEE IF YOU APPEARED ON TV!
BUT IT HAPPENED ONCE ON TUESDAY, DIDN'T IT?
WERE YOU PLAYING HOOKY?
HE PROBABLY DIDN'T HAVE SCHOOL THAT DAY!
ON THAT THREE-DAY WEEKEND, A LOT OF ELEMENTARY SCHOOLS HELD SPORTS FESTIVALS.
AT TEITAN, WE GOT TUESDAY OFF BECAUSE WE'D BEEN AT SCHOOL ALL WEEKEND FOR THE FESTIVAL!
THEN YOU LEFT THE SLEEPING PILLS TO HELP HER SLEEP WELL?
UH-HUH... MOM USED TO TAKE THEM SO SHE COULD SLEEP...
BUT WHY'D YOU DO IT?
WHY ME?
YOU LOOK LIKE HER.

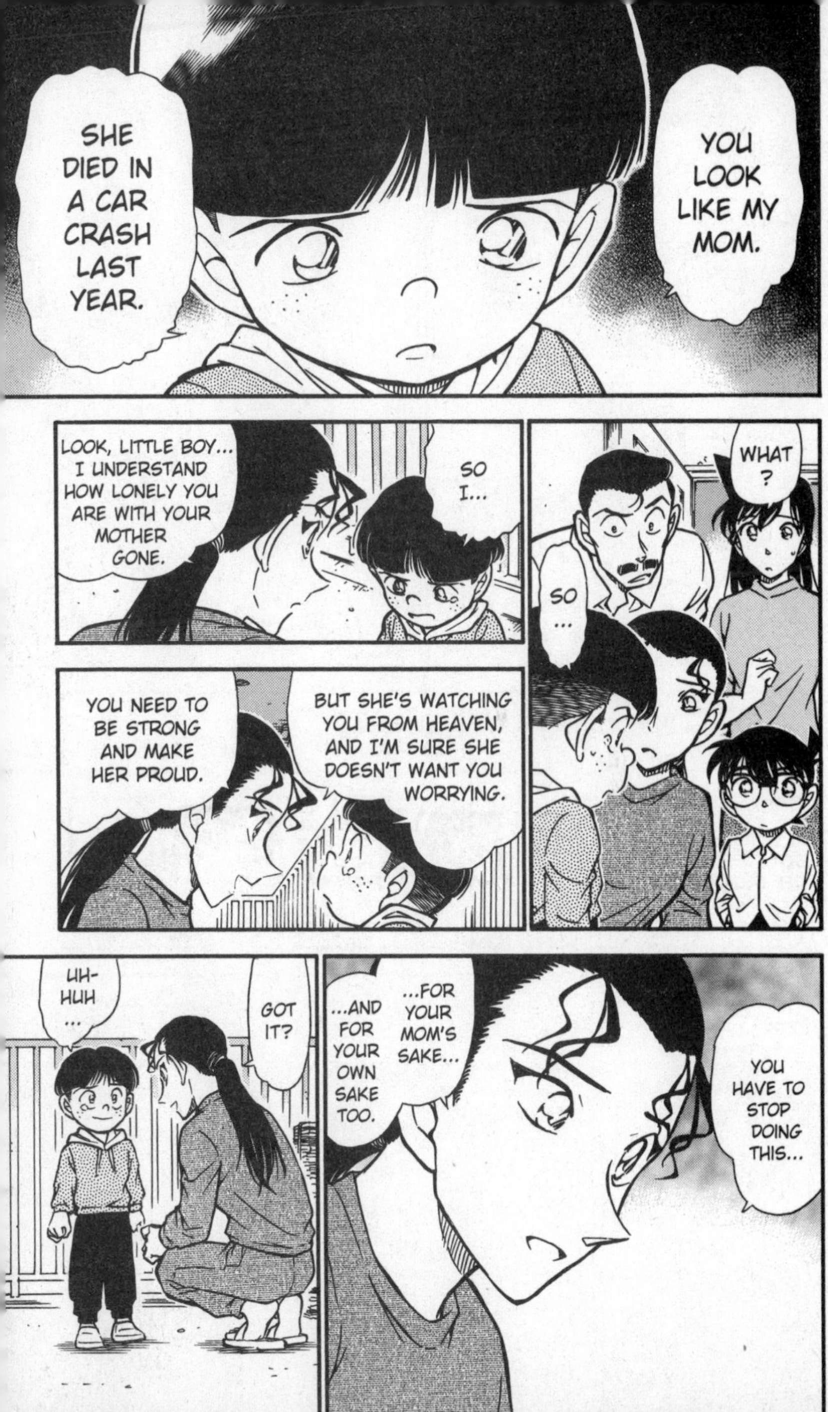
YOU LOOK LIKE MY MOM.
SHE DIED IN A CAR CRASH LAST YEAR.
WHAT?
SO ...
SO I...
LOOK, LITTLE BOY... I UNDERSTAND HOW LONELY YOU ARE WITH YOUR MOTHER GONE.
BUT SHE'S WATCHING YOU FROM HEAVEN, AND I'M SURE SHE DOESN'T WANT YOU WORRYING.
YOU NEED TO BE STRONG AND MAKE HER PROUD.
YOU HAVE TO STOP DOING THIS...
...FOR YOUR MOM'S SAKE...
...AND FOR YOUR OWN SAKE TOO.
GOT IT?
UH-HUH ...

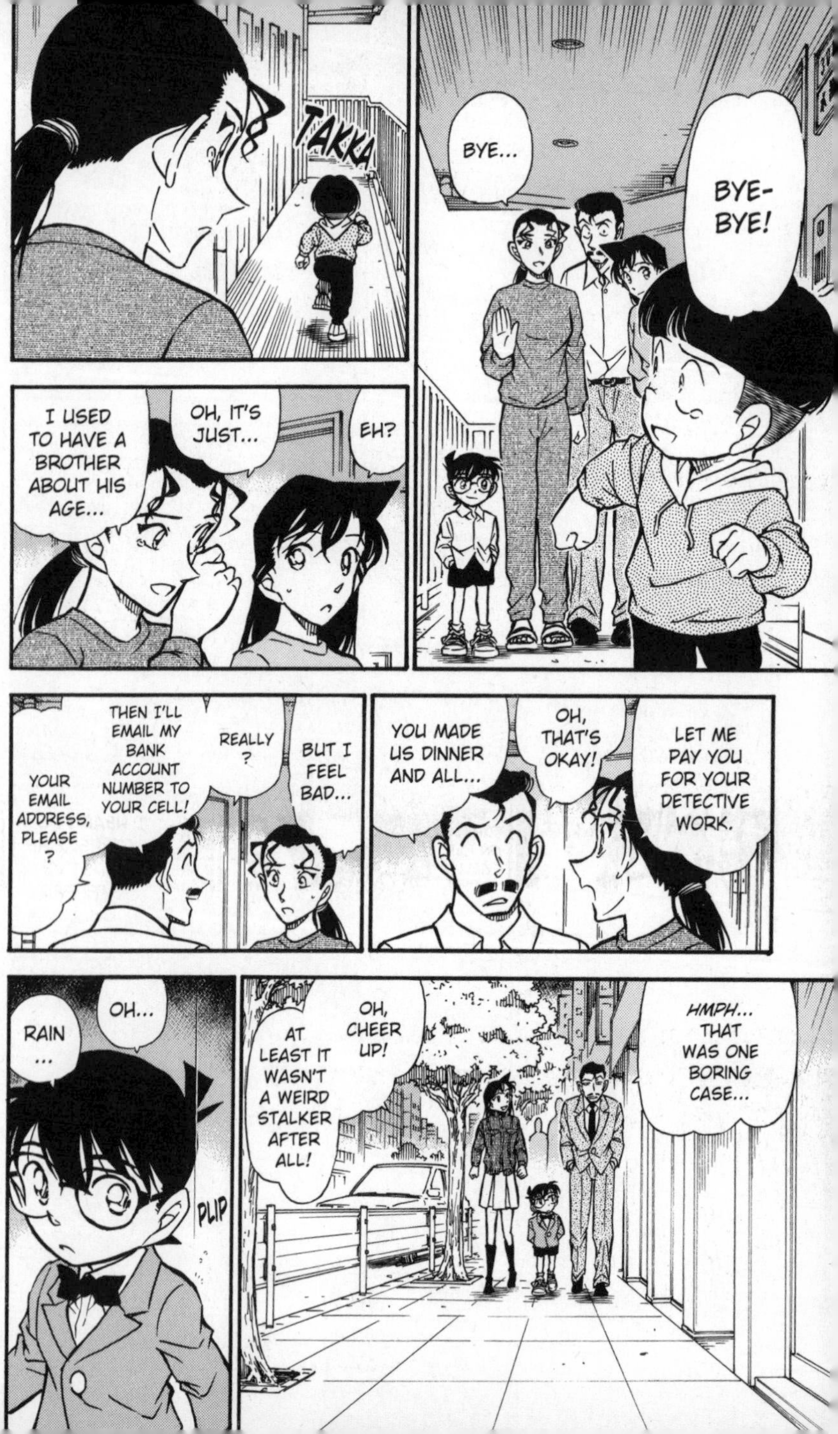

BYE-BYE!
BYE...
TAKKA
EH?
OH, IT'S JUST...
I USED TO HAVE A BROTHER ABOUT HIS AGE...
LET ME PAY YOU FOR YOUR DETECTIVE WORK.
OH, THAT'S OKAY!
YOU MADE US DINNER AND ALL...
BUT I FEEL BAD...
REALLY?
THEN I'LL EMAIL MY BANK ACCOUNT NUMBER TO YOUR CELL!
YOUR EMAIL ADDRESS, PLEASE?
HMPH... THAT WAS ONE BORING CASE...
OH, CHEER UP!
AT LEAST IT WASN'T A WEIRD STALKER AFTER ALL!
OH...
RAIN...
PLIP

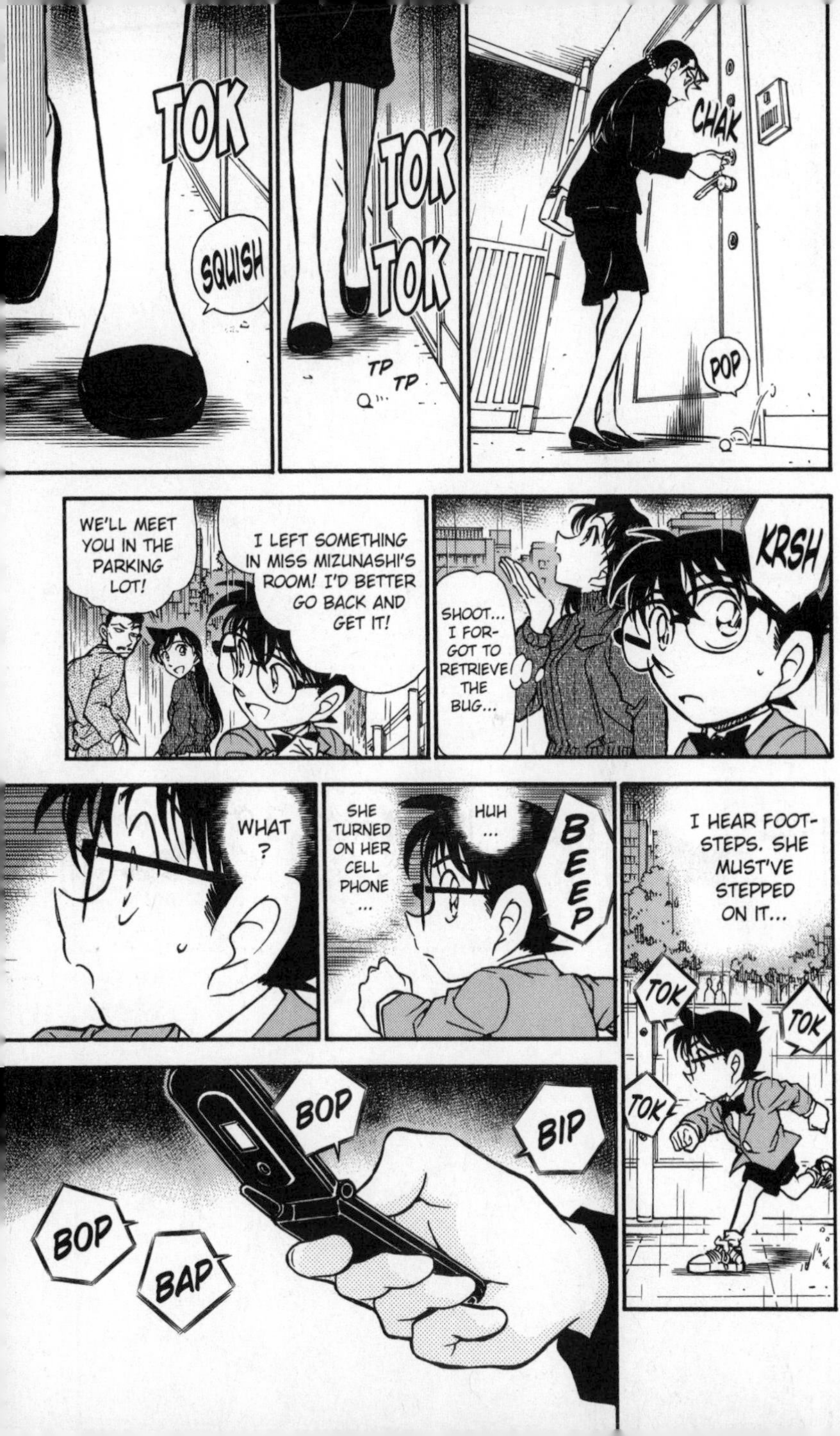
CHAK
POP
TOK
TOK
TP
TP
TOK
SQUISH
KRSH
SHOOT... I FOR-GOT TO RETRIEVE THE BUG...
I LEFT SOMETHING IN MISS MIZUNASHI'S ROOM! I'D BETTER GO BACK AND GET IT!
WE'LL MEET YOU IN THE PARKING LOT!
I HEAR FOOT-STEPS. SHE MUST'VE STEPPED ON IT...
TOK
TOK
TOK
BEEP
HUH ...
SHE TURNED ON HER CELL PHONE ...
WHAT ?
BIP
BOP
BOP
BAP

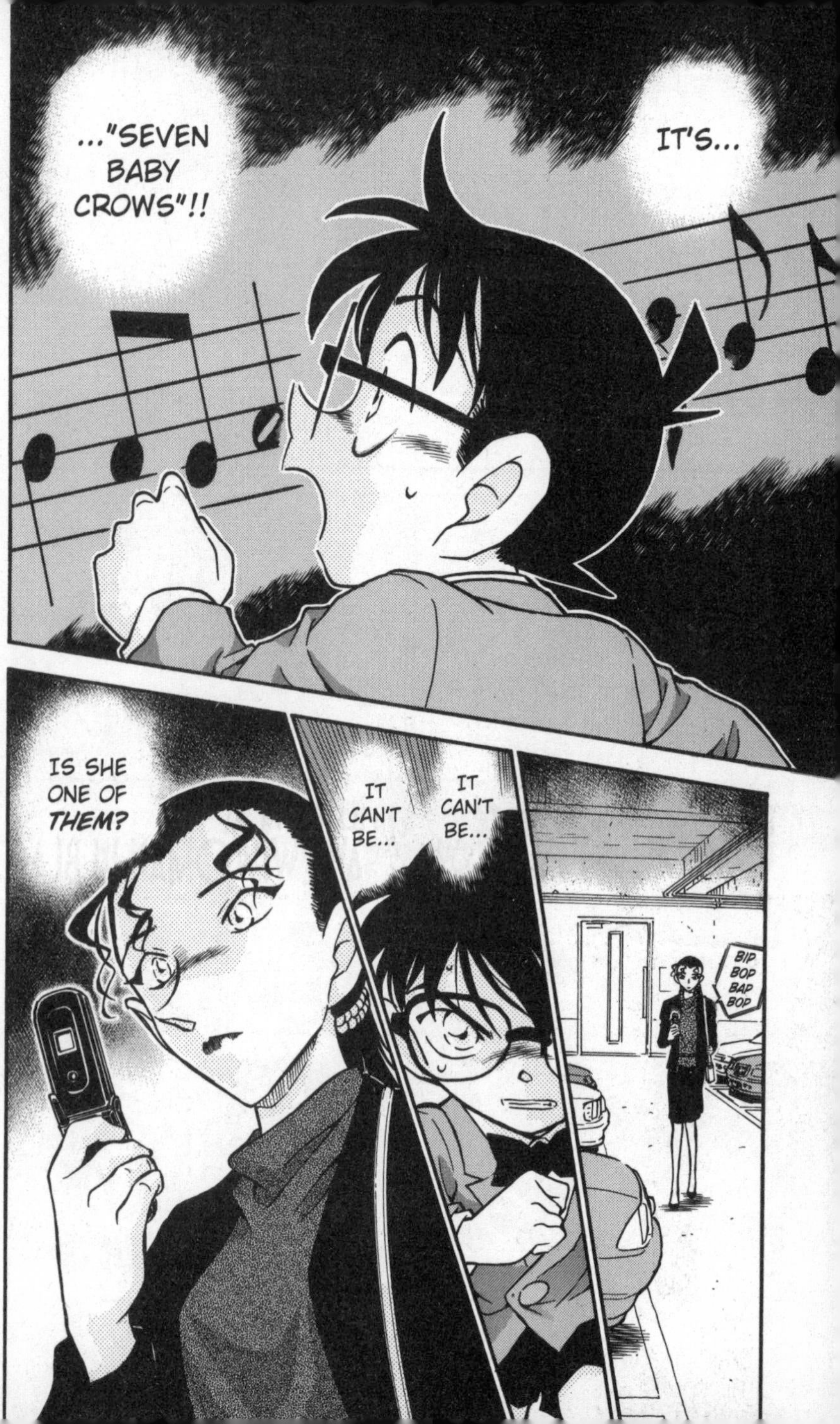
IT'S...
..."SEVEN BABY CROWS"!!
BIP BOP BAP BOP
IT CAN'T BE...
IT CAN'T BE...
IS SHE ONE OF *THEM?*

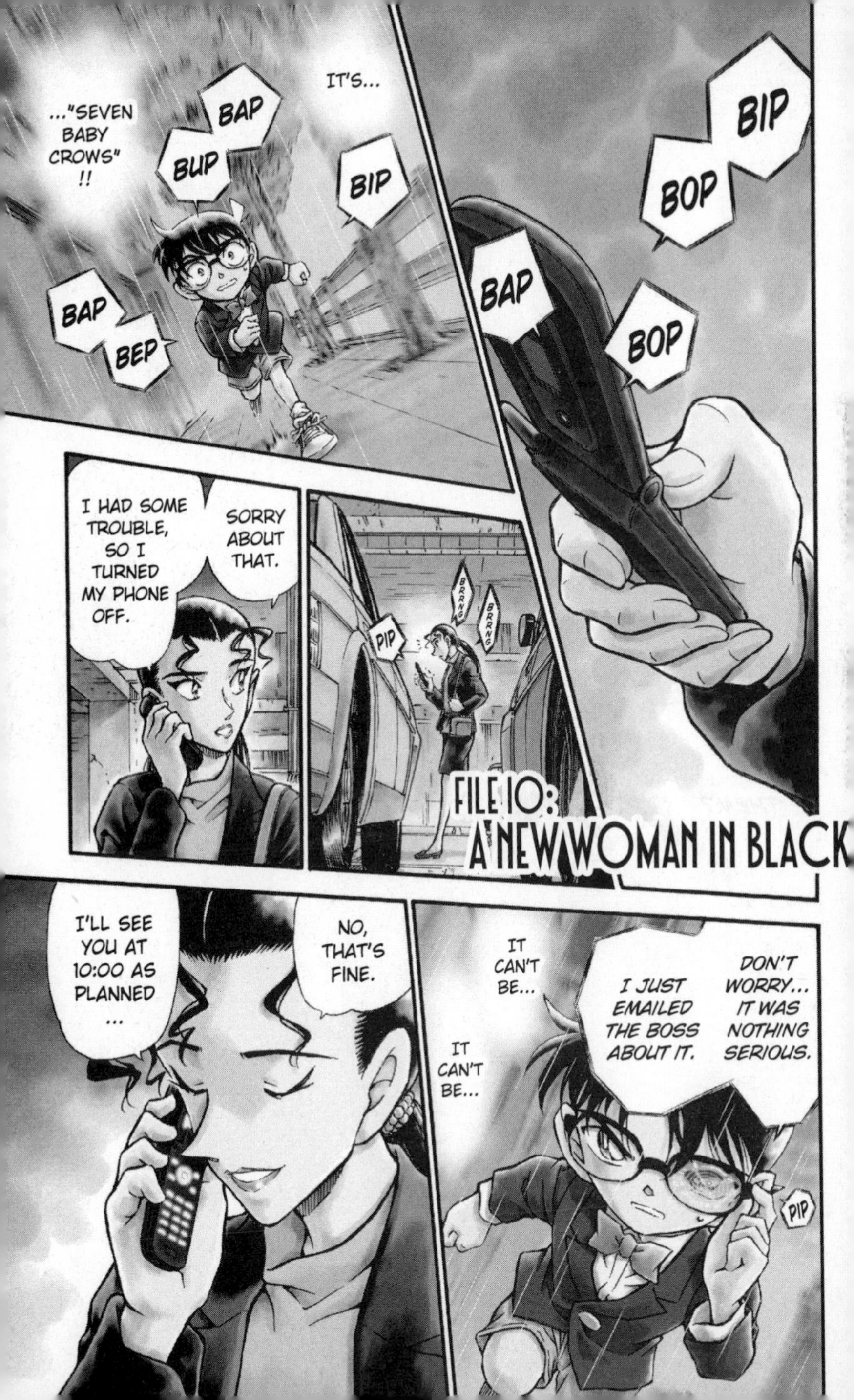
BIP
BOP
BAP
BOP
FILE 10:
A NEW WOMAN IN BLACK
IT'S...
BIP
BAP
BUP
..."SEVEN BABY CROWS"!!
BAP
BEP
BRRNG
BRRNG
PIP
SORRY ABOUT THAT.
I HAD SOME TROUBLE, SO I TURNED MY PHONE OFF.
DON'T WORRY... IT WAS NOTHING SERIOUS.
I JUST EMAILED THE BOSS ABOUT IT.
IT CAN'T BE...
IT CAN'T BE...
PIP
NO, THAT'S FINE.
I'LL SEE YOU AT 10:00 AS PLANNED...

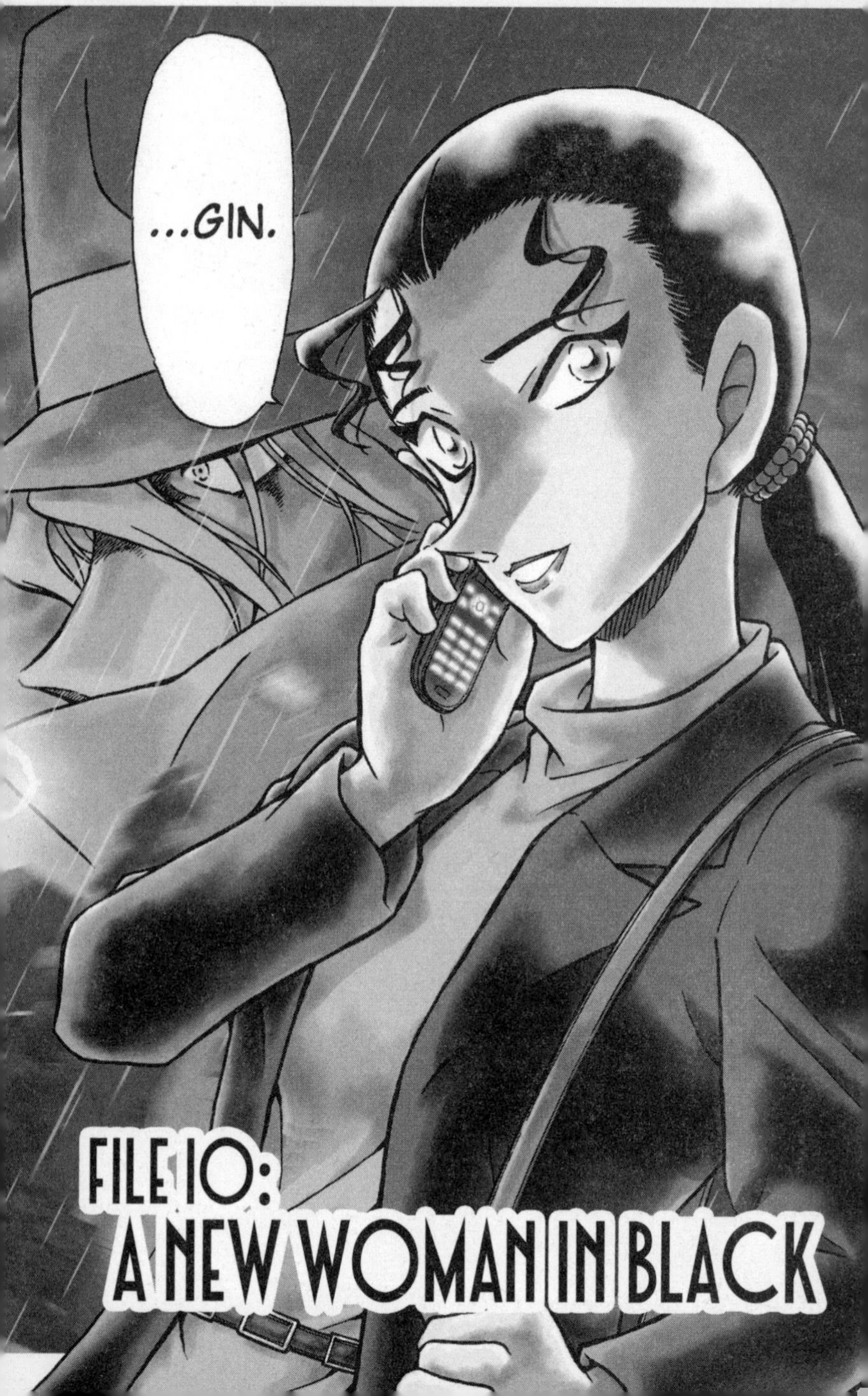
...GIN.
FILE 10:
A NEW WOMAN IN BLACK

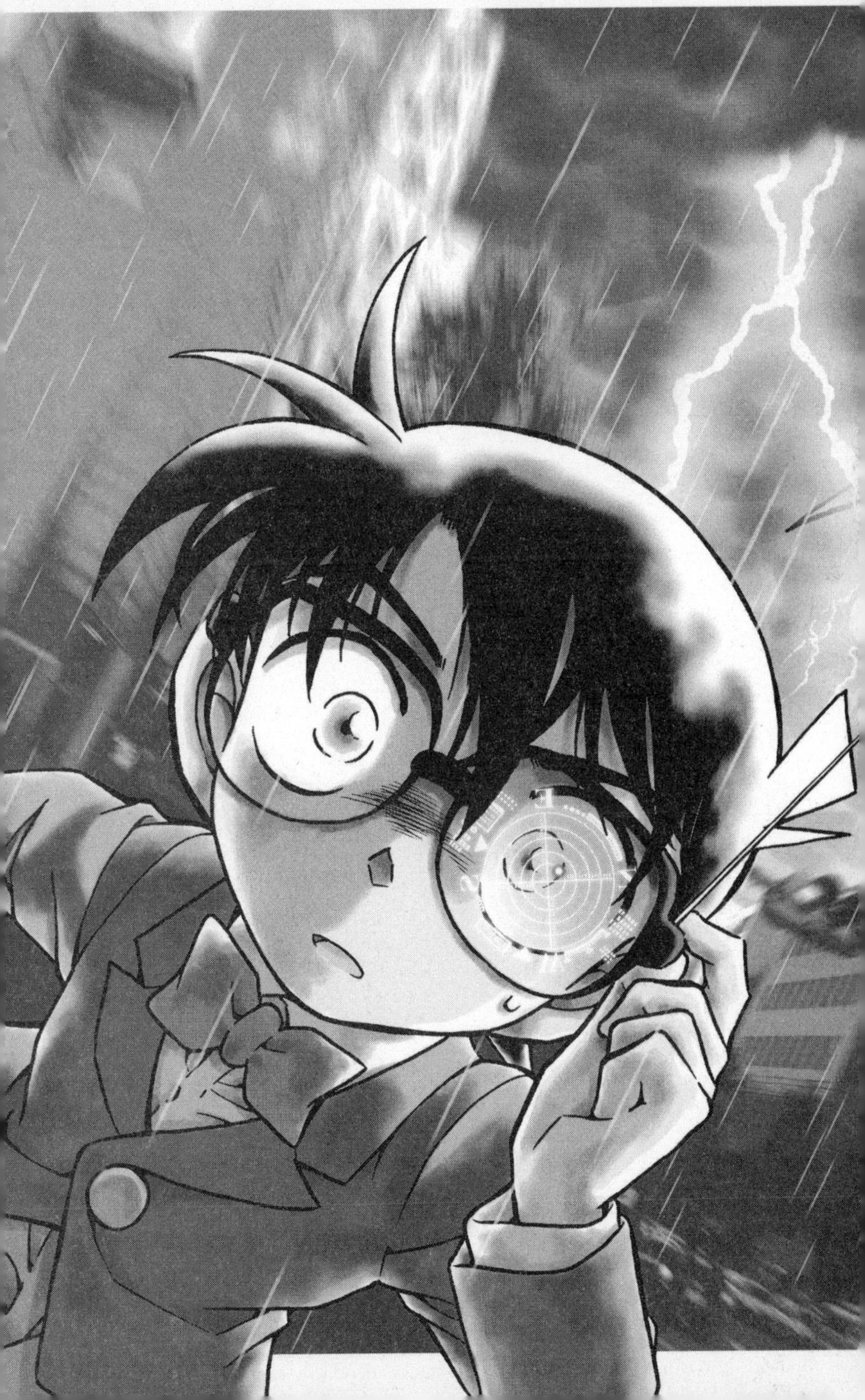

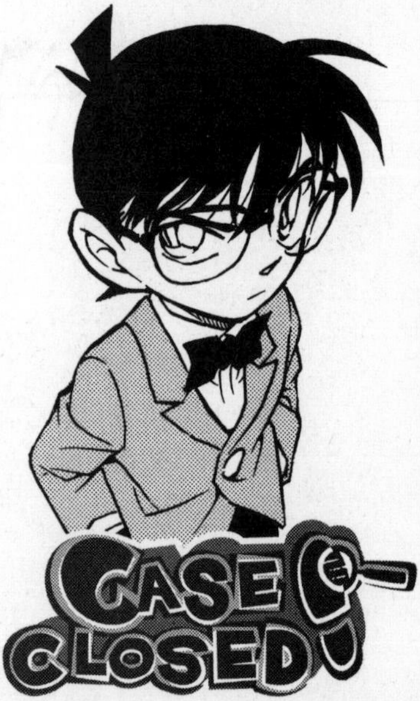
CASE CLOSED

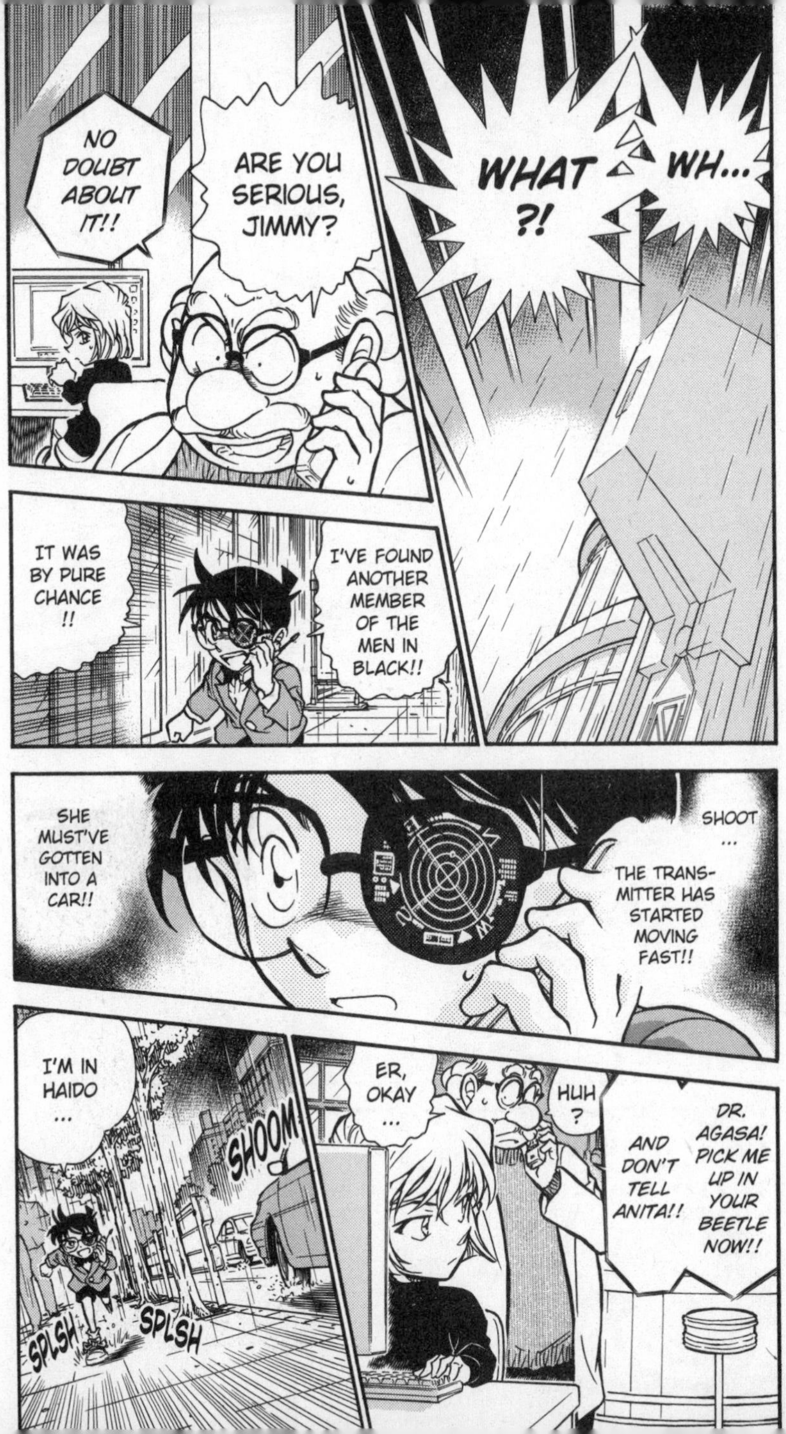
WH...
WHAT ?!
ARE YOU SERIOUS, JIMMY?
NO DOUBT ABOUT IT!!
I'VE FOUND ANOTHER MEMBER OF THE MEN IN BLACK!!
IT WAS BY PURE CHANCE !!
SHOOT ...
THE TRANS-MITTER HAS STARTED MOVING FAST!!
SHE MUST'VE GOTTEN INTO A CAR!!
DR. AGASA! PICK ME UP IN YOUR BEETLE NOW!!
AND DON'T TELL ANITA!!
HUH ?
ER, OKAY ...
I'M IN HAIDO ...
SHOOM
SPLSH
SPLSH

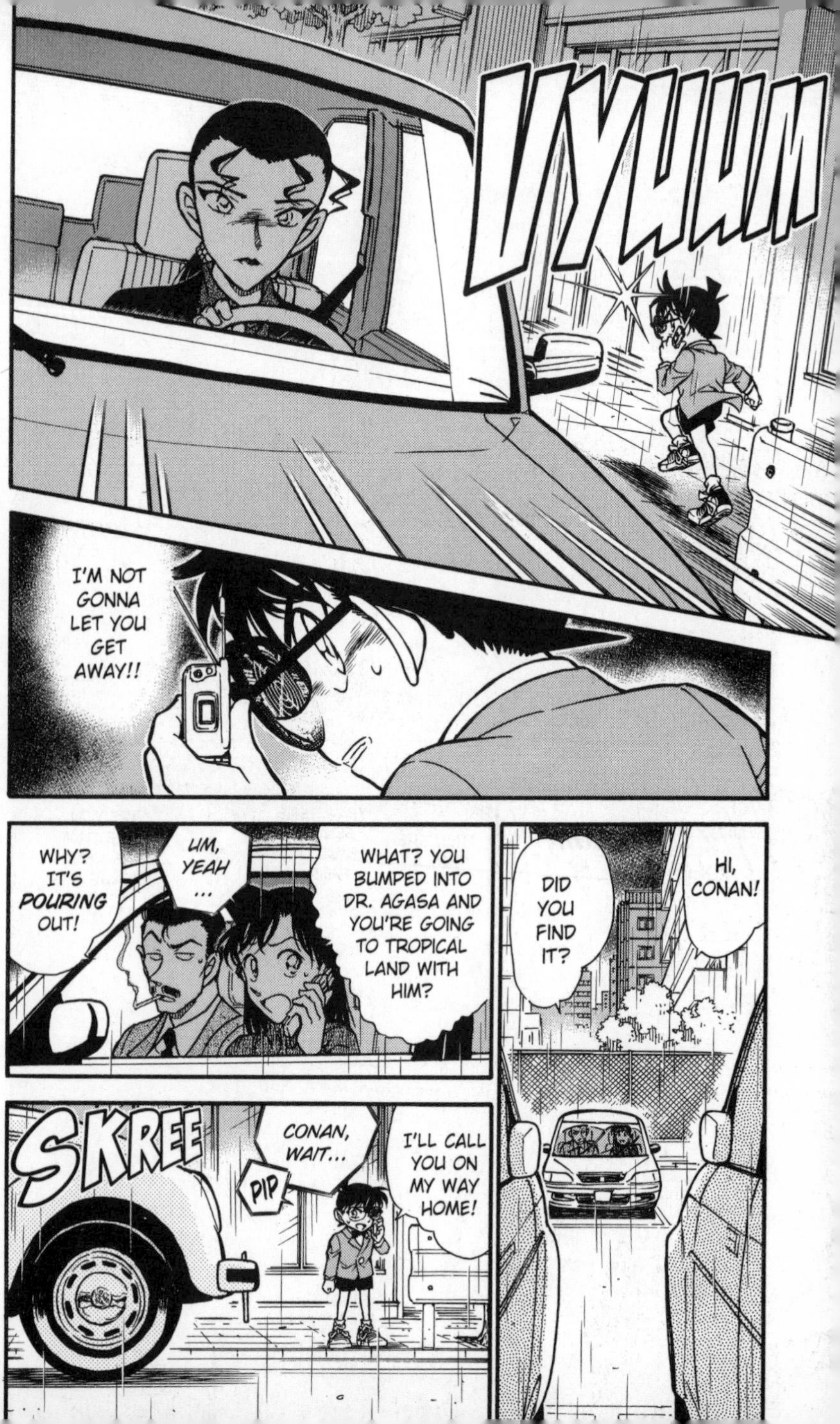
VYUUM
I'M NOT GONNA LET YOU GET AWAY!!
HI, CONAN!
DID YOU FIND IT?
WHAT? YOU BUMPED INTO DR. AGASA AND YOU'RE GOING TO TROPICAL LAND WITH HIM?
UM, YEAH...
WHY? IT'S POURING OUT!
I'LL CALL YOU ON MY WAY HOME!
CONAN, WAIT...
PIP
SKREE

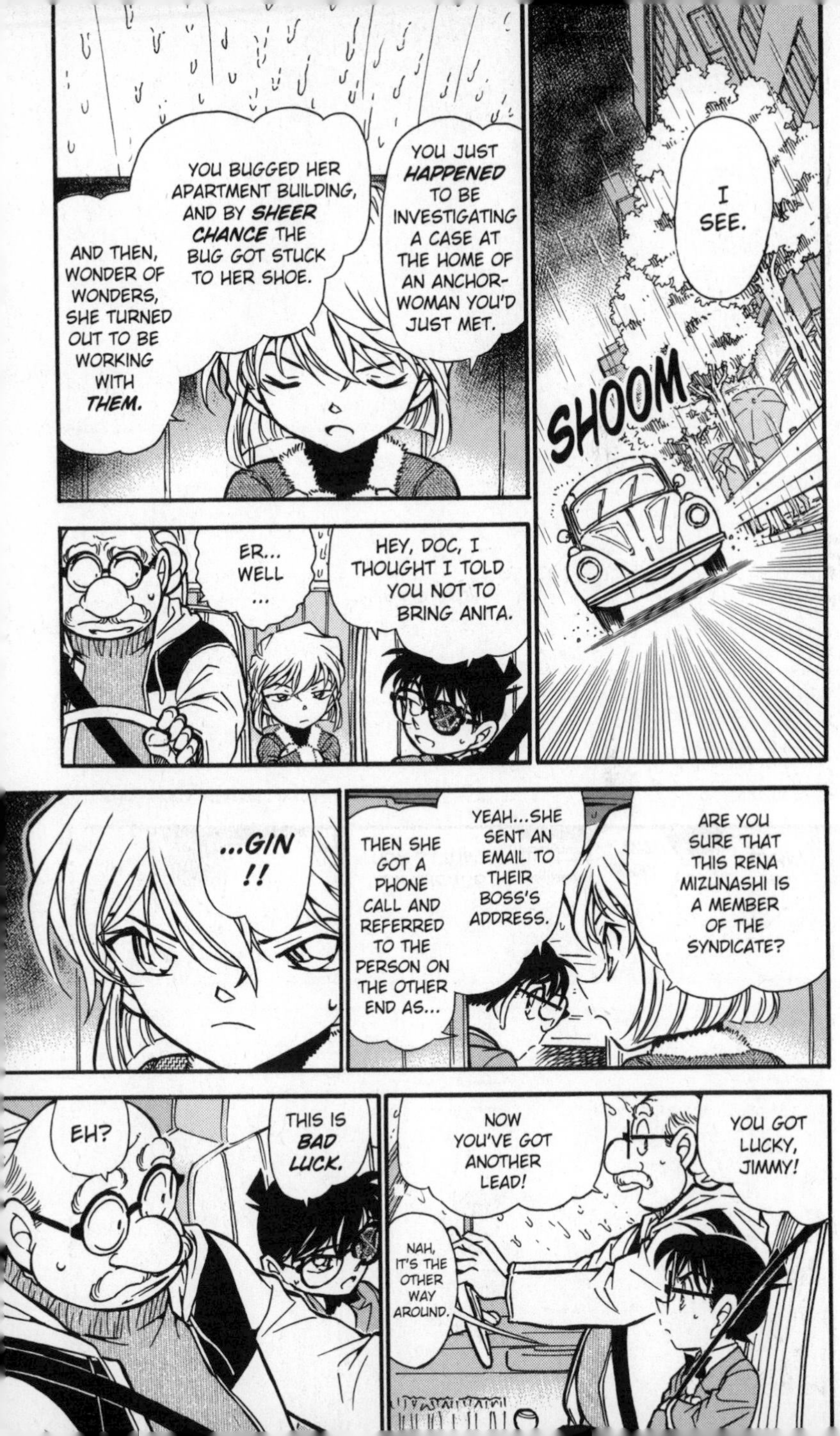
I SEE.
SHOOM
YOU JUST HAPPENED TO BE INVESTIGATING A CASE AT THE HOME OF AN ANCHOR-WOMAN YOU'D JUST MET.
YOU BUGGED HER APARTMENT BUILDING, AND BY SHEER CHANCE THE BUG GOT STUCK TO HER SHOE.
AND THEN, WONDER OF WONDERS, SHE TURNED OUT TO BE WORKING WITH THEM.
HEY, DOC, I THOUGHT I TOLD YOU NOT TO BRING ANITA.
ER... WELL ...
ARE YOU SURE THAT THIS RENA MIZUNASHI IS A MEMBER OF THE SYNDICATE?
YEAH...SHE SENT AN EMAIL TO THEIR BOSS'S ADDRESS.
THEN SHE GOT A PHONE CALL AND REFERRED TO THE PERSON ON THE OTHER END AS...
...GIN !!
YOU GOT LUCKY, JIMMY!
NOW YOU'VE GOT ANOTHER LEAD!
NAH, IT'S THE OTHER WAY AROUND.
THIS IS BAD LUCK.
EH?

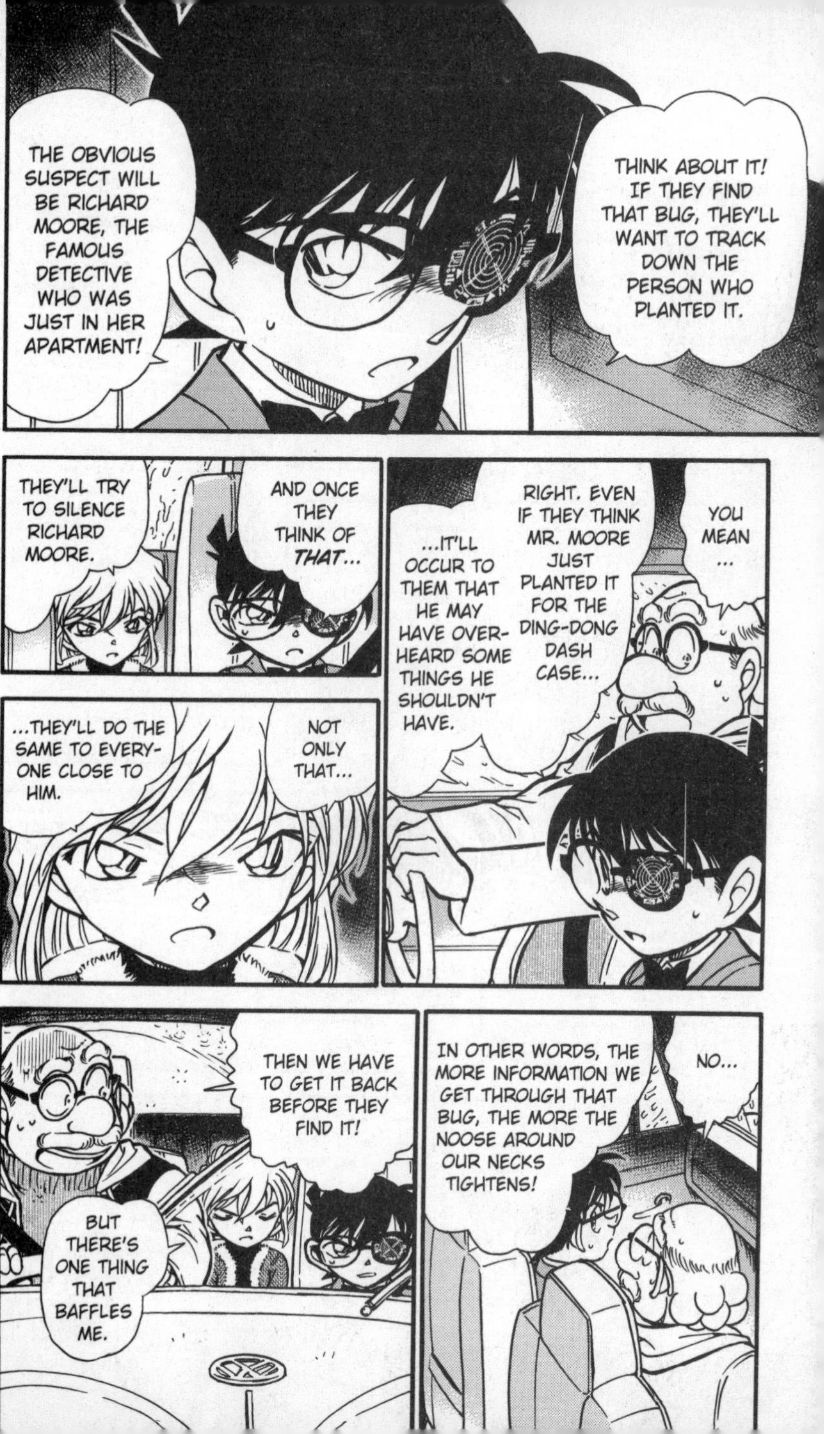
THINK ABOUT IT! IF THEY FIND THAT BUG, THEY'LL WANT TO TRACK DOWN THE PERSON WHO PLANTED IT.
THE OBVIOUS SUSPECT WILL BE RICHARD MOORE, THE FAMOUS DETECTIVE WHO WAS JUST IN HER APARTMENT!
YOU MEAN ...
RIGHT. EVEN IF THEY THINK MR. MOORE JUST PLANTED IT FOR THE DING-DONG DASH CASE...
...IT'LL OCCUR TO THEM THAT HE MAY HAVE OVER-HEARD SOME THINGS HE SHOULDN'T HAVE.
AND ONCE THEY THINK OF *THAT*...
THEY'LL TRY TO SILENCE RICHARD MOORE.
NOT ONLY THAT...
...THEY'LL DO THE SAME TO EVERY-ONE CLOSE TO HIM.
NO...
IN OTHER WORDS, THE MORE INFORMATION WE GET THROUGH THAT BUG, THE MORE THE NOOSE AROUND OUR NECKS TIGHTENS!
THEN WE HAVE TO GET IT BACK BEFORE THEY FIND IT!
BUT THERE'S ONE THING THAT BAFFLES ME.

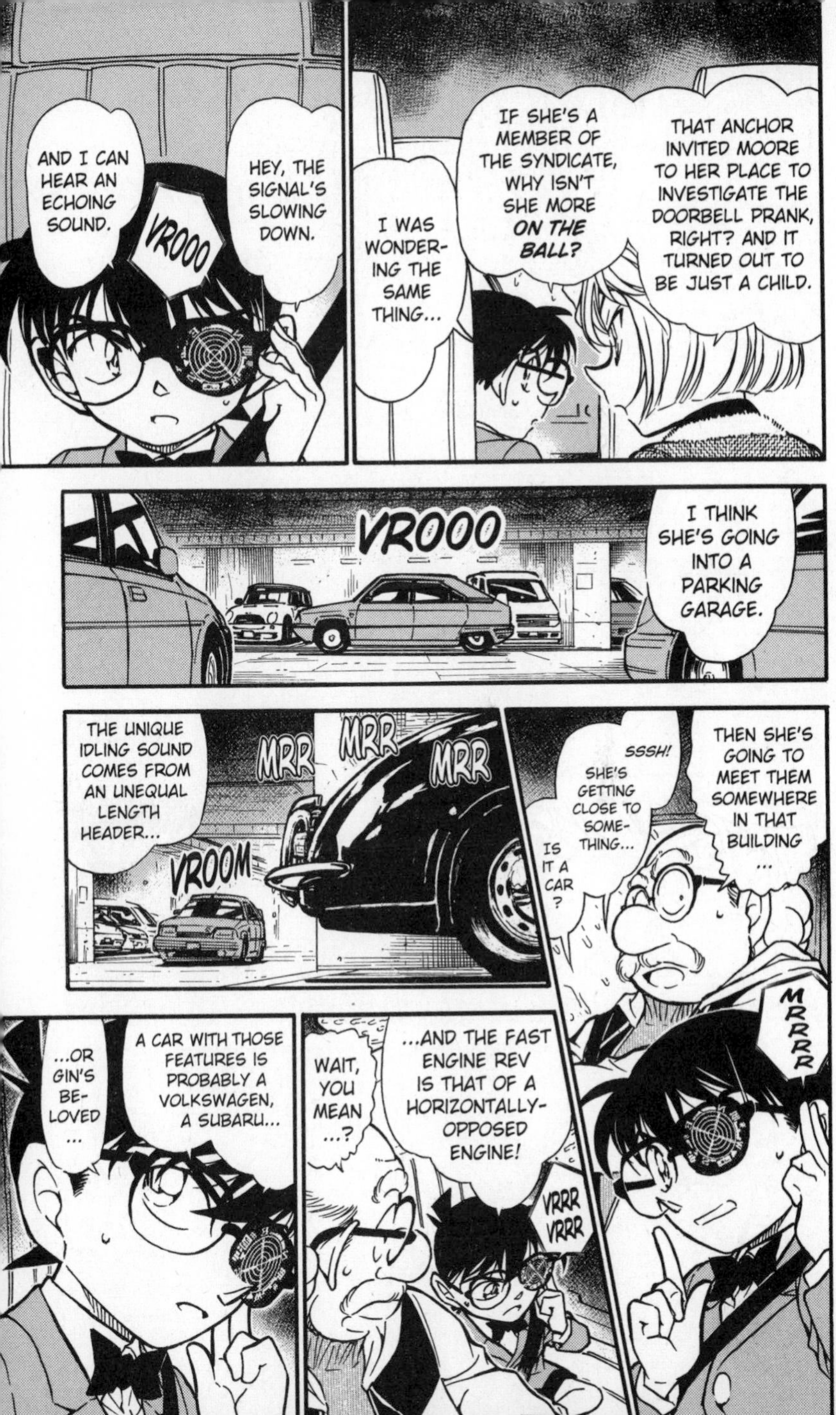
THAT ANCHOR INVITED MOORE TO HER PLACE TO INVESTIGATE THE DOORBELL PRANK, RIGHT? AND IT TURNED OUT TO BE JUST A CHILD.
IF SHE'S A MEMBER OF THE SYNDICATE, WHY ISN'T SHE MORE *ON THE BALL?*
I WAS WONDERING THE SAME THING...
HEY, THE SIGNAL'S SLOWING DOWN.
VROOO
AND I CAN HEAR AN ECHOING SOUND.
I THINK SHE'S GOING INTO A PARKING GARAGE.
VROOO
THEN SHE'S GOING TO MEET THEM SOMEWHERE IN THAT BUILDING...
SSSH! SHE'S GETTING CLOSE TO SOMETHING...
IS IT A CAR?
MRRRR
MRR MRR MRR
THE UNIQUE IDLING SOUND COMES FROM AN UNEQUAL LENGTH HEADER...
VROOM
...AND THE FAST ENGINE REV IS THAT OF A HORIZONTALLY-OPPOSED ENGINE!
WAIT, YOU MEAN ...?
VRRR VRRR
A CAR WITH THOSE FEATURES IS PROBABLY A VOLKSWAGEN, A SUBARU...
...OR GIN'S BE-LOVED ...

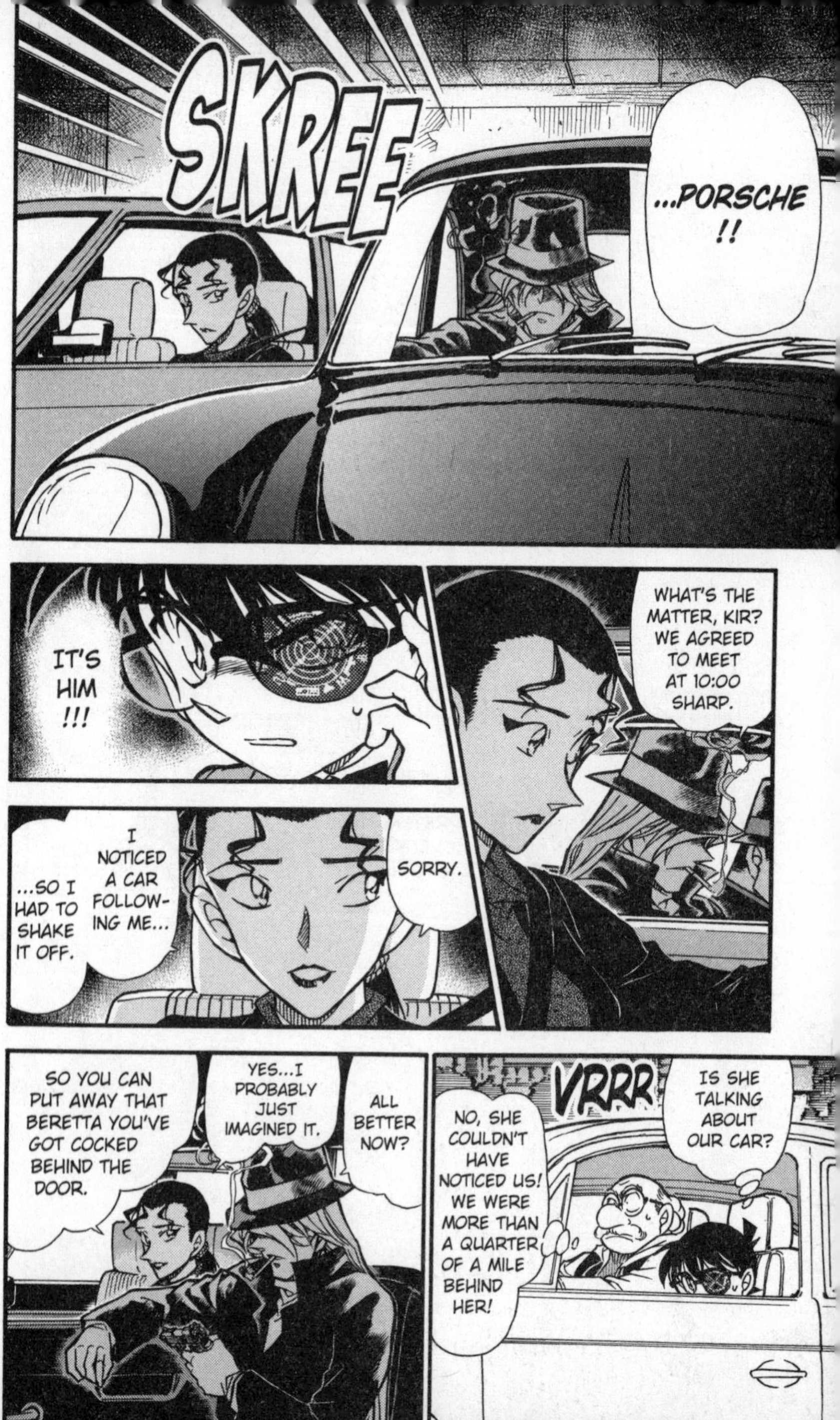
SKREE
...PORSCHE !!
WHAT'S THE MATTER, KIR? WE AGREED TO MEET AT 10:00 SHARP.
IT'S HIM !!!
SORRY.
I NOTICED A CAR FOLLOWING ME...
...SO I HAD TO SHAKE IT OFF.
VRRR
IS SHE TALKING ABOUT OUR CAR?
NO, SHE COULDN'T HAVE NOTICED US! WE WERE MORE THAN A QUARTER OF A MILE BEHIND HER!
ALL BETTER NOW?
YES...I PROBABLY JUST IMAGINED IT.
SO YOU CAN PUT AWAY THAT BERETTA YOU'VE GOT COCKED BEHIND THE DOOR.

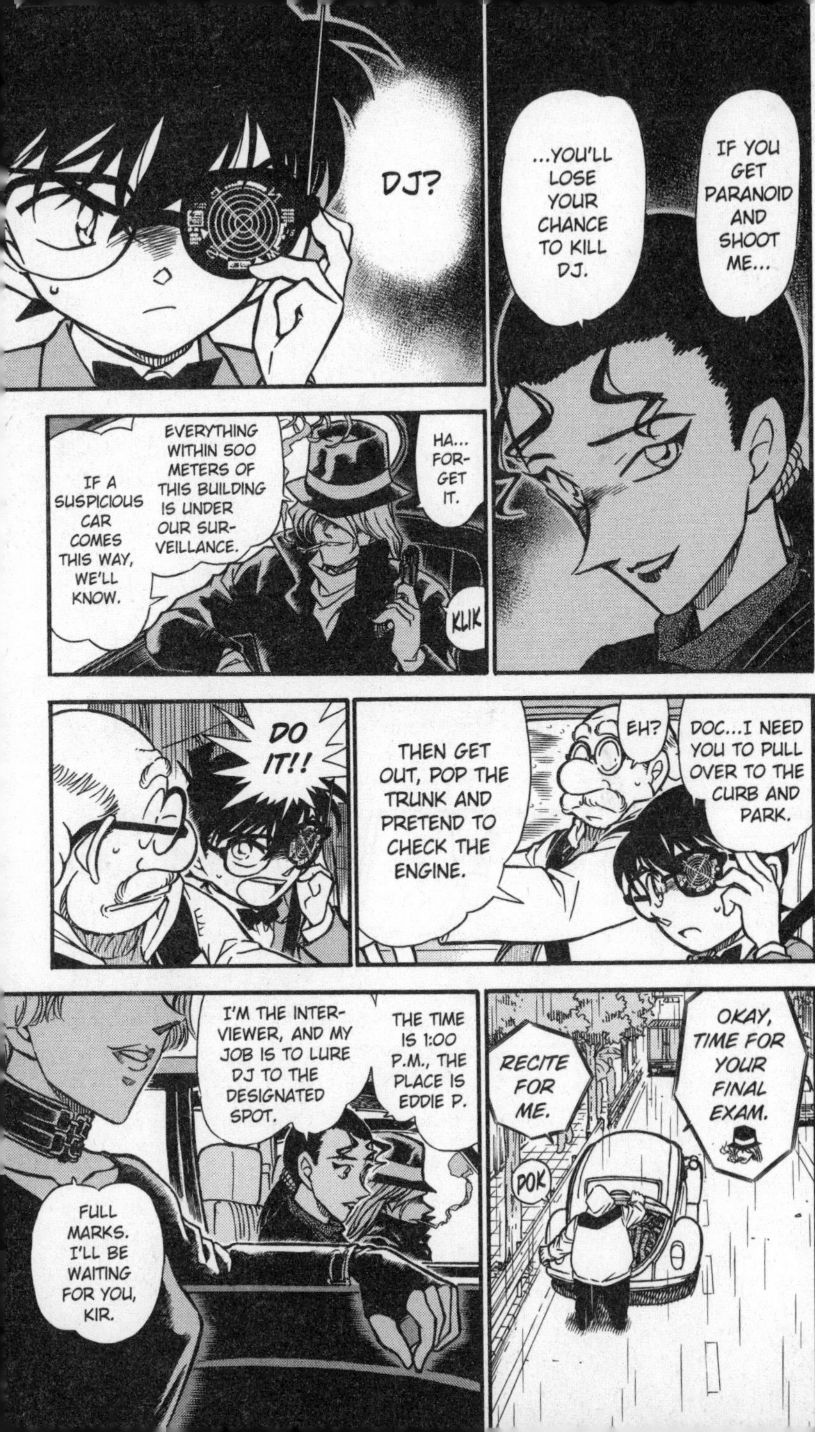
IF YOU GET PARANOID AND SHOOT ME...
...YOU'LL LOSE YOUR CHANCE TO KILL DJ.
DJ?
HA... FOR-GET IT.
KLIK
EVERYTHING WITHIN 500 METERS OF THIS BUILDING IS UNDER OUR SUR-VEILLANCE.
IF A SUSPICIOUS CAR COMES THIS WAY, WE'LL KNOW.
DOC...I NEED YOU TO PULL OVER TO THE CURB AND PARK.
EH?
THEN GET OUT, POP THE TRUNK AND PRETEND TO CHECK THE ENGINE.
DO IT!!
OKAY, TIME FOR YOUR FINAL EXAM.
RECITE FOR ME.
POK
THE TIME IS 1:00 P.M., THE PLACE IS EDDIE P.
I'M THE INTER-VIEWER, AND MY JOB IS TO LURE DJ TO THE DESIGNATED SPOT.
FULL MARKS. I'LL BE WAITING FOR YOU, KIR.

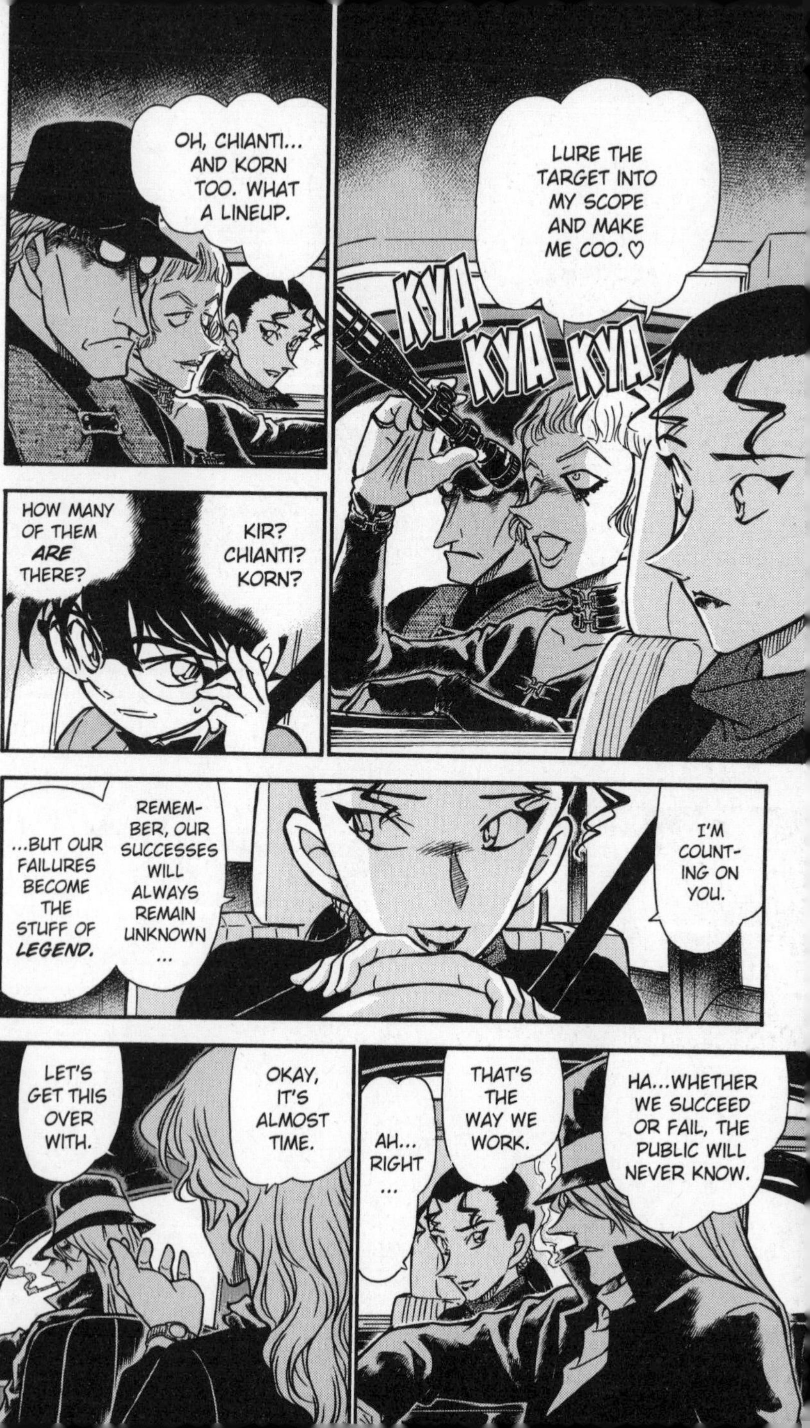
LURE THE TARGET INTO MY SCOPE AND MAKE ME COO. ♡
KYA
KYA
KYA
OH, CHIANTI... AND KORN TOO. WHAT A LINEUP.
KIR? CHIANTI? KORN?
HOW MANY OF THEM *ARE* THERE?
I'M COUNTING ON YOU.
REMEMBER, OUR SUCCESSES WILL ALWAYS REMAIN UNKNOWN...
...BUT OUR FAILURES BECOME THE STUFF OF ***LEGEND.***
HA...WHETHER WE SUCCEED OR FAIL, THE PUBLIC WILL NEVER KNOW.
THAT'S THE WAY WE WORK.
AH... RIGHT...
OKAY, IT'S ALMOST TIME.
LET'S GET THIS OVER WITH.

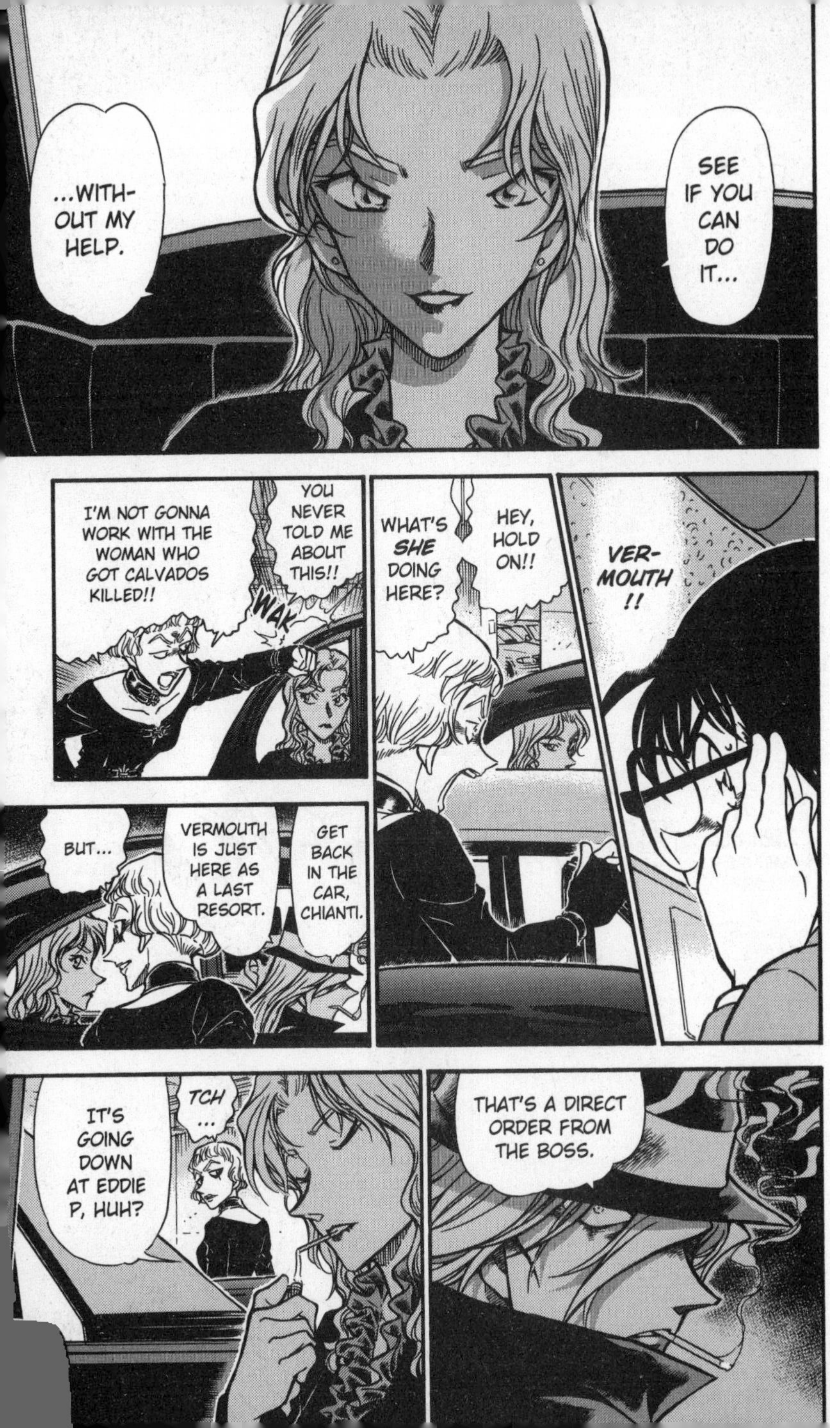
SEE IF YOU CAN DO IT...
...WITHOUT MY HELP.
VERMOUTH!!
HEY, HOLD ON!!
WHAT'S SHE DOING HERE?
YOU NEVER TOLD ME ABOUT THIS!!
I'M NOT GONNA WORK WITH THE WOMAN WHO GOT CALVADOS KILLED!!
WAK
GET BACK IN THE CAR, CHIANTI.
VERMOUTH IS JUST HERE AS A LAST RESORT.
BUT...
THAT'S A DIRECT ORDER FROM THE BOSS.
TCH...
IT'S GOING DOWN AT EDDIE P, HUH?

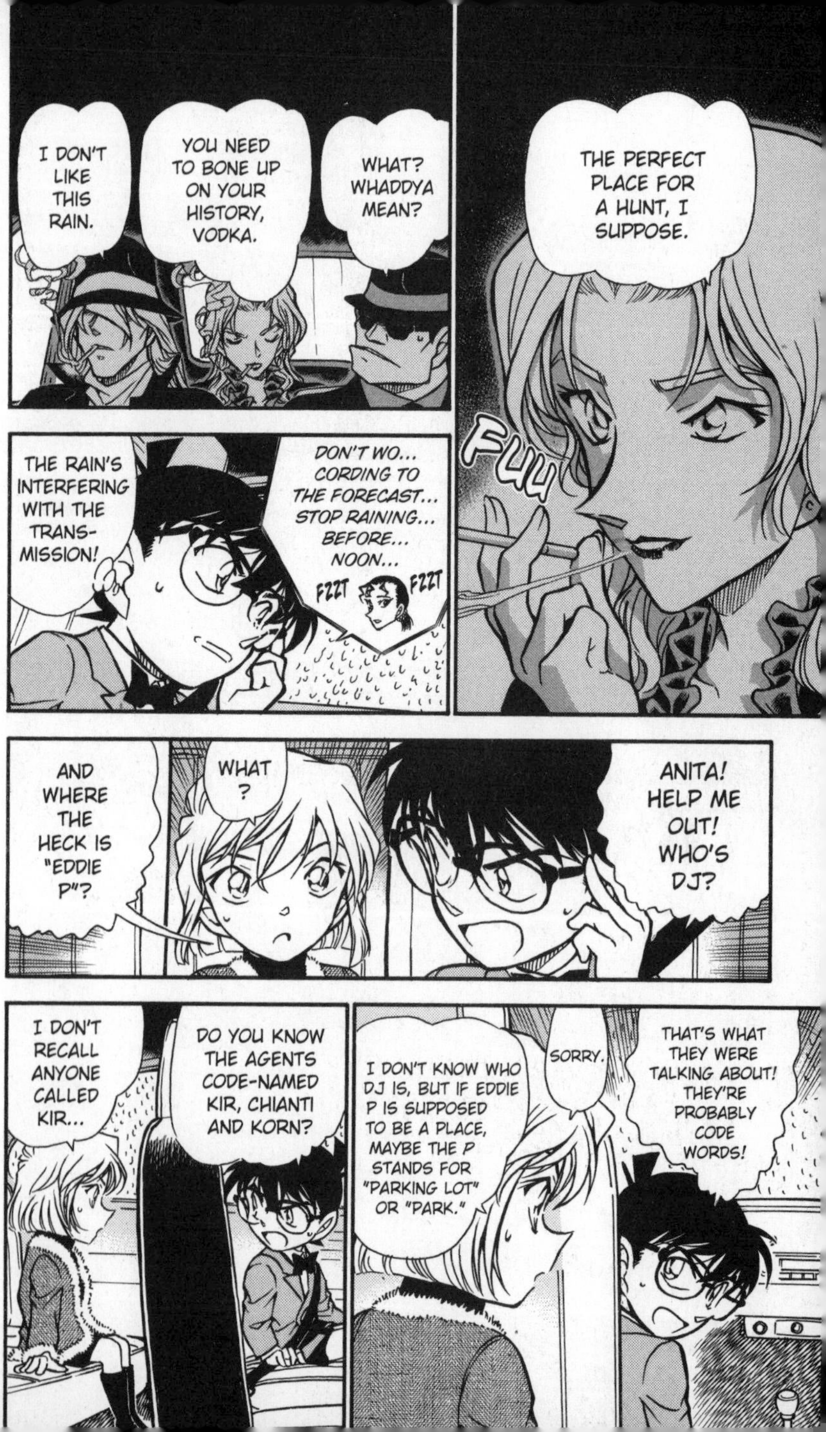
THE PERFECT PLACE FOR A HUNT, I SUPPOSE.
FUU
WHAT? WHADDYA MEAN?
YOU NEED TO BONE UP ON YOUR HISTORY, VODKA.
I DON'T LIKE THIS RAIN.
DON'T WO... CORDING TO THE FORECAST... STOP RAINING... BEFORE... NOON...
FZZT
FZZT
THE RAIN'S INTERFERING WITH THE TRANS-MISSION!
ANITA! HELP ME OUT! WHO'S DJ?
WHAT?
AND WHERE THE HECK IS "EDDIE P"?
THAT'S WHAT THEY WERE TALKING ABOUT! THEY'RE PROBABLY CODE WORDS!
SORRY.
I DON'T KNOW WHO DJ IS, BUT IF EDDIE P IS SUPPOSED TO BE A PLACE, MAYBE THE P STANDS FOR "PARKING LOT" OR "PARK."
DO YOU KNOW THE AGENTS CODE-NAMED KIR, CHIANTI AND KORN?
I DON'T RECALL ANYONE CALLED KIR...

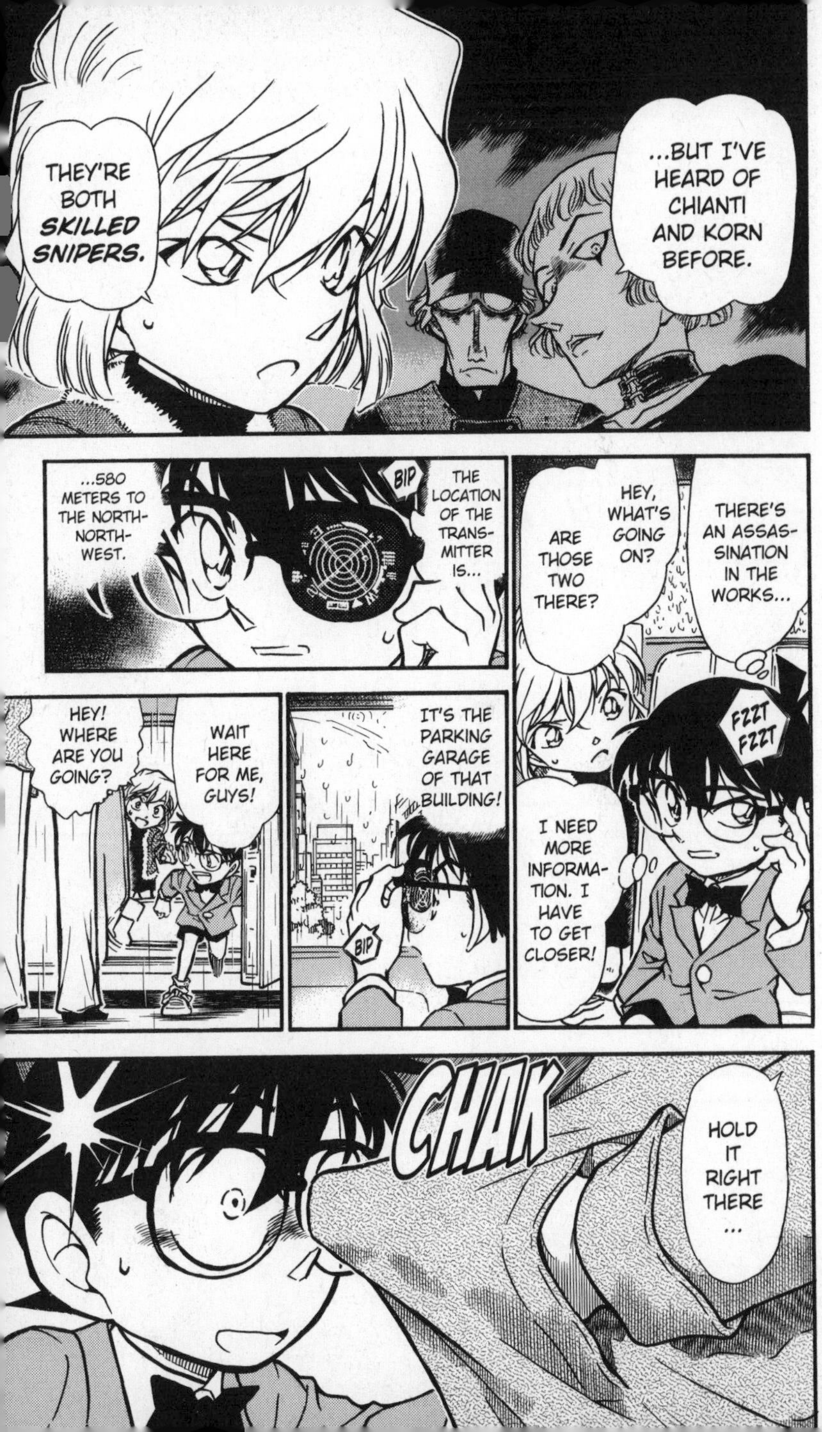
...BUT I'VE HEARD OF CHIANTI AND KORN BEFORE.
THEY'RE BOTH SKILLED SNIPERS.
THERE'S AN ASSASSINATION IN THE WORKS...
HEY, WHAT'S GOING ON?
ARE THOSE TWO THERE?
FZZT FZZT
I NEED MORE INFORMATION. I HAVE TO GET CLOSER!
THE LOCATION OF THE TRANSMITTER IS...
BIP
...580 METERS TO THE NORTH-NORTHWEST.
IT'S THE PARKING GARAGE OF THAT BUILDING!
BIP
WAIT HERE FOR ME, GUYS!
HEY! WHERE ARE YOU GOING?
HOLD IT RIGHT THERE...
CHAK

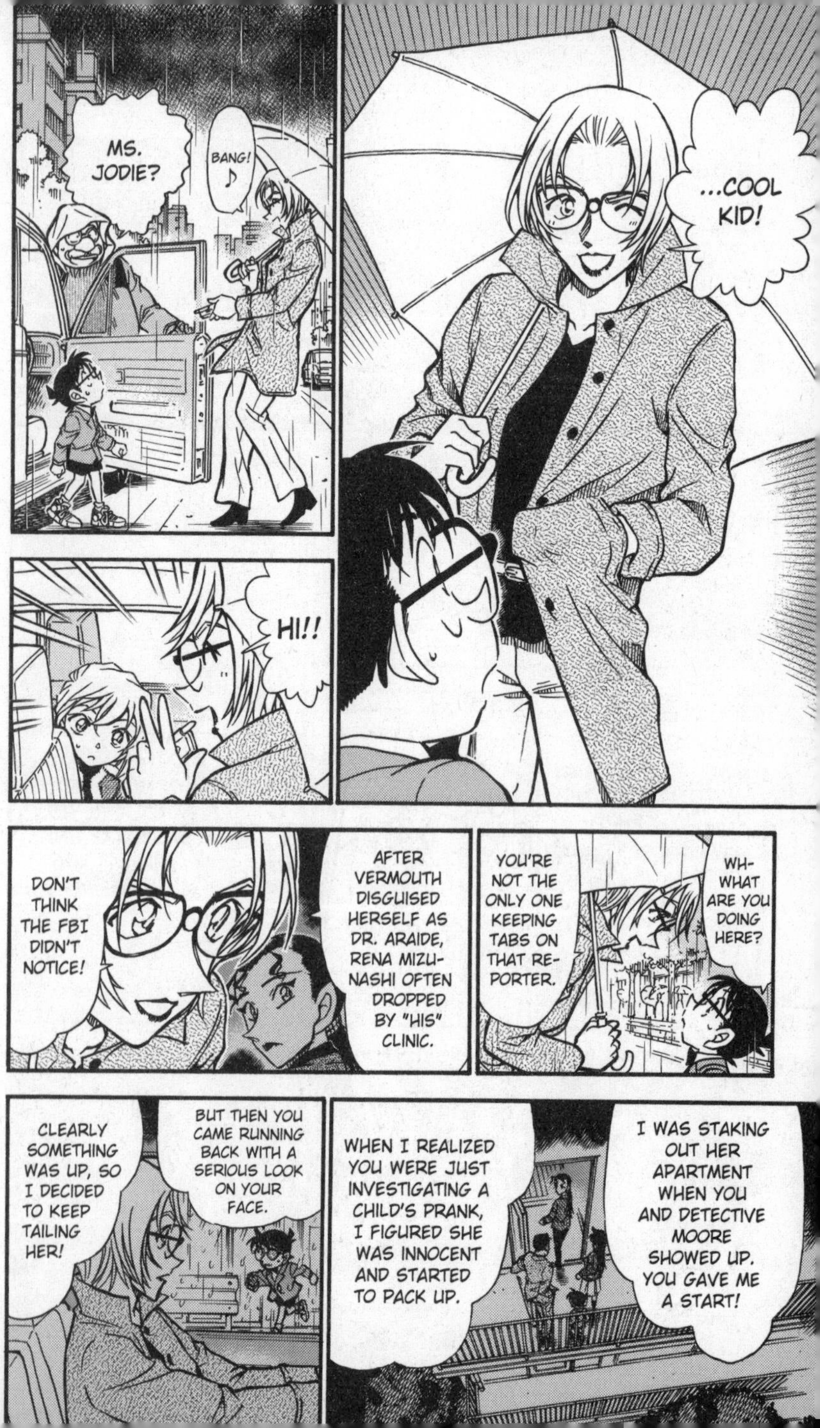
...COOL KID!
BANG! ♪
MS. JODIE?
HI!!
WH-WHAT ARE YOU DOING HERE?
YOU'RE NOT THE ONLY ONE KEEPING TABS ON THAT RE-PORTER.
AFTER VERMOUTH DISGUISED HERSELF AS DR. ARAIDE, RENA MIZU-NASHI OFTEN DROPPED BY "HIS" CLINIC.
DON'T THINK THE FBI DIDN'T NOTICE!
I WAS STAKING OUT HER APARTMENT WHEN YOU AND DETECTIVE MOORE SHOWED UP. YOU GAVE ME A START!
WHEN I REALIZED YOU WERE JUST INVESTIGATING A CHILD'S PRANK, I FIGURED SHE WAS INNOCENT AND STARTED TO PACK UP.
BUT THEN YOU CAME RUNNING BACK WITH A SERIOUS LOOK ON YOUR FACE.
CLEARLY SOMETHING WAS UP, SO I DECIDED TO KEEP TAILING HER!

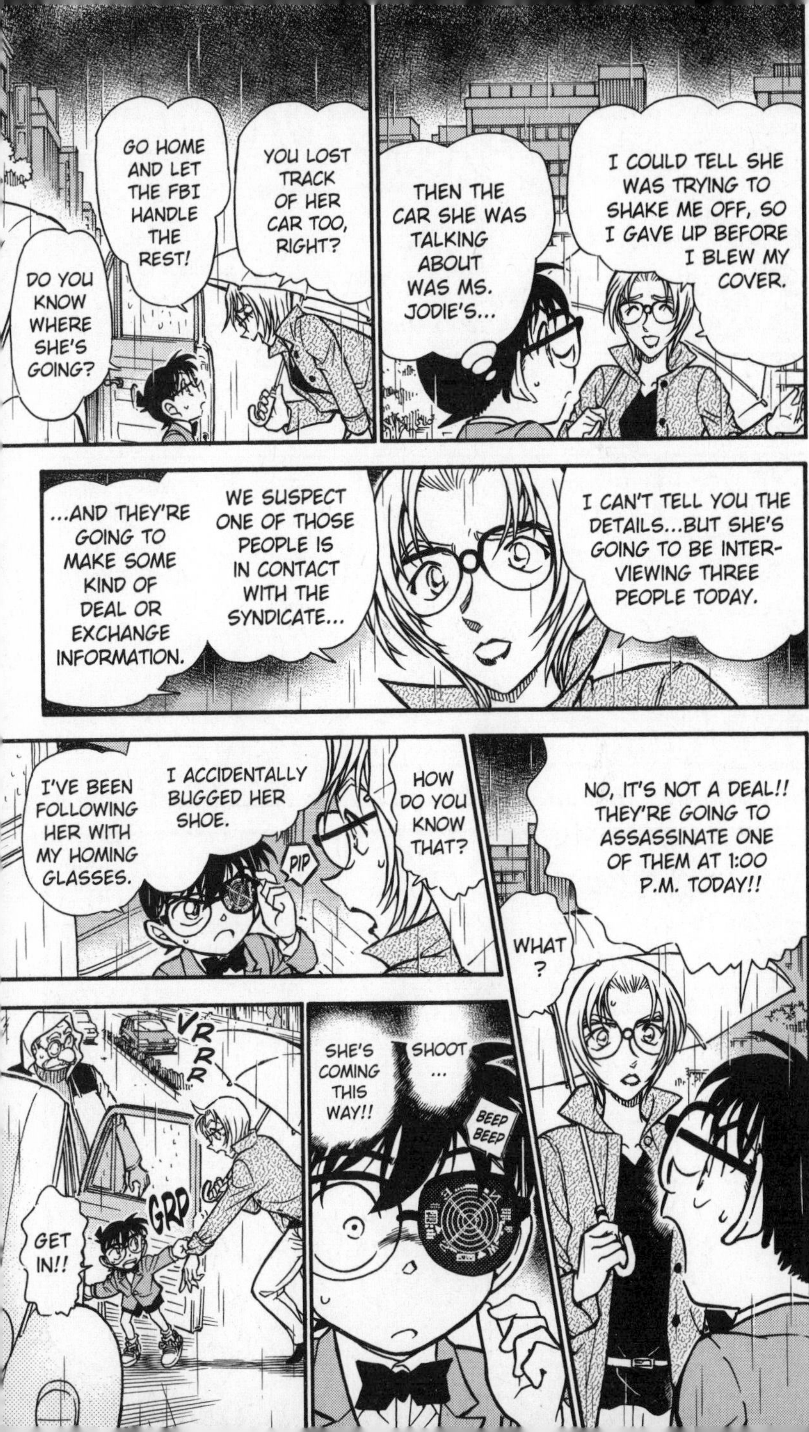

I COULD TELL SHE WAS TRYING TO SHAKE ME OFF, SO I GAVE UP BEFORE I BLEW MY COVER.
THEN THE CAR SHE WAS TALKING ABOUT WAS MS. JODIE'S...
YOU LOST TRACK OF HER CAR TOO, RIGHT?
GO HOME AND LET THE FBI HANDLE THE REST!
DO YOU KNOW WHERE SHE'S GOING?
I CAN'T TELL YOU THE DETAILS...BUT SHE'S GOING TO BE INTER-VIEWING THREE PEOPLE TODAY.
WE SUSPECT ONE OF THOSE PEOPLE IS IN CONTACT WITH THE SYNDICATE...
...AND THEY'RE GOING TO MAKE SOME KIND OF DEAL OR EXCHANGE INFORMATION.
NO, IT'S NOT A DEAL!! THEY'RE GOING TO ASSASSINATE ONE OF THEM AT 1:00 P.M. TODAY!!
WHAT?
HOW DO YOU KNOW THAT?
PIP
I ACCIDENTALLY BUGGED HER SHOE.
I'VE BEEN FOLLOWING HER WITH MY HOMING GLASSES.
BEEP BEEP
SHOOT...
SHE'S COMING THIS WAY!!
VRRR
GRP
GET IN!!

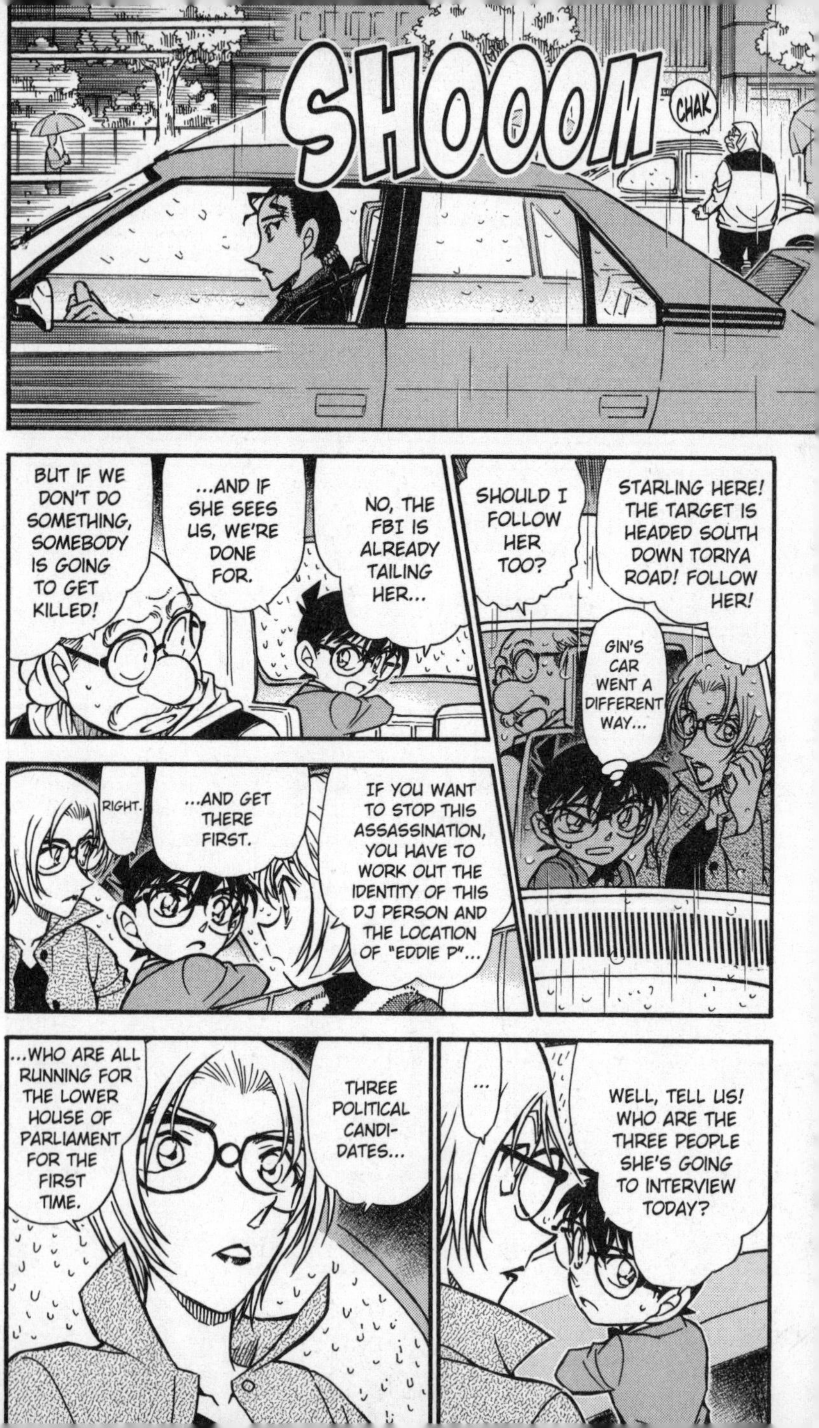
SHOOOM
CHAK
STARLING HERE! THE TARGET IS HEADED SOUTH DOWN TORIYA ROAD! FOLLOW HER!
SHOULD I FOLLOW HER TOO?
GIN'S CAR WENT A DIFFERENT WAY...
NO, THE FBI IS ALREADY TAILING HER...
...AND IF SHE SEES US, WE'RE DONE FOR.
BUT IF WE DON'T DO SOMETHING, SOMEBODY IS GOING TO GET KILLED!
IF YOU WANT TO STOP THIS ASSASSINATION, YOU HAVE TO WORK OUT THE IDENTITY OF THIS DJ PERSON AND THE LOCATION OF "EDDIE P"...
...AND GET THERE FIRST.
RIGHT.
WELL, TELL US! WHO ARE THE THREE PEOPLE SHE'S GOING TO INTERVIEW TODAY?
...
THREE POLITICAL CANDI-DATES...
...WHO ARE ALL RUNNING FOR THE LOWER HOUSE OF PARLIAMENT FOR THE FIRST TIME.

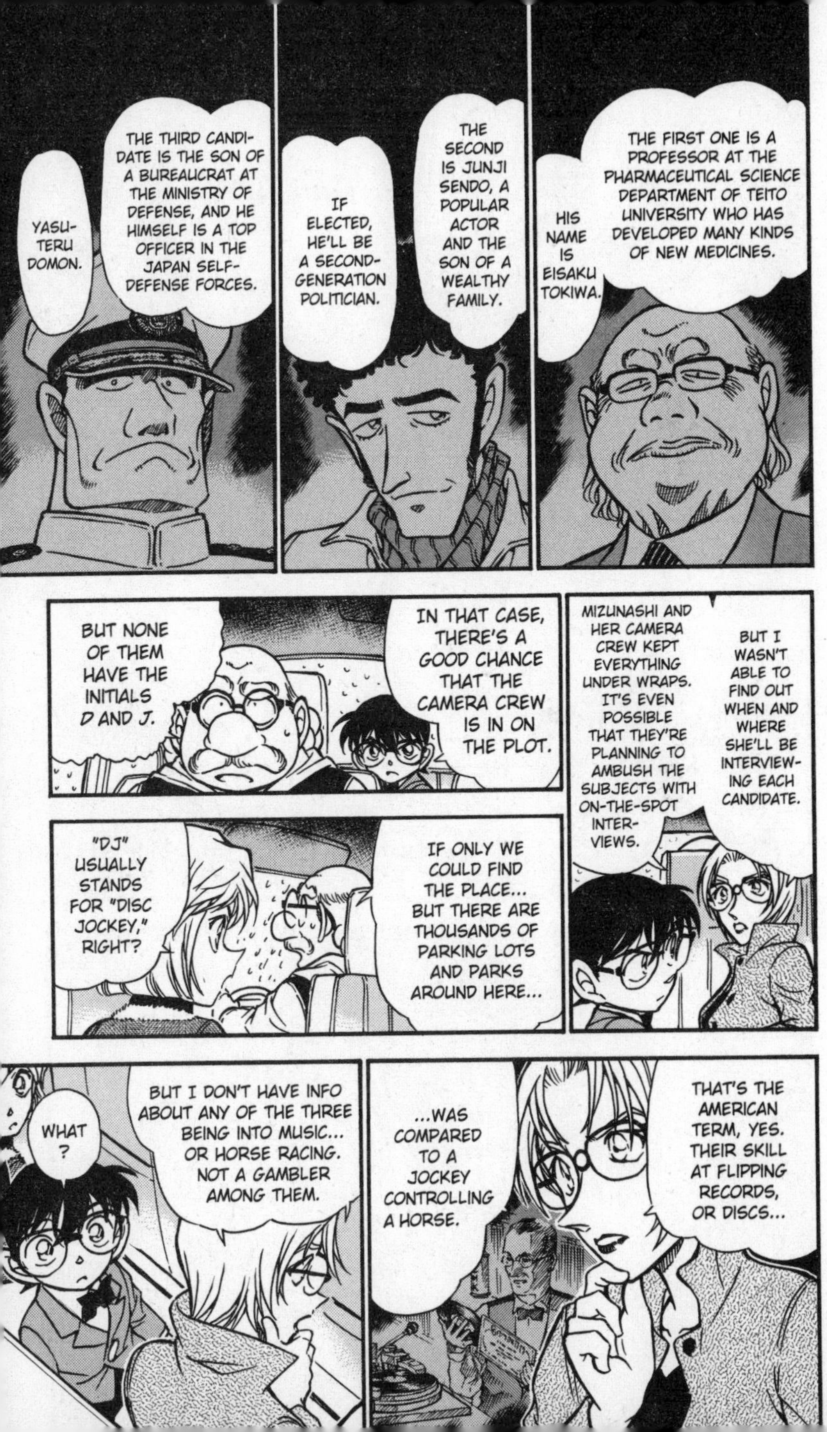
THE FIRST ONE IS A PROFESSOR AT THE PHARMACEUTICAL SCIENCE DEPARTMENT OF TEITO UNIVERSITY WHO HAS DEVELOPED MANY KINDS OF NEW MEDICINES.
HIS NAME IS EISAKU TOKIWA.
THE SECOND IS JUNJI SENDO, A POPULAR ACTOR AND THE SON OF A WEALTHY FAMILY.
IF ELECTED, HE'LL BE A SECOND-GENERATION POLITICIAN.
THE THIRD CANDIDATE IS THE SON OF A BUREAUCRAT AT THE MINISTRY OF DEFENSE, AND HE HIMSELF IS A TOP OFFICER IN THE JAPAN SELF-DEFENSE FORCES.
YASUTERU DOMON.
BUT I WASN'T ABLE TO FIND OUT WHEN AND WHERE SHE'LL BE INTERVIEWING EACH CANDIDATE.
MIZUNASHI AND HER CAMERA CREW KEPT EVERYTHING UNDER WRAPS. IT'S EVEN POSSIBLE THAT THEY'RE PLANNING TO AMBUSH THE SUBJECTS WITH ON-THE-SPOT INTERVIEWS.
IN THAT CASE, THERE'S A GOOD CHANCE THAT THE CAMERA CREW IS IN ON THE PLOT.
BUT NONE OF THEM HAVE THE INITIALS D AND J.
IF ONLY WE COULD FIND THE PLACE... BUT THERE ARE THOUSANDS OF PARKING LOTS AND PARKS AROUND HERE...
"DJ" USUALLY STANDS FOR "DISC JOCKEY," RIGHT?
THAT'S THE AMERICAN TERM, YES. THEIR SKILL AT FLIPPING RECORDS, OR DISCS...
...WAS COMPARED TO A JOCKEY CONTROLLING A HORSE.
BUT I DON'T HAVE INFO ABOUT ANY OF THE THREE BEING INTO MUSIC... OR HORSE RACING. NOT A GAMBLER AMONG THEM.
WHAT?

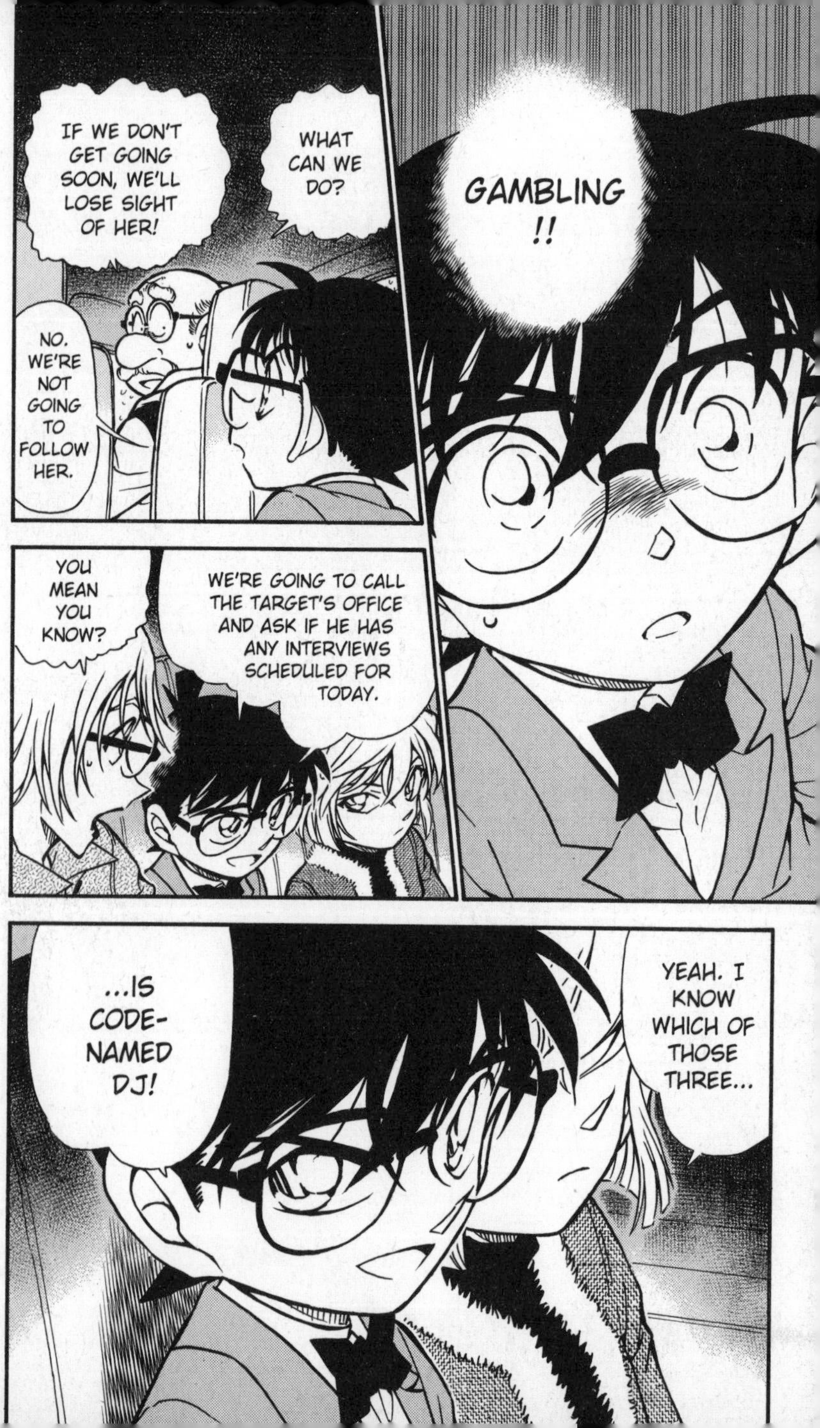
GAMBLING !!
WHAT CAN WE DO?
IF WE DON'T GET GOING SOON, WE'LL LOSE SIGHT OF HER!
NO. WE'RE NOT GOING TO FOLLOW HER.
WE'RE GOING TO CALL THE TARGET'S OFFICE AND ASK IF HE HAS ANY INTERVIEWS SCHEDULED FOR TODAY.
YOU MEAN YOU KNOW?
YEAH. I KNOW WHICH OF THOSE THREE...
...IS CODE-NAMED DJ!

Hello, Aoyama here.

I've recently gotten hooked on the American TV show *24*. The story is breathtaking, exciting and frustrating all at once. I'm the type of person who just has to get to the bottom of things, so when I watch it I literally sit through all 24 hours in a row without eating or sleeping! And so I end up missing my deadlines by a whole day... heh. I recommend the second season, which is less frustrating.

Gosho Aoyama's
Mystery Library

48

UKYO SUGISHITA

Some sleuths are so hyper-competent they have trouble working within the system.
Inspector Ukyo Sugishita, created by screenwriter Yasuhiro Koshimizu, may be the most
extreme example. He used to be a top police detective in the 2nd Investigation Division,
but his eccentric, Sherlock Holmes-like personality got him transferred to the Community
Safety Special Task Unit, otherwise known as the "Cast-Out Refuge of the Tokyo Police."
But he doesn't seem to mind one bit and keeps solving baffling cases every day.

Sugishita's greatest weapon is his outstanding deduction skills! The cold, shining eyes
behind his glasses can see through the truth of a case at a glance. His sole subordinate
officer, Sergeant Kaoru Kameyama, runs errands for him. A good-natured but hotheaded
man, Kameyama's main trait is his vigor, but he happens to be one of my favorite cops.
Heh...

I recommend *The Intent to Kill*.

Hey! You're Reading in the Wrong Direction!

This is the **end** of this graphic novel!

To properly enjoy this VIZ graphic novel, please turn it around and begin reading from **right to left.** Unlike English, Japanese is read right to left, so Japanese comics are read in reverse order from the way English comics are typically read.

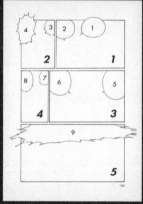

Follow the action this way

This book has been printed in the original Japanese format in order to preserve the orientation of the original artwork. Have fun with it!